Praise for Eric Tyson's *Mutual Funds For Dummies*

"Eric Tyson gets it. *Mutual Funds For Dummies* cuts through the clutter that clouds personal finance for millions of Americans. This is a must-read for the savvy investor and novice alike."

— Gerry Dick, Indianapolis Economic Development Corp., and Host, *Indiana Business This Week*, WRTV/WFYI-TV, Indianapolis

"I was clueless and intimidated by the terminology and information that I need to know about investing into mutual funds. This book has given me confidence as well as a sturdy foundation to begin investing."

— Clifford Record, Colt's Neck, NJ

"You don't have to be a novice to like *Mutual Funds For Dummies* . . .. Author Eric Tyson clearly has a mastery of his subject. He knows mutual funds and he knows how to explain them in simple English . . .. It's hard to imagine a more accessible sourcebook."

— *Kiplinger's Personal Finance Magazine*

"*Mutual Funds For Dummies* . . . is an excellent source for not only the novice investor but also for someone looking to enhance their understanding of one of the fastest growing investment tools."

— *Northwest Arkansas Times*

"I handle my mother's money and my own family's, so it is very important that I make all the right moves and decisions. I didn't have any confidence until I studied Eric Tyson's books."

— Lisa Patten, Lake Junaluska, NC

". . . injects common sense into the dizzying world of mutual funds."

— *Oakland Tribune*, CA

"I liked how easy the book is to read. I understand more now about mutual funds than I did before I read the book — it's excellent."

— Dennis Pipper, Lansing, MI

"A book that should help investors be smarter . . . readable, comprehensive . . .. Tyson's encyclopedic book is chockful of useful examples and advice for both new and experienced investors.. . ."

— *Christian Science Monitor*

"*Mutual Funds For Dummies* . . . brought me up to speed financially."

— Riccardo Heald, New York, NY

"Comprehensive, well-organized information in an easy-to-read format."

— Dianne L. Zimmerman, Rockville, MD

"*Mutual Funds For Dummies* gives good common sense advice about putting your financial house in order."

— John B. Fout, MBA

"I wish my finance teachers in college had been this interesting and informative."

— Lori Buono, reader

"Eric Tyson is far and away the best writer, most readable author, and most honest and intelligent voice in America today in the areas of personal finance and mutual fund investing."

— David Diaman, Enrolled Agent

"Never have I been as impressed with the advice and insight offered by a columnist, as I have been by Eric Tyson! Finally, there is someone in print cogently and lucidly speaking financial truth and common sense."

— Kenneth S. Imbriale, Staten Island, NY

"Accurate, easy-to-read, and humorous; 'teaches' the reader rather than preaching at the reader!"

— Victoria L. Simmons, High Point, NC

Praise for Eric Tyson's Other Best-Selling Books

Personal Finance For Dummies

"Eric Tyson . . . seems the perfect writer for a *...For Dummies* book. He doesn't tell you what to do or consider doing without explaining the why's and how's — and the booby traps to avoid — in plain English.. . . It will lead you through the thickets of your own finances as painlessly as I can imagine."

— *Chicago Tribune*

"Smart advice for dummies . . . skip the tomes, buy *Personal Finance For Dummies,* which rewards your candor with advice and comfort."

— *Newsweek*

"For those named in the title, such as myself, *Personal Finance For Dummies* is a godsend. It's bright, funny, and it can save you money, too."

— *The Los Angeles Times*

"*Personal Finance For Dummies* gives a fresh, non-threatening conversational approach to the information — I was drawn in to the author's personal touch."

— John Bennett, Fairlawn, OH

"*Personal Finance For Dummies* is easy to understand and explains every area of personal finance that I wanted to know more about. It kept my undivided attention from beginning to end."

— Rosetta Watkins, Wichita, KS

"Easy to read and helpful — gives sound advice, not 100 options. It's the best financial book I've read, and I've read many. I intend to recommend it to couples I do pre-marriage counseling with in my work as a minister."

— Pastor Claude Stayton, Seffner, FL

"Fun to read and informative. I wish all financial magazines and prospectuses were as fun to read."

— Mike Mendiola, Whittier, CA

"Worth getting. Scores of all-purpose money-management books reach bookstores every year, but only once every couple of years does a standout personal finance primer come along. *Personal Finance For Dummies*, by financial counselor and columnist Eric Tyson, provides detailed, action-oriented advice on everyday financial questions . . .. Tyson's style is readable and unintimidating."

— Kiplinger's Personal Finance Magazine

"This book helped me sort through all the hype and advertising out there and helped me increase my net worth!"

— Bryan Hailey, Fairbanks, AK

Investing For Dummies

"Simple, but informative information. The book is designed to provide advice to the pure novice and the veteran."

— Scott Minder, Warren, MI

"*Investing For Dummies* filled in all the gaps from my undergraduate investment class. It eliminates the need for full-service brokers. Thanks so much!"

— Jericho Guzman, Walnut Creek, CA

Taxes For Dummies

"*Taxes For Dummies* will make tax preparation less traumatic.. . . It's a book that answers — in plain English, and sometimes with humor — many puzzling questions that arise on the most commonly used tax forms."

— The Wall Street Journal

"... among tax advice books [it] is far and away the best. *Taxes For Dummies* is fun to read and teaches about the tax system itself. The book also provides excellent advice about dealing with mistakes — created by you or the Internal Revenue Service. And it talks about fitting taxes into your daily financial planning. In other words, it's a book you can use after April 15, as well as before."

— The Los Angeles Times

"... a witty, irreverent reference ... And since laughter is good medicine, it most definitely is what it claims. But its focus on humor does not undermine its merit as a research tool. While the guide could be used just to answer individual questions, its friendly format is such fun that you may end up reading Eric Tyson's book from cover to cover. No kidding."

— The New Orleans Times-Picayune

"User-friendly, comprehensive, ... funny! *Taxes For Dummies* made me feel I could tackle our complex tax situation."

— Kathleen Harrison, Paso Robles, CA

Home Buying For Dummies

" ... takes you step by step through the process ... humorous insights that keep the pages turning. This is a reference you'll turn to time after time."

— St. Petersburg Times

"... *Home Buying For Dummies* immediately earned a prominent spot on my reference bookshelf ... takes a holistic approach to home buying."

— San Jose Mercury News

"... *Home Buying For Dummies* provides a much-needed emotional stabilizer."

— Knight-Ridder News Service

"The humorous *Home Buying For Dummies* by Ray Brown and Eric Tyson is a favorite ... because the editorial is so good. They check their facts very well. They set out to make you understand this subject and make it fun reading and informative."

— Minneapolis Star Tribune

"The book *Home Buying For Dummies* is a primer on all the things to do and not to do when buying a home."

— FOX-TV

MUTUAL FUND$ FOR DUMMIE$®

2ND EDITION

by Eric Tyson, MBA

Foreword by James C. Collins, co-author of *Built to Last: Successful Habits of Visionary Companies*

IDG BOOKS WORLDWIDE

IDG Books Worldwide, Inc.
An International Data Group Company

Foster City, CA ♦ Chicago, IL ♦ Indianapolis, IN ♦ New York, NY

Mutual Funds For Dummies®, 2nd Edition

Published by
IDG Books Worldwide, Inc.
An International Data Group Company
919 E. Hillsdale Blvd.
Suite 400
Foster City, CA 94404
www.idgbooks.com (IDG Books Worldwide Web site)
www.dummies.com (Dummies Press Web site)

Library of Congress Catalog Card No.: 98-85433

ISBN: 0-7645-5112-4

Printed in the United States of America

10 9 8 7 6 5 4 3 2

2B/RY/RR/ZY/IN

Distributed in the United States by IDG Books Worldwide, Inc.

Distributed by Macmillan Canada for Canada; by Transworld Publishers Limited in the United Kingdom; by IDG Norge Books for Norway; by IDG Sweden Books for Sweden; by Woodslane Pty. Ltd. for Australia; by Woodslane (NZ) Ltd. for New Zealand; by Addison Wesley Longman Singapore Pte Ltd. for Singapore, Malaysia, Thailand, and Indonesia; by Norma Comunicaciones S.A. for Colombia; by Intersoft for South Africa; by International Thomson Publishing for Germany, Austria and Switzerland; by Distribuidora Cuspide for Argentina; by Livraria Cultura for Brazil; by Ediciencia S.A. for Ecuador; by Ediciones ZETA S.C.R. Ltda. for Peru; by WS Computer Publishing Corporation, Inc., for the Philippines; by Contemporanea de Ediciones for Venezuela; by Express Computer Distributors for the Caribbean and West Indies; by Micronesia Media Distributor, Inc. for Micronesia; by Grupo Editorial Norma S.A. for Guatemala; by Chips Computadoras S.A. de C.V. for Mexico; by Editorial Norma de Panama S.A. for Panama; by Wouters Import for Belgium; by American Bookshops for Finland. Authorized Sales Agent: Anthony Rudkin Associates for the Middle East and North Africa.

For general information on IDG Books Worldwide's books in the U.S., please call our Consumer Customer Service department at 800-762-2974. For reseller information, including discounts and premium sales, please call our Reseller Customer Service department at 800-434-3422.

For information on where to purchase IDG Books Worldwide's books outside the U.S., please contact our International Sales department at 317-596-5530 or fax 317-596-5692.

For information on foreign language translations, please contact our Foreign & Subsidiary Rights department at 650-655-3021 or fax 650-655-3281.

For sales inquiries and special prices for bulk quantities, please contact our Sales department at 650-655-3200 or write to the address above.

For information on using IDG Books Worldwide's books in the classroom or for ordering examination copies, please contact our Educational Sales department at 800-434-2086 or fax 317-596-5499.

For press review copies, author interviews, or other publicity information, please contact our Public Relations department at 650-655-3000 or fax 650-655-3299.

For authorization to photocopy items for corporate, personal, or educational use, please contact Copyright Clearance Center, 222 Rosewood Drive, Danvers, MA 01923, or fax 978-750-4470.

About the Author

Eric Tyson, MBA

Eric Tyson is a best-selling author and syndicated columnist. Through his counseling, writing, and teaching, he teaches people to manage their personal finances better and successfully direct their own investments.

He has been involved in the investing markets in many capacities for the past two decades. Eric first invested in mutual funds back in the mid-1970s, when he opened a mutual fund account at Fidelity. With the assistance of Dr. Martin Zweig, a now-famous investment market analyst and frequent guest on PBS's *Wall Street Week,* Eric won his high school's science fair in 1976 for a project on what influences the stock market!

Since that time, Eric has (among other things) worked as a management consultant to Fortune 500 financial service firms, and earned his Bachelor's degree in economics at Yale and an MBA at the Stanford Graduate School of Business. Despite these handicaps to clear thinking, he had the good sense to start his own company, which took an innovative approach to teaching people of all economic means about investing and money.

An accomplished freelance personal finance writer, Eric is the author of the national bestsellers *Personal Finance For Dummies* and *Investing For Dummies,* co-author of *Home Buying For Dummies* and *Taxes For Dummies,* and is an award-winning columnist for the *San Francisco Examiner.* His work has been featured and quoted in dozens of national and local publications, including *Newsweek, The Wall Street Journal, Forbes, Kiplinger's Personal Finance Magazine,* the *Los Angeles Times,* and *Bottom Line/Personal;* and on NBC's *Today Show,* ABC, CNBC, PBS's *Nightly Business Report,* CNN, CBS national radio, Bloomberg Business Radio, and Business Radio Network. He's also been a featured speaker at a White House conference on retirement planning.

Despite his "wealth" of financial knowledge, Eric is one of the rest of us. He maintains a large inventory of bumble-bee yellow-and-black-covered computer books on his desk for those frequent times when his computer makes the (decreasing amount of) hair on his head fall out.

ABOUT IDG BOOKS WORLDWIDE

Welcome to the world of IDG Books Worldwide.

IDG Books Worldwide, Inc., is a subsidiary of International Data Group, the world's largest publisher of computer-related information and the leading global provider of information services on information technology. IDG was founded more than 25 years ago and now employs more than 8,500 people worldwide. IDG publishes more than 275 computer publications in over 75 countries (see listing below). More than 90 million people read one or more IDG publications each month.

Launched in 1990, IDG Books Worldwide is today the #1 publisher of best-selling computer books in the United States. We are proud to have received eight awards from the Computer Press Association in recognition of editorial excellence and three from *Computer Currents*' First Annual Readers' Choice Awards. Our best-selling *...For Dummies*® series has more than 50 million copies in print with translations in 38 languages. IDG Books Worldwide, through a joint venture with IDG's Hi-Tech Beijing, became the first U.S. publisher to publish a computer book in the People's Republic of China. In record time, IDG Books Worldwide has become the first choice for millions of readers around the world who want to learn how to better manage their businesses.

Our mission is simple: Every one of our books is designed to bring extra value and skill-building instructions to the reader. Our books are written by experts who understand and care about our readers. The knowledge base of our editorial staff comes from years of experience in publishing, education, and journalism — experience we use to produce books for the '90s. In short, we care about books, so we attract the best people. We devote special attention to details such as audience, interior design, use of icons, and illustrations. And because we use an efficient process of authoring, editing, and desktop publishing our books electronically, we can spend more time ensuring superior content and spend less time on the technicalities of making books.

You can count on our commitment to deliver high-quality books at competitive prices on topics you want to read about. At IDG Books Worldwide, we continue in the IDG tradition of delivering quality for more than 25 years. You'll find no better book on a subject than one from IDG Books Worldwide.

IDG BOOKS WORLDWIDE

John Kilcullen
CEO
IDG Books Worldwide, Inc.

Steven Berkowitz
President and Publisher
IDG Books Worldwide, Inc.

VIII WINNER
Eighth Annual Computer Press Awards 1992

IX WINNER
Ninth Annual Computer Press Awards 1993

X WINNER
Tenth Annual Computer Press Awards 1994

XI WINNER
Eleventh Annual Computer Press Awards 1995

IDG Books Worldwide, Inc., is a subsidiary of International Data Group, the world's largest publisher of computer-related information and the leading global provider of information services on information technology. International Data Group publishes over 275 computer publications in over 75 countries. More than 90 million people read one or more International Data Group publications each month. International Data Group's publications include: **ARGENTINA:** Buyer's Guide, Computerworld Argentina, PC World Argentina; **AUSTRALIA:** Australian Macworld, Australian PC World, Australian Reseller News, Computerworld, IT Casebook, Network World, Publish, Webmaster; **AUSTRIA:** Computerwelt Osterreich, Networks Austria, PC Tip Austria; **BANGLADESH:** PC World Bangladesh; **BELARUS:** PC World Belarus; **BELGIUM:** Data News; **BRAZIL:** Annuário de Informática, Computerworld, Connections, Macworld, PC Player, PC World, Publish, Reseller News, Supergamepower; **BULGARIA:** Computerworld Bulgaria, Network World Bulgaria, PC & MacWorld Bulgaria; **CANADA:** CIO Canada, Client/Server World, ComputerWorld Canada, InfoWorld Canada, NetworkWorld Canada, WebWorld; **CHILE:** Computerworld Chile, PC World Chile; **COLOMBIA:** Computerworld Colombia, PC World Colombia; **COSTA RICA:** PC World Centro America; **THE CZECH AND SLOVAK REPUBLICS:** Computerworld Czechoslovakia, Macworld Czech Republic, PC World Czechoslovakia; **DENMARK:** Communications World Danmark, Computerworld Danmark, Macworld Danmark, PC World Danmark, Techworld Denmark; **DOMINICAN REPUBLIC:** PC World Republica Dominicana; **ECUADOR:** PC World Ecuador; **EGYPT:** Computerworld Middle East, PC World Middle East; **EL SALVADOR:** PC World Centro America; **FINLAND:** MikroPC, Tietoverkko, Tietoviikko; **FRANCE:** Distributique, Hebdo, Info PC, Le Monde Informatique, Macworld, Reseaux & Telecoms, WebMaster France; **GERMANY:** Computer Partner, Computerwoche, Computerwoche Extra, Computerwoche FOCUS, Global Online, Macwelt, PC Welt; **GREECE:** Amiga Computing, GamePro Greece, Multimedia World; **GUATEMALA:** PC World Centro America; **HONDURAS:** PC World Centro America; **HONG KONG:** Computerworld Hong Kong, PC World Hong Kong, Publish in Asia; **HUNGARY:** ABCD CD-ROM, Computerworld Szamitastechnika, Internetto online Magazine, PC World Hungary, PC-X Magazin Hungary; **ICELAND:** Tolvuheimur PC World Island; **INDIA:** Information Communications World, Information Systems Computerworld, PC World India, Publish in Asia; **INDONESIA:** InfoKomputer PC World, Komputek Computerworld, Publish in Asia; **IRELAND:** ComputerScope, PC Live!; **ISRAEL:** Macworld Israel, People & Computers/Computerworld; **ITALY:** Computerworld Italia, Macworld Italia, Networking Italia, PC World Italia; **JAPAN:** DTP World, Macworld Japan, Nikkei Personal Computing, OS/2 World Japan, SunWorld Japan, Windows NT World, Windows World Japan; **KENYA:** PC World East African; **KOREA:** Hi-Tech Information, Macworld Korea, PC World Korea; **MACEDONIA:** PC World Macedonia; **MALAYSIA:** Computerworld Malaysia, PC World Malaysia, Publish in Asia; **MALTA:** PC World Malta; **MEXICO:** Computerworld Mexico, PC World Mexico; **MYANMAR:** PC World Myanmar; **NETHERLANDS:** Computer! Totaal, LAN Internetworking Magazine, LAN World Buyers Guide, Macworld Netherlands, Net, WebWereld; **NEW ZEALAND:** Absolute Beginners Guide and Plain & Simple Series, Computer Buyer, Computer Industry Directory, Computerworld New Zealand, MTB, Network World, PC World New Zealand; **NICARAGUA:** PC World Centro America; **NORWAY:** Computerworld Norge, CW Rapport, Datamagasinet, Financial Rapport, Kursguide Norge, Macworld Norge, Multimediaworld Norge, PC World Ekspress Norge, PC World Nettverk, PC World Norge, PC World ProduktGuide Norge; **PAKISTAN:** Computerworld Pakistan; **PANAMA:** PC World Panama; **PEOPLE'S REPUBLIC OF CHINA:** China Computer Users, China Computerworld, China InfoWorld, China Telecom World Weekly, Computer & Communication, Electronic Design China, Electronics Today, Electronics Weekly, Game Software, PC World China, Popular Computer Week, Software Weekly, Software World, Telecom World; **PERU:** Computerworld Peru, PC World Profesional Peru, PC World SoHo Peru; **PHILIPPINES:** Click!, Computerworld Philippines, PC World Philippines, Publish in Asia; **POLAND:** Computerworld Poland, Computerworld Special Report Poland, Cyber, Macworld Poland, Networld Poland, PC World Komputer; **PORTUGAL:** Cerebro/PC World, Computerworld/Correio Informático, Dealer World Portugal, Mac*In/PC*In Portugal, Multimedia World; **PUERTO RICO:** PC World Puerto Rico; **ROMANIA:** Computerworld Romania, PC World Romania, Telecom Romania; **RUSSIA:** Computerworld Russia, Mir PK, Publish, Seti; **SINGAPORE:** Computerworld Singapore, PC World Singapore, Publish in Asia; **SLOVENIA:** Monitor; **SOUTH AFRICA:** Computing SA, Network World SA, Software World SA; **SPAIN:** Communicaciones World España, Computerworld España, Dealer World España, Macworld España, PC World España; **SRI LANKA:** Infolink PC World; **SWEDEN:** CAP&Design, Computer Sweden, Corporate Computing Sweden, Internetworld Sweden, it.branschen, Macworld Sweden, MaxiData Sweden, MikroDatorn, Nätverk & Kommunikation, PC World Sweden, PCaktiv, Windows World Sweden; **SWITZERLAND:** Computerworld Schweiz, Macworld Schweiz, PCtip; **TAIWAN:** Computerworld Taiwan, Macworld Taiwan, NEW ViSiON/Publish, PC World Taiwan, Windows World Taiwan; **THAILAND:** Publish in Asia, Thai Computerworld; **TURKEY:** Computerworld Turkiye, Macworld Turkiye, Network World Turkiye, PC World Turkiye; **UKRAINE:** Computerworld Kiev, Multimedia World Ukraine, PC World Ukraine; **UNITED KINGDOM:** Acorn User UK, Amiga Action UK, Amiga Computing UK, Apple Talk UK, Computing, Macworld, Parents and Computers UK, PC Advisor, PC Home, PSX Pro, The WEB; **UNITED STATES:** Cable in the Classroom, CIO Magazine, Computerworld, DOS World, Federal Computer Week, GamePro Magazine, InfoWorld, I-Way, Macworld, Network World, PC Games, PC World, Publish, Video Event, THE WEB Magazine, and WebMaster; online webzines: JavaWorld, NetscapeWorld, and SunWorld Online; **URUGUAY:** InfoWorld Uruguay; **VENEZUELA:** Computerworld Venezuela, PC World Venezuela; and **VIETNAM:** PC World Vietnam. 5/7/98

Dedication

To my wife, Judy; my family, especially my parents Charles and Paulina; my friends; and to my counseling clients and students of my courses for teaching me how to teach them about managing their finances.

Author's Acknowledgments

Many people contribute to the birth of a book, and this book is no exception. First, I owe a deep debt of gratitude to James Collins who inspired me when I was a young and impressionable business school student. Jim encouraged me to try to improve some small part of the business world by being an entrepreneur and focusing solely on what customers needed rather than on what made the quickest buck.

The technical reviewers for this book, Gary Karz and CCH INCORPORATED, helped to improve each and every chapter, and I am thankful for that.

Special thanks also to Frederic Lowrie, Chris Doyle, Brian Mattes, John Woerth, and Mariann Lindsey for helping provide forms, documents, and answers to my many questions.

Thanks to all the good people in the media and other fields who have taken the time to critique and praise my previous writing so that others may know that it exists and is worth reading. And to those too lazy to open the book just because of its bright yellow color and title I say, "Don't judge a book by its cover!"

And a final and heartfelt thanks to all the people on the front lines and behind the scenes at IDG Books who helped to make this book and my others a success. A big round of applause, please, for Kathy Cox as project editor and Diane Smith as copy editor. Special thanks to Kathy Welton, publisher, for her many timely and thoughtful ideas, and to John Kilcullen for cajoling me into writing these books in the first place. Thanks also to the Production, Graphics, Proofreading, and Indexing staff for their great efforts in producing this book.

P.S. Thanks to you, dear reader, for buying my books.

Publisher's Acknowledgments

We're proud of this book; please register your comments through our IDG Books Worldwide Online Registration Form located at `http://my2cents.dummies.com`.

Some of the people who helped bring this book to market include the following:

Acquisitions, Editorial, and Media Development

Project Editor: Kathleen M. Cox

Acquisitions Editor: Mark Butler

Senior Copy Editor: Susan Diane Smith

Technical Editor: Gary Karz, CFA

General Reviewers: Karen Notaro, Robert Kauffman, Peter Melcher, and Dave Dotson from CCH INCORPORATED

Permissions Editor: Heather Heath Dismore

Associate Permissions Editor: Carmen Krikorian

Editorial Manager: Colleen Rainsberger

Editorial Assistant: Paul E. Kuzmic

Production

Project Coordinator: Karen York

Layout and Graphics: Lou Boudreau, Linda M. Boyer, J. Tyler Connor, Angela F. Hunckler, Todd Klemme, Jane E. Martin, Drew R. Moore, Brent Savage, Janet Seib, Deirdre Smith, Michael A. Sullivan

Proofreaders: Christine Berman, Kelli Botta, Rachel Garvey, Nancy Price, Nancy L. Reinhardt, Rebecca Senninger, Janet M. Withers

Indexer: Christine Spina

Special Help

Wendy Hatch, Copy Editor

General and Administrative

IDG Books Worldwide, Inc.: John Kilcullen, CEO; Steven Berkowitz, President and Publisher

IDG Books Technology Publishing: Brenda McLaughlin, Senior Vice President and Group Publisher

Dummies Technology Press and Dummies Editorial: Diane Graves Steele, Vice President and Associate Publisher; Mary Bednarek, Director of Acquisitions and Product Development; Kristin A. Cocks, Editorial Director

Dummies Trade Press: Kathleen A. Welton, Vice President and Publisher; Kevin Thornton, Acquisitions Manager

IDG Books Production for Dummies Press: Michael R. Britton, Vice President of Production and Creative Services; Cindy L. Phipps, Manager of Project Coordination, Production Proofreading, and Indexing; Kathie S. Schutte, Supervisor of Page Layout; Shelley Lea, Supervisor of Graphics and Design; Debbie J. Gates, Production Systems Specialist; Robert Springer, Supervisor of Proofreading; Debbie Stailey, Special Projects Coordinator; Tony Augsburger, Supervisor of Reprints and Bluelines

Dummies Packaging and Book Design: Robin Seaman, Creative Director; Jocelyn Kelaita, Product Packaging Coordinator; Kavish + Kavish, Cover Design

♦

The publisher would like to give special thanks to Patrick J. McGovern, without whom this book would not have been possible.

♦

Contents at a Glance

Cartoons at a Glance

By Rich Tennant

The 5th Wave
By Rich Tennant

"It's surprising, considering his portfolio is so conservative."

page 7

The 5th Wave
By Rich Tennant
Defining your investment risk with the:
TOAST RETRIEVING RISK TOLERANCE TEST
LOW RISK Waits for toast to pop up even though it's burning.
MODERATE RISK Goes after toast with wooden toast prongs.
HIGH RISK Goes after toast with all metal butter knife.
ULTRA HIGH RISK Goes after toast with metal butter knife wearing a wet swim suit and a stainless steel colander on head.

page 135

The 5th Wave
By Rich Tennant
MY GOD! THAT'S MY FUND MANAGER!

page 289

The 5th Wave
By Rich Tennant

"Perhaps you'd like to buy these magic beans, or this charm that will give you good luck, or this stock that promises a 200% return on your investment in less than 18 months."

page 335

The 5th Wave
By Rich Tennant

"My portfolio's gonna take a hit for this."

page 363

Fax: 978-546-7747 • *E-mail:* the5wave@tiac.net

Table of Contents

Foreword

I admit it. I am a "Dummy" — at least when it comes to personal finances. But like a smart dummy, I know where to turn for trusted information and advice. Fortunately, Eric Tyson wrote *Personal Finance For Dummies*. I knew Eric so I've had a copy to serve as a valuable and trusted quick reference guide whenever I have a money question.

Like you (if you've picked up this book), I know that I should be wiser about investing my savings. Magazine articles about mutual funds clutter my desk and mutual fund literature piles up in a corner of the living room — mountains of reading that, "I'll get to later, when I have a few minutes." Friends tell me over dinner that they've invested in this fund or that fund. They spout off sage advice about "load" and "no-load" and "growth funds" and "income funds" and risk and — well, I usually just go back to the menu and try to figure out what to order for dinner.

"You know, we really should invest some of our money in a few of those funds," I might comment to my wife on the drive home. But, like most of us, I put it off or — worse — make bad decisions. Like the novice mountain climber, I know just enough to get myself into trouble.

However, unlike exotic activities such as mountain climbing, the task of managing our personal finances is one we all face. It's as if we are all stuck in the mountains, but few of us really know how to climb. Wealthy people hire personal guides to help them out. But most of us can't afford or don't feel comfortable doing that. And as Eric points out, and my own experience suggests, financial advisors may have their own agendas that conflict with yours.

I first met Eric when he was a graduate business student of mine at Stanford; I was impressed by the strength and clarity of his personal purpose: to help people at all income levels to take control of their financial futures. He nurtured his vision while he worked to pay off all his student loan obligations. Then he boldly quit his high-paying and prestigious management consulting career to devote full time to making his vision a reality. Like Henry Ford, Eric wants to make that which is available only to the wealthy widely accessible to middle-income Americans. Ford did it with automobiles; Tyson aims to do it with thoughtful financial planning. This book is yet another important step toward that goal.

We live in a knowledge age. Those who "know" will be better-off in the long run than those who "have." I do not see the widening cleavage in our society to be between the "haves" and the "have-nots," but between the "knows" and the"know-nots." Those who know will have; those who know-not...

Eric knows a lot about mutual funds and making intelligent investing decisions in funds within the context of one's overall personal financial situation. And he makes that knowledge accessible to all of us "Dummies" here in this book. I hope you learn and apply his lessons. I intend to.

James C. Collins
Co-author of the national bestseller *Built to Last: Successful Habits of Visionary Companies* and *Beyond Entrepreneurship: Turning Your Business into an Enduring Great Company.*

Introduction

Thanks for choosing *Mutual Funds For Dummies,* 2nd Edition. Whether you're a regular reader of investing books or this is your first, *Mutual Funds For Dummies* gives you practical techniques of mutual fund investing that you can put to work now and for many years to come.

Mutual funds aren't literally for dummies — in fact, they are smart investments for people at all income and educational levels. Mutual funds are investment companies that pool your money with that of thousands of other people to create a large pool of assets that can be invested in stocks, bonds, or other securities. Because your assets are part of a much larger whole, mutual funds enable you to invest in securities that you otherwise could not afford, and they give you low-cost access to professional money managers. With good money managers investing your nest egg in top-flight investments that match your financial goals, you can spend your time doing the activities in life that you enjoy. Mutual funds should improve your investment returns as well as your social life!

How This Book Is Different

Many investment books confuse folks. They present you with some newfangled system that you never figure out how to use without the help of a mainframe computer, several mathematicians, and a Nobel Laureate as your personal consultants. Books that bewilder more than enlighten may be intentional because the author may have another agenda: to get you to turn your money over to him to manage or to sell you his newsletter(s). These writers with an agenda may imply and sometimes say that you really can't invest well on your own.

Going another route, too many investment books glorify rather than advise. They place on a pedestal the very, very few who, during decidedly brief periods in the history of the world and financial markets, managed to beat the market averages by a few percentage points or so per year. Many of these books and their publishers suggest that reading them will show you the strategies that led Superstar Money Manager to the superlative performance that the book glorifies. "He did it his way; now you can, too," trumpets the marketing material. Not so. Reading a book about what made

Michael Jordan a phenomenal basketball player, Shakespeare a great playwright, or Henry Kissinger a successful Secretary of State won't help you shoot a basket, versify, or negotiate stately alliances like these famous folks. By the same token, you can't discover from a book the way to become the next Wall Street investment wizard. These types of books make their publishers wealthy, not you.

Almost as bad, most mutual fund books are too technical. Those that do a good job explaining the fundamental concepts typically don't delve into the nuts-and-bolts issues that frustrate some financial novices. Many authors lack a financial planning perspective and an "in the trenches" understanding of the challenges real investors face.

When you want to buy or sell a mutual fund, your decision needs to fit your overall financial objectives and individual situation. Fund investors make many mistakes in this regard. For example, they invest in funds instead of paying off debt or tucking money into their employer's tax-deductible retirement savings plan. It's also common for investors to choose funds that don't fit their tax situation. *Mutual Funds For Dummies,* 2nd Edition, helps you avoid those common fund-investing pitfalls.

This book also covers pesky issues completely ignored by other mutual fund books. For novice fund investors, simply finding the correct application form in the mountain of literature that fund companies send can be a challenge. And if you invest in mutual funds outside of tax-sheltered retirement accounts, you're greeted by the inevitable headache from figuring out how to report distributions at tax time. This book puts you on the path you need to be on in order to avoid these problems.

The truth is, investing is not all that difficult — and mutual funds are the great equalizer. There's absolutely no reason, except perhaps a lack of time and effort on your part, why you can't successfully invest in mutual funds on your own. In fact, if you understand some basic concepts and find out how to avoid major mistakes that occur for some fairly obvious reasons, you can be even more successful than most so-called investment professionals.

I've invested in mutual funds for more than two decades and in my practice as a financial counselor, and in the personal finance courses I teach, I help investors make successful investing decisions with mutual funds as part of comprehensive personal financial management. So I know the questions and challenges that you face when you invest in funds. I wrote this book to answer, in plain English, your fund-investing questions.

Conquering Fund Confusion

You have good reason to be reading this book because mutual funds are a huge and confusing business. Although mutual funds began in the United States in 1924, as recently as 1978 they held only $57 billion in assets. Today, thousands of mutual funds account for over four *trillion* dollars ($4,000,000,000,000 — count all those zeros!) under management — a 70-fold increase in just the last 20 years.

Although the basic principle behind mutual funds sounds simple enough — pooled money from thousands of individuals that is invested in stocks, bonds, or other securities — you have to understand the different types of investments, such as stocks and bonds, and the way they work, because funds are a package deal. And that's where the fun begins.

The second fact you have to understand is that so *many* individual funds — more than 8,000 — are available. Hundreds of companies in many different kinds of businesses (mutual fund companies, brokerage firms, insurers, banks, and so on) are trying to sell funds. Even experienced investors suffer from information overload. Lucky for you, I present short lists of great funds that work for you and your situation.

And because no investment, not even one of the better mutual funds, is free of flaws and shortcomings, I show you sound alternatives to mutual funds — and help you understand when investing in funds may not be appropriate for you.

Using This Book Effectively

You don't need to read this book cover to cover. But if you're a beginner or you want to fully immerse yourself in the world of fund investing (or if you're just an information glutton), there's no reason why you can't.

On the other hand, you may have a specific question or two that you want to focus on today, but you'll want some other information tomorrow. No problem there, either. *Mutual Funds For Dummies,* 2nd Edition, is lighter on its feet and on your brain than most reference books. Use the table of contents or index to speed your way to what you need to know and get on with your life.

The sections that follow describe the parts in this book and what they cover.

Part I: The Why and How of Mutual Funds

In Part I of this book. I take you through the investing basics. If you don't understand the different types of investments that funds are made of, such as stocks and bonds, you won't fully understand funds. Part I defines and demystifies what mutual funds are and discusses what funds are good for and when you should consider alternatives.

Before you're even ready to start investing in funds, your personal finances need to be in order, so in Part I, I give you some financial house-cleaning tips. You also discover the importance of fitting mutual funds to your financial goals. After your finances are shipshape and you've identified your goals, you are ready to find out how to pick great funds, how to avoid losers, where and how to purchase funds, and how to read all those pesky reports (such as prospectuses and annual reports) that fund companies stuff in your mailbox. Part I touches all these bases.

Part II: Establishing a Great Fund Portfolio

In Part II, I show you how to build a portfolio of mutual funds to accomplish your specific financial goals. You start off by exploring the basic strategies of portfolio construction. Then, for each of the major fund types — money market, bond, and stock — you get specific fund recommendations. A chapter of sample fund portfolios based on real life scenarios brings together the important concepts this section introduces.

Part III: Maintaining a Great Fund Portfolio

In mutual fund investing, getting started is the hard part. After you have a good fund portfolio up and running, you shouldn't have to devote much time to maintaining it. This part covers what you do need to do, including chapters on how to evaluate your funds' performance and deal with the tax consequences of your investing. I also offer some tips on how to minimize aggravations when you deal with fund companies and discount brokers.

Part IV: Evaluating Information and Advice

If you're still not full, you can find out about the scores of individuals, companies, and publications that rank and predict financial market gyrations. I warn you about the bad ones and the dangers of blindly following gurus, and I reveal which, if any, of them really are gurus. You also discover how to use the best mutual fund information sources, how to tell the difference between good and bad newsletters, and where to turn for more information. You may want to know how to use your computer to track and even invest in mutual funds using online services and software — so Part IV tells you that, too.

Part V: The Part of Tens

Broaden your thinking even further with these chapters that offer ten or more short sections about important fund issues and concepts. I discuss recent trends in the mutual fund industry, placate some fund-investing fears that you may have, and introduce some concerns that you may not have but perhaps should.

Appendix

So as to not clutter up the book unnecessarily, I stuck some useful facts at the end of book. Here you find the telephone numbers, addresses, and other vital statistics of all the top-notch funds I recommend in this book.

Icons Used in This Book

Throughout this book, you can find friendly and useful icons to enhance your reading pleasure and to flag and demarcate special types of information. So, when you meet one of these margin-hugging doodads, imagine this conversation with yourself:

Hey, I bet that Eric just pointed out something that can save me time, headaches, money, or all the above!

Uh, bombs normally ain't real popular in polite company, so maybe Eric's trying to steer me away from mistakes and boo-boos others have made when investing in mutual funds.

Sharklike life-forms dead ahead. *Some*thing around here could really cost me big bucks (maybe even an arm and a leg!) if I don't devote my most rapt attention to Eric here.

Yowza! Finally, a book that tells me what to do, where to do it, and whom to do it with. This icon denotes Eric's favorite mutual funds.

Eminently skippable stuff here (especially if something important like a call from Mother Nature is pressing upon me), but I may not seem as astute at the next cocktail party when mutual fund trivia games begin. Neat but nonessential stuff — read at leisure.

An invite from His Tysonship to get out my trenchcoat, sagging pipe, and Sherlock Holmes hat and look into something on my own. Eric's told me as much as he can, but he thinks that I may need or want to check it out more on my own before I make a move.

I bet that what Eric's telling me is *so* important that I should *make sure* that I don't forget it when I'm at large in the real world making my own fund investing decisions!

Where to Go From Here

Mutual funds can be a low-cost way to get access to the best securities and the best money management. I tell you all you need to know to get started in this book. First figure out your financial goals. Be sure to invest in retirement accounts. And then proceed to invest in efficiently managed funds that meet your needs now and for the future. The important thing is to begin. So get started.

Part I

The Why and How of Mutual Funds

"It's surprising, considering his portfolio is so conservative."

In this part . . .

In five rollicking, action-packed chapters, you get everything under your belt and into your cerebral cortex that you need to know to understand and converse about mutual funds. If you don't know the difference between a stock and a bond or between a prospectus and an expense ratio, this part gives you those key terms — and others — for an excellent grounding in the fundamentals of mutual fund investing. You also find out how to fit mutual funds neatly with the rest of your finances, and you get an inside look at how, when, and where to invest in the best mutual funds.

Chapter 1

Investments Primer

In This Chapter

- Determining your investment needs and goals
- Understanding investments
- Investment risk and returns
- Benefits of diversification

"I've made every investing mistake there is to make," said Chris in her first meeting with me. "Doing the opposite of every financial move I've ever made would have been a great strategy."

I had Chris sit down in a comfortable chair, poured her a glass of water, and — as I normally do in the first meeting with a new client — asked her to tell me the history of her financial life.

Chris's investing career began in the late 1970s when she bought stock (shares of ownership in a company) in the company that employed her. Unfortunately, the employer was a manufacturing company whose days were numbered. In 1980, Chris's company filed for bankruptcy, she got a pink slip from her boss, and, to top it off, her big pile of stock suddenly had no price per share — it was essentially worthless. Few things could have been more depressing than sitting at home unemployed and seeing company stock account statements show a balance of $0.00.

Being a little bit gun shy, Chris did not foray into another major investment until 1983. While vacationing in Florida, she went to a presentation that extolled the virtues of purchasing a share in luxury condominiums being built near Disney World. "How could you lose," the presenter asked, "with the never-ending attraction of Disney?" Chris concurred: Kids would always be dragging their money-toting parents to the Magic Kingdom.

Chris found out what far too many time-share owners know: A time-share is a grossly overpriced way to purchase an annual week's vacation in a place that you'll soon tire of visiting. Ten years later, Chris unloaded her investment for 20 percent of what she paid for it — and her 80 percent loss was *after* she'd paid annual maintenance and other unanticipated fees, all of which had been conveniently left out of the initial sales pitch (er, I mean, presentation).

Chris's next investment decision came as the result of an unfortunate family occurrence. In 1984, her father passed away and left her $200,000. Because Chris had learned from her experiences that putting too many investment eggs in one basket causes problems for investors, she was all ears when Louis, a financial consultant recommended by the attorney who handled her father's estate, advised "a diversified, professionally managed investment."

These limited partnerships (LPs), Louis assured Chris, would end her string of bad luck in investments. "Each partnership holds dozens of individual investments, so if one of them does poorly or even becomes worthless, it's just a small portion of the whole. Besides, you'll get all these great tax write-offs to boot," Louis assured her.

The advice made sense to her. Louis's investment firm advertised everywhere and had what looked like a hundred employees. Louis wore an expensive business suit, and his office looked out on to a panoramic view of the financial district. "I've invested in limited partnerships myself and so have my parents," he said.

Well, Chris reasoned, if limited partnerships were good enough for Louis's company, an obviously successful brokerage firm, and for Louis and his family, then limited partnerships were good enough for her. She put three-quarters of her inheritance money into a couple of them.

More than a decade later, here's the news on Chris's limited partnerships:

Total invested = $150,000. Current value = $8,000.

In addition to high sales commissions and high ongoing management fees, the LPs make poor investments, as I explain later in this chapter. Oh, and Chris must pay her accountant to fill out those nasty special income tax return schedules for LPs every year.

Luckily, Chris reserved $50,000 of the inheritance for a home down payment. By 1987, however, real estate prices in northern California seemed to be heading into the stratosphere, so when Louis called again with stock recommendations, Chris was receptive to his advice (it wasn't yet clear how bad the LPs would prove to be). If she could just make her money grow, Chris thought, she could afford to buy a good home that she'd be really happy with.

She bought half a dozen stocks — which promptly nose-dived 40 percent when the stock market crashed that October. Monday had never been Chris's favorite day, so when she heard on the news that the market had dropped more than 500 points (a 22+ percent plunge) on Monday, October 19, for her, that day was indeed Black Monday.

She had a hard time getting through to Louis, whose secretary said, "He's very busy today helping clients make changes with their investments." When she finally got through to him, Louis helped Chris make changes to her investments, too. "A money market fund will provide a safe haven from the turbulent financial markets," he reasoned.

Chris didn't want to jeopardize the future home purchase, so she took Louis's advice to sell her stocks and put the proceeds into a money market fund. Her $50,000 was now worth about $28,000. That's when she finally knocked on my door, both her portfolio and her ego quite deflated.

Although Chris was being hard on herself when she said that she had made every investing mistake there is to make — actually, there are many more — she had made other financial mistakes during her years of investing horrors that she wasn't even aware of:

- She had missed out on the opportunity to contribute to tax-deductible investment accounts through her employers.
- She had racked up more than $10,000 in high-interest consumer debt, mostly on credit cards, further reducing the size of her assets.

And, at the risk of having you think I enjoy finding fault, I must tell you that Chris had neither long term disability insurance nor life insurance when she called me — even though she had started a family following her marriage in 1992.

Chris made her investing mistakes for one simple reason: She didn't understand investments. She didn't know what her investing options were and why particular options were inferior or superior to others.

By reading this book, you can prevent yourself from making big investment mistakes. And you can take advantage of an excellent investment vehicle: mutual funds — the best of which offer you instant diversification and low-cost access to outstanding money managers. And you do this in the context of your overall financial plans and goals.

Now, I'm not going to try to fool you by saying that you can't make mistakes with mutual funds, because you can. But, because the best mutual funds are superior in many respects to many other investments, they help you minimize your risk while maximizing your chances of success. People from many walks of life use funds because of this. This chapter gives you an investment overview so you can see how mutual funds fit into the overall investment picture.

Mutual Funds: An Investment

At their most basic, mutual funds are an investment.

"Tell me something I don't know; I'm not *that* dumb," you say.

I know that, but please bear with me. I don't want to make the mistake that I see so many investment writers (and financial advisors) make: starting with the more advanced stuff on the assumption that you know the basics. So often I hear from people reading about mutual funds and complaining that a writer starts throwing around terms such as "small cap value stock fund" and "asset allocation" without explaining them, and before you know it, you're lost in the weeds and frustrated. You have every right to be.

TIP: If you already understand what stocks and bonds are, their risks and potential returns, terrific. You can skip this chapter. Most people, however, don't really understand the basics of investments, and that's one of the major reasons that people make investment mistakes in the first place. If you understand the specific types of securities that funds can invest in, you've mastered one of the important building blocks to understanding mutual funds.

All right, let me get more specific: A mutual fund is an investment that invests in other investments. In other words, when you invest in a mutual fund, you're contributing to a big pile of money that a mutual fund manager uses to buy other investments, such as stocks, bonds, and/or other assets that meet the fund's investment criteria.

Differences in investment criteria are how mutual funds broadly categorize themselves, analogous to the way that an automaker labels a car a "four-door sedan" or a "sport utility vehicle." This helps you, the buyer, have a general picture of the product even before you see the specifics.

On the car lot, of course, it's taken for granted that you know what "sedan" and "sport utility vehicle" mean. But what if the car salesman asks you whether you want a Pegasus or a Stegasaurus? How can you decide if you don't know what those names mean?

Mutual fund terms, such as "municipal bond fund" or "small cap stock fund," are thrown around too casually. Fact is, thanks to our spending-oriented culture, the average American knows cars a lot better than mutual funds. In this chapter and the next, I explain the investment and mutual fund terms and concepts that many writers assume you already know (or perhaps don't understand well enough themselves to explain to you).

REMEMBER

Piecing together your financial puzzle

Many people plunge into mutual funds without first coming up with an overall financial plan. Would you start out on a long trip without picking a destination? Before you ask for directions, you have to know where you're trying to go. And you have to know what you need and want to do along the way.

Some investors leap into the task of picking a fund before they know what they want their mutual funds to do. They may choose fine funds, but they also may make big financial planning mistakes that lead them to pay far more in taxes than they need to.

If you haven't planned, you're not alone. You work hard and want to have a life; developing a financial plan may be the last thing on your mind when the weekend rolls around. But in recent years, too many people have found out the hard way that recessions and natural disasters aren't just bad things that happen to other people. You need a safety net in case you lose your job or are hit with unexpected expenses. This safety net needs to be invested in something that you can sell quickly; something whose value you can count on to *not* drop at inconvenient moments (see Chapter 7).

A great deal of what's written about mutual funds completely ignores the financial planning implications of mutual fund decisions. In some cases, the writer doesn't have enough space to go into these important details. In other cases, writers simply don't know what they're overlooking.

If you've determined your financial needs and goals already, terrific! Understanding yourself is a good part of the battle. But don't shortchange yourself by diving in before you put on your mask and flippers. Be sure to dress for investing success! And be sure to read Chapter 3.

Making Sense of Investments

Our eyes can perceive dozens of different colors, and hundreds if not thousands of shades in between — so many colors that it's easy to forget what we learned back in our early school days, that all colors are based on some combination of the three primary colors: red, blue, and yellow.

Well, believe it or not, the world of investments is even simpler than that. The seemingly infinite number of investments out there is based on just two primary kinds of investments: lending investments and ownership investments.

Lending investments: Interest on your money

When your buddy Bob forgets his wallet at home (again) and you agree to spot him $7 so that he can buy lunch, you're a *lender*. Although it's your money buying Bob's lunch, Bob owns the lunch that he's buying, not you. And when he retrieves his wallet, he'll hopefully pay you back the $7.

If you loan the money to Bob with the condition that he must share his potato chips with you, you're charging interest and, therefore, profiting from the loan (unless, that is, he buys barbecue-flavored chips and you don't like them). Lending is a type of investment in which the lender charges the lendee a fee (generally known as *interest*) until the original loan (typically known as the *principal*) gets paid back.

Familiar lending investments include bank certificates of deposit, U. S. Treasury bills, and bonds issued by corporations such as AT&T. In each case, you are lending your money to an organization — the bank, the federal government, or AT&T — that pays you an agreed-upon rate of interest. You are also promised that your principal (the original amount that you loaned) will be returned to you in full on a specific date.

The best thing that can happen with a lending investment is that you are paid all the interest in addition to your original investment, as promised. (In Chapter 8, you see how you can also make money or lose money on lending investments when interest rates fall or rise.) Although getting your original investment back with the promised interest won't make you rich, this result isn't bad, given that the investment landscape is littered with the carcasses of failed investments that return you nothing — including lunch money loans to colleagues that we never see again!

The worst thing that can happen with a lending investment is that you don't get everything that you were promised. Under extenuating circumstances, promises get broken. When a company goes bankrupt, for example, you can lose all or part of your original investment.

Another risk is that you get what you were promised, but, because of the ravages of inflation, your money is simply worth less than you expected it to be worth; it has less purchasing power than you thought it would. Back in the 1960s, for example, high-quality (that is, "safe") companies were issuing long-term bonds that paid approximately 4 percent interest. At the time, such bonds seemed like a good investment because the cost of living was increasing only 2 percent a year. But when inflation rocketed to 6, 8, and then 10 percent and higher, those 4 percent bonds didn't look quite so attractive. The interest and principal didn't buy nearly the amount it did years earlier when inflation was lower.

Here's a simple example to illustrate the damages of inflation to lending investments. Suppose that you had put $5,000 into an 18-year lending type investment yielding 4 percent. You planned to use it in 18 years to pay for one year of college. Although a year of college cost $5,000 when you invested the money, college costs since then had risen 8 percent a year; so that in 18 years when you needed the money, one year of college cost nearly $20,000. But your investment would only be worth around $10,100, nearly 50 percent short of the cost of college.

A final drawback to lending investments is that you do not share in the success of the organization to which you lend your money. If the company doubles or triples in size and profits, the growth is good for the company and its owners, and you're sure to get your interest and principal back. But you don't reap any of the rewards. If Bill Gates had approached you many years ago for money to help make computer software, would you rather have loaned him the money or *owned* a piece of the company that he created — Microsoft.

Ownership investments: Your profit, your loss

Now suppose that your buddy, Bob, starts getting a little more audacious in his requests for favors. Due to a strong local economy and real estate market, the landlord wants to increase Bob's rent 15 percent, so Bob asks if he can live with you.

But you're a bit tired of lending Bob money, and you know that you don't want him to live in your spare bedroom for free. You begin to think that maybe it's time that you bought your own place to live rather than paying increasing rents yourself. So this time, you strike a deal with Bob to buy a duplex and rent him the lower unit for $800 per month.

Now you're making an ownership investment. You're an *owner* when you purchase an asset, whether a building or part of a multi-national corporation, that has the ability to generate earnings or profits. Real estate and stock are typical examples of an ownership investment.

Ownership investments can generate profits two ways. The first is through the investment's own cash flow. For example, as the owner of the duplex, you derive rental income from tenants like Bob. If you own stock in a corporation, many companies elect to pay out a portion of their annual profits (in the form of a *dividend*).

The second way to profit from ownership investments — and this is the one with the potential for really big profits — is through *appreciation* in the value of the investment. When you own a piece of real estate in an area with a healthy economy, or you own stock in a growing company, then your investment can increase in value over time. If and when you sell the investment, the difference between what you sold it for and what you paid for it is your (pre-tax) profit. (The IRS, of course, will eventually expect its share of your investment profits.) This potential for appreciation is the big advantage of being an owner versus a lender.

On the downside, ownership investments come with extra responsibilities. If the heater goes out or the plumbing springs a leak, you, as the property owner, are the one who must fix it while Bob gets to kick back in his recliner watching football games and swilling beer.

Moreover, where there is the potential for appreciation, there is the potential for depreciation. Ownership investments can decline in value. Real estate markets can slump, stock markets can crash, and individual companies can go belly up. For this reason, ownership investments tend to be riskier than lending investments.

The Major Investment Options

Once you understand that there are fundamentally only two kinds of investments — ownership and lending — you can more easily understand how a specific investment option works . . . and whether it's an attractive option to help you achieve your specific goals.

Which investment vehicle you choose for a specific goal depends on where you're going, how fast you want to get there, and what risks you're willing to take along the way. Here's a list of vehicles to choose from and some of my thoughts on which vehicle would be a good choice for your situation. Beware icons point out the ones that you should avoid.

Savings and money market accounts

Savings accounts can be found at banks; money market funds are available through mutual fund companies. Both are lending investments based on short-term loans and are about the safest in terms of risk to your investment among the various lending investments around. Relative to the typical returns on growth oriented investments such as stocks, the interest rate (also known as the *yield*) paid on savings and money market accounts, is quite low but does not fluctuate as much over time. (The interest rate on savings and money market accounts generally fluctuates as the level of overall market interest rates changes.)

Bank savings accounts are backed by the federal government through Federal Deposit Insurance Corporation (FDIC) insurance. If the bank goes broke, you still get your money back (up to $100,000). Money market funds are not insured.

TIP: Should you prefer a bank account because your investment (principal) is insured? No. Savings accounts and money market funds have almost equivalent safety, but money market funds tend to offer higher yields. Chapter 7 provides more background on money market funds.

Bonds

Bonds are the most common lending investment traded on securities markets. Bond funds also account for about *20* percent of all mutual fund assets invested.

When issued, the bond includes a specified maturity date at which you will be repaid your principal. Also specified when a bond is issued is the interest rate, which is typically *fixed* (that means it doesn't change over time).

Bonds, therefore, can fluctuate in value with changes in interest rates. If, for example, you're holding a bond issued at 8 percent, and rates increase to 10 percent, your bond decreases in value. (Why would anyone want to buy your bond at the price that you paid if it yields just 8 percent and she can get a bond yielding 10 percent somewhere else?)

Bonds differ from each other in the following ways:

- **The type of institution to which you're lending your money.** Institutions include state governments (municipal bonds), the federal government (treasuries), mortgage holders (Government National Mortgage Association, or GNMA), and corporations (corporate bonds).
- **The credit quality of the borrower to whom you lend your money.** The probability that a borrower will pay you the interest and return all your principal varies from institution to institution.
- **The length of maturity of the bond.** Short-term bonds mature in a few years, intermediate bonds in around 10 years, and long-term bonds within 30 years. Longer-term bonds generally pay higher yields but fluctuate more widely in value with changes in interest rates.

I tell you more than you ever thought you wanted to know about bonds in Chapter 8.

Stocks

Stocks are the most common ownership investment traded on securities markets. They represent shares of ownership in a company. Companies that sell stock to the general public (called *publicly held* companies) include automobile manufacturers, computer software producers, fast food restaurants, hotels, magazine and newspaper publishers, supermarkets, wineries, zipper manufacturers, and many types of other (legal) businesses!

When you hold stock in a company, you share in the company's profits in the form of annual dividends as well as an increase (you hope) in the stock price if the company grows and makes increasing profits. That's what happens when things are going well. The downside is that if the company's business declines, your stock can plummet or even go to $0 per share.

Besides occupying different industries, companies also vary in size. In the financial press, you often hear companies referred to by their *market capitalization,* which is the total value of their outstanding stock. This is what the stock market and the investors who participate in it think a company is worth.

You can choose from two very different ways to invest in bonds and stocks. You can purchase individual securities, or you can invest in a portfolio of securities through a mutual fund. You learn all about stock mutual funds in Chapter 9.

Overseas investments

Overseas investment is a potentially misleading category. The types of overseas investment options, such as stocks and bonds and real estate, are not fundamentally different from our domestic options. However, overseas investments are often categorized separately because they come with their own set of risks and rewards.

TIP

Here are some good reasons to invest overseas:

- **Diversification.** International securities markets don't move in tandem with U.S. markets, so adding foreign investments to a domestic portfolio offers you a smoother ride. During the 1987 U.S. stock market crash, for example, most international stock markets dropped far less than ours — some actually rose in value. Conversely, if you thought the growing Asian economies were *the* place to invest, you would have been mighty disappointed to have placed all your investing eggs in this basket when this sector of world hit major problems in the latter 1990s.
- **Growth potential.** Another reason for investing in international securities is this: When you confine your investing to U.S. securities, you're literally missing a world of opportunities. The majority of investment opportunities are overseas. If you look at the total value of all stocks and bonds outstanding worldwide, the value of U.S. securities is now in the minority. We are *not* the world! Many overseas economies are growing faster than ours.

Some people hesitate to invest in overseas securities because they feel that doing so hurts the U.S. economy and contributes to a loss of American jobs. Fair enough. But I have two counterarguments:

- If you don't profit from the growth of economies overseas, someone else will. If money is to be made there, Americans may as well be there to make some of it.
- America already participates in a global economy — Making a distinction between U.S. companies and foreign companies is no longer appropriate. Many companies headquartered in the U.S. also have overseas operations. Some U.S. firms derive a large portion of their revenue from their international divisions. Conversely, many firms that are based overseas also have operations in the U.S. Increasing numbers of companies are worldwide operations.

REMEMBER

You are not unpatriotic if you buy from a company that is based overseas or that has a foreign name. In fact, the product that you thought was foreign-made may be made right here at home. Profits from a foreign company are distributed to all stockholders, no matter where they live. Dividends and stock price appreciation know no national boundaries.

Real estate

Perhaps the most fundamental of ownership investments, real estate has made many people wealthy. Not only does real estate produce consistently good rates of return (averaging around 8 to 10 percent per year) over long investment periods, it can also be purchased with gobs of borrowed money. This leverage helps enhance your rate of return when real estate prices are rising.

As with other ownership investments, the value of real estate depends on the health and performance of the economy as well as on the specifics of the property that you own:

- If the local economy grows and more jobs are being produced at higher wages, then real estate should do well.
- If companies in the community are laying people off left and right and excess housing is sitting vacant because of previous overbuilding, then rents and property values are likely to fall.

TIP

For investors who have time, patience, and capital, real estate can make sense as part of an investment portfolio. If you don't want the headaches that come with purchasing and maintaining a property and being a landlord, you can buy mutual funds that invest in real estate properties (see Chapter 9).

Precious metals

Gold and silver have been used by many civilizations as mediums of exchange. One advantage of using precious metals as currency is that the government can't debase them. With a paper-based currency, such as the U.S. dollar, the government can always print more currency to pay off its debts. (To date, gold is much harder to make than paper money. Just ask Rumpelstiltskin.) This process of casually printing more and more currency can lead to a currency's devaluation — and to our old friend, inflation.

Holdings of gold and silver can provide a so-called *hedge* against inflation. In the U.S. in the late 1970s and early 1980s, inflation rose dramatically. This rise depressed stocks and bonds. Gold and silver, however, soared in value, rising more than 500 percent (even after adjusting for inflation) from 1972 to 1981.

But don't purchase precious metals futures contracts. As I discuss later in this chapter, futures are not investments; they are short-term gambles on which way prices of an underlying investment (in this case, gold or silver) may head over a short period of time. You also should stay away from firms and shops that sell coins and *bullion* (not the soup, but bars of gold or silver). Even if you can find a legitimate firm (which is not an easy task), storing and insuring gold and silver is costly. You don't get good value for your money. I hate to break the news to you, but the Gold Rush is over.

Gold and silver can profit long-term investors, but if you want to invest in precious metals, you're wise to do so through mutual funds. For more information about determining how these types of funds may fit with the rest of your investments and how to buy them, be sure to read Chapters 3 and 9.

Annuities

Annuities are investment products with some tax and insurance twists. They behave like savings accounts, except that they give you slightly higher yields, and they're backed by insurance companies.

As in other types of retirement accounts, the money that you put into an annuity compounds without taxation until withdrawal. However, unlike most other types of retirement accounts — 401(k)s, SEP-IRAs, and Keoghs — an annuity gives you no tax deductions.

Annuities also charge relatively high expenses. That's why it makes sense to consider contributing to an annuity only after you fully fund the tax-deductible retirement accounts that are available to you.

The best annuities available today are distributed by no-load (commission-free) mutual fund companies. For more information about the best annuities and situations for which annuities may be appropriate, be sure to read Chapter 10.

Life insurance

Agents love to pitch cash-value life insurance as an investment. That's because these policies that combine life insurance protection with an account that has a cash value — usually known as *universal, whole,* or *variable life* policies — generate big commissions for the agents who sell them.

Cash-value life insurance is not a good investment. First, you should be saving and investing as much as possible through tax-deductible retirement savings plans such as 401(k)s, IRAs, and Keoghs. Contributions to a cash-value life insurance plan provide you *no* up-front tax benefit. Second, you can earn better investment returns through mutual funds.

The only reason to consider cash-value life insurance is that the proceeds paid to your beneficiaries can be free of inheritance taxes. You need to have a fairly substantial estate at your death to benefit from this feature.

Term life insurance is best for the vast majority of people. Because this is not a book on insurance (thankfully), I advise you to consult my first book, *Personal Finance For Dummies,* 2nd Edition (published by IDG Books Worldwide, Inc.), which has all sorts of good stuff on life and other types of insurance.

Don't fall prey to whole life insurance agents and their sales pitches. Life insurance should not be used as an investment, especially if you haven't exhausted your ability to contribute to retirement accounts. (Even if you've exhausted contributing to retirement accounts, you can do better than cash-value life insurance by choosing tax-friendly mutual funds and/or variable annuities that use mutual funds as an investment option — see Chapters 7 through 10 for the details.)

Limited partnerships (LPs)

Always avoid limited partnerships sold directly through brokers and financial planners. They are inferior investment vehicles. That's not to say that no one has ever made money on them, but limited partnerships are so burdened with high sales commissions and investment-depleting management fees that you can do better in other vehicles.

Limited partnerships are ownership investments that invest in real estate and a variety of businesses, such as cable television, cellular phone companies, and research and development. They pitch that you can get in on the ground floor of a new investment opportunity and make big money. And usually they also tell you that while your investment is growing at 20 percent or more per year, you'll get handsome dividends of 8 percent or so per year. Sound too good to be true? It is.

Many of the yields on LPs have turned out to be bogus. In some cases, partnerships propped up their yields by paying back investors' principals (without telling them, of course). The other hook with LPs is tax benefits. What few loopholes did exist in the tax code for LPs have largely been closed. Amazingly, some investment salespeople hoodwink investors to put their retirement account money — which is already tax-sheltered, just the way that you want it — into LPs! The other problems with LPs overwhelm any small tax advantage, anyway. If you want tax-friendly investments, check out Chapters 7 through 9.

The investment salesperson who sells you such an investment stands to earn a commission of up to 10 percent or more. That means that only 90 cents (or less) per dollar that you put into an LP actually gets invested. Each year, LPs typically siphon off more of your money for management and other expenses. Efficient, no-load mutual funds, in contrast, put 100 percent of your capital to work and charge 1 percent per year or less in operating fees.

Most partnerships have little or no incentive to control costs. In fact, they may have a conflict of interest that leads them to charge more to enrich the managing partners. And, unlike mutual funds, in limited partnerships you can't vote with your feet. If the partnership is poorly run and expensive, you're stuck. That's why LPs are called *illiquid* — you can't get your own money back until the partnership is liquidated, typically seven to ten years after you buy in. (If you want to sell out to a third party in the interim, you have to sell at a huge discount. Don't bother unless you're totally desperate for cash. You're better off sticking it out.) The only thing limited about a limited partnership is its ability to make you money. If you want to make investments that earn you healthy returns, stick with stocks (using mutual funds), real estate, or your own business.

Important Investing Concepts

Now that I've covered the fundamental building blocks of the investing world, I spend much of the rest of the book helping you build with them. Of course, as the title of this book suggests, I focus on what I think is the most convenient and efficient way to put it all together — mutual funds.

But before I do, let me introduce a few key investing concepts that you continually come across as an investor.

Is there a future in commodities and options?

I hesitate to include this passage because buying options, futures, or commodities is not investing; it's gambling. You may hear some people argue that there's no difference between gambling and investing. After all, both involve exposing your money to a degree of risk.

I believe that there's an important difference, and it is this: An investment, over the long haul, is a proven winner. Sure, you'll take some losses now and again, but if you stick with it long enough and are properly diversified, you'll come out ahead. The stock and real estate markets are examples of investments because, in aggregate, over the decades they have consistently gone up.

Gambling, on the other hand, is putting your money into schemes that are sure long-term losers. That's not to say that everyone loses, or that you lose every time you gamble. However, the deck is stacked against you; how else would the casino operators make a profit? And the longer you play, the more likely you are to lose.

Futures, options, and commodities are called *derivatives* — financial instruments whose values are derived from another security (such as a stock or bond) — and they all involve betting on short-term price movements. If the market moves in the right direction at the right time, you win. If it doesn't move in the right direction, or if it moves in the right direction but not at the right time, you lose. Given that short-term market movements are largely unpredictable, you should be able to understand why I say that "investing" in derivatives is like shooting craps.

Return: Why you invest

Ultimately, the *return* is what investors pay the most attention to — perhaps a bit too much attention. I suppose that's to be expected. After all, the expectation of the return of more money than we had to begin with is the reason why we invest. Otherwise we'd just go ahead and blow the money on a big-screen TV.

Return measures how much your investment has grown (or shrunk as the case may be). Return figures are usually quoted as a rate or percentage that measures how much the value of an investment has changed over a specified period of time. So if an investment has a five-year annualized return of 8 percent, then every year for the past five years, that investment, on average, has gotten 8 percent bigger than it was the year before.

So what kind of returns can you expect from different kinds of investments? I say "can" because I'm looking at history, and history is a record of the past. Using history to predict the future, especially the near future, is dangerous. History won't exactly repeat itself, not even in the same fashion and not necessarily when you expect it to.

TIP

During the 20th century, ownership investments like stocks and real estate have returned around 8 to 10 percent per year, handily beating lending investments such as bonds (around 5 percent) and savings accounts (roughly 4 percent) in the investment performance race. Inflation has averaged around 3 percent per year, so savings accounts and bonds barely would have kept up with increases in the cost of living. Factoring in the taxes that you pay on your investment earnings, bonds and savings account returns would even be losing ground relative to the cost of living.

Wouldn't it be interesting to see where those who have some discretionary funds to toss around invest their money? They must know some secret.

Many millionaires are financially savvy; that's how some of them made their millions. But others are financial illiterates. The difference between poorly informed millionaires and poorly informed average investors is that the millionaires are (or feel) wealthy enough to hire advisors — or else they have so much money that it doesn't matter if they lose a few thousand every year on bad investments. As a group, millionaires invest most of their wealth — almost three-quarters of it — in ownership investments such as corporate stock, real estate, and businesses. The remaining quarter they invest mainly in lending-type investments.

Risk: Why you invest carefully

Obviously, you should put all your money in stocks and real estate, right? The returns sure look great. So what's the catch?

REMEMBER

The greater an investment's potential return, the greater, generally, is its risk.

The main drawback to ownership investments is volatility. For example, during this century, stocks have declined by more than 10 percent in a year approximately once every five years. Drops in stock prices of more than 20 percent have occurred about once every ten years (see Figure 1-1). Thus, in order to earn those generous long-term stock market returns of about 10 percent per year, you must be willing to tolerate volatility. That's why you absolutely should *not* put all your money in the stock or real estate market.

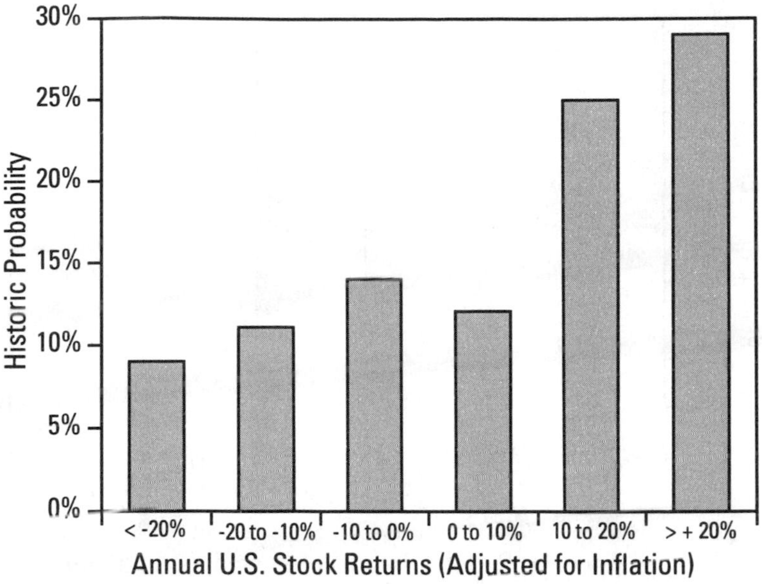

Figure 1-1: Historic probability of different U.S. stock market returns.

As you can see from Figure 1-2, bonds have had fewer years in which they have provided rates of return that were as tremendously negative or positive as stocks have. Bonds are less volatile but, as I discuss in the preceding section, on average you earn a lower rate of return.

TIP

Some types of bonds have higher yields than others, but nothing is free here, either. A bond generally pays you a higher rate of interest as compared with other bonds when it has

- **Lower credit quality,** which compensates for the higher risk of default and the higher likelihood that you will lose your investment.
- **Longer-term maturity,** which compensates for the risk that you'll be unhappy with the bond's interest rate if interest rates move up.
- **Callability,** which retains an organization's or company's right to buy back the bonds issued before the bond matures. Companies like to be able to pay back early if they have found a cheaper way to borrow the money. Early payback is a risk to bondholders because they may get their investment money returned to them when interest rates have dropped.

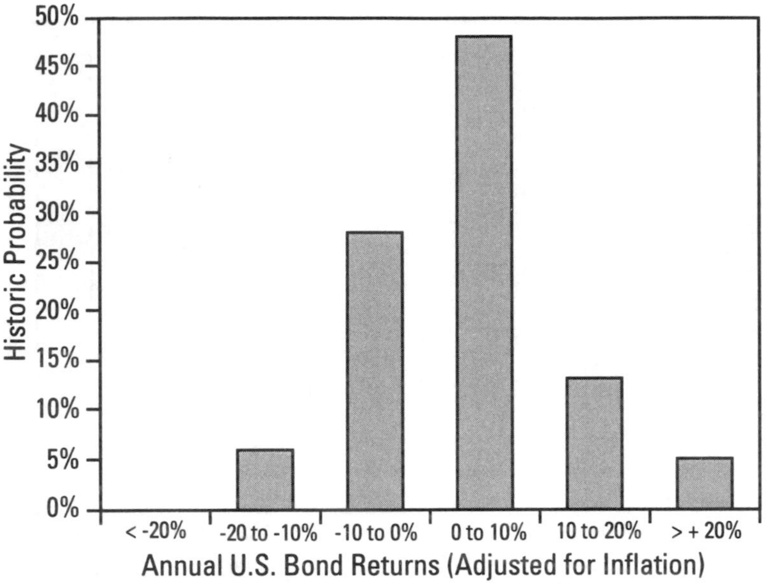

Figure 1-2: Historic probability of different U.S. bond market returns.

Diversification: Eggs in different baskets

Diversification is one of the most powerful investment concepts. All diversification really means is that you carry and save your eggs (your investments) in different baskets.

Diversification requires you to place your money in different investments with returns that are not completely correlated. Now for the plain-English translation: With your money in different places, when one of your investments is down in value, the odds are good that at least one other is up.

To decrease the odds that all your investments will get clobbered at the same time, put your money in different types or classes of investments. The different kinds of investments include money market funds, bonds, stocks, real estate, and precious metals. You can further diversify your investments by investing in international as well as domestic markets.

Within a given class of investments, such as stocks, you should diversify by investing in different types of stocks that perform well under various economic conditions. For this reason, mutual funds, which are diversified portfolios of securities, are highly useful investment vehicles. You buy into the mutual fund, which in turn pools your money with that of many others to invest in a vast array of stocks or bonds.

Risk and return go together: Beware of greed and "advisors" who encourage it

Greed has a long history of exacting harsh punishment on those who fall prey to it in the world of investing. Dating back three centuries from the tulip bulb mania in Holland in 1637, the South Sea Bubble of the 1720s in England, and the extraordinary margin and leverage investors took in the U.S. stock market in the 1920s, to the Japanese real estate market speculative bubble that finally burst in the 1980s, you'll find lessons aplenty for investors willing to learn from others' mistakes.

The 1994 Orange County investment fund debacle (not a mutual fund but a pool of money privately managed by the county treasurer in Orange County, CA) is chock full of mistakes that easily could have been avoided. The fund engaged in insanely complicated and risky investment practices — including borrowing up to 200 percent of the value of the fund to buy risky derivative investments.

Robert Citron, Orange County Treasurer, made critical investing decisions based almost exclusively on advice from commission-based brokers like Michael Stamenson of Merrill Lynch. According to *The Wall Street Journal*, Stamenson is one of Merrill Lynch's top salesmen, reported to have earned in excess of $5 million in commissions yearly during 1993 and 1994, a period during which Merrill Lynch earned an astounding $80 million in its dealings with Orange County.

Lured by the success of higher-than-average returns while interest rates were falling, Citron's fund took on greater risk and more investors. The legend of his success surely attracted many to blindly jump on board as a number of smaller city and county governments (nearly 200 in total) handed over their money to Citron and his legions of brokers to invest.

Orange County and the other governments could have avoided making the same mistake that officials of San Jose, CA, did a decade earlier when they made aggressive interest-rate risky investments that plunged when rates turned tail. Stamenson was heavily involved in this investment disaster as well, which led to Merrill Lynch and a number of other brokerage firms coughing up a legal settlement of $26 million.

Some municipalities are getting the same investing education in the school of hard knocks that individual investors got when they were sold limited partnerships by the same brokerage firms involved in the Orange County fiasco.

You can look at the benefits of diversification in two ways: First, diversification reduces the volatility in the value of your whole portfolio. In other words, when you diversify, you can achieve the same rate of return that a single investment can provide, but with reduced fluctuations in value. Another way to look at it: Diversification allows you to obtain a higher rate of return for a given level of risk.

Chapter 2

Mutual Funds: Smart Money Management for All of Us

In This Chapter

- Mutual funds versus individual securities
- Reasons to choose mutual funds
- Open-end versus closed-end funds
- Drawbacks to mutual funds
- Money-managed alternatives to mutual funds

Consider this: A young man with his first paycheck, a child with some gift money from loving grandparents, my good friend Chris from Chapter 1, and bigwigs like Steve Jobs, Hillary and Bill Clinton, Charles Schwab, Michael Jackson, Danielle Steel, and Michael Jordan all can hire the same professional money managers — for the same price — by investing in mutual funds.

I'm not sure where the "mutual" in mutual funds comes from; perhaps it's used because these funds allow many people to mutually invest their money. And while it's true that some wealthy people prefer to invest in and spend their money on things that you and I can't — such as private jets, yachts, savings and loan companies, cattle futures, or beach-front vacation homes — most well-heeled investors choose to invest in mutual funds for the same reasons that make sense for you and me:

- Easy diversification
- Access to professional money managers
- Low investment management costs

Some of the big-time investors who haven't invested in mutual funds probably wish that they had — instead of putting their money into now-vacant office buildings, barren oil fields, lame racehorses, and other "promising" investments.

What's a Mutual Fund?

A mutual fund is a collection of investment money pooled from lots of people to be invested for a specific objective. When you invest in a mutual fund, you buy shares and become a *shareholder* of the fund. A fund manager and his or her team of assistants figure out in which specific securities (for example, stocks, bonds, money market funds) they should invest the shareholders' money so they can accomplish the objectives of the fund and keep you (and your fellow shareholders) as a happy customer.

Because good mutual funds take most of the hassle and cost out of figuring out which securities to invest in, they are among the best investment vehicles ever created:

- Mutual funds allow you to diversify your investments — that is, invest in many different industries and companies instead of in just one or two.

  By spreading the risk over a number of different securities representing many different industries and companies, mutual funds lessen your volatility and chances of a large loss.

- Mutual funds enable you to give your money to the best money managers in the country — some of the same folks who manage money for the already rich and famous.

- Mutual funds are the ultimate couch potato investment! However, unlike staying home and watching *The X Files* or playing Nintendo, investing in mutual funds can pay you back big rewards.

What's really cool about mutual funds is that once you understand them, you realize that they can help you meet a bunch of different financial goals. Maybe you're building up an emergency savings stash of three to six months' living expenses (a prudent idea, by the way). Perhaps you're starting to think about saving for a home purchase, retirement, or future educational costs. You may know what you need the money for, but you may not know how to protect the money you have and make it grow.

Don't feel bad if you haven't figured out a long-term financial plan. And don't feel bad if you don't have a goal in mind for the money you're saving. Many people don't have their finances organized. That's why there are books like this one! I talk more about what kinds of goals mutual funds can help you accomplish in Chapter 3.

Financial intermediaries

A mutual fund is a type of financial intermediary. (Now that's a mouthful!) Why should you care? Because, if you understand what a financial intermediary is and how mutual funds stack up to other financial intermediaries, you'll better understand when funds are appropriate for your investments and when they probably are not. A financial intermediary is nothing more than an organization that takes money from people who want to invest and then gives the money to those who need investment capital (another term for money).

Suppose that you want to borrow money to invest in your own business. You go to your friendly neighborhood banker, who examines your financial records and agrees to loan you $20,000 at 10 percent interest for five years. The money that the banker is lending you has to come from somewhere, right? Well, the banker got that money from a bunch of people who deposited money with the banker for three years at, say, 5 percent interest. Thus, the banker acts as a financial intermediary, or middleman, one who receives money from depositors and lends it to borrowers who can use it productively.

Insurance companies do similar things with money. They sell investments such as annuities (see Chapter 1) and then turn around and lend the money — by investing in bonds, for example — to businesses that need to borrow. (Remember, a bond is nothing more than a company's promise to repay borrowed money over a specified period of time at a specified interest rate.)

The best mutual funds are better financial intermediaries for you to invest through. The reasons: they skim off less to manage your money and allow you more choice and control over what your money actually gets invested into.

Ten Reasons to Choose Mutual Funds

Good mutual funds are excellent investment vehicles for many people. To understand why funds are so sensible is to understand how and why funds can work for you. Read on to discover their many benefits.

Professional management

Mutual funds are investment companies that pool your money with the money of hundreds, thousands, or even millions of other investors. The investment company hires a portfolio manager and a team of researchers whose full-time job is to analyze and purchase investments that best meet the fund's stated objectives.

Typically, fund managers are graduates of the top business and finance schools in the country, where they learn the principles of portfolio management and securities valuation and selection. (Despite the handicap of their formal education, most of them still do a good job of investing money.) In addition to their educational training, the best fund managers typically have five or more years of experience in analyzing and selecting investments.

For most fund managers and researchers, finding the best investments is more than a full-time job. Consider the following activities (all of them unpleasant for non-investing professionals) that an investor should do before investing in stocks and bonds:

- **Analyze company financial statements.** Companies whose securities trade in the financial markets are required to issue reports every three months detailing their revenue, expenses, profits and losses, and assets and liabilities. Unless you're a numbers geek, own an HP-12C financial calculator, and enjoy dissecting tedious corporate financial statements, this first task alone is reason enough to invest through a mutual fund and leave the driving to them.
- **Talk with the muckety-mucks.** Most fund managers log thousands of frequent-flier miles and incur massive long-distance phone bills talking to the folks running the companies they're invested in or thinking about investing in. Because of the huge amount of money they manage, large fund companies even get visits from company executives, who fly in to grovel at the fund managers' feet.

  Now, do you have the correct type of china and all the place settings that etiquette demands of people who host such high-level folks? If not, avoiding this activity is another reason for you to invest through mutual funds.
- **Analyze company and competitor strategies.** Corporate managers have an irritating tendency to talk up what a great job they're doing. It's not that they fib; they just want rich investors to feel warm and fuzzy about forking over their loot. Some companies may look as if they're making the right moves, but what if their products are soon to lag behind the competition's? Fund managers and their researchers take a skeptical view of what a company's execs say — they read the fine print and check under the rugs. They also keep on top of what competitors are doing. Sometimes they discover better investment ideas this way.
- **Talk with company customers, suppliers, and industry consultants.** Another way the mutual fund managers find out if a company's public relations story is full of holes rather than reality is by speaking with the company's customers, suppliers, and other industry experts. These people often have more balanced viewpoints and can be a great deal more open about the negatives. These folks are harder to find but can provide valuable information.
- **Attend trade shows and review industry literature.** It's truly amazing how specialized the world is becoming. Do you really want to subscribe to business magazines that track the latest happenings with ball-bearing or catalytic-converter technology? They'll put you to sleep in a couple of pages. Unlike *People, Newsweek,* and *TV Guide,* they'll also cost you an arm and a leg to subscribe.

TECHNICAL STUFF

A (brief) history of mutual funds

Mutual funds date back to the 1800s, when English and Scottish investment trusts sold shares to investors. Funds arrived in the U.S. in 1924. They were chugging along and growing in assets until the late 1920s, when the Great Depression derailed the financial markets and the economy. Stock prices plunged, and so did mutual funds that held stocks.

As was common in the stock market at that time, mutual funds were *leveraging* their investments — which is a fancy way of saying that they put up only, for example, 25 cents on the dollar for investments they actually owned. The other 75 cents was borrowed. That's why, when the stock market plunged in value in 1929, some investors and fund shareholders got clobbered. They were losing money on their investments *and* on all the borrowed money, too. But, like the rest of the country, mutual funds, although a little bruised, pulled through this economic calamity.

In 1940, the Investment Company Act established ground rules and oversight by the Securities and Exchange Commission (SEC) over the fund industry. Among other benefits, this landmark federal legislation required funds to gain approval from the SEC *before* issuing or selling any fund shares to the public. Over time, this legislation has been strengthened by requiring funds to disclose cost, risk, and other information in a uniform format through a legal document called a *prospectus* (see Chapter 4).

During the 1940s, 1950s, and 1960s, funds grew at a fairly high and constant rate. From less than $1 billion in assets in 1940, fund assets grew to more than $50 billion by the late 1960s — more than a 50-fold increase.

Before the early 1970s, funds focused largely on investing in stocks. Since then, however, money market mutual funds and bond mutual funds have mushroomed. They now account for about half of all mutual fund assets.

Today, thousands of mutual funds manage more than $4 trillion. That's a mighty big number — but still less than the amount of the U.S. government's debt outstanding.

Are you, as the investor, going to do all these tasks and do them well? Nothing personal, but I doubt that you will. Even in the unlikely event that you could perform investment research as well as the best fund managers, don't you value your time? A good mutual fund management team will happily perform all the yucky research for you, do it well, and do it for a fraction of what it would cost you to do it haphazardly on your own.

REMEMBER

In short, a mutual fund management team does more research and more number-crunching and applies more due diligence than most of you could ever possibly have the energy or expertise to do in what little free time you have. Investing in mutual funds will help your friendships and maybe even your love life because you'll have more free time!

Greater value and efficiency

The concept of mutual funds sounds great, you say. But what does it cost to hire such high-powered talent to do all this dreadful research and analysis? A mere pittance, if you pick the right funds. In fact, when you invest your money in a good, efficiently managed mutual fund, it will likely cost you far less than it would to trade individual securities on your own.

When fund managers buy and sell securities, they can do it for a fraction of the cost that you would pay. Because mutual funds typically buy or sell tens of thousands of shares of a stock at a time, they get bulk discounts on their transaction fees, generally 80 to 90 percent less per share than what you would pay to buy or sell a few hundred shares on your own, even if you're using a low-cost discount broker.

But lower trading costs are only part of the reason that mutual funds are a cheaper, more communal way to get the investing job done. A mutual fund also spreads out the cost of extensive — and expensive — research over thousands of investors.

Mutual funds are also able to manage money more efficiently through effective use of technology. Innovations in information management tools enable funds to monitor and manage billions of dollars from millions of investors at a very low cost. In general, moving around $5 billion in securities doesn't cost them much more than it does to move $500 million. Larger investments just mean a few more zeros in the computer data banks.

The most efficiently managed mutual funds cost less than one percent per year in fees (bonds and money market funds cost much less — good ones charge just 0.5 percent per year or less). Some of the larger and more established funds charge annual fees as low as 0.2 percent per year. (I explain the role of fees in your investment decisions in Chapter 4.)

And today, many funds do not charge a commission to purchase or redeem shares. Commission-free funds are called no-load funds. Such opportunities used to be rare. Fidelity and Vanguard, the two largest distributors of no-load funds today, exacted sales charges as high as 8.5 percent during the early 1970s. Even today, some mutual funds known as load funds charge you for buying or selling shares in their funds.

If you decide that you want to withdraw money from a fund, most funds — particularly no-loads — do not charge you a redemption fee. (Think about that — some investments require that you pay to get your own money back!)

Diversification

Diversification is a big attraction for many investors who choose mutual funds. Here's an example of why.

Suppose you heard that Phenomenal Pharmaceuticals has developed a drug that stops cancer cells in their tracks. You run to the phone, call your broker, and invest all your savings in a few hundred shares of Phenomenal stock. Five years later, the Food and Drug Administration denies the company approval for the drug, and the company goes belly up, taking your $10,000 with it.

Your $10,000 would have been much safer in a mutual fund. A mutual fund might buy a few shares of a promising, but risky, company like Phenomenal without exposing investors like you to financial ruin. The fund owns stocks or bonds from dozens of companies, diversifying against the risk of bad news from any single company or sector. So when Phenomenal goes belly-up, the fund may barely feel a ripple.

It would be difficult — and expensive — to diversify like that on your own, unless you have a few hundred thousand dollars and a great deal of time to invest. You would need to invest money in at least 8 to 12 different companies in different industries to ensure that your portfolio could withstand a downturn in one or more of the investments.

Mutual funds typically invest in 25 to 100 securities, or more. Proper diversification ensures that the fund receives the highest possible return at the lowest possible risk, given the objectives of the fund.

I'm not suggesting that mutual funds escape without share-price declines during major market downturns. For example, mutual funds that invested in U.S. stocks certainly declined during the October 1987 U.S. stock market crash. However, the most unhappy investors that month were individuals who had all their money riding on only one or a handful of stocks. Some individual stock share prices plunged by as much as 80 to 90 percent.

Although most mutual funds are "diversified," some aren't. For example, some stock funds, known as sector funds, invest exclusively in stocks of a single industry (for instance, health care). Others focus on a single country (such as India). I'm not a fan of such funds because of this lack of diversification and because such funds typically charge higher operating fees. I talk more about narrowly focused stock funds in Chapter 9.

An "equal opportunity" investment

If you have $500 or more to invest, you should consider mutual funds. Most funds have low minimum investment requirements. Nearly a quarter have minimums of $500 or less, and nearly two-thirds have minimums of $1,000 or less. Retirement account (such as IRAs, Keoughs) investors often can invest with even less. Some have monthly investment plans — so you can start with as little as $50. Best of all, when you invest in a mutual fund, you get the same attention given to the rich and famous. With mutual funds, all investors' dollars receive the same royal treatment.

Even if you have a whole pile of money to invest, mutual funds make sense. Increasing numbers of companies and institutions with big bucks (millions) to invest are turning to the low-cost, high-quality money management services that you get from a mutual fund.

Regulatory scrutiny

Before a fund can take in money from investors, the fund must go through a tedious review process by the Securities and Exchange Commission (SEC). Once it offers shares, a mutual fund is required to publish in its prospectus (discussed in Chapter 4) historical data on the fund's earnings, its operating expenses and other fees, and its rate of trading (turnover) in the fund's investments.

It should go without saying that government regulators are far from perfect. (Remember the Savings & Loan fiasco of the 1980s?) Conceivably, a fund operator could slip through some bogus numbers. But I wouldn't lose sleep worrying about this, especially if you invest through the larger, reputable fund companies recommended in this book.

Choice of risk level

Choosing from a huge variety of mutual funds, you can select the funds that meet your financial goals and take on the kinds of risks that you're comfortable with:

- **Stock funds.** If you want your money to grow over a long period of time (and you can put up with some bad years thrown in with the good), select funds that invest more heavily in stocks.
- **Bond funds.** If you need current income and don't want investments that fluctuate as widely in value as stocks do, consider bond funds.

Are mutual funds too risky?

One of the major misconceptions about mutual funds is that they all invest entirely in stocks and, therefore, are too risky. They don't, and they're not. Using mutual funds, you can invest in a whole array of securities, ranging from money market funds, bonds, stocks, and even real estate.

You may be surprised to learn that only about half of all the money invested in mutual funds is invested in stocks. The other half is invested in money market securities and bonds.

When you hear folks talk about the "riskiness" of mutual funds, even in the media, you'll know that they're overlooking this fact: All mutual funds are not created equal.

- Some funds, such as money market funds, carry virtually zero risk that your investment will decline in value.
- Bond funds that invest in shorter-term bonds don't budge by more than several percentage points per year.

And you may be surprised to learn in Chapter 9 that some funds that invest in stocks aren't all that risky if you can plan on holding them for a decade or more.

- **Money market funds.** If you want to be sure that your invested principal does not drop in value because you may need to use your money in the short term, you may choose a money market fund.

Most investors choose a combination of these three types of funds to diversify and help meet different financial goals. I get into all that in the chapters to come.

Virtually no risk of bankruptcy

Hundreds of banks and dozens of insurance companies have failed in the past decade alone. Banks and insurers can fail because their liabilities (the money customers have given them to invest) can exceed their assets (the money they have invested or lent). When a big chunk of a bank's loans go sour at the same time that its depositors want their money back, the bank fails. That happens because banks have less than 20 cents on deposit for every dollar that you and I place with them. Likewise, if an insurance company makes several poor investments or underestimates the number of claims that will be made by insurance policyholders, it too can fail.

Such failures can't happen with a mutual fund. The situation in which the investors' demand for the return of their investment (the fund's liabilities) exceeds the value of a fund's investments (the fund's assets) simply cannot occur. Why not? Because for every dollar a fund holds for its customers, that mutual fund has a dollar's worth of redeemable securities.

That's not to say that you can't lose money in a mutual fund. The share price of a mutual fund is tied to the value of its underlying securities; if the underlying securities such as stocks decrease in value, so, too, does the share price of the fund. If you sell your shares when their price is less than what you paid for them, then you'll get back less cash than you originally put into the fund. But that's the worst that can happen; you cannot lose all your investment in a mutual fund unless every single security owned by that fund suddenly becomes worthless — an extraordinarily unlikely event.

In fact, since the Investment Company Act of 1940 was passed to regulate the mutual fund industry, no fund has ever gone under. (A money market fund run by and invested in by banks did disband after losing a small portion of principal — see Chapter 7.)

You may be interested to know that the specific stocks and/or bonds that a mutual fund buys are held by a custodian — a separate organization independent of the mutual fund company. The employment of a custodian ensures that the fund management company can't embezzle your funds and use assets from a better-performing fund to subsidize a poor performer.

Freedom from sales sharks

Stock brokers (also known as financial consultants) and commission-based financial planners make more money by encouraging trading activity and by selling you investments that provide them with high commissions — limited partnerships and mutual funds with high load fees, for example. Brokers and planners also get an occasional message from the top brass asking them to sell some new-fangled investment product. All this creates inherent conflicts of interest that can prevent them from providing objective investment and financial advice and recommendations.

No-load (commission-free) mutual fund companies do not push products. Their toll-free telephone lines are staffed with knowledgeable people who earn salaries, not commissions. Sure, they want you to invest with their company, but the size of their next paycheck does not depend on how much they can persuade you to buy or trade.

Don't fret about the crooks

Don't worry about others having easy access to the money you've invested in mutual funds. Even if someone were able to convince a fund company through the toll-free phone line that he were you (say, by knowing your account number and Social Security number), the impostor at worst could only request a transaction to occur between accounts registered in your name. You'd find out about the shenanigans when the confirmation arrived in the mail, at which time you could call the mutual fund company and undo the whole mess. (Just by listening to a tape of the phone call, which the fund company records, the company could confirm that you did not place the trade.)

No one can actually take money out of your account, either. Suppose that someone does know your personal and account information and calls a fund company to ask that a check be sent from a redemption on the account. Even in such a scenario, the check would be sent to the address on the account and be made payable to you.

The only way that someone can actually take money out of your account is with your authorization. And there's only one way to do that: by completing a full trading authorization or power-of-attorney form. I generally recommend that you not grant this authority to anyone. If you do, make sure the investment firm makes checks payable only to you, not to the person disbursing the money from the account.

Convenient access to your money

What I find really terrific about dealing with mutual funds is that they are set up for people who don't like to waste time going to a local branch office and standing in line waiting for "the next available representative." I don't know about you, but I enjoy waiting in lines, especially in places like a bank, about as much as I enjoy having my dentist fill a cavity.

With mutual funds, you can make your initial investment from the comfort of your living room by filling out and mailing a simple form and writing a check. Later, you can add to your investment by mailing in a check or by authorizing money transfers by phone from one mutual fund account to another.

Selling shares of your mutual fund for cash is just as easy. Generally, all you need to do is call the fund company's toll-free number. Some companies have representatives available by phone 24 hours a day, 365 days a year. Many mutual fund companies also allow you to wire money back and forth from your local bank account, allowing you to access your money almost as quickly through a money market fund as you can through your local bank. (As I discuss in Chapter 7, you'll probably need to keep a local bank checking account to write smaller checks and for immediate ATM access to cash.)

You may also be interested in knowing that most money market funds also offer check-writing privileges. These accounts often carry a restriction that your bank checking account doesn't have: Money market checks must be greater than a specified minimum amount — typically $250.

If you like to do some transactions in person, some of the larger fund companies, such as Fidelity, and some discount brokers, such as Charles Schwab, have branch offices in convenient locations so you can give money to or get it from another living, breathing human being. (***Note:*** Such branch offices won't give you cash on the spot the way a bank would. Schwab, for example, will issue you a check only if you give them a day's notice.)

Because you value your limited time

You work hard; you have family and friends. Chances are, the last thing you want to do with your free time is research where to invest your savings. If you're like many other busy people, you've kept your money in a bank just to avoid the hassles. Or maybe you turned your money over to some smooth-talking broker who sold you a high-commission investment you still don't understand but are convinced will make you rich.

Mutual funds — which you can purchase by writing a check or calling toll-free number — can pay you a much better rate of return over the long haul than a dreary, boring bank account or an insurance company account. And you don't have to pay high commissions.

REMEMBER

Just don't forget that mutual funds, like all investments, carry their own unique risks, which I tell you about later in this chapter. You need to understand these risks before you take the plunge into mutual funds.

Funds and Families, Open or Closed

In addition to understanding such things as fund prospectuses and performance numbers (which I discuss in Chapters 4 and 12, respectively), you need to know some important investment terms right now to avoid confusion.

Of families and funds

Throughout this book, I discuss mutual fund companies as well as individual funds. To better illustrate the difference between the two, let me draw an analogy to a nuclear family — one with parents and children.

Mutual fund companies, such as Vanguard and Fidelity, can be thought of as parent organizations that act as the distributors for a group of funds. The parent organization doesn't actually take your money. Instead, it is responsible for distributing and managing the individual mutual funds — the kids, if you will, in the family.

You actually invest your money in an individual mutual fund — one wayfaring child of the whole family — such as Vanguard's Wellesley Income Fund or the Fidelity Balanced Fund. Vanguard and Fidelity are the parent organizations. (Don't worry: Children don't actually manage the funds, although some portfolio managers are on the young side — in their 30s!)

As with real families, good parent organizations tend to produce better offspring. That's why you should understand the reputation of the parent organization that's responsible for overseeing the fund before you ever invest in it. What is the parent's track record with similar funds? How long has the parent been managing the types of funds you're interested in? Has the parent had any disasters with similar funds? The specific funds I recommend later in the book will satisfy these concerns.

Open-end or closed-end?

I'm not talking about remembering to place the cap back on the tube of toothpaste! (Though keeping the cap closed makes more sense if you don't want dried-up toothpaste.) Open-end and closed-end are general terms that refer to whether a mutual fund company issues an unlimited or a set amount of shares in a particular mutual fund.

The vast majority of funds in the marketplace are open-end funds, and they're also the funds that I focus on in this book because the better open-end funds are superior (more on this point in a moment) to their closed-end counterparts. *Open-end* simply means that the fund issues as many (or as few) shares as investors demand. In open-end funds, there's no limit to the number of investors or the amount of money in the fund.

Closed-end funds decide up front, before they take on any investors, exactly how many shares they will issue. Thus, once these shares are issued, the only way you can purchase shares (or more shares) is to buy them from an existing investor on a stock exchange.

Sorry to complicate things, but I need to clarify what I just said. Open-end funds can, and sometimes do, decide at a later date to close their fund to new investors. This does not make it a closed-end fund, however, because investors with existing shares can still buy more shares from the fund company. Rather, it becomes an open-end fund that is closed to new investors!

Generally speaking, the better open-end funds are preferable to closed-end funds for the following reasons:

- **Bigger and better.** The better open-end funds attract more investors over time. Thus, they can afford to pay the necessary money to hire better managers. That's not to say that closed-end funds don't have good managers, too, but as a general rule, open-end funds attract better talent.
- **Lower cost.** Because they can attract more investors, and therefore more money to manage, the better open-end funds charge lower annual operating expenses. Closed-end funds tend to be much smaller and therefore more costly to operate. Remember, operating expenses are always deducted before a fund pays its investors their returns. Thus, the returns for closed-end funds are depressed by higher annual fees.

  The initial sale of a closed-end fund is generally handled by brokers who receive a hefty (for them, not for you) commission. Brokers' commissions usually siphon anywhere from 5 to 10 percent out of your investment dollars. Even if you're smart and wait until after the initial offering to buy closed-end fund shares on the stock exchange, you'll still pay a brokerage commission. You can avoid these high commissions by purchasing a no-load (commission-free), open-end mutual fund.
- **Fee-free selling.** With an open-end fund, the value of a share always equals 100 percent of what the fund's investments are currently worth. And you don't have the cost and trouble of selling your shares to another investor as you must with a closed-end fund. Because closed-end funds trade like securities on the stock exchange, and because you must sell your shares to someone who wants to buy, closed-end funds sometimes sell at a discount. Even though the securities in a closed-end fund may be worth $20 per share, you may be able to get only $19 per share if sellers outnumber buyers.

  There can be a good side to a closed-end fund selling at a discount. You could buy shares in a closed-end fund at discount and hold onto them in hopes that the discount disappears or — even better — turns into a premium (which means that the share price of the fund exceeds the value of the investments it holds). Never pay a premium to buy a close-end fund and never buy one without getting at least 5 percent discount.

Unless I specify otherwise, funds discussed and recommended in this book are open-end funds.

Face-Off: Mutual Funds versus Individual Securities

According to a recent slew of books, newsletters, and magazine articles, (stock) mutual funds are not the place to be. They're boring, conservative, and totally unsexy.

And what's hip? Individual stocks. Why? Because, according to the pronouncements of the individual stock gurus, you can get rich quick by investing in these individual stocks.

Not only do these pundits say that investing in individual stocks supposedly provides Himalayan returns . . .

> "How we beat the stock market — and how you can, too. 23.4% annual return." – subtitle of *The Beardstown Ladies' Common-Sense Investment Guide*
>
> Novices can ". . .nearly double the S&P 500 posting returns in excess of 20 percent per year. . .you might be able to fish out greater than 30 percent per year on your own without assuming considerably greater risk," – David and Tom Gardner, *The Motley Fool Investment Guide*
>
> "Forget bonds . . . real estate . . . build a portfolio entirely of stocks. Returns an annual average of 34 percent." – Matt Seto, 17 years old, *The Whiz Kid of Wall Street's Investment Guide*
>
> "I have been able to obtain fantastic returns on so many stock market plays: 260,000% annualized one hour returns; 10,680% annualized in two days and so many more . . . . These trades are sort of like a magic trick. At first it seems 'stupendous' — otherworldly. But as you learn the trick, you say 'it's a piece of cake.'" – Wade Cook, *Stock Market Miracles*

but they also say anyone can do it with little effort . . .

> "It's not an exaggeration to say that fifth graders can wallop the market after one month of analysis. You can too." – *The Motley Fool Investment Guide*
>
> "An amateur who devotes a small amount of study to companies in an industry he or she knows something about can outperform 95 percent of the paid experts who manage mutual funds, plus have fun in doing it." – Peter Lynch, *Beating the Street*

Do the stock pundits' claims sound too good to be true?

Well, they are.

Beware the claims of the stock-picking gurus

It's easy to dismiss the outrageousness of the claims made by someone like Wade Cook. Even if you don't know that Cook has been in trouble with securities regulators and courts for many years now, your common sense tells you that five and six digit returns are well outside the realm of reasonable expectations for stock performance.

But what about the more believable performance claims, in the range of 20 and 30 percent, that can so easily dupe an investor into thinking they're true? Like the annualized return of 23.4% claimed by the Beardstown Ladies. Sounds reasonable, and why would a bunch of ladies from a small town in Illinois mislead you? Well, back in 1995, I asked the Beardstown Ladies to send me some account statements so that I could verify their return claims, but they turned me down, citing a decision "not to make our return an issue . . . we're not out to be bragging." (Have they told that to their publishers, who've plastered the return claims across the cover of their book?)

I even offered to have an independent accounting firm review their records and the club refused. That told me loud and clear how authentic their 23+ percent performance claims were.

Turns out their claims were indeed bogus. Shane Tritsch, a reporter for *Chicago* magazine, wrote a piece in the March 1998 issue, entitled "Bull Marketing," in which he exposed gross inaccuracies in how the Beardstown Investment Club calculated its stock market returns. Tritsch was tipped off to potential problems by a note added to the copyright page of the paperback edition of the Beardstown book in which it said that the club's 23.4 percent annualized returns were determined "by calculating the increase in their total club balance over time. Since this increase includes the dues that the members pay regularly, this return may be different from the return that might be calculated for a mutual fund . . ."

May be different? Indeed. Using documents from the investment club provided by a *The Wall Street Journal* reporter, Jim Raker, a senior research analyst at Morningstar, told me that he calculates that the investment club earned a return of a mere 9 percent per year — a far cry from the 23+ percent returns claimed by the club.

Even worse, though, is that the Beardstown investment club *under*performed the market. For the period in question (from 1983 to 1992), while the Beardstown club earned just 9 percent per year, the Standard & Poor 500 Index — the widely followed index for the U.S. stock market — returned about 16 percent. In fact, if you had invested in lower risk bonds, you would have earned nearly 12 percent per year and outperformed the stock picks of the Beardstown club!

After the *Chicago* magazine story appeared, reporters from numerous media outlets including CNBC, CBS, *The Wall Street Journal,* and the Associated Press picked up on the news. I find this somewhat ironic since the media are a large part of what brought this investment club to fame. Many in the media bought the original Beardstown investing success story hook, line, and sinker. During an appearance on the CBS morning show, then-anchor Harry Smith said, "If these ladies had a mutual fund, I'd invest!"

Perhaps Harry and other journalists should have done a little more homework. Whenever a book author, investment newsletter, or investment manager claims to have produced a particular rate of return, especially a market-beating return, I always ask for proof before I'm willing to put the claim in print myself. Otherwise, how do you know whether the claims are real or advertising hype?

Some performance claims are so ridiculous that most journalists don't fall for them. Recently, I reported in my column about how investing seminar promoter Wade Cook was promising attendees that he could teach them to earn 300 percent per year in the stock market. Although some journalists have recently been reporting on Cook's deceptions and hype, consumers have been flocking to his $4,695 seminars.

The Beardstown investment club's claim of 23.4 percent annualized returns made me suspicious as well, even though it wasn't an outrageous triple digit return. Stocks historically return just 10 percent per year, yet this club, in their book, was claiming to ". . . have been outperforming mutual funds and professional money managers 3 to 1." When the club was unwilling to document their performance claims, I assumed they were false. Now the rest of the media know it too.

And for Peter Lynch, who tells us in his book that an amateur stock-picker can easily beat 95 percent of the pros — shame on him! Widely regarded as the best mutual fund manager ever, Lynch more than anyone knows how much hard work goes into beating the market. In fact, during the years that Lynch piloted Fidelity's Magellan fund, he was known for his workaholic 70- and 80+- hour work weeks. He stated publicly that the primary reason he retired early was to spend more time with his family. He worked this hard to do something that he says anyone can do with ease? Something that you as an investor don't really need his skills for?

The notion that most average people and non-investment professionals can, with minimal effort, beat the best full-time, experienced money managers is, how should I say, ludicrous and absurd. But it does seem to appeal to some people's egos, until the returns come in (or don't, as the case may be).

Know the drawbacks behind investing in individual securities

The stock-picking cheerleaders will cite plenty of reasons and make hyped claims to get you to invest in individual stocks. But they are loathe to mention the drawbacks of selecting and trading individual securities. You won't buy their books if they can't promise you effortless riches, so you may not openly get the following information from the "stock-picking-is-easy" writers:

- **Stock-picking takes significant research time and related expenses.** Before buying an individual security, you should know a great deal about the company you're investing in. Relevant questions that you need to answer include these: What products or services does the company sell? What are the company's prospects for future growth and profitability? How does the company's performance compare to its competitors' performances — both recently and over the long haul? Are technological changes in the works that might harm or improve their business? How much debt does the company have?

  You need to do your homework on these questions, not only before you make your initial investment, but also on a continuing basis as long as you hold an investment. And you have to expend this legwork for every company you invest in and every company you consider investing in. That's how Lynch filled up his marathon work weeks as a fund manager.

  Be honest with yourself. If you're really going to research and monitor your individual securities, the extra work ultimately will take time away from other pursuits. In worst-case situations, I've seen busy people spend almost as many hours on the weekend and in the evenings with their portfolios as they do with family and friends. If you can really afford the time for this type of hobby, more power to you. But remember, no one I know of has ever said on her deathbed, "I wish I had spent more time watching my investments." You only get one chance to live your life — once squandered, your time is gone forever.

- **Stock trading incurs higher transaction costs.** Even when you use a discount broker (described in Chapter 5), the commissions you pay to buy or sell securities are not cheap. By contrast, a large institution, such as a mutual fund, that buys securities in blocks of 10,000 shares or more pays a fraction of the cost — a penny or two per share when trading. If you invest in securities on your own, you're effectively paying 20 times or more per share in commissions than mutual fund companies do.

  Note two exceptions to the rule that individual security purchases cost too much: (1) Government bonds can be purchased directly from the Federal Reserve without charge, and (2) deep discount brokers (see Chapter 5) can be quite cheap for investors making large purchases.

- **Individual stocks offer less likelihood of diversification.** Unless you have several hundred thousand dollars or more to invest in dozens of different securities, you probably can't afford to develop a diversified portfolio. For example, when investing in stocks, you should hold stock in companies belonging to different industries, in different companies within an industry, and so on. Not properly diversifying adds to the risk of losing your shirt.
- **Individual stocks bring more accounting and bookkeeping chores.** When you invest in individual securities outside retirement accounts, every time you sell a specific security, you must report that transaction on your tax return.

  Even if you pay someone else to complete your tax return, you still have the hassle of keeping track of statements and receipts. (On the plus side, however, you control selling decisions with individual securities; with funds, managers who trade can lead to capital gains distributions for you.)

Dividend reinvestment plans (DRIPs) for individual stocks

This interesting spin on investing may sound attractive, but it's often more bother than it's worth: Increasing numbers of corporations allow existing holders of shares of stock to reinvest their dividends (known as DRIPs) in more shares of stock without paying brokerage commissions. In some cases, companies allow you to make additional cash purchases of more shares of stock, also commission-free.

In order to qualify, you must generally have already bought some shares of stock in the company. Ideally, you bought these initial shares through a discount broker to keep your commission burden as low as possible.

Although DRIPs reduce your stock commissions on future purchases, DRIPs have their shortcomings.:

- Investing in DRIPs is only available and cost-effective for investments held outside retirement accounts. As I discuss in Chapter 3, most people should invest as much as possible through the retirement accounts that are available to you.
- You need to complete a lot of paperwork to invest in a number of different companies' DRIP stock plans. Life is too short to bother with these plans for this reason alone.
- Some companies that offer these plans are hungry — for whatever reason. They need to drum up support for their stock. These investments may not be the best ones for the future.
- DRIP plans don't eliminate fees. You still pay fees to buy the initial shares of stock, and many company DRIP plans charge nominal fees for additional transactions and services.

Taking these shortcomings into account, you're better off in the long run using professional money managers such as those available through no-load mutual funds.

Understand the psychology of selecting stocks

Some folks just don't, won't, or can't enjoy having all their money tied up in mutual funds. Some people say that funds are, well, kind of boring. It's true that following the trials, tribulations, successes, and failures of a favorite company can provide you plenty of excitement (sometimes more than you want). A fund, on the other hand, is a little like a black box. You pour money into it and don't have specific corporate dramas to follow.

Over the years, I've noticed some common characteristics among investors who prefer to have at least some of their portfolios in individual securities. No offense, but see if you recognize yourself:

- **The Boaster.** You only go to parties when you've just made a sweet deal in the stock market. If you couldn't tell others of your shrewd stock picks and your latest killing in the market, there'd be little point to owning securities. While the thought has, hopefully, never crossed your mind of sending copies of a brokerage statement out to friends and relatives, you've been known on more than a few occasions to offer unsolicited stock tips and investment advice.
- **The Controller.** You hate delegating jobs to others, especially important ones, because no one will do as good a job as you. Investing much or all of your money in mutual funds and leaving all the investment decisions to the fund manager won't make you a happy camper.
- **The Free Spirit.** You're the type who says, "I don't care if there's more than $4 trillion invested in mutual funds. I don't care if everyone's using word processors instead of typewriters." You like to be just a little bit different and independent.

Although investing a small portion of your money in individual securities may be a compromise, be realistic as to why you're investing in them. And before you plunk down too much money in them, remember the sage words of Jack Bogle, often called the mutual fund investor's best friend:

> "Attempting to build an investment program around a handful of individual securities is, for all but the most exceptional investors, a fool's errand. . . . Specific stock bets should be made, if at all, in small portions, and more for the excitement of the game than for the profit."

Yes, Bogle is the founder and former CEO of a large mutual fund company, Vanguard. But, no, his comments aren't self-serving: Vanguard also operates a discount brokerage company that handles individual securities trades for Vanguard customers who wish to do them.

In the long haul, you're not going to beat full-time professional managers who are investing in the securities of the same type and risk level that you are. As with hiring a contractor for home remodeling, you need to do your homework to find a good money manager. Even if you think that you can do as well as the best, remember that even superstar money managers like Peter Lynch have beaten the market averages by only a few percentage points per year.

In my experience, more than a few otherwise smart, fun-loving people choose to invest in individual securities because they think that they're smarter or luckier than the rest of us. If you're like most people, I can safely say that, in the long run, your individual investment choices will not outperform those of a full-time investment professional.

I've noticed a distinct difference between the sexes on this issue. Perhaps because of differences in how people are raised, testosterone levels, or whatever, men tend to have more of a problem taming their egos and admitting that they're better off not going with individual securities. Maybe it's genetically linked to not wanting to ask for directions.

Should you join an investment club?

Investment clubs are a little bit like having your own hands-on mutual fund. Each club member chips in a bit of money. Then the group gets together for periodic meetings to discuss stocks and make investment decisions.

These groups can be valuable as an educational forum so long as you utilize good information sources. If the group members are somewhat clueless and the meetings are rambling, these groups can end up degenerating into the blind leading the blind.

Investment clubs may have social or hobby value (which are most clubs' major benefits), but investment clubs aren't likely to help your finances much. In fact, investment clubs can hurt your checkbook more than they help.

First of all, let's face it — the members of the vast majority of investment clubs are a bunch of part-time amateurs. You could end up making some real bone-headed decisions and losing money (or not making nearly as much as if you had been in some good mutual funds).

Second, it's highly unlikely that everyone in the group is in the same tax situation. Thus, the club's investments may work for some members' tax situations but not for others.

Beware of stockbrokers who have been known to participate in investment clubs and volunteer as leaders as a so-called business development tool. Although their participation may be harmless, more often than not, these brokers have a hidden agenda to reel in new clients to whom they've been able to demonstrate their vast investment knowledge.

Consider forming a financial reading club and discussion group instead of an investment club. You can get together and discuss financial periodicals, books, and investment strategies. This way, you can advance your level of financial knowledge, learn about new resources from others, and have the fun, camaraderie, and other benefits that come from doing things in a group.

Better yet, join a bowling league or a softball team and leave the investing to fund managers!

Mutual Funds: The Drawbacks

Although I am a fan of good mutual funds, I am also well aware of the drawbacks of funds, and you need to know them, too. After all, no investment vehicle is perfect.

Still, the mutual fund drawbacks that I'm concerned about are different from the ones that some of the popular press likes to harp on. Here is my take on which mutual fund drawbacks you shouldn't worry about . . . and which ones should make you stop and think a little more.

Don't worry about these . . .

The following concerns shouldn't trouble you:

- **The investment Goliath.** One of the concerns I still hear about is the one that, because the fund industry is growing, if fund investors head for the exits at the same time, they may get stuck or trampled at the door. Here's a fear you can just chuck. Mutual funds hold just 15 percent of outstanding U.S. stocks. They're growing in importance simply because they're a superior alternative for a whole lot of people.
- **Where's the building?** Some people, particularly older folks who grew up doing all their saving through a local bank, feel uncomfortable doing business with an organization that they can reach only via an 800 number or through the mail. However, please recognize that there are some enormous benefits to mutual funds' *not* having branch offices all over the country. Branch offices cost a lot of money to operate. That's one of the reasons why bank account interest rates are so cruddy.

  TIP: If you feel better dropping your money off in person to an organization that has local branch offices, invest in mutual funds through one of the firms recommended later that maintain branch offices, such as Charles Schwab or Fidelity. Or do business with a fund company headquartered near your abode (see the Appendix for the main office address of the fund companies recommended in this book).

Do worry about these . . . (but not too much)

Make sure you consider and accommodate these factors before you invest in any mutual fund:

- **Volatility of your investment balance.** When you invest in mutual funds that hold stocks and/or bonds, the value of your funds fluctuates with the general fluctuations in those securities markets. These fluctuations don't happen if you invest in a bank certificate of deposit (CD) or a fixed insurance annuity that pays a set rate of interest yearly. With CDs or annuities, you get a statement every so often that shows steady — but slow — growth in your account value. You never get any great news, but you never get any bad news either (unless your insurer or bank fails, which could happen).

  Over the long haul, if you invest in solid mutual funds — ones that are efficiently and competently managed — you should earn a better rate of return than you would with bank and insurance accounts. And if you invest in growth-oriented funds (such as stock funds), you'll be more likely to keep well ahead of the double bite of inflation and taxes.

  But if you panic and rush to sell when the market value of your mutual fund shares drops (instead of taking advantage of the buying opportunity), then maybe you're not cut out for funds. Take the time to read and internalize the investment lessons in this book, and you'll soon be an honors graduate from my Mutual Fund University!

- **Mystery (risky) investments.** In recent years, some mutual funds (not those that I recommend) have betrayed their investors' trust by taking unnecessary and, in some cases, undisclosed risks by investing in volatile financial instruments such as futures and options (also known as derivatives). Because these instruments are basically short-term bets on the direction of specific security prices (see Chapter 1), they are very risky when not properly used by a mutual fund.

- **An arm and a leg.** Not all mutual funds are created equal. Some charge extremely high annual operating expenses (again, you won't find such funds on my recommended list in this book) that put a real drag on returns. Expense ratios, for example, in excess of 0.75 percent for bond funds and 1.25 percent for U.S. stock funds take away too much of your expected returns. I talk more about expense ratios in Chapter 3.

- **Taxes, Taxes, Taxes.** The taxable distributions that funds produce can also be a negative. When fund managers sell a security at a profit, the fund must distribute that profit to shareholders in the fund. For funds held outside tax-sheltered retirement accounts, these distributions are taxable. I fill you in on taxes and mutual funds in Chapter 6.

  Some people — especially brokers who advocate investing in individual securities — have argued that taxes on mutual fund distributions are a problem big enough to justify the avoidance of mutual funds altogether, especially for higher tax-bracket investors. They don't have to be. If you are concerned about the money you're investing outside of tax-sheltered retirement accounts, don't worry — there's a solution: See my recommended tax-friendly funds in Chapters 7 through 9.

Managed Investment Alternatives to Mutual Funds

The unbelievably wide variety of mutual funds enables you to invest in everything from short-term money market securities to corporate bonds, U.S. and international stocks, precious metals companies, and even real estate. Although mutual funds can fill many investing needs — as I discuss in Chapter 1— you may be interested in and benefit from directly investing in things such as real estate, your own business, and many other investments. Other types of privately managed investment accounts exist that have some things in common with mutual funds.

The following sections provide some background that you need to know if you're going to seriously consider these fund alternatives.

Wrap (or managed) accounts

Many of the brokerage firms that used to sell investment products on commission (for example, Prudential, Merrill Lynch, Smith Barney Shearson, Paine Webber, and Dean Witter) are moving into fee-based investment management. This change is an improvement for investors because it reduces some of the conflicts of interest caused by commissions.

On the other hand, these brokers charge extraordinarily high fees (which are usually quoted as a percentage of how much money they're managing for you, also referred to as *assets under management*) on their *managed* (or *wrap*) investment accounts.

These accounts go under a variety of names, such as "Traks" or "Consults." But they're all the same in one crucial way: For the privilege of investing your money through their chosen money managers, they all charge you a fixed percentage of the assets they're managing for you.

Wrap accounts have two major problems. First, their management expenses are extraordinarily high, often up to 3 percent per year of assets under management. Remember that stocks have historically returned about 10 percent per year before taxes. So if you're paying 3 percent per year to have the money managed in stocks, 30 percent of your return (before taxes) is siphoned off. And don't forget (because the government certainly won't) that you pay a good chunk of money in taxes on your 10 percent return as well. So the 3 percent wrap actually ends up depleting 40 to 50 percent of the profits you get to keep after you pay taxes — ouch!

No-load (commission-free) mutual funds offer investors access to the nation's best investment managers for a fraction of the cost of wrap accounts. You can invest in dozens of top-performing funds for an annual expense of 1 percent per year or less. Many excellent funds are available for far less — 0.2 to 0.5 percent annually.

So how do brokerage firms hoodwink investors into paying 3 to 15 times as much for access to investment managers? Marketing. Slick, seductive, deceptive, misleading pitches that often include some outright lies. Here are the key components of the brokers' pitch for wrap accounts — and then the real truth behind the pitch:

- **"You're accessing investment managers who normally don't take money from small-fry investors like you."**

  Not a single study shows that the performance of money managers has anything to do with the minimum account they handle. Besides, no-load mutual funds hire many of the same managers who work at other money management firms. In fact, Vanguard, the nation's largest exclusively commission-free investment firm, contracts out to hire money managers who typically handle only million-dollar-plus private-client accounts to run many of their funds. A number of other mutual funds are managed by private money managers with high entrance requirements for individual clients.

- **"You'll earn a higher rate of return, so the fees are worth it."**

  Part of the bait brokers use to hook you into a wrap account is the wonderful rates of returns they supposedly generate. You could have earned 18 to 25 percent per year, they say, had you invested with the "Star of Yesterday" investment management company. The key words here are "could have." History is history. As I discuss in Chapter 4, in the money management business, many of yesterday's winners become tomorrow's losers or mediocre performers.

  You also must remember that, unlike mutual funds, whose performance records are audited by the SEC, wrap account performance records may include marketing hype. Wrap accounts are not audited by the SEC. The most common ploy is showing the performance of only selected accounts — which turn out to be (you got it) only the ones that performed the best!

  The expenses you pay to have your investments managed have an enormous impact on the long-term growth of your money. If you can have your money managed for 0.5 to 1 percent per year instead of 2.5 to 3 percent, you've got a 2 percent-per-year performance advantage already.

- **"A wrap account is tailored to your personal needs."**

  Thousands of different mutual funds are available out there, covering every possible combination of investments and degree of risk. You can find a mutual fund that meets your objectives and risk tolerance.

Moreover, if your portfolio ever begins to drift from your objectives, buying into a new mutual fund is much easier than ending a relationship with a personal money manager.

- **"There's little difference in cost between wrap accounts and mutual funds."**

  Baloney! True, the worst and most inefficient mutual funds can have total costs approaching that of a typical wrap account. But you're not stupid — you're not going to invest in the highest-cost funds. Chapters 7 through 9 detail which mutual funds offer both top performance and low cost.

Private money managers

In the world of money management, added benefits — snob appeal and ego stroking for many — come with having your own private money manager. First of all, you generally need big bucks, often $1 million or more, to gain entrance. (Although it never ceases to amaze me how often this minimum account size is lowered if you have a friend who recommends you and already has an account with the firm — "You only have $200,000, no problem.")

A private money management company allows you to sit down and visit with a personal representative and perhaps even the investment manager. The company lavishes you with lots of attention and glossy brochures. You hear how your money will not only receive individualized and personalized treatment but also how superb the investment manager's performance has been in prior years.

Even if you've got big bucks, you probably don't need a private money manager for two simple reasons. First, the best, average, and worst private money managers earn returns comparable to their counterparts in the mutual fund business. And, as I mention earlier in this chapter, some mutual fund firms contract out to or are themselves private money managers. This gives you the best of both worlds: the SEC oversight of a mutual fund and access to some money managers you may not otherwise be able to use.

Consider what one bank CEO, speaking at a banking conference about future sources of revenue growth, had to say about private money management. Along with the credit card business, he included private money management for the wealthy as one of the few "high-return, low risk businesses" in the financial world. Knowing that you're getting soaked with high fees like the average credit card customer shouldn't make you feel so special about having a private money manager.

TIP

Prioritizing your financial goals

Only you know what's really most important to you and how to prioritize your goals. And prioritize you must. That's because, if you're like most Americans, your desires outstrip your ability to save to accomplish your goals.

Now that doesn't mean that you can't fulfill all your dreams. We're fortunate to live in a country where on an average income, you can, with proper planning of course, achieve most of the financial goals identified above. But you do have to be realistic about how many balls you can juggle at any one time.

That may mean, for example, that you have to reduce your retirement plan contributions while you save up for a down payment on a home. Or that you have to downscale the size of your dream house a bit if you really want Junior to attend a pricey private college.

Again, you're the best person to decide where to make the tradeoffs. However, because of the tax breaks that come with retirement account contributions, retirement funding should always be near the top of your priority list. ***Remember:*** Making retirement account contributions reduces your tax bill, effectively giving you more goal-chasing dollars to play with.

And, as suggested by its name, your emergency reserve fund should always be a top priority, especially if your income is unstable and/or you have no family to fall back on. On the other hand, if you've got a steady job and at least a few solvent family members, you can probably afford to build up this fund more slowly and in conjunction with other savings goals.

INVESTIGATE

If you're considering investing through private investment firms, make sure that you

- Ask to see independently audited rates of return.
- Check lots of references.
- Compare the performance and costs of the private money manager with similar mutual funds (such as those in this book).

For more ideas about evaluating money managers, see the criteria for selecting mutual funds in Chapter 4.

Hedge funds

TIP

Hedge funds, another investment reserved for big ticket investors, have the added glamour and allure of taking significant risk and gambles with their investments. Hedge funds may do this by purchasing derivatives (options, futures, and the like, discussed in Chapter 1). Or they may bet on the fall in price of particular securities by selling the securities short. When you *short sell,* you borrow a security from a broker, sell it, and then hope to buy it back later at a lower price.

When hedge fund managers guess right, they can produce high returns. When they don't, however, the fund manager can have his head handed to him on a very expensive silver platter. With short selling, because the security sold short can rise an unlimited amount, the potential loss from buying it back at a much higher price can be horrendous. And even the most experienced investing professionals can also lose a pile of money in no time when investing in derivatives.

A number of hedge funds have gone belly up, kaput, bankrupt when they guessed wrong. In other words, their investments did so poorly, investors in the fund lost all their money. As I discussed earlier in this chapter, the odds of this happening with a mutual fund, particularly from one of the larger, more established companies, are nil.

If you want more risky investments, you can find aggressive mutual funds. Or you can buy mutual funds on *margin,* meaning that you make a down payment but control a larger investment (such as when you purchase a home), through a brokerage account. See Chapter 11 for more about the risks and rewards of buying on margin.

Chapter 3

Fitting Funds into Your Financial Future

In This Chapter

- Important things to do before investing
- Goals that can be accomplished with mutual funds
- How to prioritize your goals

Justine and Max, both in their 20s, recently married and excited about planning their life together, heard about a free financial planning seminar taking place at the local Holiday Inn.

The seminar was taught by a financial planner. Among the many points made by the planner was, "If you want to retire by the age of 65, you need to save at least 12 percent of your income every single year between now and retirement."

"The longer you wait to start saving," the seminar leader continued, "the more painful it will be. Postpone your saving a mere ten years and you will have to double the amount of your annual income that you need to save."

For Justine and Max, the seminar was a wake-up call. On the drive home, they couldn't stop thinking and talking about the future. They had big plans: They wanted to buy a home, they wanted to send the not-yet-born kiddies to college, and they definitely wanted to retire by age 65. And so it was resolved: A serious investment program must begin right away. Tomorrow, they would fill out two applications for mutual fund companies that the financial planner had distributed to them.

Within a week, they had set up accounts in five different mutual funds at two firms. No more 3-percent-return bank savings accounts — the funds they chose had been returning 10 to 12 percent per year in prior years! Proud of their initiative, Justine and Max patted themselves on the back. Unlike most of their twentysomething friends, who didn't own funds or understand what funds are, they believed they were well on their way to realizing their dreams.

Although I have to admire Justine and Max's initiative (that's often the biggest hurdle to starting an investment program), I must point out the mistakes they made by investing in the way they did. The funds themselves weren't poor choices — in fact, the funds they chose were quite good: They had competent managers, good historic performance, and reasonable fees.

Among the biggest mistakes they made were:

- Justine and Max completely neglected investing in their employers' retirement savings plans. Thus, they were missing out on making tax-deductible contributions. By investing in mutual funds outside of their employers' plans, they received no tax deductions.
- Justine and Max were steered into funds that did not fit their goals. They ended up with bond funds, which were decent funds as far as bond funds go. But bond funds are designed to produce current income, not growth. Justine and Max, looking to a retirement decades away, were trying to *save* and *grow* their money, not produce more current income from their investments.
- To add tax insult to injury, the income generated by their bond funds was fully taxable, because the funds were being held outside of tax-sheltered retirement accounts. The last thing Justine and Max needed was more taxable income, not because they were rolling in money — neither Justine nor Max had a high salary — but because, as a two-income couple, they were in a high tax bracket.
- And, in their enthusiasm to get serious about their savings, Justine and Max made probably the biggest error of all: They didn't adjust their spending habits to allow for their increased savings rate.

Justine and Max *thought* they were saving more — 12 percent of their income was going into the mutual funds versus the 5 percent they had been saving in a bank account. However, as the months rolled by, their outstanding balances on credit cards grew. In fact, when they started to invest in mutual funds, Justine and Max had $1,000 of revolving debt on a credit card at 14 percent interest rate. Six months later, their debt had grown to $2,000.

The extra money for investment had to come from somewhere — and in Justine and Max's case, it was coming from building up their credit card debt. But, because their investments were highly unlikely to return 14 percent per year, Justine and Max were actually losing money in the process. No real additional saving was going on — just borrowing from Visa to invest in the mutual funds.

I tell the story of Justine and Max not to discourage you but to caution you against buying mutual funds in haste or out of fear before you have your own financial goals in mind. In this chapter, I show you how to fit mutual funds into a thoughtful personal financial plan so that the mutual funds you invest in serve your goals instead of keeping them out of reach.

Prerequisites to Investing in Funds

The single biggest mistake that mutual fund investors make is investing in funds before they're even ready to. It's like trying to build the walls of a house without a proper foundation.

You've got to get your financial ship in shape — sailing out of port with leaks in the hull is sure to lead to an early, unpleasant end to your journey. And you've got to figure out what you're trying to accomplish with your investing. Throughout this book, I impress upon you that mutual funds are specialized tools for specific jobs. I don't want you to pick up a tool that you don't know how to use.

Here, then, are the ten most important things to do so that you get the most from your mutual fund investments.

Pay off your consumer debts

Right now!

I repeat: If you carry a balance on your credit card or have an outstanding auto loan, do not invest in mutual funds until these consumer debts are paid off.

I realize that investing money makes you feel like you're making progress; paying off debt, on the other hand, just feels like you're treading water.

Shatter this illusion. Paying credit card interest at 14 or 18 percent while making an investment that generates only an 8 percent return isn't even treading water; it's sinking!

REMEMBER

You won't be able to earn a consistently high enough rate of return in mutual funds to exceed the interest rate you're paying on consumer debt such as credit cards and auto loans. Although some financial gurus claim that they can make you 15 to 20 percent per year, they can't — not year after year. Besides, in order to try and earn these high returns, you have to take great risk. If you have consumer debt and little savings, you're not in a position to take that much risk.

I'll go a step further on this issue: Not only should you delay any investing until your consumer debts are paid off, you should seriously consider tapping into any existing savings (presuming you would still have adequate emergency funds at your disposal) to pay off your debts.

Review your insurance coverage

Insurance? What's that got to do with mutual funds? Take this as my friendly little paternalistic reminder to get all of your financial house in order. Saving and investing is psychologically rewarding and makes many people feel more secure. But, ironically, even some good savers and investors are in precarious positions because they have gaps in their insurance coverage.

Do you have

- Adequate life insurance to provide for your dependents?
- Long-term disability insurance to replace your income in case a disability prevents you from working?
- Sufficient liability protection on your home and car to guard your assets against lawsuits?

If not, your mutual funds and other investments could be quickly wiped out in the event of a catastrophe. The point of insurance is to eliminate the financial downside of such a catastrophe and protect your investments.

In reviewing your insurance, you may also discover unnecessary policies or ways to spend less on insurance, freeing up more money to invest in mutual funds. (See my book, *Personal Finance For Dummies,* 2nd Edition, published by IDG Books Worldwide, Inc., to learn about the right and wrong ways to buy insurance and whip the rest of your finances into shape.)

Figure out your financial goals

To a large degree, mutual funds are goal-specific tools. And to a large degree, humans are goal-driven animals. Perhaps that's why the two make such a good match.

Most of us find saving money easier when we do so with a purpose or goal in mind — even if it's for something so undefined as a "rainy day." Because mutual funds tend to be pretty specific in what they're designed to do, the more defined your goal, the better able you'll be to make the most of your mutual fund money.

Granted, your goals and needs will change over time, so these determinations need not be carved in stone. But unless you've got a general idea of what you're going to do with the savings down the road, you won't really be able to thoughtfully choose suitable mutual funds.

Common financial goals include saving for retirement, a home purchase, an emergency reserve, and stuff like that. In the second half of this chapter, I talk more about what goals mutual funds can help you to accomplish.

Another benefit of going through this exercise is that you'll know better how much risk you need to take to accomplish your goals. Seeing the amount you need to save to achieve your dreams may encourage you to invest in more growth-oriented funds. Conversely, if you find that your nest egg is substantial given what your aspirations are, you may scale back on the riskiness of your fund investments.

Determine how much you are currently saving

If you're like most people, you're more likely to know the name of the 13th U.S. president than the amount of income you're now saving. By saving, I mean, over a calendar year, how did your spending compare with your income? For example, if you earned $40,000 last year, and $38,000 of it got "spent" on taxes, food, clothing, rent, insurance, and other fun things, you saved $2,000. Your savings rate then would be 5 percent ($2,000 of savings divided by your income of $40,000).

The vast majority of Americans haven't a clue what their savings rate is. If you already know that your rate is low, non-existent, or negative, you can safely skip this step because you also already know that you need to save much more. But figuring out your savings rate can be a real eye opener and wallet closer. (Incidentally, in case you forgot, Millard Fillmore was the 13th U.S. president.)

Examine your current spending and income

If you're saving enough to meet your goals, you can skip this step and move ahead. For the rest of the class, however, some additional work needs to be done. To save more, you need to reduce your spending, increase your income, or both. This isn't rocket science, but it's not easy to do.

For most people, reducing spending is the more feasible option. But where do you begin? First, figure out where your money's going. You may have some general idea, but you need to have facts. Get out your checkbook register, credit card bills, and any other documentation of your spending history and tally up how much you spend on dining out, operating your car(s), paying your taxes, and everything else. Once you have this information, you can begin to prioritize and make the necessary tradeoffs to reduce your spending and increase your savings rate.

Earning more income may work as well if you can get a higher paying job or increase the number of hours you're willing to work. Watch out though: Your spending has a nasty habit of soaking up increases in income. Moreover, if you're already working a lot, reining in your spending will be better for your emotional and social well-being.

Maximize tax-deferred retirement account savings

It's difficult for most people to save money. Don't make a tough job impossible by forsaking the terrific tax benefits that come from investing through retirement savings accounts. Employer-based 401(k) and 403(b) retirement plans offer substantial tax benefits. Contributions into these plans are federal and state tax-deductible. And once the money is invested inside these plans, the growth on your contributions is tax-sheltered as well.

The common mistake fund investors make is that they neglect to take advantage of retirement accounts in their enthusiasm to invest in funds in "non-retirement" accounts. This can cost you hundreds, perhaps thousands, of dollars per year in lost tax savings, and tens of thousands to hundreds of thousands of dollars over your working years.

Fund companies are happy to encourage this financially detrimental behavior. It's not detrimental to them. They lure you into their funds without educating you about using your employer's retirement plan first. Why? Because the more you invest through your employer's plan, the less you have available to invest in their mutual funds. (See the section on retirement later in this chapter to learn about the different retirement accounts you may contribute to, including plans for self-employment income.)

Don't neglect to fund retirement accounts in an effort to save money for your kids' college expenses. If you do, you'll not only pay more in taxes, but your children will have a more difficult time qualifying for financial aid, including loans that are not based on financial need (see the section on saving for college later in this chapter). If you're affluent enough that you can afford to pay for your children's college costs and fund your retirement needs, you can safely ignore this concern.

Determine your tax bracket

When you're investing in mutual funds outside of tax-sheltered retirement accounts, the profits and distributions that your funds produce are subject to taxation. So the type of fund that makes sense for you depends at least partly on your tax situation.

If you're in a high bracket, you should give preference to mutual funds such as tax-free bond funds and stock funds with low levels of distributions, particularly dividends. If you're not in a high bracket, avoid tax-free bond funds because you'll end up with less of a return than in taxable bond funds. (In Chapter 6, I explain how to select the best fund types to fit your tax status.)

Assess the risk you're comfortable with

Think back over your investing career. I know you're not a star money manager, but you've already made some investing decisions. For instance, leaving your excess money in a bank savings or checking account is a decision — it may indicate that you're afraid of volatile investments.

How would you deal with an investment that drops 10, 20, 30, 40, or even 50 percent in a year? Some of the more aggressive mutual funds that specialize in volatile securities like growth stocks, small company stocks, emerging market stocks, and long-term and low-quality bonds can fall in a hurry.

If you can't stomach big waves on the seas of the financial markets, don't get in a small boat that you'll want to bail out of in a big storm. Selling after a big drop is the equivalent of jumping into the frothing sea at the peak of a pounding storm — you're sealing your doom.

You can invest in the riskier types of securities by selecting mutual funds that mix riskier securities with more stable investments and which are well diversified. For example, you can purchase an international fund that invests in companies of varying sizes in established as well as emerging economies. That would be safer (less volatile) for you than investing money in small companies just in Southeast Asian countries, a region that got clobbered in the late 1990s.

Review current investment holdings

Many people have a tendency to compartmentalize their investments: IRA money here, 401(k) there, brokerage account somewhere else. Part of making sound investment decisions is to examine how the pieces fit together to make up the whole. That's where jargon like "asset allocation" comes into play. Asset allocation simply means how your investments are divvied up among the major types of securities or funds, such as money market, bond, U.S. stocks, international stocks, precious metals, and others.

Another reason to review your current investments before you buy into new mutual funds is that some house cleaning may be in order. You may discover investments that don't fit with your objectives or tax situation. Perhaps you'll decide to clear out some of the individual securities that you know you can't adequately follow and that clutter your life.

Consider other "investment" possibilities

Mutual funds are a fine way to invest your money, but they're hardly the only way. You can also invest in real estate, in your own business or someone else's, or you can pay down mortgage debt more quickly.

Again, what makes sense for you depends on your goals and personal preferences. If you hate taking risks and detest volatile investments, paying down your mortgage may make better sense than investing in mutual funds.

REMEMBER

Don't become so obsessed with making, saving, and investing money that you neglect the things that money can't buy: your health, friends, family, and exploration of new career options and hobbies.

Accomplishing Goals with Mutual Funds

Mutual funds can help you accomplish various financial goals. The rest of this chapter gives an overview of some of these more common goals — saving for retirement, buying a home, paying for college costs, and so on — that can be tackled with the help of mutual funds. For each goal, I mention what kinds of funds are best suited to it, and I point you to the part of the book that discusses that kind of fund in greater detail.

You'll start to see how important goal identification is in the mutual fund selection process. In most cases, only a few fund categories are appropriate for a specific financial goal. Once you've got your fund category, simply peruse Chapters 7 through 9 to find the best individual funds in that fund category.

As you understand more about this process, you'll notice that the time horizon of your goal — in other words, how much time you've got between now and when you'll need the money — largely determines what kind of fund is appropriate. If you need to tap into the money within two or three years or less, a money market or short-term bond fund may fit the bill. If your time horizon falls between three and seven years, you want to focus on bond funds. For long-term goals, seven or more years down the road, stock funds are probably your ticket.

But time horizon is not the only variable. Your tax bracket, for example, is another important consideration in mutual fund selection. (See Chapter 6 for more about taxes.) Other variables are goal-specific, so take a closer look at the goals themselves.

Throughout the rest of this chapter, I also give you plenty of non-mutual fund-related tips on how to tackle these goals. ***Remember:*** Mutual funds are just part of the overall picture.

The financial pillow — an emergency reserve

Before you save money towards anything, it's a good idea to save up an amount of money equal to about three to six months of living expenses. This fund is not for keeping up on the latest developments in stereo amplification. It's for emergencies only: for your living expenses when you're "between jobs," for unexpected medical bills, for a last-minute plane ticket to visit an ailing relative.

Basically, it's a fund to cushion your fall when life unexpectedly trips you up. Call it your pillow fund. You'll be amazed how much of a stress reducer a pillow fund is.

How much you save in this fund and how quickly you build it up depends on the stability of your income and the depth of your family support. If your job is steady and your folks are still there for you, then you can keep the size of this fund on the smaller side. On the other hand, if your income is erratic and you've got no ties to solvent, friendly family members, you may want to consider building up this fund to a year's worth of expenses.

The ideal savings vehicle for your emergency reserve fund is a money market fund. See Chapter 7 for an in-depth discussion of money market funds and a list of the best ones to choose from.

The golden egg — investing for retirement

Uncle Sam gives big tax breaks for retirement account contributions. This is a deal you can't afford to pass up. The mistake people at all income levels make with retirement accounts is not taking advantage of them, thereby delaying the age at which they start to sock money away. The sooner you start to save, the less painful it is each year, because your contributions have more years to compound.

Each decade you delay approximately doubles the percentage of your earnings you should save to meet your goals. For example, if saving 5 percent per year starting in your early 20s would get you to your retirement goal, waiting until your 30s may mean socking away 10 percent; waiting until your 40s, 20 percent; beyond that, the numbers get troubling.

Taking advantage of saving and investing in tax-deductible retirement accounts should be your number one financial priority (unless you're still paying off high-interest consumer debt on credit cards or an auto loan).

Here are the main benefits of investing in retirement accounts first:

- **Tax-deductibility.** Retirement accounts should be called tax-reduction accounts. If they were called that, people might be more excited about contributing to them. For many people, avoiding higher taxes is the motivating force that opens the account and starts the contributions.

  Suppose that you're paying about 35 percent between federal and state income taxes on your last dollars of income (see Chapter 6 to determine your tax bracket). For most of the retirement accounts described in this chapter, for every $1,000 you contribute, you save yourself about $350 in taxes in the year that you make the contribution.
- **Tax-deferred growth of your investments.** Once money is in your retirement account, any interest, dividends, and appreciation add to the amount of your account without being taxed. You defer taxes on all the accumulating gains and profits until you withdraw the money down the road. Thus, more money is working for you over a longer period of time.
- **They save you from yourself.** Retirement accounts are separate from your other personal money. The IRS also penalizes you if you want the money out of your accounts prior to age 59½. Don't let this deter you from contributing — the penalties will keep you from raiding your accounts to go to the Caribbean!

On average, most people need about 70 to 80 percent of their annual preretirement income throughout retirement to maintain their standard of living. If you've never thought about what your retirement goals are, looked into what you can expect from Social Security (okay, cease the giggling), or calculated how much you should be saving for retirement, now's the time to do it. *Personal Finance For Dummies*, 2nd Edition, goes through all the necessary details and even tells you how to come up with more money to invest and how to do it wisely.

Your retirement investing options

If you earn employment income (or receive alimony), you have the option of putting money away in a retirement-type account that compounds without taxation until you withdraw the money. With many retirement accounts, you can elect to use mutual funds as your retirement account investment option. And if you have retirement money in some other investment option, you may be able to transfer it into a mutual fund company (see Chapter 11).

In most cases, your contributions into retirement accounts are tax-deductible. The following list includes the major types of accounts and explains how to determine whether you are eligible for them.

401(k) plans

For-profit companies typically offer 401(k) plans, which typically allow you to save up to $10,000 per year (tax year 1998), subject to percentage of income limitations of no more than 20 percent. Your contributions to a 401(k) are excluded from your reported income and thus are free from federal and state income taxes, but not FICA (Social Security) taxes.

Absolutely don't miss out on contributing to your employer's 401(k) plan if your employer matches a portion of your contributions. Your company, for example, may match half of your first 6 percent of contributions (so in addition to saving a lot of taxes, you get a bonus from the company). Check with your company's benefits department for your plan's details.

Thanks to technological innovations and the growth of the mutual fund industry, smaller companies (those with fewer than 100 employees) can consider offering 401(k) plans, too. In the past, it was prohibitively expensive for smaller companies to administer 401(k)s. If your company is interested in this option, have it contact a mutual fund organization such as T. Rowe Price, Vanguard, or Fidelity, or a discount brokerage house, such as Charles Schwab or Jack White.

403(b) plans

Many nonprofit organizations offer 403(b) plans to their employees. As with a 401(k), your contributions to these plans are federal and state tax-deductible. The 403(b) plans often are referred to as tax-sheltered annuities, the name for insurance-company investments that satisfy the requirements for 403(b) plans.

For the benefit of 403(b) retirement-plan participants, no-load (commission-free) mutual funds can now be used in 403(b) plans. Check which mutual fund companies your employer offers you to invest through — I hope you have access to the better ones covered in Chapter 5.

Employees of nonprofit organizations generally are allowed to contribute up to 20 percent or $10,000 of their salaries, whichever is less. Employees who have 15 or more years of service may be allowed to contribute a few thousand dollars beyond the $10,000 limit. Ask your employee benefits department or the investment provider for the 403(b) plan (or your tax advisor) about eligibility requirements and details about your personal contribution.

If you work for a nonprofit or public-sector organization that doesn't offer this benefit, make a fuss and insist on it. Nonprofit organizations have no excuse not to offer a 403(b) plan to their employees. This type of plan includes virtually no out-of-pocket set-up expenses or ongoing accounting fees like a 401(k). The only requirement is that the organization must deduct the appropriate contribution from employees' paychecks and send the money to the investment company that handles the 403(b) plan.

Some state and local governments offer plans quite similar to 403(b) plans known as Section 457 plans. As if we don't have enough confusing retirement plan options already, the IRS and the federal government figured a 403(b) wouldn't be enough for the entire nonprofit world. In the words of the immortal Winnie the Pooh, "Oh, bother!"

SEP-IRAs

If you're self-employed, you can establish your own retirement savings plans. You can and should do this through the excellent no-load mutual fund companies discussed in this book.

Simplified employee pension individual retirement account (SEP-IRA) plans require little paperwork to set up. They allow you to sock away from about 13 percent (13.04 percent, to be exact) of your self-employment income (business revenue minus expenses) up to a maximum of $24,000 per year (tax year 1998). Each year, you decide the amount you want to contribute — there are no minimums. Your contributions to a SEP-IRA are deducted from your taxable income, saving you big-time on federal and state taxes. As with other retirement plans, your money compounds without taxation until withdrawal.

Keoghs

Keogh plans are another retirement savings option for the self-employed. They can and should be established through the no-load fund providers recommended in this book.

Keogh plans require a bit more paperwork to set up and administer than SEP-IRAs (I show you the differences in Chapter 11). The appeal of certain types of Keoghs is that they allow you to put away a greater percentage (20 percent) of your self-employment income (revenue less your expenses), up to a maximum of $30,000 per year.

Another appeal of Keogh plans is that they allow business owners to maximize the contributions to which they are entitled relative to employees in two ways that they can't with SEP-IRAs:

- First, all types of Keogh plans allow vesting schedules, which require employees to remain with the company a number of years before they earn the right to their retirement account balances. If an employee leaves prior to being fully vested, the unvested balance reverts to the remaining plan participants.
- Second, Keogh plans allow for Social Security integration. Integration effectively enables those in the company who are high-income earners (usually the owners) to receive larger percentage contributions for their accounts than the less highly compensated employees. The logic behind this idea is that Social Security taxes top out once you earn more than $68,400 (for 1998). Social Security integration allows you to make up for this ceiling.

Select the Keogh that fits you best

Anything that involves the IRS is never simple. Keoghs are no exception. You've got several options. Although these options make understanding Keoghs a bit of a headache, they also allow you to choose a Keogh plan that best meets your needs.

A *profit-sharing plan* allows for the same contribution limits as SEP-IRA and is suitable for small business owners who want to use vesting schedules and Social Security integration, which cannot be done with SEP-IRA plans. You can vary your contribution (and even contribute nothing if you'd like) each year.

Another option is a *money-purchase pension plan,* which appeals to self-employed people who want to contribute more to retirement accounts than can be contributed with profit-sharing plans or SEP-IRAs. The maximum tax-deductible contribution here is the lesser of 20 percent of your self-employment income or $30,000 per year. While allowing for a larger contribution, there is no flexibility allowed on the percentage contribution you make each year — it's fixed. Thus, these plans make the most sense for high-income earners who are comfortable enough financially to know that they can continue making large contributions.

If you dislike the rigidity of a money-purchase plan but want the ability it gives you to contribute more, check out a *paired plan,* which combines the best features of the profit-sharing and money-purchase plans. You can attain the maximum contribution possible (20 percent) that you get with the money-purchase pension plan but have some of the flexibility that comes with a profit-sharing plan. You can fix your money-purchase pension plan contribution at 8 percent and contribute anywhere from 0 to 12 percent of your net income to your profit-sharing plan.

If you are a consistently high-income earner between the ages of 45 to 50 who wants to save more than $30,000 per year in a retirement account, you have still another option: a *defined-benefit plan.*

When establishing your Keogh plan at a mutual fund or discount brokerage company, ask what features its plans allow — especially if you have employees and are interested in vesting schedules and Social Security integration.

Individual Retirement Accounts (IRAs)

Anyone with employment (or alimony) income can contribute to Individual Retirement Accounts (IRAs). You may contribute up to $2,000 each year or the amount of your employment or alimony income if it's less than $2,000 in a year. If you are a nonworking spouse, you're eligible to put $2,000 per year into a so-called spousal IRA.

Your contributions to an IRA may or may not be tax deductible. For tax year 1998, if you're single and your adjusted gross income is $30,000 or less for the year, you can deduct your IRA contribution. If you're married and file your taxes jointly, you're entitled to a full IRA deduction if your AGI (adjusted gross income) is $50,000 per year or less.

If you make more than these amounts, you can take a full IRA deduction if you are not an active participant in any retirement plan. The only way to know for certain whether you're an active participant is to look at the W-2 form that your employer sends you early in the year to file with your tax returns. Little boxes indicate whether you are an active participant in a pension or deferred-compensation plan. If either of these boxes is checked, you're an active participant.

If you are a single-income earner with an adjusted gross income above $30,000 but below $40,000, or part of a couple with an AGI above $50,000 but below $60,000, you're eligible for a partial IRA deduction, even if you're an active participant. The size of the IRA deduction that you may claim depends on where you fall in the income range. For example, a single-income earner at $35,000 is entitled to half ($1,000) of the full IRA deduction because his or her income falls halfway between $30,000 and $40,000. (***Note:*** These thresholds are for tax year 1998. They will increase every year over the next decade.)

If you can't deduct your contribution to a standard IRA account, consider making a non-deductible contribution to a new type of IRA account called the Roth IRA (also known as an IRA Plus). Single taxpayers with an AGI less than $95,000 and joint filers with an AGI less than $150,000 can contribute up to $2,000 per year to a Roth IRA. Although the contribution is not deductible, earnings inside the account are shielded from taxes, and unlike a standard IRA, qualified withdrawals from the account, including investment earnings, are free from income tax.

To make a qualified withdrawal from a Roth IRA, you must be at least $59\frac{1}{2}$ and have held the account for at least 5 years. An exception to the age rule is made for first-time home buyers, who are allowed to withdraw up to $10,000 toward the down payment on a principal residence.

TIP

Before you contribute to a Roth IRA, make sure that you're maximizing your ability to make deductible contributions to the retirement accounts available to you, such as a 401(k), Keogh, and others. If your AGI prevents you from contributing to a Roth IRA, consider making a non-deductible contribution to a regular IRA for the tax-deferred compounding of your investment earnings.

Annuities

Annuities are peculiar investment products. They are contracts that are backed by insurance companies. If you, the annuity holder (investor), should die during the so-called accumulation phase (that is, prior to receiving payments from the annuity), your designated beneficiary is guaranteed to be reimbursed the amount of your original investment. This is not life insurance!

Annuities, like IRAs, allow your capital to grow and compound without taxation. You defer taxes until withdrawal. However, unlike an IRA that has a $2,000 annual contribution limit, you can deposit as much as you want in any year into an annuity — even a million dollars if you've got it! As with a Roth IRA, you get no up-front tax deduction for your contributions. (See Chapter 10 for examples of when these may make sense and for fund company annuity plans.)

Prioritizing your retirement contributions

TIP

If you have access to more than one type of retirement account, prioritize which accounts to use by what they give you in return. Your first contributions should be to employer-based plans that match your contributions. After that, contribute to any other employer or self-employed plans that allow tax-deductible contributions. If you've contributed the maximum possible to tax-deductible plans or do not have access to such plans, contribute to an IRA.

If you've maxed out on contributions to an IRA or don't have this choice because you lack employment income, consider an annuity or tax-friendly investments (discussed in Chapter 6). Annuities get the lowest priority since your contributions are not tax-deductible and because annuities carry higher annual operating fees due to the small insurance that comes with them.

The white picket fence — saving for a home

A place to call your own is certainly the most tangible element of the American dream. A home is also an investment: Not only does it generally appreciate in value, but it also should keep you dry in a thunderstorm (assuming, of course, that you've got a good roof!).

Fortunately, it's relatively easy in this country to borrow money to buy a home; otherwise, few of us could ever afford it. Still, to get the best mortgage terms for a house, you should aim for making a down payment of 20 percent of the purchase price. For a $150,000 home, that's $30,000. So unless you have some other sources available (such as a loan from your parents), you have some saving up to do.

If you're looking to buy a home in a year or so, then a money market fund is the best place to store your down payment money (see Chapter 7). If your target purchase date is a few years off, then a short-term bond fund is the way to go (see Chapter 8).

The ivory tower — saving for college

A college education for the kiddies is certainly part of the American dream today — not surprising when you consider that a college degree has quickly replaced the high school diploma as the entrance bar to the American job market.

Unfortunately, the financial services industry has fully exploited the opportunity to deepen the American anxiety over educational expenses. While mutual funds can help to send your kids off to college, their specific role may be different from what you'd expect.

Don't get sucked into saving in child's name

Few subject areas have more misinformation and bad advice than what is dished out on paying for your children's college expenses. Some mutual fund companies, including a few of the better ones discussed in this book, publish free guides that are rife with poor advice and some scare tactics.

Their basic premise is that, by the time your tyke reaches age 18 or so, it's going to cost more money than you could possibly imagine to pay for college. Thus, you had better start saving a lot of money as soon as possible. Otherwise, you'll have to look your 18-year-old in the eyes some day and say, "Sorry, we can't afford to send you to the college you have your heart set on."

Bogus. Yes, college is expensive and it ain't gettin' any cheaper. But what the financial services companies don't like to tell you is that you don't have to pay for all of it yourself. Thanks to financial aid, most Americans don't. By financial aid, I mean more than just grants and scholarships; I am talking about low-cost loans, which are by far and away the most common form of aid.

Tips on how to afford college

So, how are you going to be able to afford sending your children to Prestige U. or even Budget Community College? Here are some tips on how to gain financial aid and plug the gap between what college costs are and what you can afford:

- **Fund your retirement accounts first:** Self-centered as it may seem, you're really doing yourself and your kids a tremendous financial favor if you fully fund your retirement accounts before tucking away money for college. First, you save yourself a boatload in taxes. As discussed earlier in this chapter, 401(k), 403(b), SEP-IRAs and Keough plans give you an immediate tax deduction at the federal and state level. And once the money is inside these retirement accounts, it compounds without taxation over the years.

  Second, the more money you save and invest outside of retirement accounts, the less financial aid (loans and grants) your child will qualify for. Strange as it may seem, the financial aid system ignores 100 percent of the money you invest *inside* retirement accounts.

- **Always, always, always apply for financial aid:** College is expensive and, unless you're affluent, you and your child will need to borrow some money. Consider these educational loans as investments in your family. Much financial aid is available regardless of need, including grants and loans. So don't make the mistake of not applying.

  The financial aid system examines your income, assets and liabilities, number of children in college, and stuff like that. Based on an analysis, the financial aid process may determine that you can afford to spend, for example, $8,000 per year on college for your child. That doesn't mean that your child can only consider schools that cost up to that amount. In fact, if your son or daughter desires to go to a $25,000-per-year private school, loans and grants may be able to cover the difference between what the financial aid system says you can afford and what the college costs.

  Apply for aid. Otherwise, you may never know what you and your child are missing out on.

- **Investigate all your options:** In addition to financial aid, you may be able to use other sources to help pay college expenses. If you're a homeowner, for example, you may be able to tap into home equity. The kids' grandparents also may be financially able to help out (it's better for them to hold the money themselves until it's needed).

- **Teach your children the value of working, saving, and investing:** If you're one of the fortunate few who can pay for the full cost of college yourself, more power to you. But even if you can, you may not be doing as well by your children as you may like to believe.

  When children set goals and learn to work, save, and make wise investments, these values pay dividends for a lifetime. So does your spending time with your children rather than working so hard to try and save enough to pay for 100 percent of their college costs.

  Encourage your children to share in the cost of their education. They can contribute in different ways, either up front or by taking over the outstanding loans after they graduate. Either way, I think you'll find that your children appreciate their education more.

What's really sad about the scare tactics some investment companies use is that it effectively encourages parents to establish investment accounts in their children's names. The financial aid system heavily penalizes money held in your child's name by assuming that about 35 percent of the money in your child's name (for example, in custodial accounts) will be used toward college costs. By contrast, only 6 percent of the non-retirement money held in your name is considered available for college expenses.

You should also know that when you place money in your child's name, your child has a legal right to that money in most states at age 18 or 21. That means your 18- or 21-year-olds could spend the money on an around-the-world junket, a new sports car, or anything else their young minds can dream up. Because there's no way of knowing in advance how responsible your children will be once they are ages 18 or 21, it's better for you to keep money earmarked for their college education out of their names.

For the few of you that can and do want to pay for the full cost of your child's education, there is an income tax incentive to put money in your child's name. Under what is known as the "kiddie tax" system, income generated by investments held in your child's name is usually taxed at a lower rate than your own. Remember, however, that by saving money in a child's name, you are reducing that child's chances for financial aid. That's why I say don't invest in your child's name unless you want to pay for it all yourself.

Using mutual funds for college cost funding

College costs have been rising at about double the rate of inflation. Although this gap is expected to decrease, educational expense rate increases will continue to outstrip inflation for the foreseeable future. That's because teaching, in its present form anyway, is labor intensive. To keep up with or stay ahead of college price increases, you must invest for growth. At the same time, you've got to keep an eye on your time horizon; kids grow up fast.

The younger your child is, the more years you have before you need to tap the money and, therefore, the greater the risk you can take. A simple rule of thumb: Take a number between 30 (if you're aggressive) and 50 (if you're more conservative) and add that to your child's age. Got that number? That's the percentage you should put in bonds; the rest should go into stocks. Be sure to continually adjust the mix as your child gets older.

For a list of good stock and bond funds to invest in, see Chapters 8 and 9. Pay particular attention to hybrid funds, which invest in both stocks and bonds and may already reflect your desired mix.

If you want to learn more about getting your finances in order and planning for college costs, read *Personal Finance For Dummies,* 2nd Edition.

Chapter 4

How to Pick Great Funds

In This Chapter

- Fund costs
- Risk and return and how funds hide their true colors
- Fund manager and fund family expertise
- Warning signs of a loser fund
- Understanding prospectuses and annual reports

When you go camping in the wilderness, you can do a number of things to maximize your odds of happiness and success. You can take maps to keep you on course, food to keep you nourished, proper clothing to stay dry and warm, and some first-aid stuff in case something awful happens, such as an outbreak of mosquitoes. But no matter how much advance preparation you do, you still may not have the best of times. You may get sick, trip over a rock and break your leg, or face inclement weather.

And so it is with mutual funds. Although they can help you reach your financial goals, they come with no guarantees. You can, however, use a number of simple, common sense criteria to greatly increase your chances of investment success. The following issues are the main ones you should consider. The mutual funds that I recommend in Chapters 7 through 9 meet these criteria.

Evaluate Gain-Eating Fees

The Investment Company Institute, a mutual fund trade association, conducted a survey that asked mutual fund buyers what information they reviewed about a fund before purchasing it. Fifth on the list, mentioned by only 43 percent of the respondents, were fees and expenses. This means that the majority of fund buyers surveyed — a whopping 57 percent — did not examine the fees and expenses for the funds that they bought.

Additionally, only 27 percent of fund buyers surveyed bothered to look at how much of a load or sales charge was levied by the fund. On the other hand, past fund performance was the most cited information reviewed by fund buyers (with 75 percent considering).

Such survey results don't surprise me. I've witnessed investors looking first — and sometimes only — at the prior performance of a fund while completely ignoring fees. Doing so is generally a mistake.

The charges you pay to buy or sell a fund and the ongoing fund operating expenses have a big impact on the rate of return you earn on your investments. Why? Because fees are deducted from your investment returns and can attack a fund from many angles. All other things being equal, high fees and other charges depress your returns, while past performance offers no guarantee. In fact, past performance is a relatively poor indicator of a fund's likely future returns. As you will see later in this chapter, many of yesterday's star funds turn into tomorrow's losers and mediocre performers. You just can't know what tomorrow will bring.

On the other hand, you *can* know a fund's expenses and fees before you buy it. Think about that for a second: Although you have no idea how much of a return you'll actually make, the fund tells you how much it is going to deduct in fees from your account both up-front (in the form of sales commissions) and ongoing (in the form of fund operating expenses). Factor these known reductions in returns into your fund-buying decisions.

Sales loads are brokers' commissions

Sales loads are commissions paid to brokers (who often call themselves something other than brokers) who sell mutual funds. Typically, commissions range from 4 percent to as high as 8.5 percent of the amount you invest. ***Note:*** Some funds sold at companies such as Fidelity and Dreyfus charge a commission even though you purchase the fund directly from them without a broker's involvement. I recommend that you avoid these funds as well. (I'll make sure that you do when I recommend specific funds later in Part II. I'll even show you how to buy some of the better funds at Fidelity without paying the loads.)

Sales loads, or "loads" for short, have their problems. As you will see in this section, loads deducted from your investment money are an additional and unnecessary cost (if you're in the market for the best funds).

Why brokers push house brands

Be wary of brokers or planners pitching house brands: for example, a Dean Witter broker recommending only Dean Witter mutual funds or an American Express financial planner only extolling the virtues of American Express mutual funds.

Salespeople often get higher commissions by pushing house brands. Many of the better load mutual funds, such as American and Franklin/Templeton, are managed by companies independent of brokerage firms. Brokerage firms are Johnny-come-latelys to the mutual fund field, and the performance of their funds reflects their lack of experience. They also have the habit of introducing new funds according to the popular fund flavor of the month, which often coincides with the worst time for investors to buy them.

Not surprisingly, those who have a vested interest in sales loads make a number of misleading arguments in favor of funds that carry sales loads. Over the years, I've heard quite a number of arguments from brokers and, in counseling clients who come to me for advice, I frequently hear them repeat arguments they've heard from investment salespeople to get them to pay a sales charge when buying a mutual fund.

Here are the common arguments for paying loads, followed by the facts:

"Don't concern yourself with commissions — I get paid by the mutual fund company."

It's true that the broker's commission is paid by the mutual fund company. But where do you think this money ultimately comes from? From your investment dollars, that's where. Brokers like to imply that you're effectively not paying for the commission since it comes from the mutual fund company. Not so.

"You get what you pay for — load funds have better fund managers."

Bunk! Five out of five objective studies that I've seen show that paying a load does not get you a better fund manager. Remember, loads wind up in the pockets of the selling brokers and don't go toward the management of the fund.

What the studies have shown is that load funds underperform no-loads. Why? It's simple: Those commissions paid to the brokers come out of the fund's returns, although you may not know that from a fund's published rankings.

Many published mutual fund rankings and ratings services completely ignore sales commissions in their calculations of funds' returns (see Chapter 15).

"No-loads have higher ongoing fees."

Not! Investment salespeople will imply or actually say that no-loads have to make it up somewhere if they aren't charging you a sales commission. Although this may sound logical, remember that sales commissions go to the broker, not toward the expenses of managing the fund.

Fact is, the reverse is true. My analysis shows that load funds, on average, have higher, not lower, annual operating expenses than no-load funds.

Brokers will also say that no-loads have to spend gobs of money marketing themselves to investors, and that these higher costs, inevitably, are reflected in no-loads' annual operating expenses. This sounds good from a broker's perspective, but it is false. Load funds also have to spend money to market themselves, both to brokers and to the investing public like you and me. And the better no-load companies, such as those recommended in the next chapter, benefit from the thousands of investors who call, based on word-of-mouth or other recommendations (such as through this book!), seeking to invest.

"No-loads have hidden costs."

Another nice try, Mr. Broker. But this is a case where a half-truth does not make a whole. Both no-load *and* load funds incur brokerage transaction costs when securities are bought and sold in the fund. These costs are not really "hidden." They are disclosed in a fund's prospectus; however, they are not included in the calculated annual operating costs for any type of mutual fund, either load or no-load (see the section "Fund expenses" later in the chapter).

"No-loads are for do-it-yourself types. People who need help buy load funds."

This either/or mentality is trumpeted not only by investment brokers but also by some financial writers in the mass media, who sometimes parrot what brokers say to them. If you need advice, you have other options. (Many brokers would like you to believe that they are your only option.) One alternative is to hire a financial advisor and pay a fee for his or her time to recommend specific no-load mutual funds. No-loads are hardly just for do-it-yourself types (see Chapter 5 for the different types of advisors you may hire), although you'll see from this book that you have what it takes to just do it yourself.

"I'll do a financial plan for you to determine your needs."

Try as they might, investment salespeople simply cannot perform objective, conflict-free financial planning. You should never pay for a "financial plan" produced by an investment salesperson. Such financial plans end up being nothing more than sales tools. And, even if you get a broker's financial plan for free, the advice probably will be detrimental to your wealth.

The problem with sales loads is the power of self-interest discussed in the next chapter. This issue is rarely talked about, but brokers' self-interest is even more important than the extra costs you pay. When you buy a load fund through a salesperson, you miss out on the chance to decide for yourself whether you should buy a mutual fund at all. Maybe you'd be better off paying debts or investing in something entirely different. But salespeople almost never advise you to pay off your credit cards or your mortgage — or to invest through your company's retirement plan — instead of buying an investment through them.

I've seen too many people get into investments without understanding what they're buying and what the risks are. People who sell mutual funds usually sell other investments, too. And some of those other products hold the allure (for the salespeople) of high commissions — vehicles such as limited partnerships, cash-value life insurance, annuities, futures, and options. Salespeople tend to exaggerate the potential benefits and obscure the risks and drawbacks of what they sell; they don't seem to take the time to educate investors.

"I can get you funds from the same no-load companies, such as Fidelity...."

Another half truth. Brokers like to imply that they can sell you basically the same funds that you could buy on your own through no-load companies. However, top no-load companies, such as Vanguard, for example, do not sell any load funds through brokers. Fidelity sells a limited number of load funds, called Fidelity Advisor funds, which are sold through commission-based brokers. These funds carry 4.75 percent sales charges and much higher ongoing fees — up to a full 1 percent more per year — than their no-load counterparts.

In recent years, increasing numbers of brokerage firms are offering their customers access to some no-load mutual funds through a service known as a *wrap* (or *managed*) *account.* To get into these funds, you must agree to pay the brokerage firm an annual investment management fee on top of the fees the underlying mutual funds charge. I explain in Chapter 2 why wrap accounts are generally not in your best interest.

"On a busy day, you won't be able to get through on the phone lines to the no-loads."

When the financial markets make wide swings or a major news event occurs, it's true that many investment firms see a pick-up in calls. Many brokers will imply that you won't be able to place your trade at a no-load company on such days. Not true. In fact, most of the major no-load mutual fund companies and discount brokers are open for business far more (some offer 24-hour-a-day phone assistance) than brokerage firms that sell load funds.

Remember also that making emotional, knee-jerk trades on days of market turmoil is bad for your investing health. The investors who sold when the market crashed in October 1987 would ultimately regret it. If anything, that crash would have been a good time to buy.

"The no-loads won't call you to tell you when to get out of the market or switch funds."

True. But far from being a disadvantage, not getting a call to switch funds is actually a plus. Although mutual funds offer daily liquidity, funds are meant to be a longer-term investment.

As for switching funds, you don't want a broker telling you when he thinks it's the right time. A broker, who stands to gain financially when you trade, is hard pressed to be a source of objective advice of when to trade funds. (In Chapter 12, I explain how to evaluate the funds you own by applying the criteria discussed in this chapter.)

"No-loads have worse performance because investors on their own are more likely to panic and bail out when the financial markets turn volatile."

This is another myth perpetuated by investment salespeople. A broker who was surfing incognito on an America Online bulletin board and dishing out investment advice said that funds sold through brokers are better to hold in a downturn because, "Scared money tends to flow fast out of no-advice funds, while brokered funds tend to lose less assets and don't force the hand of the reluctant fund manager."

No data supports this. Remember that brokers who make money when you make a trade will play on your fears and encourage you to sell when the market goes sour. Thus, there's a danger that, if your load fund goes in the tank, your broker may use this as an excuse to call and recommend selling at a time when prices are low, not high. The majority of mutual funds experiencing large redemptions in recent years have been load funds.

"No-loads are impersonal organizations."

When you call a no-load fund's 800 line, you will surely get a different representative every time. If it's important to you to have a relationship with someone at these firms, however, some representatives will give you their names and extensions (just ask) so you can reach them in the future.

Alphabet soup — do we have a (hidden) load for you . . . ABCD shares

Over the years, investors have learned about the sales loads that are deducted from their investments in load mutual funds. Perhaps you just learned this yourself. Well, the companies that specialize in selling load funds have, with the unwitting assistance of government regulators, developed new types of funds that make finding the load much harder.

Just as some jewelers flog fake diamonds on late-night TV commercials, increasing numbers of brokers and financial planners are selling funds that they *call* no-loads, when they're really *not* no-loads. By any other name, these funds are load funds: The only difference is that, with these funds, someone has taken the time to hide the sales commission.

For a given load fund, some fund companies have introduced different "classes" of shares, usually labeled by the letter A, B, C, or D. No matter what letter they slap onto it, remember that you're getting the same fund manager and the same fund. The only difference is how much the company's charging you to own it.

Shares with the traditional front-end load are usually sold as Class A shares. Class B, C, and D shares are the classes that the mutual fund marketers spend a lot of time on hiding the load, deploying tricky techniques such as *back-end loads* or ongoing commissions known as *12b-1 fees.* These commissions often end up being more expensive than the old up-front loads.

Take the back-end sales load, for example, which is the typical technique of Class B shares. Rather than assessing a load when you purchase these shares, you're charged a load when you sell them. But wait, the broker tells you, the more years you hold onto the shares, the lower the sales charge when you sell. In fact, if you hold onto the shares long enough, usually five to seven years, the load disappears altogether. This sure sounds like a better deal than the Class A shares, which charge you an up-front load no matter what.

Not so fast. The broker selling the Class B shares still gets a commission. The company simply raises the fund's operating expenses (much higher than on Class A shares) and pays the broker commissions out of that. One way or another, the broker gets his pound of flesh from your investment dollars.

How can you avoid these hidden loads? Simple. Don't buy funds through salespeople, and do buy no-loads, such as those recommended in this book.

A broker can be a personal contact who asks you about your golf game, how your family is doing, and . . . by the way . . . "What is the phone number of your rich Uncle Johnny?" Independent financial counselors who charge a fee for their time can serve the same role. Likewise, firms such as Charles Schwab and Fidelity maintain branch offices that offer a personal, local touch if you need and want it.

TIP

Invest in no-loads and avoid load funds and investment salespeople. The only way to be sure that a fund is truly no-load is to look at the prospectus for the fund. Only there, in black and white and absent all marketing hype, must the organization tell the truth about its sales charges and other fund fees. I explain how to read a prospectus later in this chapter.

Figure 4-1 is a sample of a typical fee table from a fund prospectus for a load fund. Note that the Class A shares have an up-front 6.5 percent sales commission that's deducted when you invest your money.

BEWARE

The Class B shares don't have an up-front commission but instead have a deferred sales charge, which reduces over time. *However,* note that it charges you an extra 1.00 percent per year (12b-1 marketing expense fees). Class B shares in this example (as in most real cases) cost you more in the long run because you pay this cost each year as long as you own the fund, more than making up for the gradual decline in sales charges.

Operating expenses: The unavoidable cost of doing business

One of the two costs of fund ownership — loads — is completely avoidable. Just don't pay them. Buy no-load funds.

However, you can't avoid the other cost of fund ownership — *operating expenses.* Every mutual fund — load and no-load — must charge fees to pay for the operational costs of running the fund: paying the fund manager, servicing the toll-free phone lines, printing and mailing prospectuses, buying super-duper computers to track all those investments and customer-account balances, and so on. Running a business costs money! Operating expenses also include a profit margin for the fund company, which keeps the company in business.

A fund's operating expenses are quoted as a percentage of your investment. The percentage represents an annual fee or charge. In the case of load funds, this fee is in addition to the stated load. You can find this number in the expenses section of a fund's prospectus, usually denoted by a line such as "Total Fund Operating Expenses." Or you can call the mutual fund's 800 number and ask a representative. I even tell you, for no extra charge, what the operating expenses are for the funds recommended in this book.

FEE TABLE

	Class A Shares	Class B Shares
Shareholder Transaction Expenses:		
Maximum Sales Charge Imposed on Purchase (as a percentage of offering price)	6.50%	None
Sales Charge Imposed on Dividend Reinvestments	None	None
Deferred Sales Charge	None	4.0% during the first year, decreasing 1.0% annually to 0.0% after the fourth year
Exchange Fee	None	None
Annual Fund Operating Expenses (as a percentage of average net assets):		
Management Fee	1.00%	1.00%
12b-1 Fees	None	1.00%
Other Expenses	0.25%	0.35%
Total Fund Operating Expenses	1.25%	2.35%

Example:

	Cumulative Expenses Paid for the Period of: 1 Year	3 Years	5 Years	10 Years
You would pay the following expenses on a $1,000 investment, assuming a 5% annual return, and redemption at the end of the period:				
Class A	$78	$106	$137	$229
Class B	$64	$93	$124	$265
You would pay the following expenses on the same $1,000 investment assuming no redemption at the end of the period:				
Class A	$78	$106	$137	$229
Class B	$24	$73	$124	$265

Figure 4-1: How to spot load funds.

Although all funds must charge operating expenses, some funds charge much more than others. By picking the right funds, you can minimize the operating expenses you pay. And minimize them you should: Operating expenses come right out of your returns. Higher expenses translate into a lower return to you.

Expenses matter on all types of funds, but more on some and less on others:

- Expenses are critical on money market mutual funds and are very important on bond funds because these funds are buying securities that are so similar and so efficiently priced in the financial markets.
- With stock funds, expenses are a less important (but still important) factor in picking a fund. Don't forget that, over time, stocks have averaged returns of about 10 percent per year. So if one stock fund charges 1.5 percent *more* in operating expenses than another, you're giving up an extra 15 percent of your expected annual returns.

Some people argue that stock funds that charge high expenses may be justified in doing so — *if* they are able to generate higher rates of return. *But there's no evidence that high-expense stock funds do generate higher returns.* In fact, funds with higher operating expenses, on average, tend to produce *lower* rates of return. This makes sense because operating expenses are deducted from the returns that a fund generates.

If a given fund's expenses are much higher than its peers, one of two things is usually happening: Either the fund has little money under management — and therefore has a smaller group of investors to bear the management costs — or the fund owners are greedy. Another possibility could be that the fund company is inefficiently managed (maybe its telephone reps spend half the day making long distance phone calls to friends!). In any case, you don't want to be a shareholder of such a fund.

These high-expense funds have another insidious danger built-in: In order to produce returns comparable to those of similar funds with lower costs, the manager of such a high-cost fund may take extra risks to overcome the drag of high expenses. So on top of a prospective lower performance, higher expenses may expose you to greater risk than you desire.

There's no reason to pay a lot for the best funds. Many excellent commission-free money market, bond, and stock funds from fund companies such as Vanguard, Fidelity, USAA, and T. Rowe Price have operating expenses of less than 1 percent per year; many of these cost less than 0.5 percent per year.

All mutual fund ownership fees — both loads and operating expenses — are disclosed in a fund's prospectus. That is why it's so important to obtain a fund's prospectus before you buy it. It's especially critical for funds pitched to you by brokers or by brokers who masquerade as "financial planners" and "consultants." I tell you how to decipher a fund prospectus later in this chapter.

Oh, one last point about fund expenses: People ask me how the expenses are charged and if they are itemized on your fund statement. The answer is that a fund's operating expenses are essentially invisible to you because they're deducted before you're paid any return. Because these expenses are charged on a daily basis, you don't need to worry about trying to get out of a fund before these fees are deducted.

Performance and Risk

Although a fund's *performance,* or its historic rate of return, is certainly an important factor to weigh when selecting a mutual fund, investors tend to overemphasize its importance. It's dangerous to base fund decisions on simplistic comparisons of performance numbers.

As all mutual fund materials tell you, past performance is no guarantee of future results. Analysis of historic mutual fund performance proves that some of yesterday's stars may turn into tomorrow's skid-row bums (as I discuss in the next section, "Star today, also-ran tomorrow").

WARNING!

Realize that funds with high returns achieve their results by taking on a lot of risk. Those same funds often take the hardest fall during major market declines. Remember, risk and return go hand in hand; you cannot afford to look at return independent of the risk it took to get there. Make sure you're comfortable with the level of risk your fund is taking on.

TECHNICAL STUFF

The incredible invisible brokerage costs

One of a fund's truly invisible expenses is the annual brokerage fees the fund pays to buy and sell securities for the fund. These costs are *not* included in the fund annual operating expense numbers that a fund reports. Brokerage costs reduce a fund's returns just the same as a fund's operating expenses and are ultimately reflected in the fund's annual rate of return.

The brokerage costs on a fund can range from practically nothing to as much as 2 percent or more. These costs are now required to be disclosed in a fund's prospectus (I tell you all about how to read a prospectus and identify such fees later in this chapter). Funds that frequently trade or "turn over" the securities they hold generally spend more on brokerage fees because the fund has to pay the broker on every trade. More trades mean more costs draining your returns. This may also lead to more taxable distributions.

Star today, also-ran tomorrow

The mutual fund industry has all too much in common with Hollywood. There's always a "star" of the week, the most handsome actor or actress appearing in the most recent blockbuster with the biggest box office sales. Suddenly, that actor or actress is smiling from magazine covers at the checkout aisle, nodding at jokes by David Letterman, donning the latest fashion designs at the Oscars. . . . All that attention, however, has its drawbacks. If your next flick flops, you've got that much farther to fall.

It's the same for mutual funds. Some fund manager has a fabulous quarter or year, ripping up the market with his little growth-stock fund. All of a sudden, his face is plastered across the financial magazines, he's hailed as the next Peter Lynch, and then millions of new investor dollars come pouring into his fund.

REMEMBER: Short-term (one year is a short time period) fund performance numbers don't mean much — luck can be just as big a factor as skill. Also remember that beating the pants off the market inevitably means that the manager took a lot of risk. The greater the short-term returns for that fund and manager, the greater the odds of an imminent collapse.

The history of short-term mutual fund star funds confirms this: Of the #1 top performing stock and bond funds in each of the last 15 years, an astounding 80 percent of them subsequently performed worse, over the next three to ten years, than the average fund in their peer group! Two of these former #1 funds are actually the worst performing funds in their particular category, as you will see in the sections that follow.

The following sections provide a sampling of the many examples of short-term stars becoming tomorrow's also-rans (and in some cases, losers).

REMEMBER: Fame is fleeting. But the consequences are more serious for a fund manager than a Hollywood star: When a fund flops, the manager brings all his investors down with him.

Van Wagoner Emerging Growth

With three years of stellar returns under his belt, Garrett Van Wagoner, manager of the Govett Smaller Companies Fund, decided to cash in on his exploding popularity. In late 1995, he left Govett and started his own mutual fund company. Calling Van Wagoner the hottest small company stock picker around, several of the nation's largest financial magazines recommended investing in his new Emerging Growth fund. Investor cash came flooding in — more than a billion dollars in the fund's first six months of existence.

Unfortunately for the owners of all that money, Van Wagoner had too much of the fund's assets riding on technology stocks. In the spring of 1996, many of Van Wagoner's favorite technology picks began to get clobbered. Over the ensuing year, the Van Wagoner Emerging Growth Fund had a total return of –30.4 percent, performing worse than 1901 out of 1907 U.S. stock funds. Meanwhile, the rest of the market was booming; the Standard & Poor 500 Index returned +27 percent during the same period.

Looking at Van Wagoner's previous track record reveals clues to his risky investment behavior. At the Govett Smaller Companies Fund, for example, his turnover ratio was 519 percent, meaning he held his average stock about 10 weeks before selling it! Van Wagoner was a reckless trader, and it eventually caught up to him.

Managers Intermediate Mortgage

Managed by portfolio manager Worth Bruntjen, this fund was the darling of the moment for almost every mutual fund rating service in 1993. (I talk about rating services in Chapter 15.) It earned kudos because, in its seemingly boring investment universe — government-backed mortgage securities — it was able to produce an annual rate of return 3 percent higher than that of its peers (who came in it at just 10 percent per year) over the five-year period ending in 1993. By earning 13 percent per year instead of 10 percent, MIM's performance was about 30 percent better than that of its peers.

This fund received some of the highest ratings that most mutual fund rating companies allowed for performance, and, supposedly, MIM had "below average" risk. It earned Morningstar's coveted five-star rating. (Partly to its credit, in its analysis of the fund on January 21, 1994, Morningstar said of MIM, "Its portfolio is made up entirely of volatile derivative securities," and went on to add, "If rates move back up, this fund will find it hard to maintain its great record.")

When interest rates finally did rise sharply in early 1994, this fund not only found it difficult to continue its past performance, it got clobbered. It produced a total return of –22 percent in the first half of 1994. This little six-month disaster was enough to bring the fund in dead last among 50 other mortgage bond funds for the five-year period ending June 30, 1994.

It turns out that this fund was able to achieve its temporarily high returns by taking a ton of risk. Whence came all the danger, you ask? The fund invested in complex *collateralized mortgage obligations*. Complex collateralized mortgage obligations (CMOs) are pieces of a mortgage; when you buy them, it's like buying chicken parts instead of a whole chicken at the supermarket. A mortgage gets chopped into the different years of principal and/or interest repayments. CMOs are incredibly complicated to understand, even if you surround yourself with computers and investment bankers.

Forbes magazine, which had written a glowing article praising fund manager Bruntjen on January 17, 1994, admitted that its earlier enthusiasm had been excessive — a rare and honorable thing for a financial magazine to do. *Forbes* said that the magazine had learned from the episode "not to be overly confident in historical statistics, especially those attached to complex investment products. In this case, a volatility measure calculated from a mostly bullish period turned out to be meaningless during a period when the market turned bearish."

United Services Gold

Among no-load funds, this fund was the number one overall performer four years in the past two decades.

Sounds like a real winner, right? Wrong! $10,000 invested in this fund 15 years ago is worth $3,500 today: In other words, the fund's overall return over that time period is negative. Although its up years were really up, its down years were really, really down . . . and there were more of them.

Matterhorn Growth

This aggressive stock fund skyrocketed 184 percent in 1975, the year following the end of one of the worst declines for the stock market since the Great Depression. Since the 1970s, however, this fund has been in the doghouse. It holds the distinction of being the worst stock fund during the 1980s, one of the best decades for the stock market this century. And over the most recent 10-year period, it has returned a paltry 5 percent per year average return versus almost 15 percent for comparable funds.

As money has poured out of the fund, its annual operating expenses as a percentage of assets have ballooned and now stand in excess of an astounding 4 percent per year!

Apples to apples: Comparing performance numbers

Remember back in school when the teacher handed back exams and you were delighted to get a 92 (unless you're from an overachieving family)? But then you learned that the average on the exam was a 95. You still may have been pleased, but a lot of air was let out of your balloon.

It's the same with mutual fund performance numbers: They don't mean much until they're compared to the averages. A 15 percent return sounds great until you learn that the return from the relevant index market average was 25 percent during the same period.

The trick is picking the correct benchmark to compare to. Dozens of market indexes and fund category averages measure various components of the market. You always want to compare a fund's returns to its most appropriate benchmark. It isn't fair to compare the performance of an international stock fund to that of a U.S. stock market index, just as it isn't fair to compare a sixth grader's test results on a given test to those of a tenth grader taking the same test. (See Chapter 12 for a list of benchmarks and an explanation of what markets they measure.)

You know that context matters, and mutual fund companies realize this. So in their marketing literature, fund companies usually compare their funds' returns to selected benchmarks. Keep a wary eye on these comparisons. In the great American advertising tradition, fund companies often pick benchmarks that make it easy for their funds to look good.

Here are some examples of the games funds play to make themselves look a lot better than they really are.

During 1994, the Strong Short-Term Bond Fund ran ads claiming to be the number one short-term bond fund. (I'd show you the ad, but Strong refused permission to reprint it.) The ads featured a 12-month comparison graph that compared the Strong fund's yield to the average yield on other short-term bond funds. The Strong Short-Term Bond Fund, according to the graph, consistently outperformed the competition by 2 to 2.5 percent! And, gosh, with a vibrant, solid name like Strong, how could you go wrong?

As you see in Chapter 8, where I discuss all you need to know about bond funds, a bond fund must take a *lot* more risk to generate a dividend this much higher than the competition's. And if it's taking that much more risk, then the fund needs to be compared to its true competition — which, in Strong's case, would be other funds whose investments take similarly high risks. This fund isn't a bad fund, but it isn't nearly as good as the ad would have had you think.

This fund was on steroids! The Strong Short-Term Bond Fund was not comparable to most other short-term bond funds because

- **A high percentage of its bonds were not high-quality:** Historically, about 40 percent of its bonds are rated BBB or below.
- **Many of its bonds are not short-term bonds:** Strong invests in mortgage bonds that are more like intermediate-term bonds.

You also should be suspicious of any bond fund claiming to be this good with an annual operating expense ratio of 0.80 percent. With expenses that high (as I explain in Chapter 8), you know that it has to take higher risks than supposedly comparable funds to make up for the drag of its expenses.

Strong's ad also claimed that its bond fund was ranked number one for the year. If a fund takes more risk than the funds it compares itself to, then sure, during particular, brief periods, it can easily end up at the top of the charts. But how strong a long-term performer is this "number one" fund? Over the previous five years, including the year the ad was so proud of, Strong's fund had *under*performed most short-term bond funds.

As I explain in Chapter 8, short-term bond funds managed by companies such as Fidelity, PIMCO, and Vanguard charge far lower operating expenses, take less risk, and generate equal or better returns than this fund does.

During much of 1994, ads for the Warburg Pincus Growth & Income Fund similarly trumpeted its superior performance — claiming to be the number one growth and income fund for the year and number four out of 180 funds for the previous five years. Sounds great, doesn't it? (I'd show you the ad, but, like Strong, Warburg Pincus refused to give permission to reproduce it.)

Most growth and income funds invest in U.S. companies, primarily larger ones. This fund, however, would have been more appropriately called the Warburg Pincus Global Growth Fund, because its prospectus showed that this fund had invested about 20 percent overseas and 40 percent in small company stocks.

The average growth and income pays dividends of around 3 percent, whereas this fund was paying only 0.2 percent at the time of its ad. Thus, a huge amount of this fund was focused on relatively growth-oriented, rather than dividend-oriented, securities.

Like the Strong Short-Term Bond Fund, the Warburg Pincus Global Growth (& Income) Fund is not a bad fund. But it's hardly as superior as the ad implies.

Some mutual funds choose comparative benchmarks for the sole purpose of making themselves look good. More than a few investment advisors who manage money do the same, as Chapter 20 makes clear. In Chapter 12, I talk more about matching up funds to their relevant benchmarks and recognizing which benchmarks don't really apply at all.

Fund Manager and Fund Family Expertise

Much is made of who manages a specific mutual fund. Although the expertise of the individual fund manager is important, a manager is not an island unto himself (or herself — more women are becoming fund managers nowadays). The resources and capabilities of the parent company are equally important.

Different companies have different capabilities and levels of expertise with different types of funds. Vanguard, for example, is terrific at money market, bond, and conservative stock funds, thanks to their low operating expenses. Fidelity has a ton of experience and success investing in U.S. stocks.

Other excellent mutual fund companies only offer a handful of funds, unlike such behemoths as Vanguard and Fidelity. Don't assume from their smaller size that they are newcomers to the world of money management. Firms such as PIMCO, Neuberger & Berman, and Dodge & Cox managed money privately for decades before they started offering funds to the public.

In Chapters 7 through 10, I talk more about which firms have great reputations in various fund categories. I also recommend individual funds from these various companies.

Warning Signs for (Likely) Loser Funds

Earlier in this chapter, you see how a star fund can flare for its moment of investor glory and then easily twinkle down to become just another average or worse-than-average fund. Too many of us seem to want to believe that, in every field of endeavor — sports, entertainment, business — there are superhumans who can walk on water.

REMEMBER

It's true that in the investment world there are those who shine at what they do. But compared to other fields, the gap between the star investment manager and the average one, over long time periods, typically is incredibly small.

If the stocks of large U.S. companies, for example, have advanced 13 percent per year over a decade, the money manager focusing on such securities may vault to god-like status if his fund earns 15 percent over the same time period. Don't get me wrong: An extra 2 percent per year ain't nothin' to sneeze at — especially if you've got millions invested. But a 2 percent difference is a lot smaller than what most people are chasing.

TIP

We can try to pick the future star funds and managers, but there's actually far more value in avoiding the losers. It's not hard at all for you to avoid likely future loser funds, whether they're big losers, little losers, or run-of-the-mill losers. All you have to do is follow these few simple rules with maniacal and religious zeal:

- **Avoid funds with high annual operating fees.** How high is high? That depends on the type of fund, but you should *never* own a money market or bond fund that charges more than 0.5 percent per year, a U.S. stock fund that charges more than 1 percent per year, or an international or specialty fund that charges more than 1.3 percent per year. Steel yourself against clever marketing brochures and charming salespeople. Read the fine print and walk the other way to a better fund if costs are too high.

- **Avoid fund companies with little mutual fund management experience and success.** If you need surgery, would you rather turn your body over to a surgeon who has successfully performed this operation hundreds of times, or to a rookie who has only seen it on the local cable station and tried it out on his cat?
- **Avoid novelty funds.** Mutual funds have been around for decades. Yet not a week goes by without some newfangled fund coming out with a new concept. Some of these ideas come from the fund company's marketing department, which in some companies has too much clout. Rather than come up with investments that meet investors' needs, they come up with gimmicky funds that involve extra risk and that almost always cost extra in their high annual operating expenses.

Prospectuses

Securities laws require every fund to issue a *prospectus,* and the U.S. Securities and Exchange Commission reviews the details of every single one (which probably keeps plenty of coffee and eyeglass companies in business). A prospectus is usually written and edited by an attorney who wouldn't know a lively and comprehensible sentence if it hit him on the head with a law dictionary. You can safely skip most of what's said in any prospectus, but prospectuses do contain a few things you should check out.

TIP

The most valuable information — the fund's investment objectives, costs, and performance history — is summarized in the first few pages of the prospectus. Read these. Skip most of the rest. The rest only tells you more than you could possibly want to know about how the fund is administered. Do you really want to know whether employees are paid monthly or weekly? Which brand of computers they recently bought for the accounting department? Which pizza place they call for late-night deliveries? I don't think so.

If you find prospectuses to be positively lethal in their tediousness, let me suggest a friendlier alternative: Just jump ahead to the fund recommendations in Chapters 7 through 10 of this very book. I've already checked them out for you, and they meet the criteria for good funds that I list in this book. However, if you're going to be assessing funds for purchase other than those presented in this book, you need to be able to read and understand a prospectus.

In the pages that follow, I walk you through the more useful and relevant parts of a well-done prospectus for one of Vanguard's funds, the Vanguard Wellesley Income Fund.

Cover page

The information on the first page is duplicated inside the prospectus, but the cover page provides a synopsis of pertinent facts (see Figure 4-2). The prospectus is dated so that you know how recent its information is. Don't sweat it if the prospectus is a number of months old; in general, fund companies update prospectuses annually. The cover page lists phone numbers — handy to have in case you forget or lose them — as well as what applications you need to establish an account and how much money you need to open an account.

The table of contents is a sure sign that the prospectus is too long — but then lawyers seldom use one word where 50 will do. The table of contents helps you navigate the prospectus to find whatever information you want. To illustrate here, I cover only the first few pages of this prospectus; they're the pages that contain the best stuff, anyway.

TECHNICAL STUFF

Some prospectuses (though not this one) describe more than one fund in a particular fund family. This can save a fund company printing and mailing charges when it has funds with very similar investment objectives and/or funds run by the same management.

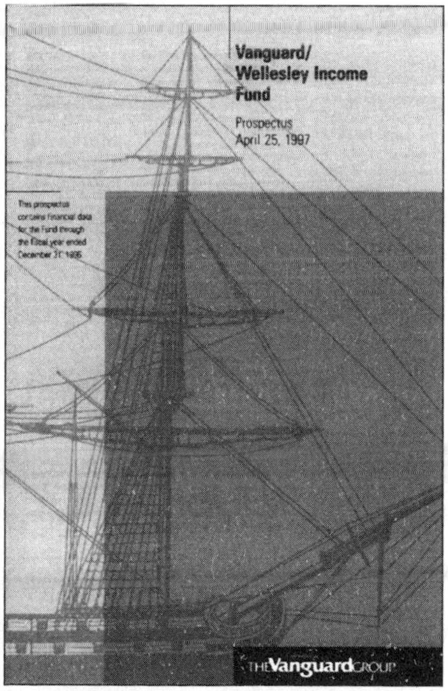

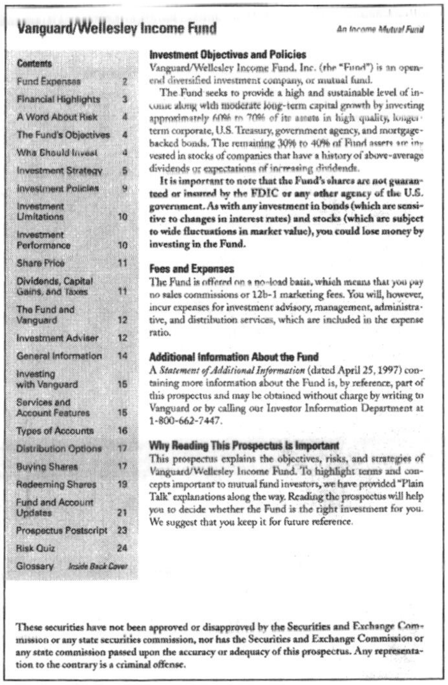

Vanguard/Wellesley Income Fund

An Income Mutual Fund

Contents

Investment Objectives and Policies

Vanguard/Wellesley Income Fund, Inc. (the "Fund") is an open-end diversified investment company, or mutual fund.

The Fund seeks to provide a high and sustainable level of income along with moderate long-term capital growth by investing approximately 60% to 70% of its assets in high quality, longer-term corporate, U.S. Treasury, government agency, and mortgage-backed bonds. The remaining 30% to 40% of Fund assets are invested in stocks of companies that have a history of above-average dividends or expectations of increasing dividends.

It is important to note that the Fund's shares are not guaranteed or insured by the FDIC or any other agency of the U.S. government. As with any investment in bonds (which are sensitive to changes in interest rates) and stocks (which are subject to wide fluctuations in market value), you could lose money by investing in the Fund.

Fees and Expenses

The Fund is offered on a no-load basis, which means that you pay no sales commissions or 12b-1 marketing fees. You will, however, incur expenses for investment advisory, management, administrative, and distribution services, which are included in the expense ratio.

Additional Information About the Fund

A *Statement of Additional Information* (dated April 25, 1997) containing more information about the Fund is, by reference, part of this prospectus and may be obtained without charge by writing to Vanguard or by calling our Investor Information Department at 1-800-662-7447.

Why Reading This Prospectus Is Important

This prospectus explains the objectives, risks, and strategies of Vanguard/Wellesley Income Fund. To highlight terms and concepts important to mutual fund investors, we have provided "Plain Talk" explanations along the way. Reading the prospectus will help you to decide whether the Fund is the right investment for you. We suggest that you keep it for future reference.

These securities have not been approved or disapproved by the Securities and Exchange Commission or any state securities commission, nor has the Securities and Exchange Commission or any state commission passed upon the accuracy or adequacy of this prospectus. Any representation to the contrary is a criminal offense.

Figure 4-2: The cover page starts you off right.

Source: The Vanguard Group.

Changes to prospectuses

Prospectuses are supposed to help you understand the fund you're buying. But they are so filled with financial and legal jargon that most do a poor job of this; some prospectuses seem like they don't want you to understand the fund at all. In 1998, the Securities and Exchange Commission passed resolutions requiring revisions to fund prospectuses that should make these documents more user-friendly.

First is the creation of a new document called the "profile" prospectus, which would summarize the key information contained in the traditional "long-form" prospectus. A particular thrust of the profile prospectus is explaining the potential risk of the fund, using graphs and tables to illustrate the fund's historic volatility. This new prospectus would replace the long-form prospectus as the document that fund companies must send to you before they sell you shares in a fund. The traditional long-form prospectus won't disappear; you will get a copy sent to you after you buy into a particular fund.

The longer form prospectus should be easier to read, thanks to new SEC requirements to replace legalese with "plain English." Specifically, the SEC rules call for shorter sentences, active voice instead of passive voice, no legal jargon, no double negatives (an example: "This fund is not without risk"), and the use of graphs and tables to illustrate complex material.

Expect to see prospectuses reflecting these new changes by early 1999.

In the "Investment Objectives" blurb, note that the Wellesley Income Fund is an open-end fund. This simply means that the fund will issue however many shares the fund has buyers for (as opposed to a closed-end fund, for which only a fixed number of shares are issued and traded; see Chapter 2 for more details on the difference).

Fund profile

The Fund profile page (see Figure 4-3) contains a synopsis of useful information about the fund, such as a description of what kind of investors should consider investing in this fund and which investors should not invest in it, fund risks, a schedule of distribution dates, who the investment adviser (fund manager) is, when the fund began, the assets under management, fees, the minimum initial investment amount, and the average historic returns, as well as a chart showing how the returns fluctuate from year to year as compared to a benchmark index. If you don't want to read the rest of the prospectus, this page at least summarizes the highlights.

Fund expenses

Thankfully, funds are required to present, in a standardized format (see Figure 4-4), the costs you'll incur for the privilege of owning the funds.

Fund Profile

Vanguard/Wellesley Income Fund

Who Should Invest *(page 4)*

- Investors seeking a balanced mutual fund as part of a diversified investment program.
- Investors seeking current income along with moderate capital growth *and* willing to invest for the long term—at least five years.

Who Should Not Invest

- Investors seeking a fund that invests exclusively in either stocks or in bonds.
- Investors unwilling to accept significant fluctuations in share price.

Risks of the Fund *(pages 4–9)*

The Fund's total return will fluctuate within a wide range, so an investor could lose money over short or even extended periods. The Fund is subject to—among other risks—interest rate risk (the chance that bond prices will decline because of rising interest rates) and stock market risk (the chance that stock prices in general will decline, sometimes suddenly and sharply).

Dividends and Capital Gains *(page 11)*

Dividends are paid in March, June, September, and December. Capital gains, if any, are paid in December.

Investment Adviser *(page 12)*

Wellington Management Company, LLP, Boston, MA.

Inception Date: July 1, 1970

Net Assets as of 12/31/96: $7.01 billion

Fund's Expense Ratio for the Year Ended 12/31/96: 0.31%

Loads, 12b-1 Marketing Fees: None

Suitable for IRAs: Yes

Minimum Initial Investment: $3,000; $1,000 for IRAs and custodial accounts for minors

Newspaper Abbreviation: Wellsl

Vanguard Fund Number: 027

Account Features *(page 15)*

- Telephone Redemption
- Vanguard Direct Deposit Service℠
- Vanguard Automatic Exchange Service℠
- Vanguard Fund Express®
- Vanguard Dividend Express℠

Average Annual Total Returns—Periods Ended December 31, 1996

	1 Year	5 Years	10 Years
Wellesley Income Fund	9.4%	10.9%	11.1%
Composite Index*	6.8	10.8	11.2

Quarterly Returns (%) 1987–1996 *(intended to show volatility of returns)*

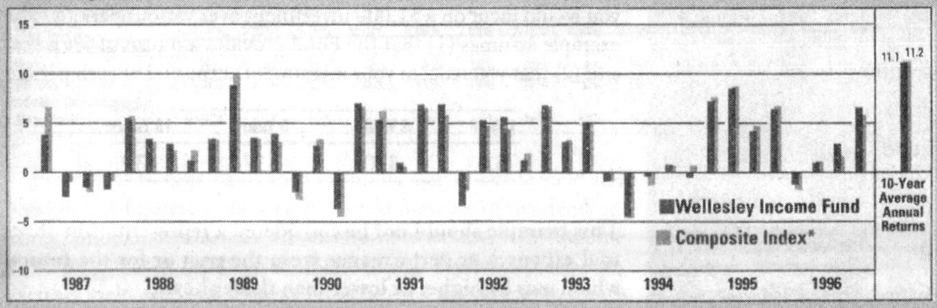

*The Composite Index is made up of 65% bonds and 35% stocks. See page 10 for details.

In evaluating past performance, remember that it is not indicative of future performance. Performance figures include the reinvestment of any dividends and capital gains distributions. The returns shown are net of expenses for the Fund, but they do not reflect income taxes an investor would have incurred. The Composite Index is a theoretical portfolio, incurring none of the advisory fees, operating expenses, and portfolio transaction costs that are borne by an operating mutual fund. Note, too, that both the return and principal value of an investment will fluctuate so that investors' shares, when redeemed, may be worth more or less than their original cost.

1

Figure 4-3: The fund profile provides a summary of the rest of the prospectus.

Source: The Vanguard Group.

PLAIN TALK ABOUT

The Costs of Investing

Costs are an important consideration in choosing a mutual fund. That's because you, as a shareholder, pay the costs of operating a fund, plus any transaction costs associated with buying, selling, or exchanging shares. These costs can erode a substantial portion of the gross income or capital appreciation a fund achieves. Even seemingly small differences in fund expenses can, over time, have a dramatic impact on a fund's performance.

PLAIN TALK ABOUT

Fund Expenses

All mutual funds have operating expenses. These expenses, which are deducted from a fund's gross income, are expressed as a percentage of the net assets of the fund. Vanguard/Wellesley Income Fund's expense ratio in fiscal year 1996 was 0.31%, or $3.10 per $1,000 of average net assets. The average balanced mutual fund had expenses in 1996 of 1.32%, or $13.20 per $1,000 of average net assets, according to Lipper Analytical Services, Inc., which reports on the mutual fund industry.

Fund Expenses

The examples below are designed to help you understand the various costs you would bear, directly or indirectly, as an investor in the Fund.

As noted in this table, you do not pay fees of any kind when you buy, sell, or exchange shares of the Fund:

Shareholder Transaction Expenses

Sales Load Imposed on Purchases:	None
Sales Load Imposed on Reinvested Dividends:	None
Redemption Fees:	None
Exchange Fees:	None

The next table illustrates the operating expenses that you would incur as a shareholder of the Fund. These expenses are deducted from the Fund's income before it is paid to you. Expenses include investment advisory fees as well as the costs of maintaining accounts, administering the Fund, providing shareholder services, and other activities. The expenses shown in the table are for the fiscal year ended December 31, 1996.

Annual Fund Operating Expenses

Management and Administrative Expenses:		0.23%
Investment Advisory Expenses:		0.05%
12b-1 Marketing Fees:		None
Other Expenses		
Marketing and Distribution Costs:	0.02%	
Miscellaneous Expenses (e.g., Taxes, Auditing):	0.01%	
Total Other Expenses:		0.03%
Total Operating Expenses (Expense Ratio):		**0.31%**

The following example illustrates the hypothetical expenses that you would incur on a $1,000 investment over various periods. The example assumes (1) that the Fund provides a return of 5% a year and (2) that you redeem your investment at the end of each period.

1 Year	3 Years	5 Years	10 Years
$3	$10	$17	$39

This example should not be considered a representation of actual expenses or performance from the past or for the future, which may be higher or lower than those shown.

2

Figure 4-4: Fund expenses.

Source: The Vanguard Group.

The first list of expenses shows *transaction expenses,* the fees you pay when you buy and sell shares. These fees are deducted at the time a transaction occurs; unfortunately, they're rarely itemized. A no-load fund such as the Wellesley Income Fund does not charge any sales commissions.

If a so-called financial advisor pitches a fund but you're not sure if he or she gets paid for selling it to you, always, always, *always* get a prospectus and check out the fund expense section. That way, you can see if commissions will erode your returns. In this case, you would see that if an advisor recommended this fund, he or she is not paid any commission — always a good sign. (Refer to Figure 4-1 for an example of a typical load-fund fee table.)

As discussed earlier in the chapter, operating expenses are fees charged on a continuous basis for all mutual funds; they cover the expenses of running a fund and include profits for the fund. In this case, they total a reasonable 0.31 percent. Because these fees are deducted from the fund's returns before your returns are paid to you, lower operating expenses translate into higher returns for you.

Financial highlights

If you get a headache looking at all the numbers on financial pages, you're not alone. Figure 4-5 looks forbidding, but this table is just a yearly summary of the value of the fund's shares and the distributions the fund has made (I cover these subjects in detail in Chapters 12 and 13).

The *Net Asset Value* (NAV) is the price per share of the fund. Tracking this value is a *terrible* measure of what you would have earned in the fund. Why? Just look at the distributions section, which details all the money paid out to shareholders each year. This fund has paid out total distributions of $14.34 per share over this ten-year period. This per-share figure is an enormous amount when you consider that the share price has only increased from $16.27 to $20.51 during the period — a modest 26 percent increase. But if you add in the distributions to the change in share price, now you're talking about a 114 percent increase (if you had reinvested these distributions, you would have had an even greater return)!

Presenting the NAV on the first line may strike you as odd and deceptive. If it does, talk to the fund regulators at the SEC to understand why they think this sort of presentation makes sense. It would make more sense to me to put the total return numbers here.

The total return represents what investors in the fund have earned historically. The returns on this type of fund, which invests in stocks and bonds, bounce around from year to year.

Financial Highlights

The following financial highlights table shows the results for a share outstanding for each of the last ten years ended December 31, 1996. The financial highlights were audited by Price Waterhouse LLP, independent accountants. You should read this information in conjunction with the Fund's financial statements and accompanying notes, which appear, along with the audit report from Price Waterhouse, in the Fund's most recent annual report to shareholders. The annual report is incorporated by reference in the *Statement of Additional Information* and in this prospectus, and contains a more complete discussion of the Fund's performance. You may have the report sent to you without charge by writing to Vanguard or by calling our Investor Information Department.

	Year Ended December 31,									
	1996	1995	1994	1993	1992	1991	1990	1989	1988	1987
Net Asset Value, Beginning of Period	**$20.44**	**$17.05**	**$19.24**	**$18.16**	**$18.08**	**$16.02**	**$16.82**	**$15.26**	**$14.57**	**$16.27**
Investment Operations										
Net Investment Income	1.17	1.13	1.11	1.14	1.21	1.27	1.30	1.32	1.23	1.24
Net Realized and Unrealized Gain (Loss) on Investments	.66	3.68	(1.95)	1.48	.29	2.06	(.72)	1.79	.69	(1.52)
Total from Investment Operations	**1.83**	**4.81**	**(.84)**	**2.62**	**1.50**	**3.33**	**.58**	**3.11**	**1.92**	**(.28)**
Distributions										
Dividends from Net Investment Income	(1.16)	(1.14)	(1.11)	(1.14)	(1.21)	(1.27)	(1.30)	(1.31)	(1.23)	(1.04)
Distributions from Realized Capital Gains	(.60)	(.28)	(.24)	(.40)	(.21)	—	(.08)	(.24)	—	(.38)
Total Distributions	**(1.76)**	**(1.42)**	**(1.35)**	**(1.54)**	**(1.42)**	**(1.27)**	**(1.38)**	**(1.55)**	**(1.23)**	**(1.42)**
Net Asset Value, End of Period	**$20.51**	**$20.44**	**$17.05**	**$19.24**	**$18.16**	**$18.08**	**$16.02**	**$16.82**	**$15.26**	**$14.57**
Total Return	**9.42%**	**28.91%**	**–4.44%**	**14.65%**	**8.67%**	**21.57%**	**3.76%**	**20.93%**	**13.61%**	**–1.92%**
Ratios/Supplemental Data										
Net Assets, End of Period (Millions)	$7,013	$7,181	$5,681	$6,011	$3,178	$1,934	$1,022	$788	$567	$495
Ratio of Expenses to Average Net Assets	0.31%	0.35%	0.34%	0.33%	0.35%	0.40%	0.45%	0.45%	0.51%	0.49%
Ratio of Net Investment Income to Average Net Assets	5.74%	5.96%	6.16%	5.79%	6.50%	7.08%	7.77%	7.68%	8.14%	7.83%
Portfolio Turnover Rate										
Bonds	29%	33%	31%	18%	24%	34%	13%	11%	19%	48%
Stocks	18%	26%	32%	26%	16%	19%	12%	10%	19%	27%
Average Commission Rate Paid	$.0334	N/A	N/A	N/A	N/A	N/A	N/A	N/A	N/A	N/A

From time to time, the Vanguard funds may advertise yield and total return figures. *Yield* is an historical measure of dividend income, and *total return* is a measure of past dividend income (assuming that it has been reinvested) plus capital appreciation. Neither yield nor total return should be used to predict the future performance of a fund.

PLAIN TALK ABOUT

How to Read the Financial Highlights Table

The Fund began fiscal 1996 with a net asset value (price) of $20.44 per share. During the year, the Fund earned $1.17 per share from investment income (interest and dividends) and $0.66 per share from investments that had appreciated in value or that were sold for higher prices than the Fund paid for them. Of those total earnings of $1.83 per share, $1.76 per share was returned to shareholders in the form of distributions ($1.16 in dividends, $0.60 in capital gains). The earnings ($1.83 per share) less distributions ($1.76 per share) resulted in a shsre price of $20.51 at the end of the year, an increase of $0.07 per share (from $20.44 at the beginning of the period to $20.51 at the end of the period). Assuming that the shareholder had reinvested the distributions in the purchase of more shares, total return from the Fund was 9.42% for the year.

As of December 31, 1996, the Fund had $7.01 billion in net assets; an expense ratio of 0.31% ($3.10 per $1,000 of net assets); and net investment income amounting to 5.74% of average net assets. It sold and replaced bonds valued at 29% of its bond holdings and stocks valued at 18% of its stock holdings.

3

Figure 4-5: Financial highlights.

Source: The Vanguard Group.

You can see how the total investments ("Net Assets") in the fund have changed over time. Assets can increase from new money flowing into the fund as well as from an increase in the value of a fund's shares.

This section of a prospectus also shows you how a fund's annual operating expenses ("Ratio of Expenses to Average Net Assets") have changed over time. They should decrease when a fund like this one has grown. If operating expenses do not decrease, their persistent levels may signal a company that maximizes its profits because of the fund's popularity. For funds only a few years old, expenses may remain higher because the fund is building its base of investors.

The line "Ratio of Net Investment Income to Average Net Assets" shows the annual dividends, or yield, that the fund has paid. (This figure is especially important for retired people, who need income to live on.) In this example, the downward trend merely reflects the overall decline in interest rates during the period. If you looked at this ratio for a similar fund, you would see the same trend for this period.

The *Portfolio Turnover Rate* tells you how much trading takes place in a fund. Specifically, it measures the percentage of the portfolio's holdings that has been traded over the year. (As this fund holds both stocks and bonds, it has chosen to show the turnover rate for each type of security.)

- A low turnover number (less than 30 percent) denotes a fund with more of a buy-and-hold strategy.
- A high turnover number (100 percent plus) indicates a fund manager who shifts things around a lot. Rapid trading is riskier and may increase a fund's taxable distributions.

Investment objectives and risks

The first section, on objectives, explains in detail what the fund is trying to accomplish (see Figure 4-6). The Wellesley Income Fund is seeking both current income and moderate growth of capital with much greater emphasis on income. It's trying to accomplish these objectives by investing in bonds (fixed-income securities) and common stocks (large, blue-chip companies) that pay decent dividends.

The investment policies or objectives can be thought of as a broad set of rules or guidelines (for example, the major type of securities that the fund invests in) that the fund operates under when investing your money. This hopefully protects you from most major surprises. And if a fund violates these guidelines — for instance, if this fund puts all of its money into

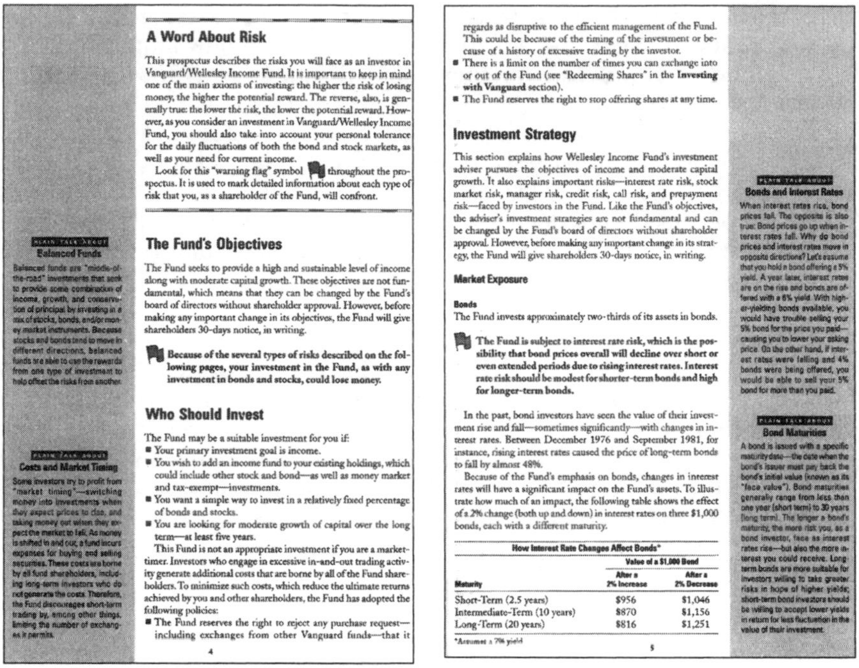

A Word About Risk

This prospectus describes the risks you will face as an investor in Vanguard/Wellesley Income Fund. It is important to keep in mind one of the main axioms of investing: the higher the risk of losing money, the higher the potential reward. The reverse, also, is generally true: the lower the risk, the lower the potential reward. However, as you consider an investment in Vanguard/Wellesley Income Fund, you should also take into account your personal tolerance for the daily fluctuations of both the bond and stock markets, as well as your need for current income.

Look for this "warning flag" symbol throughout the prospectus. It is used to mark detailed information about each type of risk that you, as a shareholder of the Fund, will confront.

PLAIN TALK ABOUT Balanced Funds

Balanced funds are "middle-of-the-road" investments that seek to provide some combination of income, growth, and conservation of principal by investing in a mix of stocks, bonds, and/or money market instruments. Because stocks and bonds tend to move in different directions, balanced funds are able to use the rewards from one type of investment to help offset the risks from another.

The Fund's Objectives

The Fund seeks to provide a high and sustainable level of income along with moderate capital growth. These objectives are not fundamental, which means that they can be changed by the Fund's board of directors without shareholder approval. However, before making any important change in its objectives, the Fund will give shareholders 30-days notice, in writing.

Because of the several types of risks described on the following pages, your investment in the Fund, as with any investment in bonds and stocks, could lose money.

Who Should Invest

The Fund may be a suitable investment for you if:

- Your primary investment goal is income.
- You wish to add an income fund to your existing holdings, which could include other stock and bond—as well as money market and tax-exempt—investments.
- You want a simple way to invest in a relatively fixed percentage of bonds and stocks.
- You are looking for moderate growth of capital over the long term—at least five years.

This Fund is not an appropriate investment if you are a market-timer. Investors who engage in excessive in-and-out trading activity generate additional costs that are borne by all of the Fund shareholders. To minimize such costs, which reduce the ultimate returns achieved by you and other shareholders, the Fund has adopted the following policies:

- The Fund reserves the right to reject any purchase request—including exchanges from other Vanguard funds—that it regards as disruptive to the efficient management of the Fund. This could be because of the timing of the investment or because of a history of excessive trading by the investor.
- There is a limit on the number of times you can exchange into or out of the Fund (see "Redeeming Shares" in the **Investing with Vanguard** section).
- The Fund reserves the right to stop offering shares at any time.

PLAIN TALK ABOUT Costs and Market Timing

Some investors try to profit from "market timing"—switching money into investments when they expect prices to rise, and taking money out when they expect the market to fall. As money is shifted in and out, a fund incurs expenses for buying and selling securities. These costs are borne by all fund shareholders, including long-term investors who do not generate the costs. Therefore, the Fund discourages short-term trading by, among other things, limiting the number of exchanges it permits.

4

Investment Strategy

This section explains how Wellesley Income Fund's investment adviser pursues the objectives of income and moderate capital growth. It also explains important risks—interest rate risk, stock market risk, manager risk, credit risk, call risk, and prepayment risk—faced by investors in the Fund. Like the Fund's objectives, the adviser's investment strategies are not fundamental and can be changed by the Fund's board of directors without shareholder approval. However, before making any important change in its strategy, the Fund will give shareholders 30-days notice, in writing.

Market Exposure

Bonds

The Fund invests approximately two-thirds of its assets in bonds.

The Fund is subject to interest rate risk, which is the possibility that bond prices overall will decline over short or even extended periods due to rising interest rates. Interest rate risk should be modest for shorter-term bonds and high for longer-term bonds.

In the past, bond investors have seen the value of their investment rise and fall—sometimes significantly—with changes in interest rates. Between December 1976 and September 1981, for instance, rising interest rates caused the price of long-term bonds to fall by almost 48%.

Because of the Fund's emphasis on bonds, changes in interest rates will have a significant impact on the Fund's assets. To illustrate how much of an impact, the following table shows the effect of a 2% change (both up and down) in interest rates on three $1,000 bonds, each with a different maturity.

How Interest Rate Changes Affect Bonds*

	Value of a $1,000 Bond	
Maturity	After a 2% Increase	After a 2% Decrease
Short-Term (2.5 years)	$956	$1,046
Intermediate-Term (10 years)	$870	$1,156
Long-Term (20 years)	$816	$1,251

*Assumes a 7% yield

PLAIN TALK ABOUT Bonds and Interest Rates

When interest rates rise, bond prices fall. The opposite is also true: Bond prices go up when interest rates fall. Why do bond prices and interest rates move in opposite directions? Let's assume that you hold a bond offering a 5% yield. A year later, interest rates are on the rise and bonds are offered with a 6% yield. With higher-yielding bonds available, you would have trouble selling your 5% bond for the price you paid—causing you to lower your asking price. On the other hand, if interest rates were falling and 4% bonds were being offered, you would be able to sell your 5% bond for more than you paid.

PLAIN TALK ABOUT Bond Maturities

A bond is issued with a specific maturity date—the date when the bond's issuer must pay back the bond's initial value (known as its "face value"). Bond maturities generally range from less than one year (short term) to 30 years (long term). The longer a bond's maturity, the more risk you, as a bond investor, face as interest rates rise—but also the more interest you could receive. Long-term bonds are more suitable for investors willing to take greater risks in hope of higher yields; short-term bond investors should be willing to accept lower yields in return for less fluctuation in the value of their investment.

5

Figure 4-6: Investment objectives and risks.

Source: The Vanguard Group.

international stocks — the SEC would spank, reprimand, and penalize Vanguard. Less ethical fund companies may be willing to pay this "small price" if they can seduce more people into their funds by showing higher returns from taking poorly disclosed risks.

If you've taken the time to look at how much money this fund has made for investors, you owe it to yourself to understand this fund's risks, too. This prospectus does an excellent job of discussing the Wellesley Income Fund's risks, using examples from earlier in this century rather than just from the past ten years, which were unusually good years for the financial markets (see Figure 4-7).

Annual Reports

Funds also produce annual reports that discuss how the fund has been doing and provide details on the specific investments that a fund holds. Look at the annual report if, for instance, you want to know which countries an international fund is currently invested in.

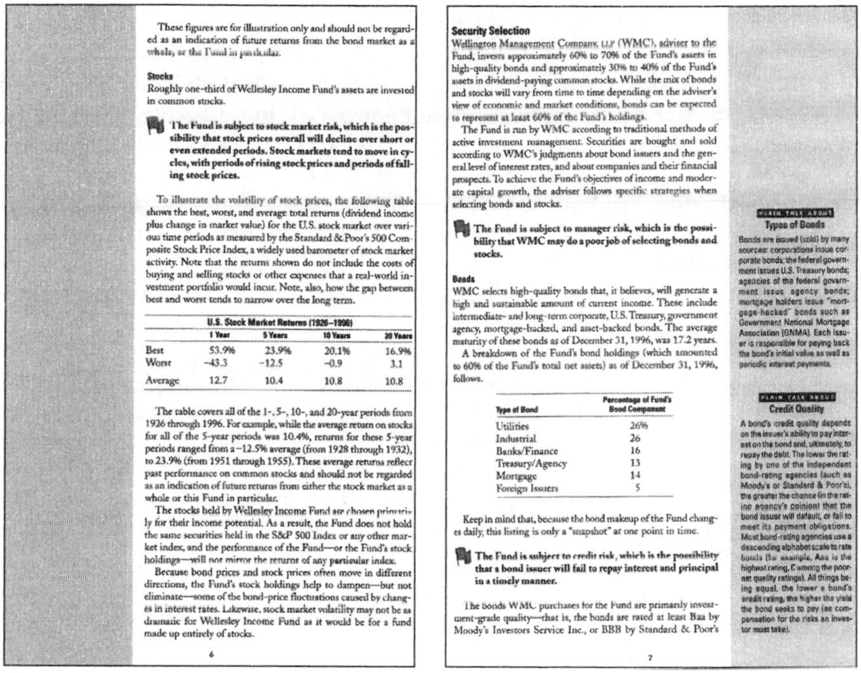

These figures are for illustration only and should not be regarded as an indication of future returns from the bond market as a whole, or the Fund in particular.

Stocks

Roughly one-third of Wellesley Income Fund's assets are invested in common stocks.

The Fund is subject to stock market risk, which is the possibility that stock prices overall will decline over short or even extended periods. Stock markets tend to move in cycles, with periods of rising stock prices and periods of falling stock prices.

To illustrate the volatility of stock prices, the following table shows the best, worst, and average total returns (dividend income plus change in market value) for the U.S. stock market over various time periods as measured by the Standard & Poor's 500 Composite Stock Price Index, a widely used barometer of stock market activity. Note that the returns shown do not include the costs of buying and selling stocks or other expenses that a real-world investment portfolio would incur. Note, also, how the gap between best and worst tends to narrow over the long term.

U.S. Stock Market Returns (1926–1996)

	1 Year	5 Years	10 Years	20 Years
Best	53.9%	23.9%	20.1%	16.9%
Worst	–43.3	–12.5	–0.9	3.1
Average	12.7	10.4	10.8	10.8

The table covers all of the 1-, 5-, 10-, and 20-year periods from 1926 through 1996. For example, while the average return on stocks for all of the 5-year periods was 10.4%, returns for these 5-year periods ranged from a –12.5% average (from 1928 through 1932), to 23.9% (from 1951 through 1955). These average returns reflect past performance on common stocks and should not be regarded as an indication of future returns from either the stock market as a whole or this Fund in particular.

The stocks held by Wellesley Income Fund are chosen primarily for their income potential. As a result, the Fund does not hold the same securities held in the S&P 500 Index or any other market index, and the performance of the Fund—or the Fund's stock holdings—will not mirror the returns of any particular index.

Because bond prices and stock prices often move in different directions, the Fund's stock holdings help to dampen—but not eliminate—some of the bond-price fluctuations caused by changes in interest rates. Likewise, stock market volatility may not be as dramatic for Wellesley Income Fund as it would be for a fund made up entirely of stocks.

6

Security Selection

Wellington Management Company, LLP (WMC), adviser to the Fund, invests approximately 60% to 70% of the Fund's assets in high-quality bonds and approximately 30% to 40% of the Fund's assets in dividend-paying common stocks. While the mix of bonds and stocks will vary from time to time depending on the adviser's view of economic and market conditions, bonds can be expected to represent at least 60% of the Fund's holdings.

The Fund is run by WMC according to traditional methods of active investment management. Securities are bought and sold according to WMC's judgments about bond issuers and the general level of interest rates, and about companies and their financial prospects. To achieve the Fund's objectives of income and moderate capital growth, the adviser follows specific strategies when selecting bonds and stocks.

The Fund is subject to manager risk, which is the possibility that WMC may do a poor job of selecting bonds and stocks.

Bonds

WMC selects high-quality bonds that, it believes, will generate a high and sustainable amount of current income. These include intermediate- and long-term corporate, U.S. Treasury, government agency, mortgage-backed, and asset-backed bonds. The average maturity of these bonds as of December 31, 1996, was 17.2 years.

A breakdown of the Fund's bond holdings (which amounted to 60% of the Fund's total net assets) as of December 31, 1996, follows.

Type of Bond	Percentage of Fund's Bond Component
Utilities	26%
Industrial	26
Banks/Finance	16
Treasury/Agency	13
Mortgage	14
Foreign Issuers	5

Keep in mind that, because the bond makeup of the Fund changes daily, this listing is only a "snapshot" at one point in time.

The Fund is subject to credit risk, which is the possibility that a bond issuer will fail to repay interest and principal in a timely manner.

The bonds WMC purchases for the Fund are primarily investment-grade quality—that is, the bonds are rated at least Baa by Moody's Investors Service Inc., or BBB by Standard & Poor's

7

PLAIN TALK ABOUT

Types of Bonds

Bonds are issued (sold) by many sources: corporations issue corporate bonds; the federal government issues U.S. Treasury bonds; agencies of the federal government issue agency bonds; mortgage holders issue "mortgage-backed" bonds such as Government National Mortgage Association (GNMA). Each issuer is responsible for paying back the bond's initial value as well as periodic interest payments.

PLAIN TALK ABOUT

Credit Quality

A bond's credit quality depends on the issuer's ability to pay interest on the bond and, ultimately, to repay the debt. The lower the rating by one of the independent bond-rating agencies (such as Moody's or Standard & Poor's), the greater the chance (in the rating agency's opinion) that the bond issuer will default, or fail to meet its payment obligations. Most bond-rating agencies use a descending alphabet scale to rate bonds (for example, Aaa is the highest rating, C among the poorest quality ratings). All things being equal, the lower a bond's credit rating, the higher the yield the bond seeks to pay (as compensation for the risks an investor must take).

Figure 4-7: Investment objectives and risks.

Source: The Vanguard Group.

You can get answers to questions like the countries a fund invests in by calling a fund's 800 number. Some of the mutual fund information sources that I recommend in Chapter 15 also report this type of information. (Or you could say, "Details, details. Just tell me what funds to buy for different needs." That's just what I do in Chapters 7 through 10.)

In this section, I review the pages from the annual report on the Vanguard Wellesley Income Fund, the same fund whose prospectus I just introduced you to. In addition to producing an annual report, each fund produces a semiannual report that (guess what?) comes out halfway between annual reports. The semiannual reports are usually a bit shorter than the full-year reports but contain the most up-to-date information on the fund's current investment holdings and performance.

When you call a fund company to ask for applications, specifically request a fund's recent annual or semiannual reports. Unlike a prospectus, most funds don't automatically send annual reports along.

Chairman's letter

The Chairman's letter is supposed to explain how well the fund has performed recently and why (see Figure 4-8). In far too many reports, the fund's chief executive uses his or her letter to the stockholders merely as an opportunity to overhype how well the fund has done — during *good* periods in the financial markets. In tougher times, too many fund execs blame subpar performance on the market. It's like fishing: On a successful day, you talk about your uncanny casting ability, your brilliant choice of lures, and your ability to keep still and quiet. When you come home empty-handed, the fish just weren't biting.

A good annual report like Vanguard's will detail the performance of the fund and compare it to relevant benchmarks and comparable funds. You hope that your fund will meet or exceed the performance of comparable funds (and perhaps even of the benchmark, too) in most periods. Don't worry if your fund periodically underperforms a little. Especially with stock and bond funds, you invest for the long haul, not just for six months or a year.

Unfortunately, more than a few fund companies use benchmarks (indexes) as comparisons for their funds' performances so that their funds look as if they perform better than they really do (such as the Warburg Pincus Growth & Income Fund, discussed earlier in this chapter). This ruse is similar to a financially savvy adult like, say, me, comparing his mutual fund selection abilities to those of, say, a child. I'm at something of an unfair advantage (at any rate, I'd better be). As you review a fund's annual report, keep in mind this tendency of some funds to fudge comparisons. I discuss ways you can make sure that you're comparing a fund's performance to an appropriate benchmark in Chapter 12.

In addition to discussing the fund's performance during the year, an annual report also covers how the overall financial markets were feeling. If you're used to a steady diet of the daily news, an overview like this can help you to better see and understand the big picture (and maybe you won't be so shocked that the fund lost 2 percent last year when you see that the benchmark index most relevant to that fund lost 2.5 percent).

Performance discussion

A good annual report is educational and honest. As you can see, Vanguard's is both. The report also does a nice job of providing a historical context for understanding this fund's performance. It explains that bonds normally are less volatile than stocks. The comparative stability of bonds means that a portfolio composed of stocks *and* bonds, like this one, is less volatile than one made up of just stocks.

FELLOW SHAREHOLDER,

Vanguard/Wellesley Income Fund earned +20.2% in 1997, a generous return made possible by an excellent environment for bonds and an even better one for stocks. The U.S. economy enjoyed strong economic growth and low unemployment, combined, somewhat surprisingly, with decelerating inflation. Reflecting lower interest rates, long-term corporate bonds provided a solid return of +13.5%, and the stock market surged to an astonishing +33.4% advance.

The table at right compares the Fund's total return (capital change plus reinvested dividends) with those of the average income fund and the unmanaged Wellesley Composite Index, which mirrors our typical balance of 65% bonds and 35% high-yielding stocks. For the year, Wellesley's return topped those of both the Index and—by a notably imposing margin—the average income-oriented mutual fund.

	Total Returns Year Ended December 31, 1997
Vanguard/Wellesley Income Fund	+20.2%
Average Income Fund	+16.4%
Wellesley Composite Index*	+19.4%

*65% Lehman Long Corporate AA or Better Bond Index, 26% S&P/BARRA Value Index, 4.5% S&P Utilities Index, and 4.5% S&P Telephone Index.

The Fund's total return is based on net asset values of $20.51 per share on December 31, 1996, and $21.86 per share on December 31, 1997, adjusted for dividends totaling $1.20 per share paid from net investment income and distributions totaling $1.445 per share from net realized capital gains. Wellesley Income Fund's annualized yield as of December 31 was 5.3%.

1

FINANCIAL MARKETS IN BRIEF

Long-term interest rates rose through the first quarter of the year on expectations that the economy's robust growth would cause inflation to accelerate. The yield on the benchmark 30-year U.S. Treasury bond peaked at 7.17% in mid-April. Then, as the news on inflation got better rather than worse, the yield turned downward, falling to 5.92% on December 31, 72 basis points below the 6.64% level at which it began the year.

Short-term interest rates bottomed out in June then began rising, apparently because of sales of short-term Treasuries by foreign central banks and investors. At year-end 1997, the yield on three-month U.S. Treasury bills was 5.35%, up just a bit from 5.17% when the year began. The spread between yields on three-month T-bills and 30-year Treasury bonds was a slim 0.57 percentage point on December 31, 1997. Such a "flattening" of the yield curve has more often than not been a precursor of a slowing economy.

On the stock side, the historic bull market that began in August 1982 continued in impressive fashion during 1997. The economy, corporate earnings, and employment grew solidly, and consumer confidence strengthened. Yet interest rates declined and inflation decelerated. In short, the domestic economic news could not have been better.

The sole dark cloud—severe turmoil in Asian economies and currencies—only briefly darkened the stock market's mood. After a sharp decline in October—the Standard & Poor's 500 Composite Stock Price Index tumbled –7% on October 27 alone—stocks resumed their climb. By the time the year was over, the Index had produced its second-highest annual return (to 1995) in the past two decades.

Figure 4-8: Chairman's letter.

Source: The Vanguard Group.

You also see a description of how this fund invested its money during 1997. The comparisons to competitors help you make sure that you're comparing your fund to Wellesley's true peers — apples to apples.

These comparisons are even more valuable and useful when applied over longer periods, as in this annual report's "Long-Term Performance Overview" section (see Figure 4-9). ***Remember:*** In the world of stocks and bonds, one year is too short a period to evaluate a fund. In this section, the chairman also looks forward and prudently reminds us that the future will likely contain both good and bad periods.

You can also see how Wellesley performed against its competitors ("average income fund") and the benchmark composite index. Wellesley beat the pants off of its competition and slightly outperformed the benchmark index by 0.3 percent per year. (The "Composite Index" is a mythical investment, which has the advantage of not having any costs deducted from it.)

Performance and its components

The performance page looks like a terrible overload of numbers, but it actually contains valuable information (see Figure 4-10).

1997 PERFORMANCE OVERVIEW

Wellesley Income Fund's return of +20.2% fell between the terrific +33.4% return of the stock market, as represented by the S&P 500 Index, and the fine +13.5% return of the long-term corporate bond market. We were a bit closer to the bond return because of the Fund's policy of emphasizing bonds. This conservative stance tends to constrain Wellesley's advances during bullish periods for the stock market, but it gives the Fund a more stable profile during the inevitable down periods for stocks.

Wellesley's bond holdings returned +14.0% during the year, ahead of the +13.5% return of the Lehman Brothers Long Corporate AA or Better Bond Index, which is the bond portion of our composite benchmark. We were aided by the bullish stance on bonds adopted by our investment adviser, Wellington Management Company. The average duration of the Fund's bond segment, at 9.1 years, is slightly longer than that of the Lehman benchmark. (The longer a bond fund's duration, the more its value rises when interest rates decline, and the more its value falls when rates rise.)

Wellesley's stock holdings returned +32.8% in 1997, a bit shy of the return on the S&P 500 Index, but ahead of the +30.7% return on the equity segment of our composite benchmark. This segment is based on the S&P/BARRA Value Index, the S&P Utilities Index, and the S&P Telephone Index, reflecting our tilt toward income-producing stocks. The shortfall against the S&P 500 can be largely attributed to the market's tilt toward growth stocks during the year. The S&P 500 Index's growth component provided a return of +36.5% during the year, well above the +30.0% return of its value component.

More than half of Wellesley's stock holdings were in the financial-services and utilities sectors, respectively the best and third-best performers within the S&P 500 Index in 1997. However, stocks we held in those groups didn't perform as well as the financial-services and utilities stocks in the S&P 500 Index. The Fund's industry concentrations were especially advantageous during the final three months of the year, when turmoil in the financial markets pushed up demand for financial and utility issues—sectors that are sensitive to interest-rate changes. In addition, we held no stocks in the technology or producer-durables sectors, two of the Index's worst-performing sectors during the year.

We held an average of about 12% of our equity assets in the market-lagging materials & processing sector—nearly twice the S&P 500 Index weight. However, this negative was mostly offset by excellent stock picks in the sector. A significant liability relative to the S&P 500 was a low commitment to health-care stocks (4.7% for our Fund, 11.0% for the Index) combined with poor stock selection in the sector.

The Fund's overall +3.8% advantage versus the average income-oriented mutual fund was the result of the fine performance of our stocks combined with the longer average maturities of our bond holdings compared to those of our competitors. We hasten to add our customary warning about comparing Wellesley Income Fund with this peer group over short periods. The income-fund group is a varied bunch, and many funds within it pursue strategies that are far different from Wellesley's.

We again achieved our objective of providing a high level of current income. Our income dividends of $1.20 per share were 3.4% higher than our 1996 dividends of $1.16 per share. As noted above, the Fund's overall yield was 5.3%. The yield on its equities was 3.4%, more than twice the record-low 1.6% yield of the S&P 500 Index.

2

LONG-TERM PERFORMANCE OVERVIEW

As shown in the table below, over the past ten years Wellesley has outperformed both its average peer and the composite index, a result that reflects both the Fund's excellent investment management and our low costs. Based on our +13.3% average annual return, which is 1.9 percentage points higher than that of our peers, a $10,000 investment in Wellesley (with dividends and capital gains distributions reinvested) would have grown over the decade to $34,983. This is $5,547 more than the $29,436 that would have accumulated in the average income fund. The "Vanguard advantage" is an impressive 55% of the initial investment.

	Total Returns 10 Years Ended December 31, 1997	
	Average Annual Rate	Final Value of a $10,000 Initial Investment
Wellesley Income Fund	+13.3%	$34,983
Average Income Fund	+11.4%	$29,436
Wellesley Composite Index*	+13.0%	$33,806

*65% Lehman Long Corporate AA or Better Bond Index, 26% S&P/BARRA Value Index, and 9% S&P Utilities Index through June 30, 1996, when the S&P Utilities component was seperated into the S&P Utilities Index and the S&P Telephone Index.

Our low expenses accounted for about half of our long-term advantage over our competitors, while the rest was earned by our investment adviser. Our expense ratio (annual expenses as a percentage of average net assets) totaled a minuscule 0.31% in 1997, one-fourth of the 1.26% expense ratio charged by our average peer. Costs matter, especially in an income-oriented fund, because operating expenses directly reduce the income that a mutual fund passes through to its shareholders.

Our performance edge over our composite index represents a significant accomplishment, given that the index does not incur the real-world expenses (for fund operations and securities transactions) that mutual funds must assume.

We stress that the returns earned during the past decade were unusually high. They encompass a ten-year period during which the U.S. stock market did not experience a single serious downturn and the bond market was buoyed by generally declining interest rates. Although financial markets are inherently unpredictable, we believe it is safe to say that returns over the next decade are virtually certain to be lower than those of the previous one.

IN SUMMARY

Returns from the U.S. stock market over the past three years—indeed, over the past 15 years—have no precedent in American financial history. Long-term bonds, too, have experienced a remarkable period as yields have generally declined since the early 1980s. While as investors we have every reason to be grateful for the bounty of the financial markets, we also have reason to regard the future with some caution. Lengthy bull markets can breed complacency and cause investors to discount the risks inherent in stocks and bonds. Make no mistake, the markets will demonstrate these risks from time to time.

However, the greatest risk is failure to invest in the first place. We believe that the best approach to dealing with risk is to hold a balanced portfolio that includes stock funds, bond funds, and money market funds—a belief that is at the core of Wellesley's

3

Figure 4-9: Performance overview.

Source: The Vanguard Group.

PERFORMANCE SUMMARY

Wellesley Income Fund

All of the data on this page represent past performance, which cannot be used to predict future returns that may be achieved by the Fund. Note, too, that both share price and return can fluctuate widely, so an investment in the Fund could lose money.

Total Investment Returns: December 31, 1977–December 31, 1997

Fiscal Year	Wellesley Income Fund Capital Return	Wellesley Income Fund Income Return	Wellesley Income Fund Total Return	Composite* Total Return	Fiscal Year	Wellesley Income Fund Capital Return	Wellesley Income Fund Income Return	Wellesley Income Fund Total Return	Composite* Total Return
1978	–4.6%	8.2%	3.6%	2.2%	1988	4.7%	8.9%	13.6%	13.7%
1979	–2.6	8.8	6.2	3.5	1989	11.8	9.1	20.9	21.0
1980	0.9	11.0	11.9	9.4	1990	–4.3	8.1	3.8	2.5
1981	–3.1	11.8	8.7	–1.7	1991	12.9	8.7	21.6	20.5
1982	10.1	13.2	23.3	36.3	1992	1.6	7.1	8.7	9.2
1983	7.1	11.5	18.6	13.2	1993	8.2	6.4	14.6	14.6
1984	4.9	11.7	16.6	13.8	1994	–10.2	5.8	–4.4	–4.6
1985	16.0	11.4	27.4	29.4	1995	21.8	7.3	28.9	30.7
1986	9.2	9.1	18.3	19.9	1996	3.3	6.1	9.4	6.8
1987	–8.1	6.2	–1.9	2.5	1997	13.8	6.4	20.2	19.4

*65% Lehman Long-Term Corporate Bond Index and 35% S&P 500 Index through December 31, 1985; 65% Lehman Long Corporate AA or Better Bond Index, 26% S&P/BARRA Value Index, and 9% S&P Utilities Index through June 30, 1996, when the S&P Utilities component was separated into the S&P Utilities Index and the S&P Telephone Index.

See *Financial Highlights* table on page 21 for dividend and capital gains information for the past five years.

9

Cumulative Performance: December 31, 1987–December 31, 1997

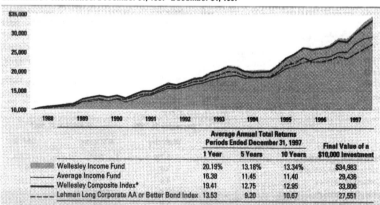

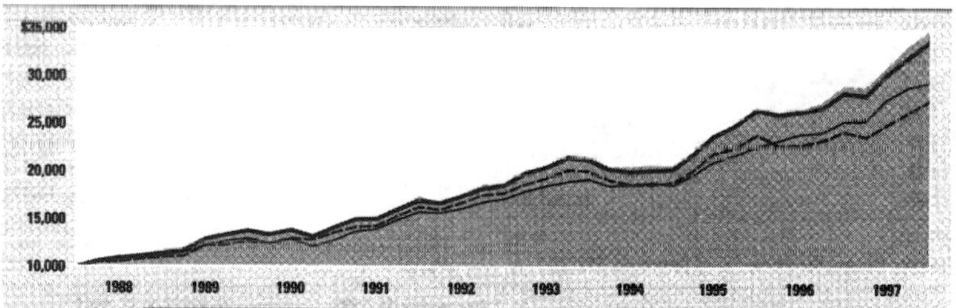

	Average Annual Total Returns Periods Ended December 31, 1997 1 Year	5 Years	10 Years	Final Value of a $10,000 Investment
Wellesley Income Fund	20.19%	13.18%	13.34%	$34,983
Average Income Fund	16.38	11.45	11.40	29,436
Wellesley Composite Index*	19.41	12.75	12.95	33,806
Lehman Long Corporate AA or Better Bond Index	13.53	9.20	10.67	27,551

*65% Lehman Long Corporate AA or Better Bond Index, 26% S&P/BARRA Value Index, and 9% S&P Utilities Index through June 30, 1996, when the S&P Utilities component was separated into the S&P Utilities Index and the S&P Telephone Index.

Average Annual Total Returns: Periods Ended December 31, 1997

	Inception Date	1 Year	5 Years	10 Years Capital	10 Years Income	10 Years Total
Wellesley Income Fund	7/1/1970	20.19%	13.18%	5.97%	7.37%	13.34%

Figure 4-10: Total investment returns.

Source: The Vanguard Group.

For example, this table shows you, on a year-by-year basis, how the Wellesley Income Fund has performed. As you can see, although the fund has produced an *average* annual return of 13.34 percent per year over the past ten years, its return varies much from year to year. In 1986, for instance, it returned 18.3 percent, but it then lost 1.9 percent in the next year. (If a swing in returns such as in this example makes you reach for your motion sickness prescription, you'd better skip investing in it. ***Remember:*** To earn better returns, you've gotta take risks.)

You also can see how much the fund paid out in dividends ("Income Return") and capital gains ("Capital Return") each year. I cover all of these details in Chapter 12 when I discuss a fund's returns.

Investment adviser's thoughts

The "Report From the Adviser" is where the portfolio managers of the fund (in this case, the Wellington Management Group) explain how the economic environment affected the fund's performance. They also look ahead and discuss what the future may hold and what investment strategy they plan to take in the near future (see Figure 4-11).

REPORT FROM THE ADVISER

Vanguard/Wellesley Income Fund outperformed its unmanaged benchmark for 1997. For the twelve months ended December 31, 1997, the Fund returned 20.2%, versus 19.4% for its benchmark. Wellesley's stock segment returned 32.8%, following increases of 24.2% in 1996 and 37.1% in 1995. These equity returns are well above historical averages and have allowed the Fund to enjoy respectable returns over the last three years.

Throughout the year the Fund maintained its traditional allocation, with 60%–65% of assets invested in longer-term investment-grade bonds and 35%–40% in dividend-paying equities. In general, the long average maturity of the Fund's bonds and our meaningful weighting in high-yielding, interest-rate-sensitive stocks make Wellesley's performance extremely sensitive to the direction of long-term interest rates. The bond portfolio's return of 14.0% for 1997 bettered the 13.5% return for the Lehman Long Corporate AA or Better Index, against which we measure that segment's performance. We increased the duration of the bond portfolio throughout 1997, and at year-end it was slightly longer than that of the Lehman index. This relatively longer duration helped performance as long-term rates fell sharply during the last three months of 1997. A longer duration than the benchmark implies that the principal value of the bond portfolio will change more dramatically with a change in interest rates.

The 32.8% return for Wellesley's equities was ahead of the 30.7% return on the equity portion of its composite benchmark, which is weighted 75% in the S&P/BARRA Value Index, 12.5% in the S&P Utilities Index, and 12.5% in the S&P Telephone Index. The stocks invested in the financial-services and utility sectors contributed handsomely to performance this year. For more details, please see the Message To Shareholders, beginning on page 1.

INVESTMENT OUTLOOK FOR 1998

Spreading economic and financial crises in Asia have caused us to lower growth expectations for the U.S. economy in 1998. Real Gross Domestic Product is now estimated to increase 2.3% on average in the year ahead, a reduction of one-half percentage point from our prior forecast. We expect exports to Asia to drop sharply, and we project that the rising U.S. dollar exchange rate will translate both into a steady stream of lower-priced imports into this country and market-share losses for industries that compete with imports. An extremely competitive pricing environment will produce declining inflation. We expect the Consumer Price Index to rise just 1.6% in 1998. Slower global growth, a strong dollar, intense pricing pressure, and some inevitable upward movement in wage rates will make it a very difficult year for corporate profits, which we now expect to rise just marginally over the next four quarters.

INVESTMENT PHILOSOPHY

The Fund reflects a belief that relatively high current income and moderate long-term growth in income and capital can be achieved without undue risk by holding 60% to 65% of assets in fixed-income securities and the balance in income-oriented common stocks. Consistent with this approach, the Fund's bond segment comprises intermediate- and long-term U.S. Treasury securities and high-quality corporate bonds; its equity segment is dominated by stocks with above-average dividend yields and strong potential for dividend increases.

7

Slower U.S. growth, a strong dollar, and falling inflation rates will end the speculation about a Federal Reserve tightening of monetary policy. Such speculation dominated the capital markets for the first nine months of 1997. Ultimately, we expect that the Fed's next move will be to lower short-term interest rates later in the year.

We also now expect a budget surplus this year, a very positive factor for the bond market. However, the fundamentals underlying 1998 will be much more of a challenge to the U.S. equity market. Valuations remain historically high, and the profit outlook has deteriorated. Nevertheless, lower long-term interest rates and stable-to-lower short-term rates will be a positive underpinning for stocks in 1998.

STRATEGY IN 1998

Our strategy remains consistent, and our allocation to stocks and bonds will vary only marginally. The maturity of Wellesley's bonds will remain long-term, with call protection to preserve the income stream. We purchase only investment-grade, U.S.-dollar-denominated bonds, emphasizing those with stable-to-improving credit fundamentals. As of December 31, approximately 86% of the bond portfolio was rated "A" or better.

Our stock portfolio strategy is to purchase companies with above-market yields across different industries. The average yield on our stocks, at 3.4%, is 113% higher than the yield on the S&P 500 Index. We began increasing our exposure to utilities because this sector benefits from declining interest rates. Also, the fundamentals for this industry should improve as companies consolidate. The primary reason for our selective sales of stocks is to dispose of issues that reach our target prices.

The dominant theme guiding the Fund's investment strategy is our ongoing obligation to shareholders to achieve an attractive absolute level of income by holding high-quality securities. Our long-term goal is to increase Wellesley's dividend by purchasing stocks of strong companies that can pass onto shareholders higher dividends generated from rising earnings. Since we wrote to you six months ago, the equities in our portfolio have had 21 dividend increases. However, we note that we avoid stocks with ultrahigh dividends that may not be sustainable over the longer term.

SUMMARY

If interest rates continue to decline, Wellesley should perform well versus more aggressive bond and stock funds. We will continue to focus on maintaining the Fund's charter and on trying to outperform the composite benchmark. Income improvement remains an objective for 1998.

Earl E. McEvoy, *Senior Vice President*
John R. Ryan, *Senior Vice President*
Wellington Management Company, LLP

January 14, 1998

8

Figure 4-11: Investment adviser's thoughts.

Source: The Vanguard Group.

Investment holdings

The "Statement of Net Assets" section lists every single solitary investment the fund owns. Here's where you get the details that tell you exactly where your money is invested. You can see here the incredible diversification your money gets in a mutual fund; you actually own a teeny, tiny sliver of each of these securities if you invest in this fund (see Figure 4-12).

For example, in this first section, you can see that this fund (as of December 31, 1997) was 46.2 percent invested in bonds issued by corporations. The corporate bond slice of the fund's pie divides further into which industries and specific companies the fund holds bonds from.

For each security, you also can see how much the fund originally invested and what each investment was worth at the end of the most recent year. (Do you need to know, should you care, will it be on the test? No, no, and no!)

More investment holdings

This includes more of the investments that the fund owns. Here you can see some of the stocks the fund owns (see Figure 4-13).

FINANCIAL STATEMENTS

December 31, 1997

STATEMENT OF NET ASSETS

This Statement provides a detailed list of the Fund's holdings, including each security's market value on the last day of the reporting period. Securities are grouped and subtotaled by asset type (common stocks, preferred stocks, bonds, etc.) and by industry sector. Other assets are added to, and liabilities are subtracted from, the value of *Total Investments* to calculate the Fund's *Net Assets.* Finally, *Net Assets* are divided by the outstanding shares of the Fund to arrive at its share price, or *Net Asset Value (NAV) Per Share.*

At the end of the Statement of Net Assets, you will find a table displaying the composition of the Fund's net assets on both a dollar and per-share basis. Because all income and any realized gains must be distributed to shareholders each year, the bulk of net assets consists of *Paid in Capital* (money invested by shareholders). The amounts shown for *Undistributed Net Investment Income* and *Accumulated Net Realized Gains* usually approximate the sums the Fund had available to distribute to shareholders as income dividends or capital gains as of the statement date. Any *Accumulated Net Realized Losses,* and any cumulative excess of distributions over net income or net realized gains, will appear as negative balances. *Unrealized Appreciation (Depreciation)* is the difference between the market value of the Fund's investments and their cost, and reflects the gains (losses) that would be realized if the Fund were to sell all of its investments at their statement-date values.

14

Wellesley Income Fund	Face Amount (000)	Market Value* (000)
CORPORATE BONDS (46.2%)		
Finance (13.0%)		
ABN AMRO Bank NV (Chicago Branch)		
7.55%, 6/28/2006	$25,000	$ 26,784
Allstate Corp.		
7.50%, 6/15/2013	20,000	21,472
Ambac, Inc.		
7.50%, 5/1/2023	5,500	5,908
American Re Corp.		
7.45%, 12/15/2026	33,000	35,583
Banc One Corp.		
7.75%, 7/15/2025	50,000	55,224
8.00%, 4/29/2027	15,000	17,067
BankBoston Corp.		
6.625%, 12/1/2005	15,000	15,106
6.875%, 7/15/2003	15,000	15,344
Boatmen's Bancshares Inc.		
7.625%, 10/1/2004	10,000	10,643
CIGNA Corp.		
7.875%, 5/15/2027	25,000	27,125
Citicorp		
6.65%, 12/15/2010 MTN	25,000	25,335
7.125%, 9/1/2005	15,000	15,593
7.625%, 5/1/2005	10,000	10,668
Comerica, Inc.		
7.125%, 12/1/2013	15,000	15,271
CoreStates Capital Corp.		
6.625%, 3/15/2005	20,000	20,181
Fifth Third Bank		
6.75%, 7/15/2005	25,000	25,395
First Bank N.A.		
7.55%, 6/15/2004	8,000	8,473
First Bank System Inc.		
6.625%, 5/15/2003	$10,000	$ 10,113
7.625%, 5/1/2005	7,500	7,997
First Chicago Corp.		
7.625%, 1/15/2003	15,000	15,851
First Union Corp.		
6.00%, 10/30/2008	15,000	14,316
7.50%, 4/15/2035	11,000	12,539
Fleet Financial Group, Inc.		
6.875%, 3/1/2003	30,000	30,622
General Electric Global Insurance Holdings		
7.00%, 2/15/2026	60,000	62,604
General Electric Capital Services		
7.50%, 8/21/2035	14,000	15,793
General Electric Capital Corp		
8.125%, 5/15/2012	10,000	11,588
GMAC		
7.00%, 9/15/2002	30,000	30,906
John Hancock		
7.375%, 2/15/2024	25,000	26,189
Liberty Mutual Insurance Co.		
8.50%, 5/15/2025	25,300	29,286
Lumbermens Mutual Casualty		
9.15%, 7/1/2026	45,000	52,045
MBIA Inc.		
7.00%, 12/15/2025	19,500	20,219
Metropolitan Life Insurance Co.		
7.80%, 11/1/2025	25,000	26,801
J.P. Morgan & Co., Inc.		
5.75%, 10/15/2008	20,000	18,797
6.25%, 1/15/2009	20,000	19,465
NBD Bank N.A.		
6.25%, 8/15/2003	20,000	19,973

Figure 4-12: Investment holdings.

Source: The Vanguard Group.

	Face Amount (000)	Market Value* (000)
Virginia Electric & Power Co.		
6.75%, 10/1/2023	$20,000	$ 19,414
Wisconsin Public Service Co.		
7.30%, 10/1/2002	6,700	7,049
		1,003,489
TOTAL CORPORATE BONDS		
(Cost $3,340,282)		**3,533,935**
FOREIGN BONDS (U.S. Dollar Denominated)(4.5%)		
Amoco Canada Petroleum Co.		
6.75%, 9/1/2023	25,000	24,620
BHP Finance USA Ltd.		
6.69%, 3/1/2006	10,000	10,045
Province of British Columbia		
6.50%, 1/15/2026	35,000	35,198
Husky Oil Ltd.		
7.55%, 11/15/2016	20,000	20,764
Republic of Italy Global Bond		
6.875%, 9/27/2023	10,000	10,470
Province of Manitoba		
6.125%, 1/19/2004	7,000	6,984
8.875%, 9/15/2021	24,041	30,906
Province of Ontario		
6.00%, 2/21/2006	25,000	24,620
7.75%, 6/4/2002	15,000	15,961
Petro-Canada		
7.875%, 6/15/2026	11,840	13,373
Province of Quebec		
7.50%, 7/15/2023	50,000	53,919
Saga Petroleum ASA		
7.25%, 9/23/2027	25,000	25,691
Province of Saskatchewan		
8.50%, 7/15/2022	19,000	23,367
Talisman Energy, Inc.		
7.125%, 6/1/2007	20,000	20,605
7.25%, 10/15/2027	25,000	25,851
TOTAL FOREIGN BONDS		
(Cost $328,156)		**342,374**
U.S. GOVERNMENT AND AGENCY OBLIGATIONS (11.6%)		
U.S. Treasury Bonds		
6.25%, 8/15/2023	250,000	257,690
7.25%, 5/15/2016	250,000	284,705
12.00%, 8/15/2013	130,000	191,599
U.S. Treasury Notes		
6.25%, 8/31/2002	100,000	102,087
6.875%, 5/15/2006	50,000	53,507
TOTAL U.S. GOVERNMENT AND AGENCY OBLIGATIONS		
(Cost $819,727)		**889,588**

	Shares	Market Value* (000)
COMMON STOCKS (36.4%)		
Auto & Transportation (2.3%)		
Chrysler Corp.	1,246,200	$ 43,851
Ford Motor Co.	2,129,900	103,700
Union Pacific Corp.	510,000	31,843
		179,394
Consumer Discretionary (2.7%)		
Eastman Kodak Co.	916,000	55,704
May Department Stores Co.	540,000	28,451
J.C. Penney Co., Inc.	1,992,600	120,179
		204,334
Consumer Staples (2.1%)		
Flowers Industries, Inc.	2,901,600	59,664
Gallaher Group PLC ADR	1,207,100	25,802
H.J. Heinz Co.	650,800	33,069
Philip Morris Cos., Inc.	475,000	21,523
Universal Corp.	521,900	21,463
		161,521
Financial Services (10.4%)		
Alexandria Real Estate		
Equities, Inc. REIT	279,100	8,809
BankAmerica Corp.	540,000	39,420
Brandywine Realty Trust REIT	332,000	8,342
CBL & Associates Properties,		
Inc. REIT	1,050,400	25,932
Camden Property Trust REIT	920,172	28,525
Chateau Communities, Inc. REIT	89,869	2,831
(1) Colonial Properties Trust REIT	1,139,900	34,339
Felcor Suite Hotels, Inc. REIT	420,000	14,910
First Union Corp.	2,720,400	139,421
General Growth Properties		
Inc. REIT	802,600	28,994
Highwood Properties, Inc. REIT	325,000	12,086
IPC Holdings Ltd.	309,300	9,898
JP Realty Inc. REIT	250,000	6,484
KeyCorp	1,679,050	118,898
Kimco Realty Corp. REIT	218,700	7,709
The Macerich Co. REIT	719,100	20,494
Mid Ocean Ltd.	179,900	9,760
National City Corp.	1,405,000	92,379
Nationwide Health		
Properties, Inc. REIT	616,000	15,708
PNC Bank Corp.	456,800	26,066
Summit Bancorp.	900,000	47,925
Sun Communities, Inc. REIT	320,600	11,522
Urban Shopping Centers,		
Inc. REIT	617,000	21,518
Wachovia Corp.	766,900	62,215
		794,185
Health Care (1.4%)		
Baxter International, Inc.	1,047,700	52,843
Pharmacia & Upjohn, Inc.	1,448,500	53,051
		105,894
Integrated Oils (5.0%)		
Amoco Corp.	1,135,000	96,617
Atlantic Richfield Co.	736,000	58,972
Equitable Resources, Inc.	1,125,000	39,797
Royal Dutch Petroleum Co. ADR	1,398,000	75,754
Texaco Inc.	733,400	39,879
USX-Marathon Group	2,188,200	73,852
		384,871

Figure 4-13: Stock holdings.

Source: The Vanguard Group.

Chapter 5

Where to Buy Funds

In This Chapter

- The best and worst places to buy funds
- What discount brokers can do for you
- How to hire an advisor

Hundreds of investment companies offer thousands of fund options. (Remember that most of the larger parent fund companies, such as T. Rowe Price, offer many individual funds in a variety of fund categories, such as money market funds, bond funds, balanced funds, and stock funds.) However, only a handful of these fund companies offer many top-notch funds, so in this chapter, I tell you which companies are the best places for your fund investing. (Turn to Part II of this book for my specific fund recommendations.)

Some other good individual funds are run by companies not mentioned in this chapter. (I discuss these funds in Part II as well.) But if you happen to stick with just the better funds from the parent companies recommended in this chapter, you can fall asleep at night knowing that your money is in good hands. In addition to recommending the best parent fund companies, I also recommend the best discount brokers. Although a slightly more expensive option, discount brokers make it easy to buy the best funds from different fund companies — la crème de la crème — and hold all the funds in a single account.

Time to Lose that Load

When the Securities and Exchange Commission deregulated brokers' commissions in 1975, total assets invested in mutual funds were less than $50 billion. The vast majority — more than 85 percent — of all mutual funds were sold through brokers. The funds they sold are known as "load" funds (load simply means commission). When you purchase a load fund through a broker, the broker is paid a commission that typically ranges from 4 percent to 8.5 percent of the amount that you invest.

Thanks in part to the deregulation of brokerage commissions and to the technological revolution of the 1980s and its accompanying explosion of low-cost computer equipment, the growth of the no-load (no commission) mutual fund industry took off. Technology provided fund companies with a cost-effective way to handle thousands of accounts for folks like you who don't have millions of dollars to invest. This also enabled fund companies to sell so-called no-load funds directly to the investor, bypassing the broker and brokers' commissions.

Today, no-load funds account for the majority of investors' mutual fund holdings, and as I discuss in Chapter 4, the best no-load funds are every bit as good, if not better, than the best load funds. Today, you can stick with the no-load (commission-free) funds and keep more of your investment dollars at work for yourself.

Table 5-1 provides a list of the major no-load and load players so that you can tell who's who.

Table 5-1 The Major No-Load and Load Companies

Major No-Load Fund Companies	*Major Load Fund Companies*	*Companies That Do Both*
Acorn	AIM	Dreyfus
American Century	Alliance	Fidelity
Columbia	American	
Federated	Dean Witter	
Harbor	Franklin/Templeton	
Invesco	IDS	
Janus	Merrill Lynch	
Neuberger & Berman	MFS (MassFinanical)	
Nicholas-Applegate	Nuveen	
PIMCO	Oppenheimer	
Schwab	PaineWebber	
Scudder	Prudential	
Stein Roe	Putnam	
Strong	Smith Barney Shearson	
T. Rowe Price	Zurich Kemper	
USAA		
Vanguard		
Warburg Pincus		

(Modern) History of Selling Investments

In the earlier decades of the 20th century, most people, even those of modest means, invested their money in what now appears to be a Neanderthalic way: They hired stockbrokers. (In those days, stockbrokers were still called stockbrokers; today, they often operate under the marketing guises of "financial consultant," "advisor," or "planner.")

Stockbrokers made their living buying and selling shares of individual stocks and bonds to investors. For this they earned commissions. Before the early 1970s, all brokers were forced by law to charge individual investors identical commissions. Investors couldn't shop around for a better deal, and "discount brokers" didn't exist.

In 1975, the Securities and Exchange Commission deregulated commissions so that brokers could discount and compete on price. This deregulation, together with technological advances, gave birth to the discount brokers and no-commission mutual funds that dominate the field today.

Places to Avoid When Buying Funds

If someone set up what looks like a hot dog stand on the street corner and started peddling mutual funds, would you buy a fund from that person? Probably not, because such an outfit would not seem like a legitimate investment management company to you. Where are the computers, the telephone equipment, and the fax machine? What about the conference room and mahogany table?

In the case of the street-corner stand, you'd be right to trust your instincts. But you can't base your investment decisions entirely on your gut. That's because some mutual fund companies have lots of branch offices with mahogany tables to make you feel comfortable, but they charge relatively high fees for their funds (to pay for all their overhead costs) or sell poorly performing funds — or both.

What types of places are likely to make you feel comfortable but lead you astray? Here's a short list of the wrong places where many people do their fund investing:

- **The First Faithful Community Bank.** Many people feel comfortable turning their money over to the friendly neighborhood banker. You've done it for years with your checking and savings accounts. The bank has an impressive-looking branch close to your home, complete with parking, security cameras, and a vault. And then there's that FDIC insurance that guarantees your deposits. So now that your bank offers mutual funds, you feel comfortable taking a little advice from the "investment specialist" or "consultant" in the branch. Besides, it's so convenient. How can you go wrong buying funds through your friendly local bank?

The Vanguard Group

With assets of more than $325 billion, Vanguard is now the second largest mutual fund company in America (after Fidelity). Vanguard's significant growth in recent years has been somewhat of a vindication for a company that was underrated during the 1980s and early 1990s. At the time that I wrote the first edition of this book, I went on record as saying that Vanguard, overall, was the best mutual fund company around and wasn't getting the recognition it deserved.

One of the reasons for Vanguard's underrating is the fact that its funds are almost never at the very tip top of the performance charts for their respective categories. As I discuss in Chapter 4, this is really a *good* sign, since many number-one-performing funds are rarely even above average over the long haul. Although Vanguard offers a spectrum of funds from low risk to high risk and everything in between, Vanguard doesn't take excessive risks with the funds it offers; thus, its funds rarely are ranked number one over short time periods.

Because of Vanguard's unique shareholder-owned structure, the average operating expense ratio of its funds — 0.30 percent per year — is lower than any other fund family in the industry. In fact, the average fund family's expense ratio is a whopping three times higher than Vanguard's.

Vanguard's low expenses translate into superior performance. Especially with money market and bond funds (markets in which even the best fund managers add relatively little value), Vanguard funds are consistently near the head of the class.

Vanguard is best at funds appealing to safety-minded investors — those who want to invest in money market, bond, and conservative stock funds. However, Vanguard offers aggressive stock funds with superior performance and low expense ratios (see Chapter 9 for a list of these). In managing stock funds, where performance is supposed to be more closely tied to the genius of the fund manager, Vanguard's thriftiness has not harmed performance.

Vanguard is increasingly becoming known for its index mutual funds, which are unmanaged portfolios of the securities that comprise a market index, such as the Standard & Poor's 500 (which tracks the stock performance of the 500 largest companies). A pioneer in the field, Vanguard was the first to offer index funds to the retail market. Today, the popularity of index funds is booming, and many fund companies have added index funds to their lists of offerings. But Vanguard is still the indexing leader, with the broadest selection of index funds and the lowest operating expenses in the business. (I talk more about the advantages of index funds in Chapter 6.)

The Bogle difference

In the early 1970s when Vanguard was formed, John Bogle, its founder and former CEO, made the big decision that to this day clearly differentiates Vanguard from its competition: Vanguard distributes funds and provides shareholder administration on an "at cost" basis — that is, with no mark-up or profit.

The seed for Vanguard was planted when Bogle was fired (over philosophical differences) in 1974 from his position as chairman of Wellington Management Company, an investment management firm. However, Bogle was chairman of the board of directors of the individual funds, which decided to keep Bogle as the funds' chairman, despite his termination by the parent company.

Over time, Bogle was given the latitude and authority to decide how his new fund company, which he named Vanguard, would operate. He insisted that the management of most of the stock funds be contracted out to private money management firms, from whom Vanguard would negotiate the best deals. Thus, Vanguard's mutual fund investors would own the company. Contrast this arrangement to that of traditional fund companies, in which the parent company owns the individual mutual funds and receives the profits from managing the funds.

Bogle felt that this unique corporate structure ensured that fund shareholders would obtain the best deals possible on money managers. "Funds ought to be run for the benefit of shareholders, not for the fund managers," Bogle reasoned. History has proven Bogle not only to be right, but also to be a mutual fund investor's best advocate.

What Vanguard doesn't offer should also appeal to you. Vanguard won't jump on the fad-of-the-month bandwagon and develop some newfangled fund designed primarily by slick marketers to line the company's coffers. Vanguard uses a customer-first approach and designs funds with the chief focus on meeting the customer's needs.

Vanguard representatives are available weekdays from 8 a.m. to 9 p.m. EST and Saturdays from 9 a.m. to 4 p.m. EST. Vanguard also offers an automated 24-hour phone service that enables customers to call for fund prices and yields, and even to enter transactions. Vanguard also has branch offices in Philiadelphia and Phoenix.

Fidelity Investments

Fidelity Investments, The Behemoth of Boston, is the largest mutual fund company in America (although Vanguard is the largest fund company that is exclusively commission-free).

Fidelity's roots trace back to the 1940s, when Edward C. Johnson II took over the then-fledgling Fidelity Fund from its president, who felt that he couldn't make enough money as the head of an investment fund! Johnson's son, Ned (Edward C. Johnson III), assumed Fidelity's top position in 1972 and has clearly proven that you can make a truckload of money operating mutual funds: He has personally made billions.

Fidelity offers a number of excellent mutual funds, particularly those that invest in U.S. stocks. The company has long had a reputation for nurturing great U.S. stock-pickers. Peter Lynch, often cited among the best mutual fund managers ever, is a Fidelity alum.

A mutual fund Goliath, Fidelity offers more mutual funds (200+) than any other mutual fund company. As evidence of Fidelity's enormous buying power, its Boston offices are visited by representatives from dozens of companies every day. Most mutual fund managers have to travel to the companies they're interested in researching; if you're a Fidelity mutual fund manager, many companies come to you.

If you're venturing to do business with Fidelity on your own, you've got your work cut out for you. One of the biggest problems novice investors have at Fidelity is discerning the good funds from the not-so-good. Relative to the best of the competition, Fidelity is weakest with the following:

- **Bond funds.** Fidelity's bond funds charge high operating expenses that depress an investor's returns. Bond fund management is an area where Fidelity's fund managers have not displayed particular investment prowess. If you want bond funds, Vanguard is generally a superior alternative.

  Note: Fidelity offers a decent series of bond funds (see Chapter 8) known as Spartan funds that have lower operating expense ratios. These funds' minimum initial investment is typically $10,000, and Fidelity charges additional fees for check writing and redemptions.

- **International stock funds.** Fidelity was late entering this field and made many hiring mistakes. Its international funds are also burdened by high fees, both sales loads and ongoing operating expenses. (See Chapter 9 for alternative international stock funds.)

- **Non-retirement investing.** Many of Fidelity's best U.S. stock funds charge 2 to 3 percent sales loads when used for non-retirement investing. (This charge is waived for most Fidelity funds when purchased inside of retirement accounts, such as for individual retirement accounts.) Fidelity funds also have a tendency to produce more capital gains distributions, which increase the tax burden for non-retirement account investors (see Chapter 6) for more about the tax consequences of mutual fund investing.

Fidelity decided to cultivate the support of the armies of commission-based securities brokers by offering them Fidelity funds that they could sell. Thus were born the "Fidelity Advisor" funds, a load family of funds that Fidelity sells through investment salespeople and that carry high sales and ongoing fees. I suggest avoiding this particular series of Fidelity funds.

Fidelity's sector funds (Select), which invest in just one industry — such as air transportation, insurance, or retailing — should also be avoided. These funds charge sales commissions of 3 percent and have high ongoing operating expenses (often in excess of 1.5 percent per year). Being industry-focused, these funds are poorly diversified and thus highly risky. Fidelity, unfortunately, encourages a trader mentality with these funds by pricing them hourly instead of daily.

One of Fidelity's strengths as a mutual fund company also explains its higher costs — it operates nearly 100 branch offices throughout the U.S. and staffs its phones 24 hours a day, 365 days a year. So if you want to have personalized attention and conduct business face to face, check your local phone directory or call Fidelity's toll-free number for the office location nearest you.

Funds with branch offices: The best of both worlds?

Many mutual fund companies have their offices in one location. If you happen to live in the town or city where they're located and want to do business with them, you can visit them in person. However, odds are that, unless you maintain several homes, you won't be living near the fund companies with which you want to do your fund investing business.

Some fund companies, such as Fidelity, have greater numbers of branch offices, which are located primarily in densely populated and more affluent areas. You may feel more comfortable dropping a check off or speaking to a live person face to face instead of being navigated through an automated voice message system. However, there's no sound financial reason that you need to go in person — everything you need to do can be done by phone and mail.

In most cases, you pay a financial cost for doing your fund investing through firms with branch offices. Operating all those branch offices in areas where rent and employees don't come cheaply costs a good chunk of money. Ultimately, firms that maintain a large branch network need to build these extra costs into their funds' fees. Higher fees lower your investment returns.

A counterargument that is made by fund companies with many branch offices is that if the branch offices succeed in enticing more investors to use the funds offered by the company, more total money is brought in. Having more money under management helps to lower the average cost of managing each dollar invested.

T. Rowe Price

T. Rowe Price is one of the oldest mutual fund companies. It is named after its founder, T. (Thomas) Rowe Price, who is generally credited with popularizing investing in growth-oriented companies. The fund company has also been a fund pioneer in international investing.

T. Rowe Price remained a small company for many years, focusing on its specialties of U.S. growth stocks and international funds. That changed in the 1990s as the company offered a comprehensive menu of different fund types. It offers 401(k) retirement plans specifically for smaller companies. The fund company also offers a series of money market and bond funds called Summit funds. Although the minimum initial investment for Summit funds is steep ($25,000), the operating expenses, at about 0.5 percent, are reasonable (although still higher than Vanguard's).

Charles Schwab & Company

Discount brokerage powerhouse Charles Schwab offers its own family of mutual funds, as well as funds from other companies (this service is discussed in the next section). The Schwab family of funds is quite small but notable for its series of *tax-friendly stock index funds* (see Chapter 9) that have low minimum initial investments compared to Vanguard's.

USAA

USAA (this acronym replaced the company's old name of United States Automobile Association) is a small family of no-load mutual funds as well as low-cost, high-quality insurance. Although you (or a family member) need to be a military officer to gain access to its homeowner and auto insurance, anyone can buy into its mutual funds. Like Vanguard, USAA is a conservative company. All of its mutual funds are no-load, and its operating fees are well below average. USAA has six branch offices scattered throughout the country.

American Century

American Century is a large fund family created by a merger between the old Twentieth Century mutual funds company and the Benham group of funds. American Century's *bond funds,* most of which were brought to the merger by Benham, have an excellent track record and low expense ratios. These old Benham bond funds have taken on the hyphenated name American Century-Benham.

PIMCO

PIMCO is a family of primarily bond funds (see Chapter 8) that normally are available only to investors who have at least $500,000 to invest. However, for as little as $1,000, you can purchase its excellent bond funds through discount brokerage firms discussed in the next section of this chapter. (These funds are managed by William Gross, who is one of the best bond fund managers in the country.) Beware of PIMCO Advisor Funds — as with Fidelity's broker-sold funds, these have high fees and should be avoided.

Hundreds of mutual fund companies offer thousands of funds. Many aren't worth your consideration because they don't meet the common-sense selection criteria I outline in Chapter 4. So if you're wondering why I didn't mention Prudential or some other fund family, it's because the record shows that its funds are high cost, low performance, managed in a schizophrenic fashion, or all of the above. Check them out against the criteria in Chapter 4 to see for yourself.

One of the beauties of all the fund choices out there is that you don't have to settle for lousy or mediocre funds. If you're wondering what to do with poor funds that you already own, read Chapter 12.

Discount Brokers: Mutual Fund Supermarkets

For many years, you could only purchase no-load mutual funds directly from mutual fund companies. If you wanted to buy some funds at, say, Vanguard, Fidelity, T. Rowe Price, and USAA, you needed to call these four different companies and request each firm's application. So you ended up filling out four different sets of forms and mailing them with four envelopes, four stamps, and four separate checks.

Soon, you received separate statements from each of the four fund companies reporting how your investments were doing. (Some fund companies make this even more of a paperwork nightmare by sending you a separate statement for each individual mutual fund that you buy through them.)

Now suppose that you wanted to sell one of your USAA funds and invest the proceeds at Fidelity. This was also a time-consuming pain in the posterior, because you contacted USAA to sell, waited days for them to send you a check for the sales' proceeds, and then sent the money with instructions to Fidelity.

Needless to say, this is a tough way to shop. Imagine wanting to make a salad and having to go to a lettuce farm, a tomato farm, and an onion farm to get all the ingredients. That's why we have supermarkets.

It wasn't until 1984 that someone came up with the idea to create a supermarket for mutual funds. It was Charles Schwab, the discount broker pioneer, who created the first mutual fund supermarket (which other discount brokers have since copied) where you can purchase hundreds of individual funds from dozens of fund companies — one-stop mutual fund shopping.

The major benefit of such a service is that it greatly simplifies the paperwork involved in buying and selling different companies' mutual funds. No matter how many mutual fund companies you wish to invest in, you need to complete just one application for the discount broker. And instead of getting a separate statement from each company, you get one statement from the discount broker that summarizes all of your mutual fund holdings. (***Note:*** You still must maintain separate non-retirement and IRA accounts.)

Moving from one company's fund into another's (for example, when an investor wants to sell a USAA fund and purchase a Fidelity fund) is a snap as well. The discount broker can usually take care of all this with one phone call from you. Come tax time, you receive just one 1099 statement summarizing your fund's taxable distributions that must be recorded on your tax return.

You weren't born yesterday, so you know that there must be a catch for all this convenience. Here's a hint: Because discount brokers serve as intermediaries for the buying and selling of funds and the time and money spent sending you statements, they expect to make some money in return. So guess what: It costs you more to use a discount broker's services.

Discount brokers charge you a transaction fee whenever you buy or sell most of the better funds that they offer. Although the transaction fee has the same impact as a sales commission — it's deducted from your investment — discount brokers' transaction fees (typically in the neighborhood of 0.5 percent or less) are substantially less than the sales commissions that you would pay to buy a load fund (usually 4 to 8.5 percent).

Buy direct or use a discount broker?

One method of buying funds is not inherently better than the other. For the most part, it's a tradeoff that boils down to personal preference and individual circumstances. It's a bit like deciding to stay in or go out to eat: Cooking at home is cheaper, but you have to clean up after yourself. Going out is more expensive, but you don't have to do the dishes.

BEWARE

Not all discounters are created equal

The discount brokerage industry has done much good for investors since its birth in the mid-1970s when brokerage commissions were deregulated. By employing salary-based representatives, discounters eliminated the inherent conflicts of interest (see Chapter 4) that traditional brokers, such as Prudential, Dean Witter, Smith Barney Shearson, and others, still have today.

However, don't pick your discount broker blindly, because they are not all created equal. Some discount brokers sell load (commission) mutual funds. A handful of discounters (for example, Olde Discount and Kennedy Cabot) *only* sell load funds.

Discounters such as Olde Discount also engage in the practice of saying that you can purchase stocks free of any brokerage commissions. This is not quite true because in many cases, the firm is making a *spread* — the difference between the buy and sell price — on the trade. When you call them for information, Olde's brokers, who earn commissions, even ask for your phone number, which they use for follow-up sales calls.

Reasons to buy direct

Here, I sum up some of the reasons to buy direct:

- **You're thrifty.** And you can take that as a compliment. Being vigilant about your investing costs boosts your returns. By buying direct from no-load fund companies, you avoid the discount brokerage transaction costs.
- **You don't have much money to invest.** If you're investing less than $5,000 per fund, the minimum transaction fees of a discount broker will gobble up a large percentage of your investment. There are no transaction fees when you buy direct from a no-load fund company.
- **You're content investing through one of the bigger fund companies with a broad array of good funds.** For example, if you deal directly with one mutual fund company that excels in all types of funds (such as Vanguard), you can minimize your fees and maximize your investment returns. Given the breadth and depth of the bigger companies' fund selections, you should feel content centralizing your fund investments through one of the better companies. However, if you sleep better at night investing through multiple fund companies' funds, I won't try to change your mind.

As I discuss later in this chapter, given the fact that most of the major fund companies such as Vanguard, Fidelity, and T. Rowe Price have discount brokerage divisions offering mutual funds from companies other than their own, you could use one of these companies as your base and have the best of both worlds. Suppose, for example, that you decide you'd like to invest a large portion but not all of your money in Fidelity funds. By establishing a discount brokerage account at Fidelity, all of your Fidelity fund purchases would be free of transaction fees; then, through that same account, you could also buy other fund companies' funds.

Reasons to buy through a discount broker

Here, I sum up some of the reasons to go with a discount broker:

- **You want to invest in funds from many fund companies.** In general, different fund companies excel in different types of investments; you may want to build a portfolio that draws on the specific talents of these various companies. Although you can buy directly through each individual fund company, there eventually comes a point where the hassle and clutter are just not worth it. The one-stop shopping of a discount broker may well be worth the occasional transaction fee.
- **You hate paperwork.** Perhaps this is just a restatement of the above point, but it's worthy of reiteration for those of you out there whose hatred of paperwork is so fierce that it keeps you from doing things that you're supposed to do.
- **You want easy access to your money.** Some discount brokerage accounts offer such bells and whistles as debit cards and unlimited check writing privileges, making it as easy as a bank checking account to tap into your money. (That's not necessarily a good thing; after all, you're supposed to be investing the money, not spending it!)
- **You want to buy into a high-minimum fund.** One unique feature available through some discount broker's mutual fund services is the ability to purchase some funds not normally available to smaller investors (PIMCO is one of these funds).
- **You want to buy funds on margin.** Another interesting but rarely used feature that comes with a brokerage account is that you can borrow on margin (take out a loan from the brokerage firm) against mutual funds and other securities held in a non-retirement account, which are then used as collateral. Borrowing against your funds is generally lower-cost than your other loan options, and it's potentially tax-deductible.

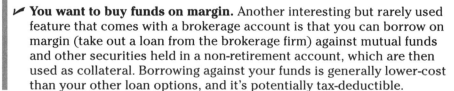

TIP

There is a way to buy and sell your funds and use a discounter but reduce the total transaction fees that you pay: Purchase your funds initially from the mutual fund company and then transfer the shares at no charge into a discount brokerage account. Conversely, when you're ready to sell shares, you can transfer shares from the discounter to the mutual fund company before you're ready to sell (see Chapter 11 for details about transfer forms).

"No Transaction Fee" funds — free funds?

After several years of distributing funds for all of these different fund companies, it was just a matter of time before the discount brokers came up with another innovation. Discount brokers were doing a lot for mutual fund companies (for instance, handling the purchase and sale of funds, as well as the ongoing account recordkeeping and reporting), but they were not being paid for all their work. In 1992, Charles Schwab & Company changed all that with its *Mutual Fund OneSource program.*

Under OneSource, Schwab negotiated with some mutual fund companies to pay his firm an ongoing fee to service and handle customer accounts. Initially, this was a hard sell because the fund companies were used to receiving this shareholder servicing for free. Eventually, however, Schwab succeeded in charging fund companies fees.

Today, through Schwab and other discount brokers who copied this service, you can purchase several hundred funds without paying any transaction fees (that is, you pay the same cost as if you had bought the funds through the mutual fund company itself). These are called *No Transaction Fee* (NTF) funds.

On the surface, this certainly sounds like a great deal for you, the mutual fund investor wanting to buy funds from various companies through a discount brokerage account: You get access to many funds and one account statement without paying transaction fees.

BEWARE

This is a case of something sounding much better than it really is. Although some discount brokers will say or imply that NTF funds are "free," they're hardly free. Discount brokers are able to waive the transaction costs only because the participating fund companies have agreed to foot the bill. In a typical arrangement, the participating fund company shares a small percentage of its annual operating expense ratio with the discount broker handling the account. But as you know if you read Chapter 4, annual operating expenses are drawn from the shareholders' investment dollars. So in the end, you're still the one paying the transaction costs.

As a group, NTF funds are inferior to the best no-load funds that you pay the discounters a transaction fee to purchase:

- Because they have to cut a share to the discount broker, NTF funds tend to have higher operating expenses than non-NTF funds.
- NTF funds also tend to be offered by smaller, less-experienced fund companies who may be struggling to compete in the saturated mutual fund market. You'll notice that big, well-established fund companies (including the ones discussed earlier in this chapter, such as Vanguard, Fidelity, and T. Rowe Price) don't participate in NTF programs. They don't have to; there's plenty of demand for their funds even with transaction costs.

Also be aware that, in their rush to sign up more NTF funds, some discounters have ignored the quality of the NTF funds they offer. In addition, some financial publications encourage and effectively endorse this lack of quality control by giving higher ratings to those discounters offering more "free" funds to customers. As with food, more isn't always better — quality counts as well!

Whenever you make a mutual fund investment decision through a discount broker, try not to be influenced by the prospect, or lack thereof, of a transaction fee. In your efforts to avoid paying a small fee today, you could end up buying a fund with high ongoing fees and subpar performance. If you're so concerned about paying additional fees, you're better off dealing directly with mutual fund companies and bypassing the discount brokers and their transaction fees.

The best discount brokers for fund shopping

More discount brokers open shop all the time. Here is a short list of the best firms for mutual fund investors wanting one-stop fund shopping. Decide which firm is best for you based on your needs and what is important to you.

Charles Schwab & Company

Charles Schwab was the pioneer in offering no-load mutual funds in the discount brokerage field. Among discounters, Schwab is one of the most expensive firms when it comes to the transaction fees charged to buy and sell no-load mutual funds. So why would you want to do business with this pricier firm?

- Schwab offers an extensive array of quality no-load mutual funds. (That's not to say that all the funds they sell are good.)
- Schwab has a bunch of branch offices (more than 200) if you want to deal face-to-face with a real person instead of calling an 800 number or sending stuff in the mail.
- Schwab is always open when you have free time to think about your investments. At 10 p.m. on Sunday night or at 8 a.m. on New Year's Day, Schwab is open — in fact, it's open 24 hours a day, 365 days a year.
- If you like using technology, you'll love Schwab. You can access your account and place trades through Schwab's proprietary software, over its Web site, or with a touch-tone telephone (see Chapter 16 for details on using your computer for fund investing).

If you're fee-sensitive and don't need fancy technology or a firm with branch offices, don't use Schwab. Read on to find other choices.

Jack White & Company

ERIC'S PICKS

Jack White & Company is a deep discount broker: Its fees are discounted from even the other discount brokers' charges. For example, White's mutual fund transaction fees on typical size trades are 50 to 70 percent *less* than what the larger discounters (such as Schwab, Fidelity, Quick & Reilly, and Waterhouse) charge. On really large trades ($100,000+), White's fees can be up to 90 percent less than the competition's!

You know that you usually don't get something for nothing. So you may be asking if White has telephones and computers, and whether it will be in business tomorrow. You may also be wondering who the heck Jack White is — he's not exactly a household name.

TIP

Jack White really does exist. He is, in my opinion, a nice, ethical fellow, like Chuck Schwab. His firm does a terrific job doing what it does, but White's firm isn't a giant like Schwab's. The main difference between these two firms is the level of hand-holding and service options each offers. White offers little; Schwab offers quite a bit. For example, White doesn't have branch offices (although you're welcome to visit the firm's headquarters if you're in the San Diego area).

White is not the low-cost leader in all areas. Self-employed folks who establish a Keogh plan (discussed in Chapter 3) with White should know that the annual fee charged can be substantially higher than at the competition. White's money market funds also generally have sub-par yields.

White also offers a service, called Connect, which pays you to sell your load funds and allows you to buy some load funds (the selection is limited) without the load. Connect allows holders of load mutual funds to sell their shares to another buyer. The buyer pays a flat $200 fee instead of the normal 4 to 8.5 percent commission that an investment salesperson earns. For purchases of $5,000 or more, this service can save a buyer hundreds or thousands of dollars. The seller benefits, too — getting paid $100 to sell a load fund through White's service.

Fund companies turned discounters

The world of mutual funds is one of increasingly fuzzy borders. Although I've spoken of mutual fund companies and discount brokers as separate entities, the line between them has blurred in recent years. You may already have heard me talk about Schwab, which started as a discount broker but later began selling its own mutual funds. Other companies started selling mutual funds but have now moved into the discount brokerage business.

The biggest and most obvious example is Fidelity, which offers discount brokerage services through which you can trade individual securities or buy many non-Fidelity mutual funds.

Vanguard and T. Rowe Price have also launched discount brokerage divisions. Although these firms don't offer nearly as many funds from other fund companies as Fidelity, the funds that they do offer are generally of higher quality. Most of the best funds I recommend in this book can be bought through Vanguard's and T. Rowe Price's services.

Keep in mind that the brokerage services of a fund company, if rigorously compared to those of a discounting specialist such as Schwab or White, will fall short in certain areas. After all, these are fund companies first, discounters second.

The discount brokerage services of Fidelity, Vanguard, or T. Rowe Price make a lot of sense if you plan on doing the bulk of your fund investing through Fidelity, Vanguard, or T. Rowe Price funds. Remember, you only have to pay brokerage transaction fees on funds offered by other fund companies; buying a Fidelity fund from Fidelity, or a Vanguard fund from Vanguard, or a T. Rowe Price fund from T. Rowe Price is always free of brokerage fees.

For example, if you're planning on building a portfolio of mostly aggressive U.S. stock funds from Fidelity, but you also recognize the importance of investing internationally and know that Fidelity's foreign stock funds are less than stellar, you can complement your portfolio with one or two good international funds from T. Rowe Price or Vanguard. In this case, it makes absolute sense for you to open up an account with Fidelity rather than a discount broker such as Schwab. With Fidelity, you only pay transaction costs on the T. Rowe Price funds; with Schwab, you pay transaction fees on them all.

Other discounters

More and more discount brokers are adding mutual fund services to their repertoires. Muriel Siebert & Company, for example, offers a significant number of funds as well as low transaction fees (although not as low as Jack White's).

Another discounter to keep an eye on, especially if you're comfortable on the computer, is E-Trade, a pioneer in the online-only discount brokerage business. By limiting its business to trades placed over the Internet, E-Trade has eliminated the need for branch offices and armies of customer service reps. With such low overhead, E-Trade can afford to charge transaction fees that vastly undercut other discount brokers. This online broker got its start dealing in individual securities but has since applied its business model to the mutual fund market. E-Trade's fund selection is fairly good, but the company has many load funds and doesn't offer some of the better no-load fund families, such as Fidelity and USAA.

Should You Hire an Advisor?

You may decide that it's too much trouble to research mutual funds and plan the rest of your finances. So you'll be tempted to find a financial advisor to relieve you of the burden. Dealing directly with various fund companies or simply selecting funds from among the many offered through a discount brokerage service may seem overwhelming to you.

Don't hire an advisor until you've explored the real reasons why you want to hire help. If you're like many people, you may hire an advisor for the wrong reason. Or you'll hire the wrong type of advisor, an incompetent one, or one with major conflicts of interest.

The wrong reason to hire an advisor

Don't hire an advisor because of what I call the *crystal ball phenomenon.* Although you know that you're not a dummy, you may feel that you can't possibly make informed and intelligent investing decisions because you don't closely follow or even understand the financial markets and what makes them move.

REMEMBER

No one that you're going to hire has a crystal ball. No one can predict future movements in the financial markets to know which investments will do well, and which ones won't. Besides, the financial markets are pretty darn efficient — meaning that lots of smart folks are following the markets, so it's highly unlikely that you or an advisor could predict what's going to happen next. Investing intelligently in mutual funds isn't that complicated. You bought this book. Read it, and you'll learn what you need to know to invest intelligently in funds.

The right reasons to hire an advisor

Consider hiring an advisor if

- You are too busy to do your investing yourself.
- You always put off investing because you don't enjoy doing it.
- You are uncomfortable making investing decisions on your own.
- You want a second opinion.
- You need help establishing and prioritizing financial goals.

Beware of conflicts of interest

In Chapter 3, I review important things to do before investing. If you're thinking about hiring a financial planner to help plan your financial future as well as make mutual fund investing decisions, read on to learn how to avoid another big mistake made by Justine and Max (our friends from Chapter 3) — listening to the wrong advisor.

BEWARE

The field of investment and financial planning is pockmarked with land mines awaiting the naive investor. A particularly dangerous one is the enormous conflict of interest that is created when "advisors" sell products that bring them commissions.

The vast majority of *financial planners* and *financial consultants* sell products and work on commission. If a planner sells products and works on commission, he's a salesperson, not a planner. There's nothing wrong with salespeople — you just don't want one spouting suggestions when you're looking for objective investment and financial planning advice.

The Consumer Federation of America said it best in its review of the investment industry: "Today's investors go up against a deadly combination of abusive securities industry practices and regulatory inattentiveness when investing their money."

Here are some of the problems created by commission-based advice:

- **Products that carry commissions can pit your interests against those of the broker selling them.** The bigger the commission on a particular investment product, the greater the incentive the broker/planner/advisor has to sell it to you, even if it's not an investment that's in your best interest.
- **Products that carry commissions mean that you have fewer dollars working in the investments you buy.** Commissions are immediately siphoned out of your investment dollars. When it comes to returns, non-commission investments have a head start over commission ones.
- **Products that carry the highest commissions also tend to be among the costliest and riskiest financial products available.** They're inferior products; that's why they need high commissions to motivate salespeople to sell them.
- **Planners who work on commission have an incentive to *churn* your investments.** Commissions are paid out whenever you buy or sell an investment — in other words, every time you make a trade. So some commission-greedy brokers/planners encourage you to trade frequently, attributing the need to changes in the economy or the companies in which you've invested. Not only does heavy trading fatten the broker's/advisor's wallet at your expense, but it's also a proven loser as an investment strategy (see Chapter 6 for more about investment strategies and your portfolio).

Here are problems and conflicts of interest that both planners working on commission and those deriving ongoing fees from managing your money have:

- **Not keeping your overall financial needs in mind.** It may well make sense for you to fund your employer-sponsored retirement plan or pay off your mortgage or credit card debt before you start investing. The commission-based and money managing planner have no incentive to recommend such strategies for you; that would give you less money to invest through them.
- **Creating dependency.** Planners may try to make things seem so complicated that you believe you can't possibly manage your finances or make major financial decisions without them.

Your best options for help

You must do your homework *before* hiring any financial advisor. The first step is to learn as much as you can about what you're seeking help with. That way, if you do hire someone to help you make investment and other financial decisions, you'll be in a better position to evaluate his or her capabilities and expertise.

Realizing that you need to hire someone to help you make and implement financial decisions can be a valuable insight. Even if you have a modest income or modest assets, spending a few hours of your time and a few hundred dollars to hire a professional can be a good investment. The services that advisors and planners offer, their fees, and their competence, however, vary tremendously.

Financial advisors make money in one of three ways: from commissions based on sales of financial products, from fees based on a percentage of your assets that they are investing, or from hourly consultation charges. You already know why the first option is the least preferred choice (if you really want to or are forced to work with an investment broker who works on commission, be sure to read the last section in this chapter).

A better choice than a commission-based planner is one who works on a fee basis. In other words, the planner is paid by fees from clients such as yourself rather than from the investments and other financial products that he or she recommends that you buy. This compensation system removes the incentive to sell you products with high commissions and churn your investments through lots of transactions to generate more commissions. However, as I discussed earlier in this chapter, this compensation system still has potentially significant conflicts of interest.

The most cost-effective method is to hire an advisor who charges an hourly fee and doesn't sell investment and other financial products. Because he doesn't sell any financial products, his objectivity is maintained. He doesn't perform money management, so he can help you get your financial house in order and make comprehensive financial decisions, including selecting good mutual funds.

Your primary risk in selecting a planner, hourly-based or otherwise, is hiring one who is competent. You can address this by checking references and learning enough yourself to discern between good and bad financial advice.

You have further risk if you and the advisor don't clearly define the work to be done and the approximate total cost before you begin. Don't forget to set your parameters up front.

A drawback of an entirely different kind occurs when you don't follow through on your advisor's recommendations. You paid for this work but didn't act on it; the potential benefit is lost. If part of the reason that you're hiring an advisor in the first place is that you're too busy or not interested enough to make changes to your financial situation, then you should look for this support in the services you buy from the planner.

If you just need someone as a sounding board for ideas or to recommend some specific no-load mutual funds, hire an hourly-based planner for only one or two sessions of advice. You save money doing the legwork and implementation on your own. Just make sure that the planner is willing to give you specific enough advice that you can implement it on your own. Some planners will intentionally withhold specific advice and recommendations to create the need for you to hire them to do more, perhaps even to manage your money.

If you have a lot of money that you want managed among a variety of mutual fund investments, you can hire a financial advisor who charges a percentage of your assets under management. Some of these advisors also offer financial planning services. Some just manage money in mutual funds and other investments.

In the chapters ahead, I give you enough information for you to make wise mutual fund investing decisions. You owe it to yourself to read the rest of the book *before* deciding whether to hire some financial help. Also, be sure to pay extra close attention to Chapter 20, which covers the ten issues to consider and questions to ask when hiring an advisor to help with mutual fund investing.

If you must have a salesperson

Despite the additional (and hence, avoidable) sales charges that apply when you purchase a load fund instead of a no-load fund, you may be forced to, or actually want to, buy a load fund through a salesperson working on commission. Perhaps you work for an employer that set up a retirement plan with only load funds as the investment option. Or your Uncle Ernie, who's a stockbroker, will put you in the family doghouse if you transfer your money out of his firm and into no-load funds. Maybe you really trust your broker because of a long-standing and productive investment relationship (but ask yourself, is it because of the broker or the financial markets?).

Protect yourself

If you're comfortable and willing to pay commissions from 4 percent up to as much as 8.5 percent to invest in mutual funds, there are a number of ways that you can protect your money and well-being when working with brokers:

- First, be aware that you're working with a broker. Unlike the real estate profession in which an employee's title — real estate broker or agent — clearly conveys how she makes her money, many investment salespeople today have appellations that obscure what they do and how they make money. A common misnomer: financial planner, financial consultant, or financial advisor as a name for salespeople who used to be called stock, securities, or insurance brokers.
- Make sure that you've already decided what money you want to invest and how it fits into your overall financial plans. This is one of the most important things to do if you're going to invest through a commission-based investment salesperson. Guard against being pushed into dollar amounts and/or investments that are not part of your financial plan.

Make sure you get the best funds

If you've optimized the structuring of your finances and you have a chunk of money that you're willing to pay as a sales charge to invest in load funds, make sure that you're getting the best funds for your investment dollars. The criteria to use in selecting those load funds are no different from those used to select no-load funds:

- Invest in funds managed by mutual fund companies and portfolio managers that have track records of expertise, that take a level of risk that fits your needs, and that charge reasonable annual operating expenses.
- Pay attention to the annual operating expenses that both load and no-load funds charge. These fees are deducted from your funds' investment returns in much the same way that IRS taxes are deducted from your paycheck, with one critical difference: Your pay stub shows how much you pay in taxes, whereas your mutual fund account statement will never show the fund's operating expense charges. You need the prospectus for that.

- Never invest in a mutual fund without knowing all the charges — sales charges, annual operating expenses, and any annual maintenance or account fees. You can find all these in a fund's prospectus (discussed in Chapter 4) or by calling the fund company's toll-free number.

Part II
Establishing a Great Fund Portfolio

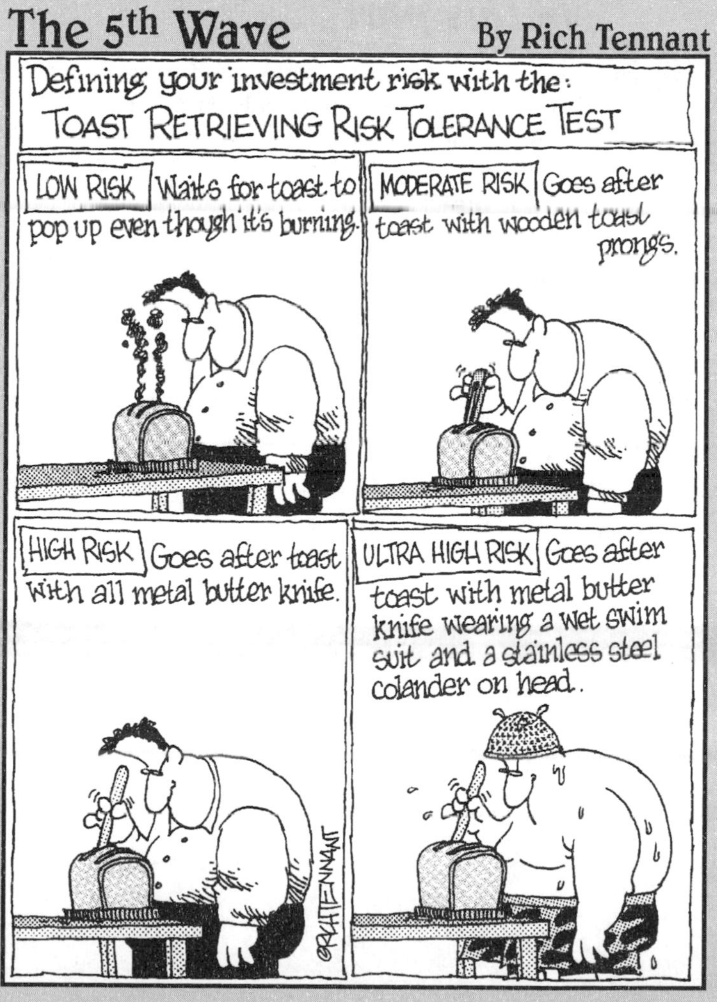

The 5th Wave
By Rich Tennant
Defining your investment risk with the:
TOAST RETRIEVING RISK TOLERANCE TEST
LOW RISK
Waits for toast to pop up even though it's burning.
MODERATE RISK
Goes after toast with wooden toast prongs.
HIGH RISK
Goes after toast with all metal butter knife.
ULTRA HIGH RISK
Goes after toast with metal butter knife wearing a wet swim suit and a stainless steel colander on head.
©RICHTENNANT

In this part . . .

Now you're ready to start building a portfolio of funds to help you meet your goals. First, I explain the fundamentals of putting a portfolio together. Then I recommend the best money market, bond, and stock funds for the job. And just to make sure that I don't leave you hanging, I pull it all together for you in a chapter that shows you how real, live people fit funds into their overall financial plans. The last chapter of this part walks you through the paperwork you need to fill out to build your fund portfolio.

Chapter 6

Constructing a Portfolio

In This Chapter

- Creating the right mix of funds for your situation
- Finding out why taxes matter when selecting funds
- Recognizing wise and unwise investing strategies
- Executing your investment plan

Once you understand how to construct a portfolio of funds to accomplish your specific needs, all you need to know to finish the job are the particular mutual funds you'll invest in. In the three chapters that follow this one, I get specific about which money market, bond, and stock funds you should consider.

Although "portfolio" usually describes a group of funds, it doesn't have to. For certain goals, one or two funds is all that you may need (for example, a short-term bond fund and a money market fund for a home down-payment). Even for a long-term goal such as retirement, you may choose to have a portfolio of just one fund; some mutual fund companies offer funds of funds, which, as the name suggests, are mutual funds comprised of other mutual funds. (I cover funds of funds in Chapter 9.)

And although a portfolio is sometimes held inside one account, it doesn't have to be. The funds that make up your retirement portfolio, for example, could be scattered across various accounts from different investment companies.

In this chapter, I show you how to draw up a blueprint for your investing goals. Consider three main issues when settling upon a portfolio design:

- **Asset allocation.** How you divvy up your portfolio among different types of investments — stocks, bonds, international securities, and so on — depends mostly on the time horizon of the portfolio's goal. But asset allocation also depends on your personality: How much risk are you willing to take without feeling the need to track the financial market's minute-by-minute movements every business day?
- **Tax implications.** For portfolios held outside of tax-sheltered retirement accounts, you must pay attention to how much of your returns you lose to federal and state income taxes. By choosing certain kinds of funds, you can reduce the damage taxes cause to your portfolio's performance.
- **Investing strategy.** You may be concerned that stock prices appear high, and therefore you may want to hold back on investing much of your money in the market just now. Or you may have heard about index funds and are wondering how they differ from actively managed mutual funds, and which one is best for your situation. I discuss how to deal with these concerns in this chapter as well.

The sections that follow provide a closer look at each part of portfolio design.

Asset Allocation: An Investment Recipe

Don't let the six syllables fool you; asset allocation is a simple concept that you're probably already familiar with. Have you ever ordered a pizza for a group of friends, and to please everybody, you got pepperoni on one half and mushrooms on the other, with extra cheese on half of the mushroom half? Divvying up the pizza pie and selecting appropriate toppings for each portion is similar to selecting different types of funds in particular portions to complete a fund portfolio. When it comes to your money, instead of pizza toppings, you're dealing with different kinds of investments: stocks, bonds, international investments, and so on. (I define and describe these in Chapter 1.)

Asset allocation simply describes the proportion of different investment types that make up your mutual fund portfolio. So if someone asks, "What's your asset allocation?" a typical response may be, "I have 60 percent in stocks, a third of which is in foreign stocks, and 40 percent in bonds."

You may hear a mutual fund nerd spout off about his allocation between "large-cap" and "small-cap" stocks, or between "growth funds" and "value funds." Don't worry about these terms for now (for the nerd in you, you'll be happy to know that I cover these other fund subcategories in Chapter 9). Even after you finish reading this book and become a mutual fund hotshot, you should be mostly concerned with the general asset allocation decisions: namely, allocating between stocks and bonds, and between U.S. stocks and international stocks.

Why should you allocate assets?

You wouldn't have to worry about asset allocation if it weren't for a simple investment truth: *The greater an investment's potential return, generally the greater the chance of a short-term loss.*

If there were no chance of loss, you could throw asset allocation out the window. No matter what your savings goal, you could put all your money into stocks. After all, as I discuss in Chapter 1, in comparison to bonds and money market investments, stocks should give you the biggest returns. If you had no chance of loss investing in stocks, every dollar you save would go to creating wealth in stocks. Your net worth would balloon.

In the real world, however, stocks are a volatile investment. Although providing the highest long-term gains, stocks also carry the greatest risk of short-term loss.

Asset allocation, then, is all about striking the right balance between your desire for high returns and your ability to withstand a short-term loss. All things being equal, all of us prefer higher returns. And, although each of us has a different personality and temperament about accepting risk, your realistic ability to withstand a loss depends primarily on your time horizon.

Your time horizon

The *time horizon* of a financial goal is the length of time between now and when you'll need the money to accomplish that goal. If you're 30 years old and want to retire by age 60, then the time horizon of your retirement investments is 30+ years. (Even though you'll begin to use some of your retirement money at age 60, some of it won't be spent until later in your retirement.) If you're saving to buy a home by the time you're 35 years old, then the time horizon of that goal is five years.

TIP

The longer your time horizon, the better able you are to withstand the risk of a short-term loss. If you have a 30-year time horizon for retirement investments, then a short-term loss is not a big deal — your investments have plenty of time to recover. Thus, you probably want more of your retirement dollars in growth investments such as stocks. On the other hand, if you're investing money that you'll need in a year, a short-term loss, such as those suffered by the stock market, could be devastating to your plans. A money market fund or other short-term investment would be better suited to your needs.

Allocating assets for short-term goals

Asset allocation for goals with short time horizons is quite simple:

- **Less than two years:** If you have less than two years, you're generally best off sticking to money market funds. Stocks and bonds are volatile, and although you have the potential for earning higher returns in stocks and bonds, a money market fund offers a great combination of safety and decent returns. See Chapter 7 for more on money market funds and a list of the best ones available.
- **Between three and seven years:** If your time horizon is between three and seven years, then consider using shorter-term bond funds. (If you have between two and three years, you can use both money market and bond funds.) When you're able to keep your money in an investment for at least several years, then the extra potential returns for bonds begin to outweigh the risk of short-term loss from possible bond market fluctuations. See Chapter 8 for the specifics on bond funds.
- **Seven or more:** If your time horizon is seven years or more, then I think that you have a long enough time horizon to start investing in stocks as well as bonds.

Long-term goals such as retirement and college tuition require more complex asset allocation decisions, which I discuss in the following sections.

Allocating assets for retirement and other long-term goals

If you're like most people and retire in your mid 60s, your retirement portfolio will need to fund your living expenses for 20 or more years. That's a tall order. Unless you have vast wealth in comparison to your spending desires, the money you've earmarked for retirement will need to work hard for you. That's why a retirement portfolio, particularly during your earlier working years, should be heavily weighted toward growth investments like stocks.

TIP

Your current age and the number of years you must wait until you retire should be the biggest factors in your retirement asset allocation decision. The younger you are and the more years you have before retirement, the more comfortable you should be with growth-oriented (and more volatile) investments, such as stock funds.

As you approach retirement age, however, you should gradually scale back the risk and volatility of your portfolio. That's why, as you get older, bonds should become an increasingly bigger piece of your portfolio pie. Although their returns are generally lower, bonds are less likely to suffer a sharp downswing in value that could derail your retirement plans.

Table 6-1 in the next section lists some guidelines for allocating money you've earmarked for long-term purposes such as retirement. All you need to figure out is how old you are (I told you investing was easier than you thought!) and the level of risk you're comfortable with.

Factoring your investment personality

In Table 6-1, you see a new variable to the asset allocation decision: your *investment personality* or tolerance for risk. Even if you and another investor are the same age, and you both have the same time horizon for your investments, you could very well have different tolerances or desires to accept and deal with risk. Some people are more apt to lose sleep over their investments, just as some people are scared by roller coasters whereas other people get a thrill from them.

Table 6-1 Asset Allocation for the Long Haul

Your Investment Attitude	*Bond Allocation (%)*	*Stock Allocation (%)*
"Play it safe"	Age	100 – age
"Middle of the road"	Age – 10	110 – age
"Aggressive"	Age – 20	120 – age

Be honest with yourself and invest accordingly. If you're able to accept who you are instead of fighting it, you'll be a happier and more successful investor. Here's my advice for how to categorize yourself:

- **"Play it safe."** Indicators of this investment personality include little or no experience or success investing in stocks or other growth investments, fear of the financial markets, and risk-averse behavior in other aspects of life. You may desire to be conservative with your investments if you have enough saved already to afford a lower rate of return on your investments.
- **"Middle of the road."** Indicators of this investment personality include some experience and success investing in stocks or other growth investments, and some comfort with risk-taking behavior in other aspects of one's life.

- **"Aggressive."** Indicators of this investment personality include past experience and success investing in stocks or other growth investments, and a healthy desire and comfort with risk-taking behavior in other aspects of one's life. You may also want to be more aggressive if you're behind in saving for retirement and you want your money to work as hard as possible for you.

What does it all mean, you ask? Consider this example. According to Table 6-1, if you're 35 years old, don't like a lot of risk but recognize the value of striving for some growth to make your money work harder (a middle-of-the-road type), you should put 25 percent (35 – 10) into bonds and 75 percent (110 – 35) into stocks.

Divvying up your stock between home and abroad

Your next major asset allocation decision is to divvy up your stock investment money between U.S. and international funds. This is an important step for keeping your portfolio properly diversified. Although some consider international markets risky, what's even riskier is putting all your stock market money into just one country, even a relatively large and familiar one such as the United States. When the U.S. market slumps, some markets overseas continue to do well. Moreover, developing countries have the potential for greater economic growth and stock market returns than the U.S. market. Here's the portion of your stock allocation I recommend investing overseas:

20 percent for *play it safe*

33 percent for *middle-of-the-road*

40–50 percent for *aggressive*

So if you're a 35-year-old, middle-of-the-road type who is investing 75 percent of your portfolio in stocks, you would then put 33 percent of that stock money into international stock funds. Multiplying 33 percent by 75 percent works out to be about 25 percent of the entire portfolio.

So here's what a 35-year-old, middle-of-the-road investor's asset allocation would look like:

Bonds	25 %
U.S. stocks	50 %
International stocks	25 %

That isn't so complicated, is it?

Gradual change is better than abrupt change. If you've had little or no experience or success investing in stocks, it's better to start with the "play it safe" allocation and then work your way to more aggressive allocations as you develop more comfort and knowledge.

Allocating for college

As I discuss in Chapter 3, be careful if you're saving money for your child's college education. Doing so the wrong way can harm your child's chances of getting needed financial aid and can increase your tax burden.

The strategy for developing a college savings portfolio can be similar to allocating for retirement. Assuming that your child is young, the goal is relatively long-term, so the portfolio should emphasize growth investments such as stocks. However, as the time horizon decreases, bonds should play a bigger role.

The big difference, of course, between investing for your retirement and investing for your child's college costs is that the time horizon for college depends not on your age but on the age of the child for whom you are investing.

Here's my rule for investing college money for your kids: Take the following number:

50 to 60 for *play-it-safe*

40 to 50 for *middle of the road*

30 to 40 for *aggressive*

and add that number to your child's age. That's the percentage you should put in bonds; the rest should go into stocks (with at least a third of those stocks overseas). Using this rule, adjust the mix as your child gets older.

Taxes: It's What You Keep That Matters

For mutual funds held in non-retirement accounts, Uncle Sam gets to grab a share of your returns. Part of what makes up a mutual fund's returns are dividend distributions and capital gains, which are subject to taxation.

For this reason, when you're investing outside of tax-sheltered retirement accounts, you must distinguish between pre-tax and post-tax returns. Think of it as the business world difference between revenue and profit. Revenue is what a business makes from selling products and services; profit is what a business gets to keep after paying all of its expenses, and in the end, that's what really matters to a business. Likewise, what should matter most to you when investing your money is not your pre-tax return but your after-tax return.

Unfortunately, all too many investors (and often their advisors) ignore the tax consequences and invest in ways that increase their tax burdens and lower their effective returns. For example, when comparing two similar mutual funds, most people would prefer a fund earning returns of 14 percent per year to a fund earning 12 percent. But what if the 14 percent per year fund causes you to pay a lot more in taxes? What if, after factoring in taxes, the 14 percent per year fund nets you just 9 percent, while the 12 percent per year fund nets you an effective 10 percent return?

When you're constructing a mutual fund portfolio outside of a tax-sheltered retirement account, pay attention to tax implications. Like asset allocation, taxes are a fundamental part of portfolio construction.

Fitting funds to your tax bracket

How much of your investment returns you have to pay to the federal and state taxing authorities depends in part on your income tax bracket. The higher your bracket, the bigger the government's cut of your dividends and capital gains, and the lower your overall returns.

Fortunately, you can pick your funds in such a way as to minimize the federal and state government's share of your returns. Some funds, for example, are managed to minimize distributions, and certain government bond funds focus on investments not subject to specified taxes.

But to choose the right funds for your investment purposes, you must know your *marginal tax rate,* which is the rate you pay on the last dollar you earn. For example, if you earned $35,000 last year, the marginal rate is the rate you paid on the dollar that brought you from $34,999 to $35,000. The government charges you different tax rates for different parts of your annual income.

You pay less tax on your *first* dollars of earnings and more tax on your *last* dollars of earnings. For example, if you're single and your taxable income totaled $30,000 during 1998, you paid federal tax at the rate of 15 percent on the first $25,350 of taxable income and 28 percent on income above $25,350 up to $30,000.The rate you pay on those last dollars of income — 28 percent — is your marginal rate.

Your marginal tax rate allows you to quickly calculate how much tax you'll owe on certain additional non-salary income, such as investment income. Suppose that on top or your $30,000 salary you have a couple of mutual funds in a non-retirement account that distributed $1,000 of dividends during the year. Because you know your marginal tax rate — 28 percent — you know that Uncle Sam gets $280 of that $1,000 distribution ($1,000 × 28 percent). Note that states generally also levy income taxes.

Table 6-2 shows federal tax rates for singles and for married households filing jointly.

Table 6-2 1998 Federal Income Tax Brackets and Rates

Singles Taxable Income	*Married-Filing-Jointly Taxable Income*	*Federal Tax Rate*
Less than $25,350	Less than $42,350	15%
$25,350 to $61,400	$42,350 to $102,300	28%
$61,400 to $128,100	$102,300 to $155,950	31%
$128,100 to $278,450	$155,950 to $278,450	36%
More than $278,450	More than $278,450	39.6%

Minimizing taxes on funds

Armed with knowledge about your tax bracket, the following sections explain how to select tax-friendly mutual funds when investing outside of retirement accounts:

Use tax-free money market and bond funds

Certain kinds of money market and bond funds invest only in bonds issued by governments, and depending on the type of government they invest in, their dividends may not be subject to state and/or federal tax.

Such funds are typically identified by the word "Treasury" or "municipal" in their fund titles. A Treasury fund buys federal government-issued Treasury bonds (also called Treasuries), and its dividends — although federally taxable — are free of state taxes. The dividends of a municipal bond fund, which invests in local and state governments, are free of federal tax, and if the fund's investments are limited to one state and you live in that state, the dividends are free of state taxes as well.

The catch (you knew there'd be one): Because everybody knows that Treasuries and municipal bonds are not subject to complete taxation, the governments issuing these bonds can pay a lower rate of interest than, say, comparable corporate bonds (the dividends on which are fully taxable to bondholders). Therefore, before taxes are taken into account, tax-free bond and money market funds appear to yield less than their taxable equivalents.

TIP

However, after taxes are taken into account, you may find that with tax-free money market or bond funds, you come out ahead of comparable taxable funds if your tax bracket is high enough. Because of the difference in taxes, the earnings from tax-free investments *can* end up being greater than what you're left with from comparable taxable investments. If you're in the 28 percent federal bracket or higher, see Chapters 7 and 8 for details on tax-free money market and bond funds.

Don't buy tax-free funds inside retirement accounts. Your returns inside a retirement account are already sheltered from taxation. You can ignore the taxability of funds and go for the highest yields.

Invest in tax-friendly stock mutual funds

Unfortunately, stock mutual funds don't have a tax-free version like bond and money market funds do. Unless they're held inside a retirement account, stock fund distributions are always taxable, period. If you're in a high enough tax bracket, these stock distributions can be a significant tax burden. Unfortunately, with stock funds more than any other type of fund, investors often focus exclusively on the pre-tax historical return, ignoring the tax implications of their fund picks.

Although there are no tax-free stock funds, you can invest in stock funds that are "tax-friendly" — in other words, funds whose investing style keeps distributions to a minimum. Here's how stock funds can minimize taxable distributions:

- **Buy and hold investing.** There are two types of stock fund distributions: dividends and capital gains. Capital gains distributions are generated when a fund manager sells a stock for a profit; that profit must then be given out to the shareholders annually. Some fund managers are always tinkering with their portfolios, and, because of their frequent trading, their funds tend to produce more distributions — each time the fund is sold for a gain, you pay tax on it. But other fund managers are buy and hold investors. These managers produce fewer capital gains distributions than their peers who make frequent trades.

  Index mutual funds, which maintain more stable investment portfolios, tend to produce fewer capital gains distributions because they hold their securities longer. (For more on indexing, see the index funds section later in this chapter, as well as Chapter 9 for more details on stock index funds.)

- **Focusing on growth stocks.** Some corporations that issue stock, especially older, larger, more established companies, typically distribute a portion of their annual profits in the form of dividends to their shareholders. Companies can also choose not to issue dividends. In fact, rather than issuing dividends, many fast-growing companies (especially smaller ones) reinvest profits back into the company to fuel further growth. When done successfully, what you as an investor in such a company "lose" in dividends can be more than made up by appreciation in the stock price, which reflects the growth of the company. By focusing on stocks of such companies — known as *growth stocks* — mutual funds can minimize taxable dividend distributions.

- **Offsetting gains with losses.** If a fund manager sells some stock for a gain of $10,000 but sells other stock for a loss of $10,000, then capital gains net out to zero. Some funds, managed specifically to minimize distributions, employ this offsetting technique to lower their capital gains. I identify the best of these tax-managed stock funds in Chapter 9.

REMEMBER

For investments inside a retirement account, you don't have to worry about the tax friendliness of your mutual fund selections. They can generate all the distributions they want; the federal and state governments get none of your annual returns (at least, not until you withdraw the money).

Watch the time of year

TIP

When purchasing stock mutual funds outside of tax-sheltered retirement accounts, consider the time of year at which you purchase shares in funds. December is the most common month in which mutual funds make capital gains distributions.

You don't want to jump into a fund just before it makes a large distribution. You're not reaping any gains from the capital gains distribution because, right after such a distribution, the fund's share price decreases to reflect the size of the payout. You are, however, effectively making yourself liable for taxes on gains you did not share in.

When making purchases late in the year, find out whether and when the fund may make a significant capital gains distribution. A large December payout generally happens when a fund has had a good performance year. For funds I recommend, the month of distribution is listed in the Appendix.

Invest in tax-sheltered retirement accounts

REMEMBER

Of course, the easiest way to avoid a tax bite on your mutual funds is to purchase them inside tax-sheltered retirement accounts. Then you don't have to worry about capital gains distributions or at what time of year you're making a fund purchase. Inside a retirement account, funds distributions are simply not taxed. Your money is able to grow tax-deferred until withdrawal.

Fund Investing Strategies

In this chapter, I cover asset allocation — how to divvy up your money among stocks and bonds and foreign and domestic securities — and how to choose funds that fit your tax situation. Here, I discuss some of the different investing strategies and philosophies that you can use to direct a mutual fund portfolio, and I also explain which are best for you and which are best avoided.

Market timing versus buy and hold investing

Over the past two centuries, stocks have produced an average return of about 10 percent per year. Some individual years are better, with stocks returning up to 20 or even 30 percent or more; other years are worse, with stocks losing 20 percent or more in value. But when taken over a period of decades, the good years and the bad years historically net out to returns of about 10 percent per year.

Despite the long-term healthy returns stocks generally produce, it's disconcerting to some people to invest their money into something that can drop far and fast. Many newsletters, advisors, and the like purport to predict the future movement of the financial markets. On the basis of such predictions, these folks advocate timing the purchase and sale of securities such as stocks to maximize returns and minimize risks.

Although market timing sounds good in theory, a wealth of studies and evidence show that market timing simply doesn't work in practice. (In Chapter 15, I discuss the poor track record of investment newsletters that attempt market timing.) In fact, those who try to time the markets inevitably do worse than those simply buying and holding because they miss the right times to buy and sell.

Market timing is based on that age-old investment mantra, "Buy low, sell high." It sounds so simple and logical; perhaps that's what makes it such an attractive concept. One fundamental problem, however, collapses the logic: Recognizing a low or a high comes only with hindsight; market movements, especially in the short-term, are unpredictable. Telling someone to buy low and sell high is no different than telling someone that it's okay to drive his car if he expects not to have an accident and that he should stay out of his car if he expects to have an accident.

If buying and holding had an investment mantra, it would be "Buy now, sell a lot later." Rather than betting on short-term market movements, buy and hold investors bank on long-term trends and are not so concerned with *when* to get in and out of the market as much as *how long* they are actually in there. Buy and hold investors know that if they hang in there through the inevitable tough times, the good years will outnumber the bad, and they'll come out ahead.

Unfortunately, too many mutual fund investors engage in market timing. I know this from all the studies I've seen showing that the typical mutual fund investor ends up earning less from his investments than the funds he's invested in earn. A study by Dalbar Inc., a leading provider of analytical information for the financial services industry, found that over a 12-year period, a strategy of simply buying and holding funds outperformed the average fund investor's returns (which were diminished by trading and market timing) by more than 3 to 1.

Don't trade in and out of funds. Stay invested. Once you've bought into a decent fund, there are few good reasons to move out of it (see Chapter 12). Not only does buy and hold investing offer better returns, but it's also less work.

Active versus index (passive) fund managers

Unlike other mutual funds, in which the portfolio manager and a team of analysts scour the market for the best securities, an index fund manager passively invests to match the performance of an index. Index funds are funds that can be (and, for the most part, are) managed by a computer. Managers invest an index fund's assets so as to replicate an underlying index, such as Standard & Poor's 500 Index — the 500 companies with the greatest market value of stock outstanding in the United States. In fact, an S&P 500 Index fund buys and holds exactly the same 500 stocks, and in exactly the same amounts, that comprise the S&P 500 Index.

Index funds are perhaps the most underrated stock funds in existence. Like the offensive linemen in football or people who do a lot of good and don't seek or receive publicity, index funds don't get the credit they deserve. Index funds are a little bit like Jaime Escalante, that Garfield High School math teacher of poor Hispanic children in the ghettos of Los Angeles. In a school where kids often dropped out and were lucky to learn some algebra, Escalante got his kids to learn calculus. In fact, he got *entire classes* to work hard and pass the college advanced placement exam for calculus. (The College Board that administers the AP test couldn't believe so many kids from this school could pass this exam, so the kids were investigated for cheating — that's how Escalante's story was learned and he finally got credit for all the great work that he did. Rent the movie, *Stand and Deliver,* to see Escalante's facianating story.)

Index funds work hard by keeping expenses to the minimum, staying invested, and not trying to jump around. So, like Escalante's kids, index funds are virtually guaranteed to be at the top of their class. Over long periods (ten years or more), index funds outperform about three-quarters of their peers! Most other so-called actively managed funds cannot overcome the handicap of high operating expenses that pulls down their funds' rates of return. Because significant ongoing research need not be conducted to identify companies to invest in, index funds can be run with far lower operating expenses.

The average U.S. stock fund has an operating expense ratio of 1.4 percent per year (some funds charge expenses as high as 2 percent or more per year). That being the case, a U.S. stock index fund with an expense ratio of just 0.2 percent per year has an average advantage of 1.2 percent per year. A 1.2 percent difference may not seem like much, but in fact, it is a significant difference. Because stocks tend to return about 10 percent per year, you're throwing away about 12 percent of your expected stock fund returns. If you factor in the taxes you pay on your fund profits, these higher expenses gobble perhaps a quarter of your after-tax profits.

Another overlooked drawback to actively managed stock funds: Your fund manager can make costly mistakes, such as not being invested when the market goes up, being too aggressive when the market plummets, or just being in the wrong stocks. An actively managed fund can easily underperform the overall market index that it is competing against. An index fund, by definition, can't.

Table 6-3 lists the worst-performing U.S. Stock Funds over the past decade. Note how much worse these bowser funds performed versus the major U.S. stock market indexes (the performance of which one could replicate by investing in an index fund).

Table 6-3 Worst Performing U.S. Stock Funds Over the Past Decade

Annualized Total Return (load adjusted)	
Steadman Technology Growth	-18.1% per year
Steadman American Industry	-11.2% per year
Centurion T.A.A.	-3.8% per year
Steadman Investment	-3.8% per year
Comstock Partners Capital Value	-1.3% per year
Stock market indexes	
Standard & Poor's 500 Index+	18.0% per year
Wilshire 5000 Index+	17.6% per year

When you invest in index funds, you'll never see your funds in the list of the top ten funds — but then you'll never see your funds in the list of the bottom ten funds, either. Don't overestimate your ability to pick *in advance* the few elite money managers who manage to beat the market averages by a few percentage points per year in the long run. And then don't overestimate the pros' ability to consistently pick the right stocks.

TIP

Index mutual funds are tax-friendlier

Mutual fund managers of actively managed portfolios, in their attempts to increase their shareholders' returns, buy and sell individual securities more frequently. This process increases the chances of a fund needing to make significant capital gains distributions.

Thus, for money invested outside of retirement accounts, index funds have an added advantage: Fewer taxable distributions are made to shareholders because less trading of securities is conducted and a more stable portfolio is maintained. For mutual funds held outside of tax-sheltered retirement accounts, this reduced trading effectively increases an investor's total rate of return.

Index funds make sense for a portion of your investments, especially when investing in bonds and larger, more conservative stocks, where it's very difficult for portfolio managers to beat the market. Index funds also make sense for investors who are terrified that fund managers may make big mistakes and greatly underperform the market.

As for how much you should use index versus actively managed funds, it's really a matter of personal taste. If you're happy as a clam knowing that you'll get the market rate of return and knowing that you can't underperform the market, there's no reason you can't index your entire portfolio. On the other hand, if you enjoy the game of trying to pick the better managers and want the potential to earn better than the market level of returns, don't use index funds at all. A happy medium is to do some of both. (You may be interested to know that John Bogle, founder of the Vanguard Group of mutual funds and pioneer of index funds, has about 40 percent of his money invested in index funds.)

Putting Your Plans into Action

Constructing a mutual fund portfolio is a bit like constructing a house: There's a world of difference between drawing up a plan and executing it. If you're the architect drawing up the plan, your world is all clean lines on white paper. But if you're the general contractor responsible for executing the plan, things are generally messier; you may face such challenges as inclement weather, unsuitable soil, and tired construction workers.

Like the contractor, you're bound to meet challenges in the execution of the plan — in your case, constructing a mutual fund portfolio rather than a house. Some of these challenges come from the funds themselves; your personal circumstances are the source of others. With patience and persistence and a healthy helping of my advice, all are surmountable. Investing in funds is much, much easier than building a house — which is why you can do this yourself if you so desire.

How many funds and families?

Suppose that you've nailed down an asset allocation for your retirement portfolio: 25 percent in bonds, 50 percent in domestic stocks, and 25 percent in international stocks. That's all very specific, except for the fact that these percentages tell you nothing about how many funds and how many fund families you should use to meet these percentages.

Let me start with the family issue. Given the sheer number and quality of funds that the larger and better fund companies such as Vanguard, T. Rowe Price, and Fidelity offer, you could do all of your investing through one family of funds. Centralizing your investments in one family saves on administrative hassles by cutting down on the number of applications to complete, envelopes to open, statements to file, tax statements to deal with, and so forth. Plus, you're more likely to learn your way around better at a company that you spend more of your time interacting with.

There's a good argument against doing this, though: Even the best mutual fund companies don't handle every type of fund the best way. By not spreading out your funds over different fund families to take advantage of their particular strengths, you may be sacrificing a little bit of return.

Discount brokerage firms offer some of the best of both approaches. You get one-stop shopping and one statement for all of your holdings, but you also have access to funds from many families. The downside: You pay small transaction fees to purchase many of the better funds through discounters. (I discuss discount brokerage services in detail in Chapter 5.)

You'll find no one right answer as to how many fund families to work with and whether to use a discount brokerage account. Choose the approach that works best for your needs. I use a combination of these approaches by maintaining accounts through a giant mutual fund company while also using discount brokers to buy funds from some of the smaller fund families that are more of a hassle to work with. This strategy allows me to maximize centralization while minimizing the extra transaction fees I have to pay.

As for the number of individual funds to hold in your portfolio, again, there's no one right answer. The typical mutual fund is quite diversified to begin with, so you needn't invest in too many. In fact, because some funds invest across different types of investments (known as hybrid funds) or even across other funds (known as funds of funds), you can achieve your desired asset allocation by investing in just one fund.

So the answer to the question, "How many funds?" is based less on science than it is on what's practical for you and how much money you have to invest. At a minimum, own enough funds so that you're able to diversify not only across the general investment types (stocks, bonds) you've targeted but also across different types of securities within those larger categories — bonds of various maturity lengths, stocks of various sized companies (I explain these in Chapters 8 and 9).

As your savings allow, I generally recommend that you invest at least $3,000 to $5,000 per fund. If you're investing outside of a retirement account, most of the better mutual funds require an initial investment of this magnitude anyway. Inside a retirement account, you may invest far less — typically only $500 per fund — to get going. However, because most retirement accounts annually ding you about $10 per fund as an account maintenance fee, you should aim to invest the higher amounts so that you don't have your small investment devoured by high relative fees. (A $10-per-year fee diminishes a $500 investment by 2 percent per year.) Some fund companies will waive this fee if you keep more than a certain amount — $5,000, for example — in their funds.

As you have larger sums to invest, it makes sense to use more funds. Suppose that you have $300,000 and want to divide it equally, putting a third each into bonds, U.S. stocks, and international stocks. You could put $100,000 into each of three funds: one bond fund, one U.S. stock fund, and one international stock fund. But with that much money to invest, why not use at least two of each of the different types of funds? That way, if the one international stock fund you've chosen does poorly, all of your money earmarked for overseas investing is not doing poorly in that fund. There's no reason that you can't use three different funds within each category. The more money you have, the more sense this strategy makes.

And one more point: Don't invest in more funds than you've got time to track. If you can't find the time to read your funds' semi-annual and annual reports, that's a sign that you have too many funds. Extra diversification does not make up for a lack of monitoring.

Matching fund allocation to your asset allocation

One thing that can trip up your asset allocation plans is the fact that mutual funds have their own asset allocations. For example, a hybrid fund may invest 60 percent in stocks and 40 percent in bonds. Perhaps you, on the other hand, want to invest 75 percent in stocks and 25 percent in bonds. How the heck do you fit that kind of fund into your portfolio?

TIP

One option is to forget it. Take Thoreau's advice to simplify your (investing) life: Avoid funds that invest in different investment types. Buy purebreds — stock funds that are 100 percent (or close to 100 percent) invested in stocks, bond funds that invest only in bonds, and international stock funds that are entirely invested overseas.

That way, your asset allocation calculations stay simple. Take the desired mix of our hypothetical 35 year old from earlier in this chapter: 25 percent in bonds, 50 percent in U.S. stocks, and 25 percent in international stocks. If she has $10,000 to invest and sticks to purebred funds, then figuring out how much money to put into each kind of fund is a simple matter of multiplying the desired allocation percentage by the $10,000 total to invest. In this case, she should put $2,500 in a pure bond fund (25% × $10,000), $5,000 in a U.S. stock fund, and $2,500 in an international stock fund.

If that seems a little too easy, you're right. Even if they label themselves as purebreds, plenty of mutual funds are given leeway in their charters to dabble in other investment types. Read the annual report of a so-called U.S. stocks fund and you may find that up to 20 percent of its assets are invested in bonds or international stocks. (Fidelity stock funds are notorious for this.)

Some hybrid funds are excellent funds, and it seems a bit silly to eliminate them simply to avoid a math problem with an extra step. Although I encourage you to focus on purebred funds, it will occasionally make sense to fit a hybrid fund, or a hybrid disguised as a purebred, into your portfolio.

Let me get back to the example of the 35-year-old investor, the one who wants a portfolio of 25 percent bonds, 50 percent U.S. stocks, and 25 percent international stocks. Suppose that she has picked out three funds she wants to buy: a U.S. stock fund (100 percent stocks), an international stock fund (100 percent international stocks), and a hybrid fund (60 percent U.S. stocks, 40 percent bonds).

Because the hybrid fund is the only one with bonds, our investor needs to figure out how much to put into the hybrid fund so that she'll end up with about 25 percent (overall) in bonds. Because 40 percent of the hybrid fund is invested in bonds, the arithmetic looks like this:

$.40 \times \text{Amount to be invested in fund} = .25$

$\text{Amount to be invested in fund} = .25 \div .4$

$\text{Amount to be invested in fund} = .625$ or 62.5 percent

I like nice round numbers, so I rounded 62.5 off to 60. Here's how much money she should put into each fund to get her desired investment mix:

60 % Hybrid fund (60 percent in U.S. stocks, 40 percent in bonds)

15 % U.S. stock fund (100 percent in stocks)

25 % International stock fund (100 percent in international stocks)

Allocating when there's not much to allocate

What a drag. If you're just starting out, there's not a lot to allocate. Here you've invested all this time exploring how to design a terrific portfolio. Then, thanks to minimum initial investment requirements, you may realize that you only have enough money to buy one of the five funds you've selected!

TIP

Fear not. You have several ways around this problem:

- Buy a hybrid fund or a fund of funds whose asset allocation is similar to your desired mix. Don't sweat the fact that you can't find a fund with the exact mix you want. For now, getting close is good enough. When you're able to afford it, you can, if you so desire, move out of the hybrid fund and into the funds you originally chose.
- Buy your desired funds one at a time as you're able to afford them. I call this little trick *diversifying over time,* and it's a perfectly legitimate way to go.

  One twist on this strategy that will test and perhaps improve your mutual fund investing habits is to start by investing in the type of fund (for example, bond or international stock) that is currently doing the most poorly — that is, buy when things are "on sale." Then, the next year, add the fund type that is doing the most poorly at *that* time. (Make sure to buy the better funds within the type that is doing poorly!)

(For more ideas, see Chapter 10 for sample portfolios for beginning investors.)

Lumping or averaging large amounts?

Most people invest money as they save it. If you're saving through a company retirement plan, such as a 401(k), this option is ideal: It happens automatically, and you're buying at different points in time, so even the world's unluckiest person gets to buy some funds at or near market bottoms.

But what if you have what to you seems like a whole *lot* of money that's lolligagging around in a savings or money market fund awaiting further instructions and direction? Maybe it's just piled up because you're thrifty, or maybe you recently inherited money or received a windfall from work that you've done. You're discovering more about how to invest this money, but once you decide what types of investments you'd like to purchase, you may be terrified at the thought of actually buying them.

Some people in this situation feel a sense of loss, failure, or even guilt for not making better use of the money than just letting it sit in a savings or money market account. Always remember one important thing: At least you're earning a positive return in the bank or money fund, and it beats the heck out of rushing into an investment that you don't understand and in which you may lose 20 percent or more. Of course, there's no reason to not find the best parking spot that you can for your money (see Chapter 7 for recommendations of the best money market funds).

So how do you invest your lump? One approach is to *dollar-cost average* it into the investments you've chosen. All this means is that you invest your money in equal chunks on a regular basis, such as once a month or per quarter. For example, if you have $50,000 to invest, and you want to invest it once a quarter over a year, you would invest $12,500 per quarter until it's all invested. Meanwhile, the money that's awaiting future investment happily continues accumulating interest in a good money market fund.

The attraction of dollar-cost averaging is that it allows you to ease into riskier investments instead of jumping in all at once. The benefit may be that, if the price of the investment drops after some of your initial purchases, you can buy some later at a lower price. If you had dumped all your money at once and then the financial markets get walloped, it's human to think, "Why didn't I wait?"

History has proven that dollar-cost averaging is a great risk-reducing investment strategy. If you had used dollar-cost averaging during the worst decade for stock investors this century (1928 to 1938), you still would have averaged 7 percent per year in returns despite the Great Depression and a sagging stock market.

The flip side of dollar-cost averaging is that if your investments do what they're supposed to and increase in value, you may wish that you had invested your money faster. Another possible drawback of dollar-cost averaging is that you may get cold feet continuing to invest money in an investment that's dropping in value. Some who are attracted to dollar-cost averaging are afraid to continue boarding a sinking ship.

Dollar-cost averaging also can cause headaches with your taxes when it's time to sell investments held outside of retirement accounts. If you buy an investment at many different times and prices, the accounting is muddied as you sell blocks of the investment. Also, try not to purchase funds, particularly stock funds that have had a good year, late in the year because most of these funds distribute capital gains in December.

TIP

In my opinion, dollar-cost averaging is most valuable when the money you want to invest represents a large portion of your total assets and you can stick to a schedule. It's best to make it automatic so that you're less likely to chicken out and discontinue investing if your initial investment purchases have declined in value from when you bought them.

Most mutual fund companies offer automatic exchange services. Pick a time period that makes sense for you. I like to do dollar-cost averaging once per quarter early in the quarter (the first of January, April, July, and October). If you feel comfortable investing and want to get on with the program, "averaging" your money in over one year is fine, but it's riskier. If you have big bucks to invest and you're cautious, there's no reason you can't average the money over two to five years (you can use some CDs or Treasury bills as holding places in this case to get a better return than on the money fund).

What to do with your existing investments

A final question that I'm frequently asked by people who want to start a comprehensive mutual fund investment program, but who also have existing portfolios, is what to do with their existing investments. Here are my thoughts:

- **Keep the good non-fund investments.** Although I'm a fan of mutual funds, there's no compelling reason for you to invest all your spare dollars in funds. If you enjoy investing in real estate or securities of your own choosing, go right ahead. You can account for these other investments when you tally up your asset allocation. As for evaluating the mutual funds you may already own, see Chapter 12.
- **Get rid of high fee, poorly performing investments.** As you understand more about the best mutual fund investments, you may come to realize by comparison how lousy some of your existing investments are. I won't stand in your way of dumping them!

- **Pay attention to tax consequences.** When you're considering selling a non-retirement account investment, especially one that has appreciated considerably since its original purchase, be mindful of taxes. Assets held for at least 18 months now are eligible for the more favorable capital gains tax rates (see Chapter 13).

Chapter 7

Funds That Beat the Bank — Money Market Funds

In This Chapter

- What are money market funds?
- How do money market funds invest your money?
- How do you choose the right fund for you?
- Which money market funds are best?

Just over a generation ago, people had hundreds of alternatives for safely investing their spare cash — they could schlep around town and shop among banks, banks, and still more banks. Although it may seem that safe money investors had many alternatives, they really didn't. As a result, yields weren't all that great compared with what a large institutional investor with millions of dollars to invest could obtain by purchasing ultra-safe short-term securities.

Back in the early 1970s, money market mutual funds were born. The concept was fairly simple. The money market mutual fund would invest in the same safe, higher-yielding financial instruments (which I discuss in the section, "Securities your money fund invests in," later in this chapter) that only those with big bucks could buy. The money fund would then sell shares to investors who didn't have the big bucks to invest. By pooling together the money from thousands of investors, the money fund could offer investors a decent yield (after charging a reasonable fee to cover the fund's operational expenses and make a profit).

In their first years of operation, these "people's" money funds had little cash flowing in. By 1977, less than $4 billion were in money market funds. But then interest rates rose precipitously as inflation took hold. Soon, bank depositors found that the rates of interest they could earn could rise no more, because banks were limited by federal regulations to paying 5 percent interest.

As interest rates skyrocketed in the late 1970s and investors learned that they could earn higher yields by switching from bank accounts to money market funds, money flooded into money market mutual funds. Within just four years, money market fund assets mushroomed more than 50-fold to $200 billion.

Money Market Funds Defined

Money market funds are a type of mutual fund. This fact often gets lost in financial discussions and writings in which many people equate mutual funds with stocks.

Money market mutual funds are a large and unique part of the mutual fund industry's offering. *Money market funds are the only type of mutual fund whose share price does not fluctuate in value.* The share prices of stock and bond mutual funds fluctuate from day to day depending on how the stock and bond markets are doing. Money market funds, in stark contrast, are locked in at a $1 per share.

So how do you make money with money market funds, you ask? By earning dividends, similar to the interest you earn on bank savings accounts. However, money market mutual funds offer several significant benefits over bank savings accounts:

- **Higher yields**. What first attracted investors to money market funds (back when interest rates zoomed up in the late 1970s and early 1980s) still holds true today. The best money market mutual funds pay a higher yield than equivalent bank accounts, despite the deregulation of the banking industry.

  TECHNICAL STUFF

  How and why do banks continue to pay less interest than most money funds? Two reasons:

  - Banks have a lot of overhead due to all of the branch offices they operate.
  - Banks know that they can get away with paying lower yields because many of their depositors, perhaps including you, believe that the FDIC insurance that comes with a bank savings account makes it safer than a money market mutual fund. I dispel this myth in the section, "Money market funds lack FDIC insurance," later in the chapter.

- **Multiple tax flavors.** Besides the lower rate of return, another problem with bank savings accounts is that they come in one — and only one — tax flavor: taxable. There is no such thing as a bank savings account that pays you tax-free interest. Money market funds, however, come in a variety of tax-free versions, paying dividends free of federal or state tax or both. So, if you're in a high federal or state (or both) income tax bracket, money funds offer you advantages that a bank savings account simply can't.
- **Check-writing privileges.** Another useful feature that comes with money market mutual funds is the ability to write checks, without charge, against your account. Most mutual fund companies require that the checks be written for larger amounts — typically at least $250. They don't want you using these accounts to pay all of your small household bills because checks cost money to process.
- **Convenient access to other mutual funds.** After you've established a money market mutual fund at a particular fund company, investing in other funds offered by that company becomes a simple toll-free phone call. (And, as I discuss in Chapter 5, if your chosen fund company has a discount brokerage division, you may also be able to invest in mutual funds from other parent companies.) One centralized account eliminates the need to complete additional application forms every time you want to invest in a new fund and reduces the ongoing paperwork involved in tracking your funds. Paperwork nirvana!
- **No lines and traffic jams.** Because you can invest and transact in mutual funds over the phone and through the mail, you can save yourself considerable hassle. No more wasting gas driving to the bank branch; no more waiting in long lines after you get there.

TECHNICAL STUFF

Sometimes, you'll get stuck on hold for a short time when you call a mutual fund company. The better companies (recommended in this book) generally won't leave you hanging for more than 15 to 30 seconds. If they do, please write me in care of the publisher and let me know so that together we can hassle them or delete them from the next edition of this book.

Banks have developed their own money market deposit accounts (MMDAs) that are money fund wannabees. Unlike normal money funds, the interest rate on MMDAs is set at the discretion of the bank and is generally lower than what you could get from one of the better money market mutual funds. Check writing on MMDAs, if it's available, is usually restricted to just a few checks per month.

Scrambling now as late-comers in the mutual fund business, some banks are offering real money market mutual funds, including tax-free funds. Again, the better money market mutual funds offered by mutual fund companies are generally superior (see recommendations in the section, "Finding the best money market funds" later in this chapter) to those offered by banks. The reason: Most bank money market funds have higher operating expenses and hence lower yields than the best money funds offered by mutual fund companies.

Uses for money funds

The best money market funds are the ideal substitute for a bank savings account; they offer all the safety of a bank, but a much better yield. Here are some of the purposes for which a money market fund is well-suited:

TIP

- **Your emergency cash reserve.** Money market funds are a good place to keep your emergency cash reserve (see Chapter 3). Because you don't know what the future holds in store, it's wise to prepare for the unexpected — events such as job loss, unanticipated medical bills, or a leaky roof. Six months worth of living expenses is a good emergency reserve target for most people (for example, if you spend $2,000 in an average month, keep $12,000 reserved).

  You may be able to skinny by with just three months' living expenses if you have other accounts such as a 401(k) or family members and close friends that you could tap for a loan. Consider keeping up to one year's expenses handy if your income fluctuates wildly. If your profession involves a high risk of job loss and if finding another job could take a long while, you also need a significant cash safety net.

- **Short-term savings goals.** If you're saving money for a big-ticket item that you hope to purchase within the next couple of years — whether it's a fishing boat or a down payment on a home — a money market fund is a terrific place to accumulate and grow the money. With such a short time horizon, you cannot afford to expose your money to the gyrations of stocks or longer-term bonds. A money market fund offers not only a safe haven for your principal but also a yield that should keep you a step ahead of the inflation rate.

- **A parking spot for money awaiting investment.** Suppose that you have a chunk of money you want to invest for longer-term purposes, but you don't want to invest all at once for fear that you may buy into stocks and bonds just before a big drop. A money market fund can be a friendly home to the money awaiting investment as you purchase into your chosen investment gradually over time. (This technique is known as *dollar-cost averaging,* which I explain in Chapter 6.)

- **Personal checking accounts.** Money market funds with no restrictions on check writing can be established and used for household checking purposes. The discount brokerage firms that offer accounts with a check-writing option downplay the fact that an investor is allowed to write an unlimited number of checks (in any amounts) on his or her account. You can leave your bank altogether — some money funds even come with debit cards that can be used at bank ATMs for a nominal fee! Later in this chapter (in the section, "Finding the best money market funds"), I point out which funds offer unlimited checking.
- **Business accounts.** Just as you can use a money market fund for your personal purposes, you can open a money market fund for your business. You can use this account for depositing checks received from customers and holding excess funds, as well as for paying bills via the check-writing feature. Some money funds allow checks to be written for any amount, and these funds can completely replace a bank checking account. My business checking account has been in a money market mutual fund for years.

TIP

You can also establish direct deposit with most money market funds. You can have your paycheck, monthly Social Security benefit check, or most other regular payments you receive from larger organizations zapped electronically into your money market mutual fund account.

Common concerns about money market funds

Investors new to money market mutual funds sometimes worry about what they're getting themselves into. It's good to be concerned and educated *before* you move your money into securities you've never invested in.

Most people don't worry about the money they keep in the bank. They should — well, at least a tiny bit. First of all, banks get burglarized and defrauded more than mutual funds! (A thief created a bogus ID card and visited five branches of my local bank, posing as me, and succeeded in withdrawing $400 from my bank checking account. The bank covered the loss, but I chose to take my business elsewhere.)

The biggest risk of keeping extra money in a bank savings account is that the purchasing power of your money will be eroded by inflation because of the paltry interest you're getting. And, remember that the FDIC insurance system is a government insurance system — that's hardly an ironclad, 100 percent safety guarantee.

The following sections present the concerns that I hear from people like you about money market funds, and the reasons I think that you shouldn't worry about them.

Money market funds lack FDIC insurance

Some people are nervous about money market mutual funds because they are not insured. Bank accounts, on the other hand, come with insurance that protects up to $100,000 you have deposited in a bank (assuming that your bank participates in the FDIC system). So, if a bank fails because it lends too much money to people and companies that go bankrupt or abscond with the funds, you should get your money back.

But consider this: Part of the reason that money market funds are not insured is that they don't really need to be. Mutual fund companies can't fail because they have a dollar invested in securities for every dollar you deposited in their money fund. Banks, on the other hand, are required to have available just 12 cents for every dollar you hand over to them; no wonder they need insurance.

One money market fund did "break the buck." A newspaper article dramatically headlined, "Investors Stunned as a Money Fund Folds," went on to say, "The fund's collapse is the latest blunder to shake investors' confidence in the nation's mutual fund industry." Although such hype may help to fill readers with anxiety (and perhaps sell more newspapers), it obscured several important facts. This particular fund didn't collapse but was liquidated because its investors, who were all small banks, owned the fund, and they decided to disband it. The fund did not hold money from retail investors like you and me. If it had, the fund company surely would have bailed it out, as other fund companies have done. You should also know that only 6 percent of the investing banks' money was lost. Hardly a collapse — and I doubt that anyone was stunned!

It's possible that a money market fund's investments may decline slightly in value — thus reducing the share price of the money market fund below a dollar. In a few cases, money market funds bought some bad investments. However, in each and every case except one, the money market fund was *bailed out* — that is, cash was infused into the money fund by the mutual fund company, thus enabling the fund to maintain a price of $1 per share.

WARNING!

If you have more than $100,000 in one bank and that bank fails, you can lose the money over the $100,000 insurance limit. I've seen more than a few cases where people had several hundred thousand — in one case, a person who came to me for advice had nearly $2 million — sitting in a bank account! Now that's risk! Since 1980, more than 1,000 banks have failed. In recent years, because the government has taken a hard line on not going beyond the $100,000 insurance limit, bank depositors have lost hundreds of millions of dollars.

TIP

When the bank or credit union may be better for you

Although I advocate use of the best money market funds, I realize that a bank or credit union savings account is sometimes the most practical place to keep your money. Your local bank, for example, may appeal to you if you like being able to do business face to face. Perhaps you operate a business where a lot of cash is processed; in this case, you can't beat the convenience and other services that a local bank offers. And if you have only $1,000 or $2,000 to invest, a bank savings account may be your only choice; many money market funds require a higher minimum initial investment.

For investing short-term excess cash, you may first want to consider keeping it in your checking account. This option may make financial sense if the extra money helps you avoid monthly service charges because your balance occasionally dips below the minimum. In fact, keeping money in a separate savings account rather than in your checking account may *not* benefit you if service charges wipe out your interest earnings.

Don't forget to shop around for the best deals on your checking account because minimum balance requirements, service fees, and interest rates vary quite a bit among banks. Credit unions offer some of the best deals, although they usually don't offer extensive access to free ATMs. The largest banks with the most ATM machines in the most areas — you know, the ones that spend gobs of money on advertising jingles and billboards — usually offer the worst terms on checking and savings accounts.

Stick with larger mutual fund companies if you're worried about the lack of FDIC insurance. They have the financial wherewithal and the most incentive to save a floundering money fund. Fortunately, the larger fund companies have the best money funds anyway.

The check may get lost or stolen

If you have the kind of mail delivery that I had when I lived in San Francisco (in a typical year, I had about a dozen different mail carriers and every month I seemed to have a problem with the mail), I can understand your concerns. However, if you're worried about a deposit being lost in the mail, don't. If it does happen (which is rare), all you do is have the check(s) reissued and stop payment (which, unlike banks, most money funds don't charge you to do) on the first check.

No one can legally cash a check made payable to you. Don't mistakenly think that going to your local bank in person is any safer — you could slip on some dog droppings or get carjacked.

TIP

If you're really concerned about the mail, use a fund company or discount broker with branch offices. I would not recommend spending the extra money and time required to send your check via registered or certified mail. You'll know if your check got there when you get the statement from the fund company processing the deposit. If you're depositing a check made payable to you, just be sure to endorse the check with the notation "for deposit only" under your signature.

I may have trouble accessing my money

Although it may appear that you can't easily and quickly access your money market fund holdings, you can, in fact, efficiently tap your money market fund in a variety of ways. (***Note:*** You can use these methods at most fund companies, particularly the larger ones.)

- **Write a check.** The most efficient way to access your money market fund is to write a check. Suppose that you have an unexpectedly large expense that you can't afford to pay out of your bank checking account. Just write a check on your money market mutual fund.
- **Telephone redemption.** Another handy way to access your money (which may be useful if your money fund checkbook is hidden under a mountain of papers somewhere in the vicinity of your desk) is to call the fund company and ask them to mail you a check for whatever amount you'd like from your money fund. Many money funds also allow you to call in to have money sent electronically from the money market fund to your bank account or vice versa.
- **Automatic withdrawal plans.** If you need money regularly sent from your money market fund to, say, your local bank checking account, you can set up an automatic withdrawal plan. On a designated day of the month, money will be sent electronically from your money market fund to your checking account. These transfers can also be done on an as-needed basis.
- **Wiring.** If you need cash in a flash, many money market funds offer the option of wiring money to and from your bank. Both the money market fund and the bank usually assess a small charge for this service. Most companies will also send you money via an overnight express carrier, such as Federal Express, if you provide them with an account number.
- **Debit cards.** Brokerage account money funds that offer debit cards allow access to your money via bank ATMs, as I discuss later in the chapter.

TECHNICAL STUFF

Chapter 11 explains how to establish these account features. Unlike when you visit a bank, you can't simply drop by the branch office of a mutual fund company and withdraw funds from your account. They don't keep money in branch offices because they're not banks. However, you can establish the preceding account features through the fund's branch office if you didn't set them up when you originally set up your account.

Securities in which your money fund invests

Under SEC regulations, money market funds can invest only in the most credit-worthy securities, and their investments must have an average maturity of less than 120 days. The short-term nature of these securities effectively eliminates the risk of money funds being sensitive to changes in interest rates.

The securities that money market funds use are extremely safe. General-purpose money market funds invest in government-backed securities, bank certificates of deposits (CDs), and short-term corporate debt issued by the largest and most credit-worthy companies and the U.S. government (although that may not be much comfort to some of you). The following sections provide the rundown on the major types of securities that money funds hold.

Commercial paper

Corporations, particularly large ones, often need to borrow money to help make their businesses grow and prosper. In the past, most companies needing a short-term loan had to borrow money from a bank. In recent decades, it has become easier to issue short-term debt or IOUs — *commercial paper* — directly to interested investors.

Money market funds buy high-quality commercial paper that matures typically within 60 to 90 days and is issued by large companies (such as AT&T, Hewlett-Packard, Intel, Sears, and Texaco), finance firms (such as Ford Motor Credit), banks, and foreign governments.

If you had hundreds of thousands of dollars to invest, you could purchase commercial paper yourself rather than buying it indirectly through a money market fund. If you do have lots of money to invest, I don't recommend this approach. You incur fees when you purchase commercial paper yourself, and you probably don't have the expertise to know what's a good purchase, what's not, and what's a fair price to pay. The best money funds charge a very small fee to do all this analysis for you, plus offer perks such as check-writing privileges.

Certificates of deposit

You can go to your local bank and invest some money in a certificate of deposit (CD). A CD is nothing more than a specific-term loan that you make to your banker — ranging anywhere from a month to some number of years.

Money market funds can buy CDs as well. The only difference is that they invest a lot more money — usually millions — in a bank's CD. Thus, they can command a higher interest rate than you can obtain on your own. Money funds buy CDs that mature within one to three months. The money fund is only insured up to $100,000 per bank CD, just like the bank insurance that you and I receive. As with other money fund investments, the money fund does research to determine the credit quality of banks and other institutions that it invests in. Remember that money funds' other investments are not insured.

Money market funds may hold some other types of CDs. Yankee CDs are CDs issued by U.S. branches of foreign banks. Eurodollar CDs are simply CDs issued by foreign banks or the foreign branches of U.S. banks.

Government debt

McDonald's, the burgermeisters, in many locations have signs saying billions and billions served. Well, our federal government serves up billions and billions — of debt, that is — in the form of Treasury securities. A truckload of federal government debt is outstanding — about $5 trillion (a trillion is a thousand billion, for those of you who missed that math class).

Most money market funds invest a small portion of their money in Treasuries soon to mature. Money funds also invest in short-term debt issued by government-run-and-sponsored agencies such as the Federal Home Loan Bank, which provides funds to the nation's savings and loans, and the Federal National Mortgage Association, which packages and sells government-backed mortgages.

TECHNICAL STUFF

Derivatives and money funds

Derivatives — high risk financial instruments, which I describe in Chapter 1 — are sometimes held in a money market fund in an attempt to pump up yield. If you stick with the better and larger money market funds that I recommend in this chapter, you needn't be concerned about derivatives. Otherwise, there's really no way to know if a particular money fund is playing with risky derivatives. Money fund managers I've talked to have said that even they can't tell from other money funds' annual reports whether those funds hold derivatives.

Historically, some managers didn't disclose derivative information because, until derivatives lost money for some investors in 1994, no one cared (or understood them). Today, responsible managers know people care, but some managers are still not disclosing — some may have something to hide. The SEC should be tougher and require greater uniformity of disclosure.

Government agency debt, unlike Treasuries, is not backed by the "full faith and credit of the U.S. government." However, no federal agency has ever defaulted on its debt. Although one should never say never, this situation is unlikely to ever happen; the folks back in Washington are certain to avoid the loss of faith in government-issued debt that would surely follow such a default.

As I discuss in more detail later in the chapter, some money market funds specialize in certain types of government securities which distribute tax-free income to their investors. Treasury money market funds, for example, buy Treasuries and pay dividends that are state tax-free, but federally taxable. State-specific municipal money market funds invest in debt issued by state and local governments in one state. The dividends on state money funds are federal and state tax-free (if you're a resident of that state).

Other types of securities

Other types of securities typically make up small portions of a money fund's holdings. *Repurchase agreements (repos)* are overnight investments that money funds send to *dealers* (banks and investment banks' securities divisions), and the money fund receives Treasury securities overnight as collateral.

Bankers' acceptances are more complex; they are issued by banks guaranteeing corporation debt incurred from trade. For example, if Sony sends televisions to the U.S. by freight but doesn't want to wait for its money until the ship comes in and stores pay them for the televisions, Sony can get paid right away by borrowing from a bank based on the expected delivery of the televisions. The stores get the televisions and pay for them, and then Sony's loan gets repaid.

Choosing a Great Money Fund

A money market is probably the easiest type of mutual fund to select. The downside to not making a good choice is not horrendous: You may lose out on some interest, be a little irritated by mediocre customer service, and need to fill out more paperwork later to access better mutual funds through other companies. To save you time and make you the most money, the following sections describe the major issues to consider in selecting the best money fund to meet your needs.

Money funds 20 percent off!

Some money market mutual funds aren't above resorting to the marketing tricks that retailers use. Beware of money fund managers running "specials" or "sales." They try to lure investors by temporarily waiving (also known as *absorbing*) operating expenses. These sales tricks create money fund yields that are a lot like muscles on steroids: artificially pumped up.

When the fund managers start thirsting for profits — and with time they will, because these aren't charities — they simply reinstate operating expenses, and then you can watch the air go out of the yield balloon. Some bond mutual funds (see Chapter 8) engage in this deceptive practice as well.

Unlike a retail purchase, the decision to invest in a money fund is usually a long-term proposition. Fund companies such as Dreyfus run sales because they know that a large portion of the fund buyers lured in won't bother leaving (or knowing) when the operating expenses are jacked up. Why the SEC allows this poor disclosure is beyond me.

To get the highest long-term yield from money funds, you're best off sticking with funds that maintain "everyday low prices" for operating expenses. You can ensure that your fund isn't running a special by asking what the current operating expense ratio is and whether the fund is waiving some portion of the expenses. You may also discern this status by checking the annual operating expense ratio in the fund's prospectus (see Chapter 4).

If you want to move your money to companies having specials and then move it back out when the special's over, you may come out a little ahead in your yield. If you have lots of money and don't mind paperwork, this strategy may be worth the bother. But don't forget the value of your time, lost interest when a check is in the mail, and the chance that you may not stay on top of the fund's expense changes.

Understanding why yield and expenses go hand-in-hand

Within a given category of money market fund (general, Treasury, municipal), money fund managers are investing in the same basic securities. The market for these securities is pretty darned efficient, so "superstar" money fund managers may eke out an extra 0.1 percent of yield over their competitors, but not much more.

However, money funds can differ significantly from one another in yield due to expenses. For money market funds more than for any other kind of fund, operating expenses are the single biggest determinant of return. All other conditions being equal (which they usually are with money market funds), lower operating expenses translate into higher yields for you.

TIP

For money market funds, you should not tolerate annual operating expenses greater than 0.5 percent. Top quality funds charge 0.25 percent or less annually.

Remember, lower expenses don't mean that a fund company is cutting corners or providing poor service. Lower expenses are possible in most cases because a fund company has been successful in attracting so much money to invest. As I discuss in Chapter 8, fund companies with consistently low expenses on their money funds also generally offer good bond funds.

Looking at your tax situation

You've probably heard the expression, "It's not what you make, it's what you keep." What you keep on your investment returns is what is left over after the federal and state governments take their cut of your investment profits. If you're investing money held outside of a retirement account and you're in a high tax bracket (particularly the federal 31 percent or higher bracket), you should come out ahead by investing in *tax-free* money market funds instead of taxable ones. If you're in a high-tax state, a state-specific money market fund, if a good one is available in your state, may be a sound move. (See recommended funds in the "Funding the best money market funds" section.)

Tax-free refers to the taxability of the dividends paid by the fund. Don't confuse term with the effective tax deductions you get on contributions to a retirement account such as a 401(k).

Deciding where you want your home base

Convenience is another important factor in choosing where to establish a money market fund. For example, if you're planning on investing in stock and bond mutual funds at T. Rowe Price, then that may be the best place for you to open up a money market fund as well. Although you may get a slightly higher money market yield from another fund company, opening up a separate account may not be worth the administrative hassle, especially if you don't plan on keeping much cash in the money fund.

TIP

If you don't mind the extra paperwork, why not net the extra yield? Calculate (based on the yield difference) the costs of keeping a lower-yielding money fund. Every tenth (0.1) of a percent per $10,000 invested costs you $10 in lost dividends annually.

TIP

Determining whether tax-free money market funds net you more

If you're in the federal 31 percent tax bracket (see the tax rate chart in Chapter 6), you will usually come out ahead in tax-free investments. If you're in the federal 28 percent tax bracket, you may or may not earn more in tax-free money funds. The only way to know is to crunch the numbers.

In order to do the comparison properly, factor in federal as well as state taxes. Suppose, for example, that you call Vanguard, which tells you that its Prime Portfolio money market fund currently yields 4.5 percent. The yield or dividend on this fund is fully taxable.

Suppose further that you are a resident of California and that Vanguard's California money market fund currently yields 3.0 percent. The California tax-free money market fund pays dividends that are free from federal *and* California state tax. Thus, you get to keep all 3.0 percent that you earn. The income you earn on the Prime Portfolio, on the other hand, is taxed. So here's how you compare the two:

yield on tax-free fund ÷ yield on taxable fund

.03 (3 percent) ÷ .045 (4.5 percent) = 0.67

In other words, the tax-free fund pays a yield of 67 percent of that on the taxable fund. Thus, if you must pay more than 33 percent (1 minus 0.67) in federal and California state tax, you net more in the tax-free fund.

If you do this analysis comparing some funds today, be aware that yields bounce around. The difference in yields between tax-free and taxable funds widens and narrows a bit over time.

Seeing eye to eye — keeping your investments close to home

Most mutual fund companies don't have many local branch offices. Generally, maintaining few offices helps fund companies keep their expenses low and their yields high. You may open and maintain your money market mutual fund through the fund's toll-free phone line and the mail.

Except for psychological security, selecting a fund company with an office in your area doesn't offer much benefit. But I don't want to downplay the importance of your emotional comfort level. Fund providers Fidelity and Schwab have the largest branch networks. Depending on where you live, you may be near one of the other fund companies I recommend (see the Appendix for locations).

Considering other issues

Most, but not all, money market funds offer other useful services, such as free check-writing privileges, fund exchange and redemption by telephone, and automated, electronic exchange services with your bank account. The fund companies I recommend generally offer all these features, so these shouldn't be a deciding factor when debating among fund options.

As I mention earlier in this chapter, most money market funds require that you write checks for at least $250 or $500. Some funds don't have this restriction, which may be important to you if you want to pay smaller bills out of the account.

Another potentially important issue is the initial minimum investment required to open an account. Most funds require a minimum investment of $3,000 or so, although some require heftier amounts. If you drop below the minimum at most money market funds, it's no big deal and no charge is assessed. Some money funds do, however, charge small fees for use of certain features. I discuss these fees in the next section.

Finding the best money market funds

Using the criteria I just discussed, in this section I recommend the best money market funds: those that offer competitive yields, check writing, access to other excellent mutual funds, and other commonly needed money market services. Vanguard funds predominate the list because they offer rock-bottom expenses as well as most of the other goodies.

Taxable money market funds

Money market funds that pay taxable dividends are appropriate for retirement account funds awaiting investment as well as non-retirement account money when you're not in a high federal tax bracket (less than 31 percent federal) *and* not in a high state tax bracket (less than 5 percent). Here are the best taxable money market funds to consider. (Call the fund companies for current yields.)

Vanguard's Money Market Reserves Prime Portfolio has a microscopic operating expense ratio of 0.3 percent per year. Like most Vanguard funds, it requires $3,000 to open for a non-retirement account ($1,000 for a retirement account) and allows check writing in amounts greater than $250. ☎ 800-662-7447.

Fidelity's Spartan Money Market has a much higher initial investment minimum than Vanguard's: $20,000 for non-retirement accounts, $10,000 for retirement accounts. Its expense ratio is 0.5 percent. Fidelity Spartan money funds charge $2 per check written, $5 for a redemption, exchange, or closing of the account. These fees are waived if your balance is greater than $50,000. If you're seeking maximum money market returns and don't keep big balances, Vanguard's a better choice. ☎ 800-544-8888.

If you can't afford Spartan's high minimums, Fidelity has other taxable fund options for the proletariat: only a $2,500 minimum initial investment for **Fidelity Cash Reserves** and a $5,000 minimum for **Fidelity Daily Income Trust.** Both funds have an operating expense ratio of 0.5 percent. The check writing minimum for the Cash Reserves fund is $500. Daily Income Trust, on the other hand, has no minimum check amount requirement, but it does charge $1 per check for amounts under $500.

If you're doing the bulk of your investing through a fund company other than heavyweights Vanguard or Fidelity, it's your call whether or not you should do your money fund investing there as well. USAA offers competitive yields. Its taxable money market fund, **USAA Mutual Money Market,** has an annual operating expense ratio of 0.5 percent, a $3,000 minimum initial investment for all types of accounts, and check writing for amounts above $250. ☎ 800-382-8722. **T. Rowe Price Summit Cash Reserves** has a minimum initial investment of $25,000, an expense ratio of 0.5 percent per year, and check writing for amounts of $500 or more. ☎ 800-638-5660.

Looking at discount brokerage accounts, **Schwab Value Advantage Money Market** also has a high minimum: $25,000 for non-retirement accounts, $15,000 for retirement accounts. Its expense ratio is 0.4 percent. A $5 fee is assessed in any month in which the balance drops below $20,000 for non-retirement accounts and $15,000 for retirement accounts. ☎ 800-435-4000.

If you want to use Schwab but don't have big bucks, consider the **Schwab Money Market.** It has a minimum initial investment amount of $1,000 for non-retirement accounts, but it weighs in with a hefty 0.8 percent annual operating expense ratio. If you're using Schwab for discount brokerage services, this is your main option for money awaiting investment; given its high expenses, I'd keep as little money in this fund as possible.

If you use **Jack White** for your discount brokerage services, be advised that its money market fund offerings are terrible. The taxable **Alliance Capital Reserves** has an outrageous 1.00 percent annual operating fee. If you use White to take advantage of the lower transaction fees its mutual fund service offers (which I describe in Chapter 5), keep your money market balance to the absolute minimum.

Money fund options in "all-in-one" discount brokerage accounts

As I discuss in Chapter 5, discount brokers such as Schwab and Fidelity have developed "all-in-one" accounts that combine unlimited check writing with investing. These accounts can certainly reduce the paperwork in your life: Everything from your monthly utility bills to your mutual fund holdings is consolidated on one account statement.

These accounts are usually built around some kind of "hub," a temporary holding place for the money that is waiting to be either spent or invested. This is the part of the account you can write checks against, take dividends into, and purchase investments with. You are usually given an option on how you want to hold this hub money. Look at your options carefully, and don't make the mistake of leaving your money in the default option.

For example, Fidelity's all-in-one brokerage account, called the Ultra Service Account, calls the hub your "core account." Your first option for the core account is to keep it in cash. Although you do earn interest on it, that interest is fully taxable and offers a much lower yield than you would get from a taxable money market fund.

Especially if you're in a higher tax bracket, the better choice is to use the Fidelity Municipal Money Market fund, the dividends on which are free of federal tax. You also have the option to put your cash in a state specific money market fund if you happen to live in a state for which Fidelity has such a fund: This strategy will shield your dividends from state as well as federal taxes.

You are not limited to the options Fidelity gives you. As a Fidelity account holder, you're perfectly welcome to invest money in any of Fidelity's money market offerings (such as the ones I discuss earlier in this chapter) through an Ultra Service Account. Of course, money funds outside of the Ultra Service Account's core options don't give you features such as unlimited check writing, but you may be able to get a higher yield. You can always keep a small amount of money in one of the core options to cover any check writing needs.

U.S. Treasury money market funds

U.S. Treasury money market funds are appropriate if you're not in a high federal tax bracket (less than 31 percent) but *are* in a high state tax bracket (5 percent or higher).

Vanguard Money Market Reserves U.S. Treasury Portfolio has a $3,000 minimum and 0.3 percent operating expense ratio. For big-balance investors who can handle the $50,000 minimum initial investment requirement, **Vanguard's Admiral U.S. Treasury Money Market Portfolio** offers a higher yield, thanks to this fund's 0.15 percent annual expense ratio. ☎ 800-662-7447.

ERIC'S PICKS

The **American Century** fund family has two U.S. government money market funds — **American Century Benham Capital Preservation,** with an expense ratio of 0.5 percent, and **Benham Government Agency,** with an expense ratio of 0.5 percent. You need a $2,500 minimum initial investment for both funds. ☎ 800-345-2021.

USAA's Treasury Money Market has a 0.4 percent operating cost and a $3,000 minimum initial investment. ☎ 800-345-2021.

Fidelity's Spartan U.S. Treasury Money Market has an expense ratio of 0.5 percent. This fund's minimum initial investment is $20,000 for non-retirement accounts. Fidelity Spartan money funds charge $2 per check written and $5 for a redemption, exchange, or closing of the account. These fees are waived if your balance is greater than $50,000. So if you're seeking maximum money market returns and don't keep big balances, use Vanguard. ☎ 800-544-8888.

TIP

You can bypass Treasury money market funds and their operating fees by purchasing Treasury bills directly from your local Federal Reserve bank for no fee. Although you save yourself expenses by going this route, you lose convenient access to your money. You have no check writing privileges; if you need to tap the Treasuries before they mature, it's a bit of an administrative hassle and will cost you a brokerage fee. With Vanguard's expense ratios on their Treasury money funds, it's "costing" you $30 per year with a $10,000 balance; $75 per year with a $50,000 balance in Admiral.

Municipal tax-free money market funds

Municipal (also known as muni) money market funds invest in short-term debt issued by state and local governments. All municipal money funds are free of federal taxes. Those investors who limit their investing to just one state are free of state taxes as well (provided you live in that state). So if you live in New York and buy a New York municipal bond fund, you shouldn't have to pay any tax, state or federal, on your dividends.

Obviously, you're saying to yourself, state-specific muni funds are the way to go. Well, not for everybody. You may not have to worry about shielding your dividends from state taxes if you live in a state that meets any of the following criteria:

- Doesn't impose any income tax, such as Florida (you lucky dog)
- Charges a lower income tax (less than 5 percent), such as Indiana
- Has a higher income tax but no decent state-specific money market funds to invest in

If you live in any of those states and if you're in a high federal tax bracket (31 percent and up), you're likely best off with one of the following national money market funds, whose dividends are free of federal but not state tax. (Call the fund companies for current yields.)

Vanguard Municipal Money Market has a 0.2 percent annual expense ratio and requires a $3,000 minimum initial investment to open. ☎ 800-662-7447.

Fidelity Spartan Municipal Money Market has a 0.5 percent annual expense ratio and requires a $25,000 minimum initial investment to open. Fidelity Spartan money funds charge $2 per check written and $5 for a redemption, exchange, or closing of the account. These fees are waived if your balance is greater than $50,000. (If you're seeking maximum money market returns and don't keep big balances, use Vanguard.) ☎ 800-544-8888.

USAA Tax-Exempt Money Market, has a 0.4 percent annual expense ratio and requires a $3,000 minimum initial investment to open. ☎ 800-382-8722.

The state-specific money market funds in Table 7-1, whose dividends are free of both federal and state taxes if you live in the specified state, are appropriate when you're in a high federal (31 percent and up) *and* a high state tax bracket (5 percent or higher). If none is listed for your state, or you're only in a high federal tax bracket, remember that you need to use one of the nationwide muni money markets just described.

Table 7-1 State and Federally Tax-Free Money Market Funds

Fund	*Operating Expense*	*Minimum to Open*
Fidelity Spartan AZ Muni Money Market	0.5%	$25,000
USAA Tax-Exempt CA Money Market	0.4%	$ 3,000
Vanguard CA Tax-Free Money Market	0.2%	$ 3,000
Fidelity Spartan CA Muni Money Market	0.5%	$25,000
American Century–Benham CA Tax-Free Money Market	0.5%	$2,500
Fidelity Spartan FL Muni Money Market	0.5%	$25,000
USAA Tax-Exempt FL Money Market	0.5%	$ 3,000
Fidelity Spartan MA Muni Money Market	0.5%	$25,000
Fidelity Spartan NJ Muni Money Market	0.5%	$25,000

(continued)

Table 7-1 *(continued)*

Fund	*Operating Expense*	*Minimum to Open*
Vanguard NJ Tax-Free Money Market	0.2%	$ 3,000
Fidelity Spartan NY Muni Tax-Free Money Market	0.5%	$25,000
Vanguard NY Tax-Free Money Market	0.2%	$ 3,000
USAA Tax-Exempt NY Money Market	0.5%	$ 3,000
Vanguard OH Tax-Free Money Market	0.2%	$ 3,000
Vanguard PA Tax-Free Money Market	0.2%	$ 3,000
Fidelity Spartan PA Muni Money Market	0.5%	$25,000
USAA Tax Exempt TX Money Market	0.5%	$ 3,000
USAA Tax-Exempt VA Money Market	0.5%	$ 3,000

If you're filling out an application for any kind of municipal money market fund, make sure that the application specifically states that you are investing in a *money market* fund. If you're doing an exchange over the phone, be sure that you say *money market* (and that the telephone representative gets it)! Otherwise, you may end up in a municipal bond fund (which I discuss in the next chapter) that fluctuates in value and is intended as a longer-term investment. See Chapter 11 for how to complete application forms correctly.

Chapter 8

Bond Funds — When Boring Is Beautiful

In This Chapter

- Understanding how bond funds differ from one another
- Knowing when and why to invest in bond funds
- Selecting short-, intermediate-, and long-term bonds
- Considering CDs, GICs, and other alternatives to bond funds

Many investors, both novice and expert, think that the "b" in bonds is for boring. And they're partly correct. No one gets excited by bonds — unless they're an investment banker or broker who deals in and makes fat paychecks from them.

But you should take the time to learn about bonds. They may seem boring, but they offer higher yields than bank accounts without subjecting you to the amount of volatility that stocks do.

So what the heck is a bond? Let me try to explain with an analogy. If a money market fund is like a savings account, then a bond is similar to a certificate of deposit (CD). With a five-year CD, for example, a bank agrees to pay you a predetermined annual rate of interest — such as, say, 6 percent. If all goes according to plan, at the end of five years of earning the 6 percent interest, you get back the principal that you originally invested. (Actually, the bank will likely send you a form letter just days before your CD is due to mature. The letter will announce that if the bank doesn't hear from you very soon, it'll roll your CD over "for your convenience"!)

Bonds work about the same way, only instead of being issued by banks, they're issued by corporations or governments. For example, you can purchase a bond, scheduled to mature five years from now, from a company such as computer software giant Microsoft. A Microsoft five-year bond may pay you, oh, 7 percent. As long as Microsoft doesn't have a financial catastrophe, after five years of receiving interest payments (also known as the *coupon rate*) on the bond, Microsoft will return your original investment to you. (***Note:*** *Zero coupon* bonds pay no interest but are sold at a discounted price to make up for it.)

The worst that can happen to your bond investment is that, if Microsoft's newest software were to devour the hard drives in users' computers, causing Microsoft to suffocate under a class-action lawsuit and file bankruptcy, then you may not get back *any* of your original investment, let alone the remaining interest.

For several important reasons, though, you shouldn't let this unlikely but plausible scenario scare you away from bonds:

- **Bonds can be safer than you think — many companies need to borrow money (issue bonds) and are good credit risks.** If you own bonds in enough companies — say, in several hundred of them — if one or even a few of them unexpectedly take a fall, their default would affect only a sliver of your portfolio and wouldn't be a financial catastrophe. This is what a bond mutual fund and its management team can provide for you: a diversified portfolio of many bonds.
- **You'll be rewarded with higher interest rates than comparable bank investments.** The financial markets and those who participate in them — people like you and me — aren't dumb. If you take extra risk and forsake FDIC insurance, you should receive a higher rate of interest investing in bonds. Guess what? All the Nervous Nellie savers who are comforted by the executive desks, the vault, the guard in the lobby, and the FDIC insurance logo at their local bank should remember that they're being paid less interest at the bank because of all of those "comforts."

  If you like the government backing afforded by the FDIC program, you can replicate that protection in bond mutual funds that specialize in government-backed securities. (See the section, "Recommended Bond Funds," later in this chapter.)
- **Bond alternatives aren't as safe as you might like to believe.** Any investment that involves lending your money to someone else or to some organization carries risk. That includes putting your money into a bank or buying a Treasury bond issued by the federal government. (Although I'm not a doomsayer, any student of history knows that governments and civilizations fail. It's not a matter of whether they will fail; it's a question of when.) In the last section of this chapter, I discuss some potentially higher-yield alternatives to investing in bond funds. You will see that with those higher yields comes far greater risk. There's no free lunch in the investing world.

Sizing Up a Bond Fund's Personality

Bond funds aren't as complicated and unique as people, but they're certainly more complex than money market funds. And, thanks to some shady marketing practices by some mutual fund companies and some salespeople who sell funds, you have your work cut out for you in getting a handle on what many bond funds really are investing in and how they differ from their peers. But don't worry: I take the time to explain the good funds that I recommend later in this chapter.

Maturity: Bonds act their age

In everyday conversation, *maturity* refers to that quiet, blessed state of grace and wisdom that we all develop as we get older (ahem). But that's not the kind of maturity I'm talking about here. Maturity, as it applies to bonds, simply means: When does the bond pay you back — next year, five years from now, 30 years from now, or longer? Maturity is the most important variable by which bond funds are differentiated and categorized.

You should care *plenty* about how long a bond takes to mature. Why? Because a bond's maturity gives you a good (although far from perfect) sense of how volatile a bond will be if interest rates change (see Table 8-1). If interest rates fall, bond prices rise. See Chapter 1 for an explanation of why interest rates and bond prices move in opposite directions.

Table 8-1 Interest Rate Increases Depress Bond Prices

Price Changes of Bonds of Differing Maturities	***If Rates Were to Suddenly Rise 1 Percent****
Short-term bond (2-year maturity)	–2%
Intermediate-term bond (7-year maturity)	–5%
Long-term bond (20-year maturity)	–10%

*Assumes that bonds are yielding approximately 7 percent. If bonds were assumed to be yielding more, then a 1 percent increase in interest rates would have less of an impact. For example, if interest rates are at 10 percent and rise to 11 percent, the price change of the 20-year bond is –8 percent.

Bond funds are portfolios of dozens — and in some cases hundreds — of individual bonds. You won't want to know the maturity of *every* bond in a bond mutual fund. A useful summarizing statistic to know for a bond fund is the *average maturity* of its bonds. In their marketing literature and prospectuses, bond funds typically say something like, "The Turbocharged Intermediate-Term Bond fund invests in high-quality bonds with an average maturity of 7 to 12 years."

Bond funds usually lump themselves into one of these three maturity categories:

- **Short-term bond funds** concentrate their investments in bonds maturing in the next few years.
- **Intermediate-term bond funds** generally hold bonds that typically come due within seven to ten years.
- **Long-term bond funds** usually hold bonds that typically mature in 15 to 20 years or so.

These definitions are not hard and fast. One "long-term" bond fund may have an average maturity of 14 years while another has an average of 25 years.

Now, you may be wondering why only three categories? Why not five? Or a dozen? I'm suspicious that it's a conspiracy on the part of all the bond fund companies that have less-than-stellar bond funds; there are more than a few of those! With so few maturity categories, potential fund investors may not be sure that they're comparing funds of the same type. For example, one bond fund has an average maturity of seven years and another has a maturity of 12 years, but both call themselves "intermediate-term." However, a five-year difference in maturity generally translates into a significant difference in interest rates and risk.

You run into problems when one "intermediate-term" fund starts bragging that its returns are better than another's. When you learn that the braggart fund has an average maturity of 12 years and the other fund has a maturity of 7, then you know that the 12-year fund is using the "intermediate-term" label to make misleading comparisons. The fact is, a fund with bonds maturing on average in 12 years *should* be generating higher returns than a fund with bonds maturing on average in 7 years. As a tradeoff, the 12-year fund is also more volatile when interest rates change.

TIP

So much for maturity and average maturities. If you're trying to determine the sensitivity of bonds and bond funds to changes in interest rates, *duration* may be a more useful statistic. A duration of ten years implies that if interest rates rise by 1 percent, then the value of the bond fund should drop by 10 percent. (Conversely, if rates fall 1 percent, the fund should rise 10 percent.)

Trying to use average maturities to determine what impact a 1 percent rise or fall in interest rates will have on bond prices forces you to slog through all sorts of ugly calculations. Duration gives you no fuss, no muss — and it gives you one big plus, too. Besides saving on number crunching, duration enables you to compare funds of differing maturities. If a long-term bond fund has a duration of, say, 12 years, and an intermediate fund has a duration of 6 years, then the long-term fund should be about twice as volatile to changes in interest rates.

Okay, if duration is easier to work with *and* a better indicator than average maturity, why do so many financial types talk about average maturity so much? Simply because average maturity is easier for most people to comprehend. A fund's duration isn't that easy to understand. Mathematically, it represents the point at which a bondholder receives half (50 percent) of the present value of her total expected payments (interest plus payoff of principal at maturity) from a bond. Present value adjusts future payments to reflect changes in the cost of living.

If you know a bond fund's duration, you know almost all you need to know about its sensitivity to interest rates. However, duration hasn't been a foolproof indicator; some funds have dropped more as interest rates have risen than the funds' durations predicted. But bear in mind that some heavy investing in unusual securities (such as derivatives) was required to make duration unreliable — so the duration values of the better funds, which I recommend in this chapter, should work just fine as a guide. Also be aware that other factors — such as changes in the credit quality of the bonds in a fund — may affect the price changes of a bond fund over time.

Credit quality: Would you lend them your money?

Bond funds also differ from one another in terms of the creditworthiness of the bonds that they hold. That's just a fancy way of saying, "Hey, are they gonna stiff me or what?"

Every year, bondholders get left holding nothing but the bag for billions of dollars when the bonds they own default. So what should you do? Common sense suggests that you purchase bonds that are unlikely to default, otherwise known as high-credit-quality bonds. Credit rating agencies exist — Moody's, Standard & Poor's, Duff & Phelps, and so on — that do nothing except rate bonds based on credit quality and likelihood of default.

The credit rating of a security depends on the company's (or the government entity's) ability to pay back its debt. Bond credit ratings are usually done on some sort of a letter-grade scale: AAA is the highest rating, with ratings descending through AA and A, followed by BBB, BB, B, CCC, CC, C, and so on.

Funds that mostly invest in

- **AAA and AA rated bonds** are considered a high-grade or high-credit-quality bond fund; this type of fund's bonds have little chance of default.
- **A and BBB rated bonds** are considered a general bond fund (moderate-credit-quality).

- **BB or lower rated bonds** are known as junk bond funds (or by their more marketable name, *high-yield* funds). These funds expect to suffer more defaults — perhaps as many as a couple of percent of the total value of the bonds per year.

REMEMBER

Lower-quality bonds are able to attract bond investors by paying them a higher interest rate. The lower the credit quality of a fund's holdings, the higher the yield you can expect a fund to pay.

Issuer: Who's doing the borrowing?

In addition to their credit ratings, bonds differ from each other according to which type of organization is issuing them — that is, according to which kind of organization you're lending your money to. Here are the major options:

- **Treasuries.** These are IOUs from the biggest debtor of them all, the U.S. federal government. Treasuries include Treasury bills (which mature within a year), Treasury notes (which mature between one and ten years), and Treasury bonds (which mature in more than ten years). All Treasuries pay interest that is state tax-free but federally taxable.
- **Municipals.** *Munis* are state and local government bonds that pay interest that's federally tax-free and state tax-free to those who reside in the state of issue. The governments that issue municipal bonds know that the investors who buy municipals don't have to pay most or any of the income tax that normally would be required on other bonds — which means that the issuing governments can get away with paying a lower rate of interest. Later in this chapter (in the section, "To muni or not to muni?"), I explain how to determine if you're in a high enough tax bracket to benefit from muni bonds.
- **Corporates.** Issued by companies such as Microsoft and Toys"R"Us, corporate bonds pay interest that's fully taxable.
- **Mortgages.** You remember that mortgage you took out when you purchased a home? Well, you can actually get back some of the interest you're paying on that mortgage by purchasing a bond fund that holds it! Yes, some bonds funds specialize in buying mortgages and collecting the interest payments. Strange concept isn't it, buying a mortgage? The repayment of principal on these bonds is usually guaranteed at the bond's maturity by a government agency such as the Government National Mortgage Association (GNMA, or Ginnie Mae — cute, huh?) or the Federal National Mortgage Association (FNMA, or Fannie Mae — what cuteness *won't* our government think of next!).
- **Convertibles.** These are hybrid securities, bonds that you can convert into a preset number of shares of stock in the company that issued the bond. Although these bonds do pay interest, their yield is lower than non-convertible bonds because convertibles offer you the upside potential of being able to make more money if the underlying stock rises.

- **International bonds.** Most of the preceding bonds can be bought from foreign issuers as well. In fact, international corporate and government bonds are the primary bonds that foreign bond mutual funds may hold. International bonds are riskier because their interest payments can be offset by currency price changes.

So now you know four *very* important facts about bond funds: You know about maturity, credit rating, and the different entities that issue bonds (and, therefore, the tax consequences on those bonds). Now you can put the four together to understand how mutual fund outfits came up with so many different types of bond funds. For example, you can buy a corporate intermediate-term high yield (junk) bond fund, or a long-term municipal bond fund. As you can see, the combinations are endless.

Management: Passive or active?

Some bond funds are managed like an airplane on autopilot. They stick to investing in a particular type of bond (such as high-grade corporate), with a target maturity (for example, an average of ten years). Index funds that invest in a relatively fixed basket of bonds — so as to track a market index of bond prices — are a good example of this passive approach.

At the other end of the spectrum are aggressively managed funds. Managers of these funds have significant freedom to purchase bonds that they think will perform best in the future. For example, if a fund manager thinks that interest rates will rise, he'll buy shorter-term bonds (remember that shorter-term bonds are less sensitive to interest rate changes than longer-term bonds) and keep more of a fund's assets in cash. The fund manager may be willing to invest more in lower-credit-quality bonds if he thinks that the economy is going to improve and that more companies will prosper and improve their credit standing.

Aggressively managed funds gamble. If interest rates fall instead of rise, the fund manager who moved into shorter-term bonds and cash suffers worse performance. If interest rates fall because the economy sinks into recession, lower-credit-quality bonds will suffer from a higher default rate and depress the fund's performance even further.

Some people think that it's fairly easy to predict which direction interest rates or the economy is heading. The truth is that economic predictions are *difficult*. In fact, over long periods of time (10+ years), meaningful predictions are almost impossible. In 1993, for example, few investors expected interest rates to plummet as far as they did. On the highest-quality bonds, short-term interest rates plunged to 3 percent, long-term rates to under 6 percent. A few figured that this was the bottom. But then almost no one expected rates to rise as high as they did over the next year as short-term and long-term rates grew about 3 percent by late 1994. The few who figured that this rise was going to happen were largely a different group than those who guessed right in 1993.

Investing some of your bond fund money in funds that try to be well positioned for changes in the economy and interest rates may be a good move. But remember that, if these fund managers are wrong, you can lose more money. Over the long-term, you'll do best in efficiently managed funds that stick with an investment objective — such as holding intermediate-term, high-quality bonds — and that don't try to time and predict the bond market. If you or a bond fund manager consistently knew which way interest rates were headed, you could make a fortune trading interest-rate futures that leverage your investment. But none of us can know — so don't even try!

Trying to beat the market can lead to getting beaten. In recent years, increasing numbers of bond funds have fallen on their faces after risky investing strategies backfired (see Chapter 4). Interestingly, bond funds that charge sales commissions (loads) and higher ongoing operating fees are the ones more likely to have blow-ups. This trend may be because these fund managers are under more pressure to try and pump up returns to make up for these higher fees.

Investing in Bond Funds

Now that you know a fair amount about bonds and bond funds and how they differ, it's time to get down to how and why you might use bonds. Bonds may be boring, but they can be more profitable for you than super-boring bank savings accounts and money market funds. Bonds pay more than these investments because they involve more risk: You're purchasing an investment that is meant to be held for a longer period of time relative to savings accounts and money market funds.

That doesn't mean that you have to hold a bond until it matures, because there is an active market for them — the bond market — where you can sell your bond to someone else (which is exactly what a bond fund manager does for you if you want out of your bond fund). You may receive more — or less — for the bond than you paid for it depending on what has happened in the financial markets since then.

As I discuss earlier in this chapter (in the section, "Maturity: Bonds act their age"), bond funds are riskier than money market funds and savings accounts because their value can fall if interest rates rise. However, bonds tend to be more stable in value than stocks (see Chapter 1).

Bond fund uses and abuses

Investing in bonds is a time-honored way to earn a better rate of return on money that you don't plan to use within the next couple of years. As with other mutual funds, bond funds are completely liquid on a day's notice, but I advise you to view them as longer-term investments. Because their value fluctuates, you're more likely to lose money if you are forced to sell the bond fund sooner rather than later. In the short-term, the bond market can bounce every which way; in the longer-term, you're more likely to receive your money back with interest.

Don't invest your emergency money in bond funds — that's what a money fund is for (see Chapter 7). You will get less money from a bond fund (and could even lose money) if you need it in an emergency. Avoid using the check-writing option that comes with many bond funds. Every time you sell shares (which is what you're doing when you write a check) in a bond fund, this transaction must be reported on your annual income tax return. When you write a check on a money market fund, by contrast, that is not a so-called *taxable event* because a money fund has a fixed share price, so you're not considered to be adding to or subtracting from your income.

You also shouldn't put too much of your longer-term investment money in bond funds. With the exception of those rare periods when interest rates drop significantly, bond funds won't produce the high returns that growth-oriented investments such as stocks, real estate, and your own business can.

Here are some common financial goals to which bond funds are well-suited:

- **A major purchase** that won't happen for at least two years, such as the purchase of a home. Short-term bond funds should offer a higher yield than money market funds. However, bond funds are a bit riskier, which is why you should have at least two years until you need the money to allow time for recovery from a dip in your bond fund account value.
- **Part of a long-term, diversified portfolio.** Because stocks and bonds don't move in tandem, bonds are a great way to hedge against downswings in the stock market. In fact, in a terrible economic environment such as the Great Depression, bonds may appreciate in value if inflation is declining. In Chapter 6, where I talk about asset allocation, I explain how to incorporate bonds into long-term portfolios for goals such as retirement.
- **Generating current income.** If you're retired or not working, bonds are better than most other investments for producing a current income stream.

Aren't higher interest rates better if I need income?

In late 1993, after a multiyear plunge, interest rates were at what seemed like rock-bottom levels compared to those of the previous decade. High-quality, short-term bonds of six months were paying 3.5 percent; intermediate-term bonds were yielding around 5 percent; and long-term bonds were paying about 6 percent. These rates represented less than half of what rates had been a decade earlier.

Generally speaking, lower interest rates are great for the economy because they encourage consumers and businesses to borrow and spend more money. But if you were a retiree trying to live off the income being produced by your bonds, low interest rates seemed like the worst of all possible economic worlds.

For each $100,000 that a retiree invested in intermediate-term bonds, CDs, or whatever when interest rates were 10 percent, the retiree received $10,000 per year in interest or dividends. A retiree purchasing intermediate-term bonds in fall 1993, however, received 50 percent less dividend income because rates on the same bonds and CDs were just 5 percent. So for every $100,000 invested, only $5,000 in dividend or interest income was paid.

If you're trying to live off the income being produced by your investments, a 50 percent reduction in that income may cramp your lifestyle. So higher interest rates are better if you're living off your investment income, right? Wrong!

Never forget that the primary driver of interest rates is the rate of inflation. Interest rates were much higher in the early 1980s because the United States had double-digit inflation. If the cost of living was increasing at the rate of 10 percent per year, why would you as an investor lend your money out (which is what you're doing when you purchase a bond or CD) at 5 percent? Of course, you *wouldn't* lend money at that rate — which is exactly why interest rates were so high in the early 1980s.

In late 1993, interest rates were so low because the inflation dragon seemed to have been slain. So the rate of interest that investors could earn by lending their money dropped accordingly. Although low interest rates reduce the interest income, the corresponding low rate of inflation doesn't devour the purchasing power of your principal balance as quickly.

So what's an investor to do if she lives off the income from her investments but can't generate enough income because present interest rates are too low? A financially simple but psychologically difficult solution is to use up some of the principal to supplement the interest and dividend income. In effect, this is what happens anyway when inflation is higher — the purchasing power of the principal erodes more quickly.

I'm gonna make how much?

When comparing bonds funds of a given type (for example, high-quality, short-term corporate bond funds), most people want to pick the one that's going to make the most money for them. But be careful; your desire for high returns is easily exploited by mutual fund companies. They love to lure you into a bond fund by emphasizing high past performance and current yield, deflecting your attention away from the best predictor of bond fund performance: operating expenses.

Don't overemphasize past performance

The first mistake novice bond fund investors make is to look at recent performance and assume that those are the returns they're going to get in the future. Investing in bond funds based only on recent performance is tempting right after a period when interest rates have declined, because declines in interest rates pump up bond fund total returns. Remember that an equal but opposite force is waiting to counteract pumped-up bond returns — bond prices fall when interest rates rise, which they eventually will.

Don't get me wrong: Past performance is an important issue to consider. But in order for performance numbers to be meaningful and useful, you must compare the same type of bond funds to each other (such as intermediate-term funds that invest exclusively in high-grade corporate bonds) and against the correct bond market index or benchmark (which I discuss in Chapter 12).

Be careful with "current yield" quotes

A fund's *yield* measures how much the fund is currently paying in dividends; it is quoted as a percentage of the fund's share price: say, 6.4 percent. This statistic certainly seems like a valid one for comparing funds. Unfortunately, it has been abusively exploited by some fund companies.

Don't confuse a bond fund's yield with its return. Dividends are just one part of a fund's return, which includes capital gain distributions as well as changes in the bond fund's share price. Over a given period of time, a bond fund could have a positive yield but a negative overall return.

Some unscrupulous fund companies try to obscure the difference between yield and return. *Forbes* magazine once reported on an advertisement sent out by the Fundamental U.S. Government Strategic Income Fund. In huge type on the cover of this brochure, the fund boasted of its 11.66 percent yield, an impressive number because the 30-year Treasury bonds were yielding less than 8 percent at the time. One can only assume that the designers of this promo piece hoped that you wouldn't check out the back cover, where the small print stated that the fund's overall return for the previous year was negative 15.7 percent.

Bond funds and the mutual fund companies that sell them can play more than a few games of creative accounting to fatten a fund's yield. Such sleight of hand makes a fund's marketing and advertising departments happy because higher yields make hawking the bond funds easier for the salespeople. But always remember that yield-enhancing shenanigans can leave you poorer. Here's what to watch out for:

- **Lower quality.** You may compare one short-term bond fund to another and discover that one pays 0.5 percent more and therefore looks better. However, if you look a little further, you discover that the higher-yielding fund invests 20 percent of its assets in junk bonds (a BB or less credit-quality rating), whereas the other fund is fully invested in high-quality bonds (AAA and AA rated). In other words, the junk bond fund is not necessarily better; given the risk it's taking, it should be yielding more.
- **Lengthened maturities.** Bond funds can usually increase their yield just by increasing maturity a bit. (Insiders call this gambit *going further out on the yield curve.*) So when comparing yields on different bond funds, be sure that you're comparing them for funds of similar maturity. Even if they both call themselves "intermediate-term," if one bond fund invests in bonds maturing on average in seven years, while another fund is at ten years for its average maturity, comparing the two is a classic case of comparing apples to oranges. Because longer-term bonds usually have higher yields (due to increased risk), the ten year average maturity fund should yield more than the seven year average maturity fund.
- **Giving your money back without your knowledge.** Some funds return a portion of your principal in the form of dividends. This move artificially pumps up a fund's yield but depresses its total return. Investors in this type of bond fund are rudely awakened when, after enjoying a healthy yield for a period of time, they examine the share price of their bond fund shares and find that they are worth less than they paid for them.

  When you compare bond funds to each other by using the information in the prospectuses, make sure that you compare their total return over time (in addition to making sure that the funds have comparable portfolios of bonds and durations).
- **Waiving of expenses.** Some bond funds, particularly newer ones, waive a portion or even all their operating expenses to temporarily inflate the fund's yield. Yes, you *can* invest in a fund that is having a sale on its operating fees, but you also buy yourself the bother of having to monitor the fund to determine when the sale is over. Bond funds engaging in this practice often end sales quietly when the bond market is doing well. Don't forget that if you sell a bond fund (held outside of a retirement account) that has appreciated in value, you owe taxes on your profits.

Do focus on costs

Like money market funds, bond fund returns are extremely sensitive to costs. After you've identified a particular type of bond fund to invest in, expenses should be your number one criterion for comparing funds.

TIP

For bond funds, do not tolerate operating expenses higher than 0.5 percent. Amazingly, about half of the thousands of bond funds charge more than 1 percent annually.

Like money market investments, the market for bonds is very efficient. For any two bond managers investing in a particular bond type — say long-term municipal bonds — picking bonds that outperform the other's over time is difficult. But if one of those bond funds charges lower fees than the other, that difference provides the low fee fund with a big head start in the performance race.

REMEMBER

You can earn a higher yield from a bond fund in one of three major ways: by investing in funds that

- Hold longer-term bonds
- Hold lower-credit-quality bonds
- Have lower operating expenses

TIP

After you've settled on the type of bonds you want, a bond fund's costs — its sales commissions and annual operating fees — are a huge consideration. Stick with no-load funds that have lower annual operating expenses.

How bond funds calculate their yields

When you ask a mutual fund company for a fund's current yield, make sure that you understand the time period the yield covers.

Fund companies are supposed to report the *SEC yield,* which is a standard yield calculation that allows for fairer comparisons among bond funds. The SEC yield reflects the bond fund's so-called *yield to maturity.* This is the best yield to use when you compare funds because it captures the effective rate of interest an investor will receive looking forward.

Funds also calculate a *current yield,* which only looks at the recently distributed dividends relative to the share price of the fund. Funds can pump up this number by purchasing particular types of bonds. For just that reason, current yield is not nearly as useful a yield number to look at (although brokers who sell funds love to use it because it makes some funds look better than they really are).

Where does a bond fall on the yield curve?

Higher yields compensate you for taking more risk. Earlier in the chapter, I show you the greater risk of longer-term bonds, which suffer price declines greater than do short-term bonds when rates rise.

Most of the time, longer-term bonds pay higher yields than do short-term bonds. You can look at a chart of the current yield of bonds plotted against when they mature. This type of chart is known as a *yield curve*. Most of the time, this curve slopes upward (see Figure 8-1). Most financial newspapers and magazines carry a current chart of the yield curve.

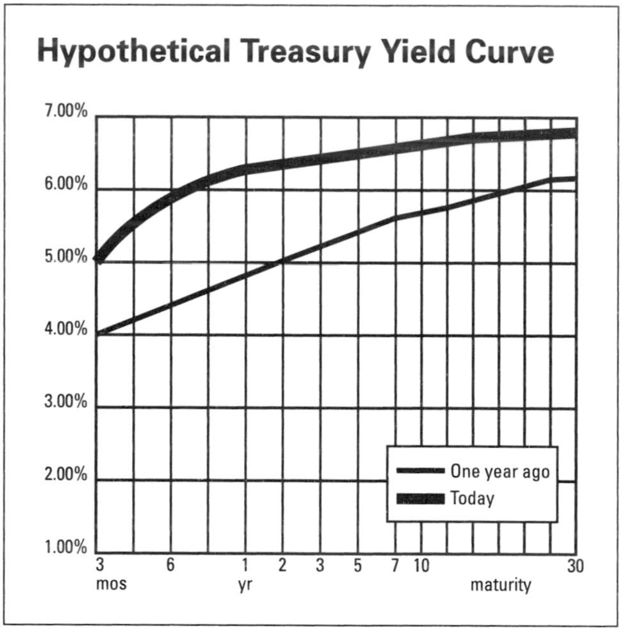

Figure 8-1: A yield curve chart.

To muni or not to muni?

Just as money market funds can produce taxable or tax-free dividends, so too can bond funds. In order to produce tax-free income, a bond fund must invest in municipal bonds (also called muni bonds or munis) issued by state or local governments.

As long as you live in the United States, municipal bond funds are federally tax-free to you. Funds that specialize in muni bonds issued just in your state pay dividend income that's free of your state's taxes as well.

TIP If you're in a high tax bracket (31 percent or higher for federal tax) and you want to invest in bonds outside of tax-sheltered retirement accounts, you'll probably do better in a muni fund than in a bond fund that pays taxable dividends (see Chapter 6 to determine your tax bracket). If you're in the 28 percent federal bracket, you may or may not come out ahead with munis; you are on the borderline. At less than 28 percent, don't muni.

The new inflation-indexed Treasury bonds

In 1997, the U.S. federal government introduced a new type of Treasury bond that is inflation-proof: inflation-indexed Treasuries. In theory, these relatively new Treasury bonds should better meet the needs of inflation-fearing investors. However, these bonds don't make sense for most investors, especially given the tax and related complications.

An investor with, say, $10,000 to invest could recently have bought a 10-year, regular Treasury bond that yielded 6.4 percent interest, or about $64, annually. Now, contrast this regular Treasury bond with its new inflation-indexed brethren. The 10-year inflation-indexed bonds issued at the same time yielded 3.4 percent. Before you think that this very low yield is a rip-off, know that this is a real (as in not affected or eroded by inflation) rate of return of 3.4 percent.

The other portion of your return with these inflation-indexed bonds comes from the inflation adjustment to the $10,000 principal you invested. The inflation portion of the return gets put back into principal. So if inflation runs at, say, 2.3 percent, after one year of holding your inflation-indexed bond, your $10,000 of principal would increase to $10,230.

So, no matter what happens with the rate of inflation, the investor who bought the inflation-indexed bond will always earn a 3.4 return above and beyond the rate of inflation. If inflation leaps to 10, 12, 14 percent or more, as it last did in the early 1980s, the holders of inflation-indexed Treasuries will not have the purchasing power of their principal or interest eroded by inflation. Holders of regular Treasury bonds, however, won't be as fortunate because at a continued double-digit annual inflation rate, holders of these 6.4 percent yield bonds would have a negative real (after inflation) return.

Because the new inflation-indexed Treasuries protect the investor from the ravages of inflation, they represent a less risky security. In the investment world, lower risk usually translates into lower returns. In fact, the total return that investors are earning from the new inflation-indexed bonds supports this. With inflation running well below 3 percent, as it has in recent years, inflation-indexed bonds are earning around 1 percent less than their non-inflation-indexed counterparts.

Of course, the rate of inflation can and will change in the future. But, for the 10-year bonds chosen in my example, inflation would need to exceed 3.0 percent per year for the holders of the inflation-indexed bonds to come out ahead of those holding the regular Treasury bonds. If inflation were running at, say, 4 percent per year, the total return of inflation-indexed bonds would be 7.4 percent, exceeding the 6.4 percent on the regular Treasury bonds.

(continued)

(continued)

Income-minded investors need to know that the inflation-indexed Treasuries only pay out the real return, which in the preceding example was just 3.4 percent. The rest of the return, which is for increases in the cost of living, are added to the bond's principal. Thus, relative to regular Treasury bonds, which pay out all their returns in interest, the inflation-indexed Treasuries pay little usable interest. Therefore, they don't make sense for non-retirement account investors who seek maximum income to live on.

To add insult to injury, non-retirement account investors face a tax problem with these new bonds. Although the amount for the inflation adjustment that is added back to principal does not come to the inflation-indexed-Treasury-bond holder as cash, the bond holder does have to pay income taxes on the amount. Owing taxes on money not paid out as a cash dividend further depletes the small income these bonds pay out.

Two fund companies recommended in this book — American Century-Benham and PIMCO — have both come out with inflation-indexed Treasury mutual funds. Although each has a relatively low 0.5 annual operating expense ratio, this fee represents a significant share of the potential return on this kind of fund. Also know that regular bond fund managers may invest some of their fund's assets in inflation-indexed Treasuries if they appear attractive relative to other bonds.

Recommended Bond Funds

If you've read through this chapter, you now know more about bond funds than you probably ever imagined possible; so now it's time to get down to brass tacks: selecting bond funds for a variety of investing needs.

Using the logic laid out earlier in this chapter, I present you with a menu of choices. Although thousands of bond funds are available — an overwhelming number of choices — not that many are left to consider after you eliminate high-cost funds (those with loads and ongoing fees), low-performance funds (which are often the just mentioned high-cost funds), and funds managed by fund companies and fund managers with minimal experience investing in bonds.

I've done the winnowing out for you, and the funds I present in the sections that follow are the best of the best for meeting specific needs. I've organized the funds by the average maturity and duration of the bonds that they invest in, as well as by the taxability of the dividends that they pay. If you're investing in bonds inside retirement accounts, then you want taxable bonds. If you're investing in bonds outside retirement accounts, as I discuss in the previous section, the choice between taxable versus tax-free depends on your tax bracket.

Use the following funds only if you have sufficient money in your emergency reserve (see Chapter 3). If you're investing money for longer-term purposes, particularly retirement, come up with an overall plan for allocating your money among a variety of different funds, including stock and bond funds. For more on allocating your money, be sure to read Chapter 6.

Short-term bond funds

Short-term bond funds, if they live up to their name, invest in short-term bonds (which mature in a few years or less). Of all bond funds, these are the least sensitive to interest rate fluctuations. Their stability makes them the most appropriate bond funds for money on which you want to earn a better rate of return than a money market fund could produce for you. But, with short-term bond funds, you also have to tolerate the risk of losing a percent or two in principal value if overall interest rates rise.

Short-term bonds work well for investing money to afford major purchases that you expect to make in a few years, such as a home, a car, or a portion of your retirement account investments that you expect to tap in the near future.

Taxable short-term bond funds

Bond funds that pay taxable dividends are appropriate if you're not in a high tax bracket (less than 28 percent federal) and for investing inside retirement accounts. (Call the fund companies for current yields.)

Vanguard Short-Term Corporate Portfolio invests about 85 percent of its portfolio in high- and moderate-quality, short-term corporate bonds (the average credit rating is A to AA). Typically, it keeps the rest of its portfolio in U.S. Treasuries. It may even stray a bit overseas and invest several percent of the fund's assets in promising foreign bonds. This fund maintains an average maturity of two to three years, and duration currently is 2 years.

Ian MacKinnon and Robert Auwaerter have co-managed Vanguard's Short-Term Corporate fund since the early 1980s (between them, MacKinnon and Auwaerter boast four decades of bond investing experience). All told, this fund invests in about 200 bonds (imagine having to keep track of all of them by your poor little old lonesome!). This fund maintains a wafer-thin 0.3 percent operating expense ratio and has a $3,000 minimum initial investment ($1,000 for retirement accounts). ☎ 800-662-7447.

PIMCO Low Duration is a more aggressive short-term bond fund than Vanguard's Short-Term Corporate. The fund invests mostly in corporate bonds, as well as in mortgage bonds with maturities that typically range from one to five years depending on fund manager William Gross's outlook for inflation and the economy.

Gross, who has managed this fund since 1987, has two decades of experience managing money in the bond market. He makes relatively wide swings in strategy and has had periods during which the fund has concentrated its investments in money market securities (more than 40 percent at times) when Gross saw interest rates rising and wanted to protect principal.

Gross has also ventured up to 20 percent into foreign bonds, some junk bonds (around 10 percent), and even a sprinkling of derivatives, such as futures and options, to slightly leverage returns. Despite this aggressiveness, the fund has had low volatility. The fund's duration is between 2 and 3 years. PIMCO Low Duration maintains a low 0.4 percent annual operating expense ratio. Although this fund may seem intended for heavy hitters, given its normally stratospheric $1,000,000 minimum initial investment, select discount brokers such as Jack White (see Chapter 5) offer this fund's purchase for $25,000.

U.S. Treasury short-term bond funds

U.S. Treasury bond funds are appropriate if you prefer a bond fund that invests in U.S. Treasuries (which have the safety of government backing) or if you're not in a high federal tax bracket (less than 28 percent), but you *are* in a high state tax bracket (5 percent or higher).

I don't recommend Treasuries for retirement accounts because they pay less interest than fully taxable bond funds. (Call the fund companies for current yields.)

Vanguard Short-Term Treasury invests in U.S. Treasuries maturing within two to three years — you can't get much safer than that. Duration currently is 2 years. Like Vanguard's Short-Term Corporate, this fund is managed by the bond dynamic duo of MacKinnon and Auwaerter. Although the fund has that lean Vanguard expense ratio of 0.3 percent annually, don't forget that you can buy Treasuries direct from your local Federal Reserve bank if you don't need liquidity. $3,000 is the minimum initial investment.

Vanguard Admiral Short-Term U.S. Treasury does what the Short-Term Treasury fund does, except that it does it even cheaper. Its annual expense ratio is 0.15 percent. But — and, yes, this is a *big* but — you need a $50,000 minimum initial investment to get in the door. ☎ 800-662-7447.

Municipal tax-free short-term bond funds

Unfortunately, short-term bond funds that are free of both federal and state taxes are scarce. However, some good short-term funds are free of federal but not state taxes. These are appropriate if you're in a high federal bracket (28 percent and up) but in a low state bracket (less than 5 percent).

If you live in a state with high taxes, consider a state money market fund, which I cover in Chapter 7. (Call the fund companies for current yields.)

Vanguard Municipal Short-Term Portfolio invests in the *crème de la crème* of the federally tax-free muni bonds issued by state and local governments around the country (its average credit rating is AAA). The fund's average maturity ranges from one to two years and duration currently is about 1 year.

Vanguard Municipal Limited-Term does just what the short-term fund does (and has the same manager), except that it does it a while longer. This fund's average muni bond matures in two to five years, although its average credit rating is a respectable AA. Both the short-term and limited-term funds have a parsimonious annual operating expense ratio of 0.2 percent and require a $3,000 minimum initial investment. ☎ 800-662-7447.

Intermediate-term bond funds

Intermediate-term bond funds hold bonds that typically mature in a decade or so. They are more volatile than shorter-term bonds but should be more rewarding. The longer you can own an intermediate-term bond fund, the more likely you are to earn a higher return on it than on a short-term fund, unless interest rates keep rising over many years.

You should not purchase an intermediate-term fund unless you expect to hold it for a minimum of three to five years — or even longer, if you can. Therefore, the money you put into this type of fund should be money that you don't expect to use during that period. Also, if you invest in these funds in a non-retirement account, be sure that you're not in a high tax bracket — 28 percent or more federal. (Call the fund companies for current yields.)

Taxable intermediate-term bond funds

Vanguard Index Total Bond Market is an index fund that tracks the index of the entire bond market, the Lehman Brothers Aggregate Bond Index. The fund is managed by Ian MacKinnon, Kenneth Volpert, and a computer. The index that this fund seeks to replicate has about 5,000 bonds, but this fund typically holds only about 10 percent of those bonds by using a sampling to mirror the index. Investment-grade corporate bonds and mortgages make up half of the investments, although the other half are U.S. government and agency securities. Annual operating expenses are a paltry 0.2 percent. To encourage longer-term investors and discourage trading, the fund charges a $10 annual account maintenance fee for balances under $10,000. You need a $3,000 minimum initial investment to open ($1,000 for retirement accounts). ☎ 800-662-7447.

PIMCO Total Return is managed in much the same way as the PIMCO Low Duration fund (which I describe in the section, "Taxable short-term bond funds"), and the two funds even share the same fund manager, William Gross. The Total Return fund's main distinction is that it invests in bonds that mature in roughly ten years (plus or minus a few years). The annual operating expense ratio is 0.4 percent. See my description of PIMCO Low Duration earlier in the chapter (in the section "Taxable short-term bond funds") for more details on PIMCO Total Return and how to purchase it.

PIMCO Total Return III is almost identical to Total Return, except that it invests in bonds issued by companies deemed to be socially responsible (a class of funds that I cover in Chapter 9).

Vanguard GNMA invests in residential mortgages that people just like you take out when they purchase a home and borrow money from a bank. Like other GNMA funds, this one has very low credit risk (its average credit rating is AAA). Why? Because the principal and interest on GNMAs is guaranteed by the federal government (which makes most people — Americans, anyway — feel warm and fuzzy). All GNMA funds have prepayment risk (if interest rates fall, mortgage holders refinance). But this GNMA fund has less risk than most because it minimizes the purchase of mortgage bonds that were issued at higher interest rates — and are therefore more likely to be refinanced and paid back early.

This fund is managed by Paul Kaplan at Wellington Management, a private money management firm that Vanguard uses for many of its other funds. GNMA doesn't invest in some of the more exotic mortgage securities and derivatives abused by other firms' bond funds. Like all other bond funds, this one has interest rate risk, though it's comparable to other intermediate-term bond funds despite the longer maturity of most of this fund's holdings. Duration is currently around 5 years and the fund's yearly operating expense ratio is 0.3 percent. $3,000 is the minimum initial investment, $1,000 for retirement accounts. ☎ 800-662-7447.

Other noteworthy GNMA bond funds include these delectable morsels:

- **American Century-Benham GNMA.** Boasts an excellent track record back to 1985, although it has suffered numerous manager changes in recent years. It has a 0.6 percent annual operating expense ratio. $2,500 is the minimum initial investment for non-retirement accounts, $1,000 for retirement accounts. Often, it can be purchased through discount brokers without additional fees. ☎ 800-345-2021.
- **USAA GNMA.** One of the many solid funds offered by USAA. Its track record, however, dates back only to 1991. Annual operating expense ratio is 0.3 percent. $3,000 is the minimum initial investment, $250 for retirement accounts. ☎ 800-382-8722.

U.S. Treasury intermediate-term bond funds

U.S. Treasury bond funds are appropriate if you prefer a bond fund that invests in U.S. Treasuries (which have the safety of government backing) and if you're not in a high federal tax bracket (less than 28 percent), but you *are* in a high state tax bracket (5 percent or higher). I don't recommend Treasuries for retirement accounts because they pay less interest than fully taxable bond funds. (Call the fund company for current yields.)

Vanguard Intermediate-Term Treasury invests in U.S. Treasuries maturing in five to ten years. **Vanguard Admiral Intermediate-Term U.S. Treasury** is for higher balance customers (see the descriptions for the short-term U.S. treasury funds for minimum initial investments and expense ratios). ☎ 800-662-7447.

Municipal tax-free intermediate-term bond funds

Consider *federally* tax-free bond funds if you're in a high federal bracket (28 percent and up) but a relatively low state bracket (less than 5 percent). If you're in a high federal *and* state tax bracket, see the state and federally tax-free bonds later in this section. (Call the fund company for current yields.)

Vanguard Municipal Intermediate-Term does what Vanguard's short-term muni funds do, except that it invests in slightly longer-term muni bonds (the average credit rating is AA). The annual operating expense ratio is 0.2 percent. $3,000 is the minimum initial investment. ☎ 800-662-7447.

The state and federally tax-free bond funds listed in Table 8-2 may be appropriate if you're in high federal (28 percent and up) *and* high state (5 percent or higher) tax brackets. (If one is not listed for your state or if you're only in a high federal tax bracket, remember to use the nationwide Vanguard municipal bond fund that I describe in the preceding paragraph.)

Table 8-2 State and Federally Tax-Free Intermediate-Term Bond Funds

Fund	*Operating Expense*	*Minimum to Open*
American Century-Benham CA Tax-Free Intermediate-Term	0.5%	$5,000
Schwab CA Short-Intermediate Tax-Free	0.5%	$1,000
Vanguard CA Tax-Free Insured Intermediate Term	0.2%	$3,000

Long-term bond funds

Long-term bond funds are the most aggressive and volatile bond funds around. If interest rates on long-term bonds increase substantially, you can easily see the principal value of your investment decline 10 percent or more.

TIP

Long-term bond funds generally are used for retirement investing in one of two situations:

- For investors not expecting to tap their investment money — ideally — for a decade or more
- For investors wanting to maximize current dividend income and who are willing to tolerate volatility

WARNING!

Definitely don't use these funds for investing money you plan to use within the next five years, because a bond market drop could leave your portfolio with a bit of a hangover (use intermediate-term and short term bond funds instead). And don't use these funds in a non-retirement account if you're in a high tax bracket — 28 percent or more federal. (Call the fund companies for current yields.)

Taxable long-term bond funds

ERIC'S PICKS

Dodge and Cox Income is run by a conservative management team at an old San Francisco investment firm that has been managing money for private accounts since 1930 and running mutual funds since 1931. This fund, which focuses on government securities and high grade corporate debt, is less volatile than most long-term bond funds. The operating expense ratio is 0.5 percent. $2,500 is the minimum initial investment ($1,000 for retirement accounts). ☎ 800-621-3979.

ERIC'S PICKS

Vanguard Long-Term Corporate is comprised mostly of high-grade corporate bonds, but it sometimes holds around 10 percent in Treasuries and foreign and convertible bonds. Long-term bonds such as these can produce wide swings in volatility. For example, this fund lost more than 9 percent of its principal value in 1987, its worst year in a decade. The dividends of 9.2 percent paid that year brought the fund back to produce a total return of 0.2 percent. The fund is managed by Wellington Management's Earl McEvoy, who was new to the fund in 1994, but Wellington itself has managed this fund since its inception in 1973. It has an annual operating expense ratio of 0.3 percent, with a $3,000 minimum initial investment ($1,000 for retirement accounts).

ERIC'S PICKS

Vanguard High Yield Corporate invests in lower-quality (also known as junk) corporate bonds. These pay more and are for more aggressive investors stretching for greater yield. Remember that long-term junk bonds are among the most volatile available: They not only are interest-rate-sensitive, but they're also susceptible to changes in the economy. For example, this fund lost *nearly 18 percent* of its principal value in 1990. Unlike other high-yield funds, this fund invests little (if any) of its funds in lower-rated junk bonds; it invests in the best of the junk! This fund has been managed since 1984 by Earl McEvoy at Wellington Management. The fund has been around since 1978, a degree of longevity that makes it one of the longest- and best-performing junk bond funds. Yearly operating expenses are 0.3 percent. $3,000 is the minimum initial investment ($1,000 for retirement accounts). ☎ 800-662-7447.

PIMCO High Yield has turned in an impressive performance since its inception in 1992. This is due to both the fund's low operating expenses (0.5 percent) and manager Benjamin Trosky's willingness to take calculated risks with a small portion of the portfolio — for example, investing in emerging-markets debt. However, Trosky manages to keep the overall fund relatively conservative for a junk bond fund: Average credit quality is BB and duration hovers around 4. See "PIMCO Low Duration" in the section "Taxable short-term bond funds" for information on how to buy into PIMCO funds.

U.S. Treasury long-term bond funds

U.S. Treasury bond funds are appropriate if you prefer a bond fund that invests in U.S. Treasuries (which have the safety of government backing) and if you're not in a high federal tax bracket (less than 28 percent), but you *are* in a high state tax bracket (5 percent or higher). I don't recommend Treasuries for retirement accounts because they pay less interest than fully taxable bond funds. (Call the fund companies for current yields.)

Vanguard Long-Term Treasury invests in U.S. Treasuries with average maturities around 20 years. Currently, duration is about 10 years. **Vanguard Admiral Long-Term U.S. Treasury** is for higher balance customers. (See the descriptions in the section, "U.S. Treasury short-term bond funds," for minimum initial investments and expense ratios.) ☎ 800-662-7447.

Municipal tax-free long-term bond funds

Vanguard Municipal Long-Term does what Vanguard's short-term muni funds do, except that it invests in long-term muni bonds (the average credit rating is AA). Another twist on Vanguard's Long-Term muni fund is the **Vanguard Municipal Insured Long-Term** fund, which also buys long-term munis, but only those that are insured (the average credit rating is AAA). Both of these funds have annual operating expense ratios of 0.2 percent and a $3,000 minimum initial investment. ☎ 800-662-7447.

The state and federally tax-free bond funds listed in Table 8-3 may be appropriate if you're in a high federal (28 percent and up) *and* high state (5 percent or higher) tax brackets. (If Table 8-3 doesn't list a fund for your state or if you're only in a high federal tax bracket, use the nationwide Vanguard Municipal bond funds I describe in this section.) (Call the fund companies for current yields.)

Table 8-3 State and Federally Tax-Free Long-Term Bond Funds

Fund	*Types of Muni Bonds*	*Operating Expenses*	*Minimum to Open*
American Century-Benham CA Tax-Free Long-Term	CA	0.5%	$5,000
Vanguard CA Tax-Free Insured Long-Term	Insured CA	0.2%	$3,000
Fidelity Spartan CT Muni Income	Lower-quality CT	0.5%	$10,000
Fidelity Spartan FL Muni Income	Lower Quality FL	0.5%	$10,000
USAA FL Tax-Free Income	FL	0.5%	$3,000
Vanguard FL Insured Tax-Free	FL	0.2%	$3,000
Fidelity Spartan MA Muni Income	Lower-quality MA	0.6%	$10,000
Fidelity Spartan MD Muni Income	Lower Quality MD	0.5%	$10,000
Fidelity Spartan MI Muni Income	Lower-quality MI	0.6%	$10,000
Fidelity Spartan MN Muni Income	MN	0.6%	$10,000
Fidelity Spartan NJ Muni Income	Lower Quality NJ	0.5%	$10,000
Vanguard NJ Tax-Free Insured Long-Term	Insured NJ	0.2%	$3,000
Vanguard NY Insured Tax-Free	Insured NY	0.2%	$3,000
USAA NY Bond	NY	0.5%	$3,000
Vanguard OH Tax-Free Insured Long-Term	Insured OH	0.2%	$3,000

Fund	*Types of Muni Bonds*	*Operating Expenses*	*Minimum to Open*
Vanguard PA Tax-Free Insured Long-Term	Insured PA	0.2%	$3,000
USAA TX Tax-Free Income	TX	0.5%	$3,000
USAA VA Bond	VA	0.5%	$3,000

Exploring Alternatives to Bond Funds

Bond mutual funds are hardly the only way to "lend" your money and get paid a decent yield. In the following sections, I talk you through the pros and cons of other alternatives, some of which have acronyms you can impress your friends and family with — or confirm that you're an investments geek. Regardless of which investment type(s) you end up purchasing, remember to do your big-picture thinking first: What do you plan to use the money for down the road? How much risk can you take — and how much are you willing to take? What's your tax situation?

Most of these bond fund alternatives have one thing in common: They offer psychological solace to those who can't stomach fluctuations in the value of their investments. After I tell you more about these alternatives (including information that you're not likely to hear in a marketing pitch from the company or person who's trying to sell you on them), those low-cost bond funds will probably look more attractive.

Certificates of deposit

For many decades, bank certificates of deposit (CDs) have been the investment of choice for folks with some extra cash that is not needed in the near-term. The attraction is that you get a higher rate of return on a CD than on a bank savings account or money market fund. And unlike a bond fund, a CD's principal value does not fluctuate. Of course, you also enjoy the peace of mind afforded by the government's FDIC insurance program.

INVESTIGATE

All these advantages of CDs are not nearly as attractive as they may seem on the surface. I start with the FDIC insurance issue. Bonds and bond mutual funds are not FDIC-insured. The lack of this insurance, however, shouldn't trouble you on high-quality bonds because these bonds rarely default. Even if a fund held a bond that defaulted, it probably would be a tiny fraction (less than 1 percent) of the value of the fund, so it would have little overall impact.

You may believe that's there's no chance you'll lose money on a CD — but banks have failed and will continue to fail. Although you're insured for $100,000 in a bank, if the bank crashes, you'll likely wait quite a while to get your money back — and you'll probably settle for less interest than you expected, too.

Here's another myth about CDs: The principal value of your CD does not fluctuate. Sure it does; you just don't see the fluctuations! Just as the market value of a bond drops when interest rates rise, so too does the "market value" of a CD and for the same reasons. At higher interest rates, investors expect a discounted price on fixed-interest-rate CDs because they always have the alternative of purchasing a new CD at the higher prevailing rates. Some CDs are actually bought and sold among investors — on what's known as a *secondary market* — and they trade and behave just like bonds.

So a lot of those advantages CDs seem to have aren't as impressive as some may believe. In fact, compared to bonds, CDs have a number of drawbacks:

- **Early withdrawal penalties.** Money in a CD is not accessible unless you cough up a fairly big penalty — typically, six months' interest. With a no-load (commission-free) bond fund, if you need some or all of your money next month, next week, or even tomorrow, you can access it without penalty.
- **Restricted tax options.** Another seldom-noted drawback of CDs is that they come in only one tax flavor — taxable. Bonds, on the other hand, come both in tax-free (federal and/or state) and taxable flavors. So if you're a higher-tax bracket investor, bonds offer you a tax-friendly option that CDs can't.
- **Lower yield.** For a comparable maturity, CDs yield less than a high-quality bond. Often, the yield difference is 1 percent or more. If you don't shop around — if you lazily purchase CDs from the bank that you use for your checking account, for example — you may be sacrificing 2 percent or more in yield.

  Don't forget about the unfriendly forces of inflation and taxes. They may gobble up all the yield that your CD is paying, thus leaving you no real growth on your investment. An extra percentage point or two from a bond can make a big difference in the long-term.

TIP

In the long run, you'll earn more and have better access to your money in bond funds than in CDs. And bond funds make particular sense if you're in a higher tax bracket and would benefit from tax-free income on your investments. If you're not in a high tax bracket (a federal rate of less than 28 percent) and you get gloomy whenever your bond fund's value dips, then consider CDs.

CDs may make the most sense if you know, for example, that you can invest your money for one year, after which you'll need the money for some purchase you expect to make. Just make sure that you shop around to get the best interest rate.

If what attracts you to CDs is the U.S. government backing that comes with FDIC insurance, then you might consider Treasuries, which are government-backed bonds. Treasuries often pay more interest than the better CDs available.

Individual bonds

"Why buy a bond fund and pay all those ongoing management fees, year after year, when you can buy high-rated bonds that pay a higher yield than that fund you're looking at?"

"You can create your own portfolio of bonds and purchase bonds with different maturities. That way, you're not gambling on where interest rates are headed, and you won't lose principal as you may in a bond fund."

Maybe you've had thoughts like these. More likely, you've listened to a broker — who was trying to sell individual bonds to you — make these sorts of comments. Does the purchase of individual bonds make sense for you? Although the decision depends on several factors, I can safely say that most types of individual bonds probably are *not* for you. (Treasuries that you can buy directly from a local Federal Reserve bank without charge are notable exceptions to the comments that follow.) Here are some strong reasons why you're probably better off with a good bond mutual fund instead:

- **Diversification.** You don't want to put all your investment money into a small number of bonds that are issued by companies in the same industry or that mature at the same time. Building a diversified bond portfolio with individual issues is difficult unless you have a hefty chunk (at least several hundred thousand dollars) that you desire to invest in bonds.
- **Commissions.** If you purchase individual bonds through a broker, you're going to pay a commission. In most cases, it's hidden; the broker quotes you a bond price that includes the commission. Even if you go through a discount broker, transaction fees take a healthy bite out of your investment. The smaller the amount invested, the bigger the bite. On a $1,000 bond, the fee can equal up to 5 percent.
- **Life's too short.** Do you really want to research bonds and go bond shopping? You have better things to do with your time. Bonds and the companies that stand behind them aren't that simple to understand. For example, did you know that some bonds can be "called" before their maturity date? Companies often do this to save money if interest rates drop significantly. After you purchase a bond, you need to do the same things that a good portfolio manager would need to do, such as tracking the issuer's creditworthiness and monitoring other important financial developments.

In terms of costs, you can purchase terrific bond funds with yearly operating expense ratios of just 0.2 percent. And remember, a bond mutual fund buys you tons of diversification and professional management so that you can spend your time doing activities you're good at and enjoy. You can increase your diversification by purchasing bond funds with different maturity objectives (short, intermediate, and long) or an index bond fund that covers the range.

If you already own individual bonds and they fit your financial objectives and tax situation, you can hold them until maturity because you've already incurred a commission when they were purchased; selling them now would just create an additional fee. When the bond(s) mature(s), think about moving the proceeds into bond funds if you want to continue owning bonds.

Don't mistakenly think that your current individual bonds are paying the same yield as when they were originally issued (that yield is the number listed on your brokerage account statement in the name of the bond). As the market level of interest rates changes, the yield that's on your bonds fluctuates to rise and fall with the market level of rates. So if rates have fallen since you bought your bonds, the value of those bonds has increased — which in turn reduces the effective yield that you're currently earning.

Guaranteed-investment contracts

Guaranteed-investment contracts (GICs) are sold and backed by an insurance company. Typically, they quote you a rate of return projected one or a few years forward. So, like that of a CD, a GIC's return is always positive and certain. With a GIC, you experience none of the uncertainty that you normally face with a bond fund that fluctuates with changes in interest rates and other economic upheavals.

The attraction of GICs is that your account value does not fluctuate (at least, not that you can see). For people who would panic the moment a bond fund's value slips, GICs soothe the nerves. And they usually provide a higher yield than a money market or savings account.

As a rule, the insurance company invests GIC money mostly in bonds and maybe a bit in stocks. The difference between the amount these investments generate for the insurer and the amount they pay in interest is profit to the insurer. The yield is usually comparable to that of a bond fund. Typically, once a year, you'll receive a new statement showing that your GIC is worth more — thanks to the newly added interest.

Some employers offer GICs in their retirement savings plans as a butt-covering option or because an insurance company is involved in the company's retirement plan. More and more companies are eliminating GICs as investment options because of the greater awareness about GICs' drawbacks. First, insurance companies (like banks) have failed and will continue to fail. Although failed insurers almost always get bailed out — usually through a merger into a healthy company — you can take a haircut on the promised interest rate if your GIC is with a failed insurance company. Second, by having a return guaranteed in advance, you pay for the peace of mind in the form of lower long-term returns.

Mortgages

Another way that you can invest your money for greater dividend income is to lend your money via mortgages and second mortgages. These "deals" are often arranged by mortgage brokers. They appeal to investors who don't like the volatility of the stock and bond markets. With a mortgage, you don't have to look up the value every day in the newspaper; a mortgage seems safer because you can't watch your principal fluctuate in value.

What's amazing is that people who invest in these types of mortgages don't realize that they're getting a relatively high interest rate *only because they are accepting relatively high risk.* The risk is that the borrower can default — which would leave you holding the bag. More specifically, you could get stuck with a property that you may need to foreclose on. And if you don't hold the first mortgage, you're not first in line with a claim on the property.

If a property buyer could obtain a mortgage through a conventional bank, he would. Banks offer the lowest interest rates. So if a mortgage broker is offering you a deal to lend your money at 12 percent when the going bank rate is 9 percent, that means you'll be lending money to people that the bank considers high risk. If a bank, with its millions of dollars of assets on hand, is not willing to lend money to somebody, ask yourself whether you should. Your mortgage investment also carries interest rate risk: If you need to "sell" it early, you'd probably have to discount it, perhaps substantially if interest rates have increased since you purchased it.

If you're willing to lend your money to borrowers who carry a relatively high risk of defaulting, check out the high-yield bond fund I discuss earlier in the chapter (under "Taxable long-term bond funds"). With this fund, you at least diversify your money across many borrowers, and you benefit from the professional review and due diligence of the fund management team. If the normal volatility of a bond fund's principal value makes you queasy, then don't follow your investments so closely!

If you're selling some real estate and are willing to act as the bank and provide the financing to the buyer in the form of a first mortgage, that can be a viable investment. Be careful to check the borrower's credit, employment, and income situation; get a large down payment (at least 20 percent); and try not to lend so much money that it represents more than, say, 10 percent of your total investments.

Chapter 9

Funds for Longer-Term Needs: Stock Funds

In This Chapter

- How, when, and why to invest in stock funds
- The different types of stock funds
- Recommended hybrid, index, and U.S. funds
- Recommended international funds
- Specialty funds — real estate, precious metals, and the like
- Socially responsible funds

To some, the stock market is nothing more than legalized gambling. To others, it's a ticket to great wealth if they can figure out what makes it tick.

As you enter this perhaps most important of investing chapters, I may need you to revise your expectations of the stock market so that you and I can see eye to eye. I don't want you to be wounded by the stock market, which can be punishing and unrelenting during bad times. Nor do I want you to fear the market, because (as FDR once said under slightly different circumstances) there's nothing to fear but fear itself.

Here's what you and I need to agree on:

- People who make money in the stock market make money not because they're smarter, luckier, or more clairvoyant than anyone else. They make money by simply being more patient and using three simple investment methods available to people of varying economic means and intellectual abilities:
  - Invest in a diversified portfolio of stocks.
  - Continue to save money and add to your investments.
  - Don't try to time the market. In other words, save, invest, and sit on your hands!

About 1 percent of professional investors appear to be "smarter" than the rest of us. They make a couple of percent more per year on average (some say that they're just lucky or statistical aberrations). You (and I) aren't going to be part of this 1 percent. If you were, you wouldn't need this book!

- People who get soaked in the stock market are those who make easily avoidable mistakes. I define *investment mistake* as *a bad decision that you could or should have avoided,* either because better options were available, or because the odds were heavily stacked against your making money. Investment mistakes result from not understanding risk and how to minimize it, ignoring taxes and how your investments fit into your overall financial plans, paying unnecessary and exorbitant commissions and fees to buy and hold your investments, surrendering to a sales pitch (or salesperson), and trading in and out of the market. Give up the search for a secret code — there isn't one. Focus on avoiding major gaffes.
- The stock market is not the place to invest money that you'll need to tap in the near future (certainly not money you'll need to use within the next five years). If your stock holdings take a dive, you don't want to be forced to sell when your investments have lost value. So come along for the ride — but only if you can stay for a while!

If you're looking for magic ways to build a vast fortune without peril, you've come to the wrong book. But, gentle reader, if you want insights for how you can tap into one of the best investment funds to make your money *grow,* read on.

Stock Funds: A Place to Grow Your Money

As I explain in Chapter 1, stocks represent a share of ownership in a company and its profits. As companies (and economies in general) grow and expand, stocks represent a way for investors to share in that growth and success.

Over the last two centuries, investors holding diversified stock portfolios earned a rate of return averaging about 10 percent per year, which ended up being about 7 percent higher than the rate of inflation. Earning 7 percent per year more than the rate of inflation may not seem like much (especially in a world with gurus and brokers telling you that they can make you 20 percent, 50 percent, or more per year). But don't forget the power of compounding: At 7 percent per year, the purchasing power of your invested money doubles about every ten years.

Contrast this return with bond and money market investments, which have historically returned just a percent or two per year over the rate of inflation. At these rates of return, the purchasing power of your invested money takes several decades or more to double.

Your investment's return relative to the rate of inflation determines the growth in purchasing power of your portfolio. What's called the *real growth rate* on your investments is the rate of return your investments earn per year minus the yearly rate of inflation. If the cost of living is increasing at 3 percent per year and your money is invested in a bank savings account paying you 3 percent per year, you're treading water — your *real* rate of return is zero. (On top of inflation, when you invest money outside of a tax-sheltered retirement account, you end up paying taxes on your returns, which could lead to a *negative* real "growth" in your money's purchasing power!)

Be patient . . .

Disclaimer: The 10 percent historic return in stocks that I quote is not guaranteed to be the same in the future. Consider some of these unexpected storms that hammered the stock market over the past century (see Table 9-1).

Table 9-1 Great Plunges (20 Percent or More) in the Dow Jones Industrial Average Index of Large Company Stocks

Years	*Percent Decline**	*Years*	*Percent Decline**
1890–1896	47%	1946–1949	24%
1899–1900	32%	1961–1962	27%
1901–1903	46%	1966	25%
1906–1907	49%	1968–1970	36%
1909–1914	29%	1973–1974	45%
1916–1917	40%	1976–1978	27%
1919–1921	47%	1981–1982	24%
1929–1932	89%	1987	36%
1937–1942	52%		

** Please note that the returns that stock market investors earned during these periods would differ slightly from the above figures, which ignore dividends paid by stocks. The returns also ignore changes in the cost of living, which normally increases over time and thus makes these drops seem even worse. The Great Depression is the exception to that rule: The cost of living dropped then.*

As you see in Table 9-1, the stock market can take a beating. But before you let the chart convince you to avoid the stock market at all costs for the rest of your life, look at the time periods during which those great plunges occurred. Notice how short most of those periods are. During the last century, major stock market declines have lasted less than two years on average. Some of the 20 percent-plus declines lasted less than one year. The longest declines (1890–1896, 1909–1914, 1929–1932, 1937–1942, and 1946–1949) lasted six, five, three, five, and three years, respectively.

Table 9-1 tells less than half the story. True, the stock market can suffer major losses. But over the long haul, stocks make more money than they lose. That's how they end up with that 10 percent average annual long-term return I've been telling you about.

Stock market crashes may be dramatic, but consider the powerful advances (see Table 9-2) that have happened after big market declines.

Table 9-2 Great Surges in the Dow Jones Industrial Average after Major Market Declines

Years	*Percent Increase*
1896–1899	173%
1914–1916	114%
1932–1937	372%
1942–1946	129%
1949–1956	222%
1962–1966	86%
1970–1973	67%
1974–1976	76%
1987–1998	420%

These stock market increases more than made up for the previous declines. In other words, wait long enough, and time will bail you out! This is why I emphasize that stocks are for long-term investors and long-term goals. If you're going to invest in stocks, you must have the time on your side to wait out a major market decline. If you don't, you face the risk that you'll have to sell your stocks for a loss. Don't keep your emergency money in stocks. Only invest money that you don't plan on using for at least five years, preferably ten or more.

Add regularly to your stock investments

Although the stock market may be able to double the purchasing power of your money on average every ten years, the real key to creating wealth with stocks is investing in them regularly. Put $1,000 into stocks, and ten years later, you'll probably have $2,000. But if you put $1,000 into stocks *every year* for ten years, you end up with $14,000 — that's 700 percent more. Remember the power of combining these two simple but powerful financial concepts: *Regular savings* and *investing in growth-oriented investments* lead to simply amazing long-term results.

Another advantage of buying in regular chunks (some call this strategy *dollar-cost averaging,* a subject I cover in Chapter 6) is that it softens the blow of a major decline. Why? Because you'll make some of your stock investments as the market is heading south; perhaps you'll even buy at or near the very bottom. After the market rebounds, you'll show a profit on some of those last purchases you made, which will help to soothe the rest of your portfolio — as well as your bad feelings about the stock market. If you had used-dollar cost averaging during the worst decade for stock investors this century (1928–38), you still would have averaged 7 percent per year in returns despite the Great Depression and a sagging stock market.

Stocks and Funds

Mutual funds are the way to go when you want to invest in stocks. Stock funds offer you tons of diversification and a low-cost way to hire a professional money manager. In Chapter 2, I discuss at length why purchasing individual stocks on your own doesn't make good financial sense. (If you haven't read Chapter 2 yet and you believe that buying individual stocks is the best route for you to take, please read it.)

Stock funds reduce risk and increase returns

There's really no way around it: Invest in stocks, and you expose yourself to risk. But that doesn't mean that you can't work to minimize unnecessary risk. One of the most effective risk-reduction techniques is *diversification* — owning lots of different stocks to minimize the damage of any one stock's decline. Diversification is why mutual funds are such a great way to own stocks.

Unless you have a lot of money to invest, you can only cost effectively afford to buy a handful of individual stocks. If you end up with a lemon in your portfolio, it could devastate the returns of your better performing stocks. Companies are quite capable of going bankrupt. Even those that survive a rough period can see their stock prices plummet by huge amounts — 50 percent or more — and sometimes in a matter of weeks or months.

Even with the extended bull market in recent years (a bull market is one in which stock prices are rising; its opposite is a bear market), certain individual stocks have taken it on the chin. A good example is the technology stock ATC Communications, which was widely touted on Internet message boards in late 1996 after a seven-fold rise in price over the prior year. After peaking in the mid- 20s in October 1996, the stock plunged more than 90 percent in a matter of months and didn't rebound. Problems can take many years to develop as well. IBM was once considered to be among the more reliable and safe blue chip stocks. After trading as high as 175 in the early 1980s, it plunged 77 percent to a low of almost 40 in 1993. As of this writing, it's up to about 115.

Of course, owning any stock in a company that goes bankrupt and stays that way means that you lose 100 percent of your investment. If this stock represents, say, 20 percent of your holdings, the rest of your stock selections must increase about 25 percent in value just to get your portfolio back to even.

Stock mutual funds reduce your risk by investing in many stocks, often 50 or more. If a fund holds 50 stocks and one drops to zero, you lose only 2 percent of the value of the fund if the stock was an average holding. If the fund holds 100 stocks, you lose 1 percent, and a 200-stock fund loses only 0.5 percent if one stock goes. And don't forget another advantage of stock mutual funds: A good fund manager is more likely to sidestep investment disasters than you are.

Another way that stock funds reduce risk (and thus their volatility) is by investing in different types of stocks across various industries. Some funds also invest in U.S. and international stocks (even though the fund names may hide this fact).

Different types of stocks don't always move in tandem. So if smaller-company stocks are being beaten up, larger-company stocks may be faring better. If growth companies are sluggish, value companies may be in vogue. If U.S. stocks are in the tank, international ones may not be. (I discuss these different types of stocks later in this chapter.)

You can diversify into different types of stocks by purchasing several stock funds, each of which focuses on different types of stocks. There are two potential advantages to this diversification. First, not all of your money is riding in one stock fund and with one fund manager. Second, each of the different fund managers can focus on and track particular stock investing possibilities.

How stock funds make money

When you invest in stock mutual funds, you can make money in three — count 'em — three ways! They are:

- **Dividends.** Some stocks pay dividends. Most companies make profits and pay out some of these profits to shareholders in the form of dividends. Some high-growth companies reinvest most or all of their profits right back into the business. As a mutual fund investor, you can choose to receive your fund's dividends as cash or reinvest them by purchasing more shares in the mutual fund.

  Unless you need the income to live on (if, for example, you're retired), reinvest your dividends into buying more shares in the fund. If you do this outside of a retirement account, keep a record of those reinvestments because those additional purchases should be factored into the tax calculations you'll make when you sell the shares. (Find the lowdown on the relationship between fund investments and taxes in Chapter 13.)

- **Capital gains distributions.** When a fund manager sells stocks for more than he or she paid for them, the resulting profits, known as capital gains, must be netted against losses and paid out to the fund's shareholders. As with dividends, your capital gains distributions can be reinvested back into the fund.

- **Appreciation.** The fund manager isn't going to sell all the stocks that have gone up in value. Thus, the price per share of the fund should increase (unless the fund manager made poor picks or the market as a whole is doing poorly) to reflect the gains in unsold stocks. For you, these profits are on paper until you sell the fund and lock them in. Of course, if a fund's stocks decline in value, the share price will depreciate.

If you add together dividends, capital gains distributions, and appreciation, you arrive at the *total return* of a fund. Stocks (and the funds that invest in them) differ in the proportions that make up their total returns, particularly with respect to dividends. Utility companies, for example, tend to pay out more of their profits as dividends. But don't buy funds that concentrate on utility stocks thinking that you'll make more money because of the heftier dividends. Utilities and other companies paying high dividends tend not to appreciate as much over time because they aren't reinvesting as much in their businesses and growing.

Stock fund choices

Stock mutual funds, as their name implies, invest in stocks. These funds are often referred to as *equity* funds. Equity (not to be confused with equity in real estate) is another word for stocks.

Stock funds and the stocks that they invest in usually are pigeonholed into particular categories based on the types of stocks they focus on. Categorizing stock funds often is tidier in theory than in practice, though, because some funds invest in an eclectic mix of stocks. Here are the major ways that funds and the stocks that they hold differ from one another:

- **Size of company.** Just as you can purchase shirts or sweaters in small, medium, and large sizes, you can purchase stock in small, medium, and large companies. The size of a company is defined by the total market value (capitalization) of its outstanding stock. Small companies are generally defined as those that have total market capitalization of less than $1 billion. Medium-sized companies have market values between $1 billion and $5 billion. Large-capitalization companies have market values greater than $5 billion. These dollar amounts are somewhat arbitrary. (***Note:*** The term "capitalization" is routinely shortened to "cap," as in small-cap company or large-cap stock.)

  Why care what size of companies a fund holds? Smaller companies typically pay smaller dividends but appreciate more. They have more volatile share prices but tend to produce greater total returns. Larger companies' stocks tend to pay greater dividends and on average are less volatile but produce slightly lower total returns than small company stocks. Medium-sized companies, as you may suspect, fall between the two.

- **Growth or value?** Stock fund managers and their funds are further categorized by whether investments are made in growth or value stocks. *Growth* stocks are public companies that are experiencing rapidly expanding revenues and profits. These companies tend to reinvest most of their earnings in the company to fuel future expansion; thus, these stocks pay low dividends. For example, IDG Books Worldwide, Inc. (the company that published this book) reinvests much of its profits back into publishing more good books. (You can't buy stock in IDG though, because the company is private.)

  Value stocks are public companies priced cheaply in relation to the company's assets, profits, and potential profits. It's possible that such a company is a growth company, but that's unlikely because growth company stocks tend to sell at a premium compared to what the company's assets are worth.

- **Geography.** Stocks and the companies that issue them are further categorized by the location of their main operations and headquarters. Is a company based in the United States or overseas? Funds that specialize in U.S. stocks are (surprise, surprise) called U.S. stock funds; those focusing internationally are typically called "international" or "overseas" funds.

What do all of those other names mean?

If small and large, value and growth, U.S. and international haven't created enough mind-numbing combinations of stock fund options, here are a few more names that you'll confront.

Start with all the variations on growth. *Aggressive growth* funds are, well, more aggressive than the other growth funds. Not only does an aggressive growth fund tend to invest in the most growth oriented companies, but the fund may also engage in riskier investing practices, such as making major shifts in strategy and trading in and out of stocks frequently (turning over the fund's investments several times or more during the year).

Then consider *growth-and-income* funds and *equity-income* funds. Both of these fund types invest in stocks (equities) that pay decent dividends, thus offering the investor the potential for growth and income. Growth-and-income and equity-income are basically one and the same. The only real difference between them is trivial: Equity-income funds tend to pay slightly higher dividends (although some growth-and-income funds have higher dividends than equity-income funds!). They may pay higher dividends because they invest a small portion of their portfolios in higher-dividend securities, such as bonds and convertible bonds.

Income funds tend to invest a healthy portion (but by no means all) of their money in higher-yielding stocks. Bonds usually make up the other portion of income funds. As you see later in this chapter, other fund names designate those funds investing in both stocks and bonds — names such as *balanced* funds. Income funds are really quite similar to some balanced funds.

The term *international* typically means that a fund can invest anywhere in the world except the United States. The term *worldwide* or *global* generally implies that a fund can invest anywhere in the world, including the United States. I generally recommend avoiding worldwide or global funds with just one manager for two reasons. First, it's difficult for a fund manager to thoroughly follow the companies and financial markets across a truly global investment landscape. (It's hard enough to follow either solely U.S. or solely-international markets.) Second, most of these funds charge high operating expenses — often well in excess of 1 percent per year — which drags down investors' returns.

Don't get bogged down in the names of funds. Remember that funds sometimes have misleading names and don't necessarily do what their names may imply. What matters are the investment strategies of the fund and the fund's typical investments. I tell you what these strategies are for the funds recommended in this book and show you how to combine great funds together into a portfolio in Chapter 10.

By putting together two or three of these major classifications, you can start to appreciate all of those silly and lengthy names that mutual fund companies give to their stock funds. You can have funds that focus on large-company value stocks or small-company growth stocks. These categories can be further subdivided into more fund types by adding in U.S., international, and worldwide funds. For example, you can have international stock funds focusing on small company stocks or growth stocks.

The Best Stock Funds

Using the selection criteria outlined in Chapter 4, the following sections describe the best stock funds worthy of your consideration. The funds differ from one another primarily in terms of the types of stocks they invest in. Keep in mind as you read through these funds that they also differ from each other in their "tax-friendliness" (see Chapter 6). If you're investing inside a retirement account, you don't need to care about this issue.

Because stock funds are used for longer-term purposes, the subject of stock funds usually raises another important issue: How do you divvy up your loot into the different types of investments for purposes of diversification and to make your money grow? Chapter 6 answers that very question.

Mixing it up: Recommended hybrid funds

Hybrid funds invest in a mixture of different types of securities. Most commonly, they invest in both bonds and stocks. These funds are usually less risky and less volatile than funds that invest exclusively in stocks; in an economic downturn, bonds usually hold up better in value than stocks do.

TIP

Hybrid funds make it easier for investors who are skittish about investing in stocks to hold stocks while they avoid the high volatility that normally comes with pure stock funds. Oh, you *could* place 60 percent of your investment moneys into a pure stock fund and the other 40 percent into a pure bond fund — but you can do just that by investing in one hybrid fund that has the same overall 60/40 mix. Because bonds and stocks often don't fluctuate in unison, movements of one can offset those of the other. Hybrid funds are excellent choices for retirement account investing, particularly where an investor doesn't have much money to start with.

The two main types of hybrid mutual funds are *balanced* funds and *asset allocation* funds. Balanced funds try to maintain a fairly constant percentage of investment in stocks and bonds. For example, a balanced fund may state that its objective is to have 60 percent of its investments in stocks and 40 percent in bonds. (Some balanced funds are exceptions to this rule and will, like asset allocation funds, adjust their mix over time.)

Asset allocation funds adjust the mix of different investments according to the portfolio manager's expectations. Essentially, the fund manager keeps an eye on the big picture — watching both the stock and bond markets — and moves money between them in an *attempt* to get the best value. The manager's efforts mean that you don't have to worry about whether to move some money from your bond mutual fund to your stock fund, or vice versa. You can spend more time in your garden.

You should note, however, that most managers have done a dismal job in beating the market averages by shifting money around rather than staying put in sensible investments (see the next section on the Rodney Dangerfield of mutual funds: index funds).

One of the brighter spots on the mutual fund landscape is the increasing number of mutual funds that invest in a variety of different funds offered by their parent companies. They're known as "funds of funds," and they're the ultimate couch-potato way to invest! Each of the Vanguard LifeStrategy

Taxes and hybrid funds

Because hybrid funds hold bonds and therefore pay decent dividends, they are not appropriate for many investors who are purchasing funds outside tax-sheltered retirement accounts. If you're in a higher tax bracket (federal 31 percent and higher), bonds that you hold outside a retirement account should be tax-free.

With the exception of the Vanguard Tax-Managed Balanced Fund (which I discuss in the next paragraph), you should avoid the hybrid funds if you're in this situation. Buy separate tax-friendly stock funds (which I cover later this chapter) and tax-free bond funds (see Chapter 8).

Vanguard Tax-Managed Balanced is the one hybrid fund that is tax-friendly enough to be considered for investments held outside tax-sheltered retirement accounts. Why? Because the bonds that it holds (typically half or more of this fund's investments) are federally tax-free municipal bonds. Be forewarned, though, that this fund has a steep initial minimum of $10,000 and is intended for investors who will hold the fund for at least five years. Otherwise, a 1-to-2 percent transaction fee is charged against your sale proceeds and paid into the fund.

The bond portion of the portfolio is managed by Vanguard's bond fund king, Ian MacKinnon; the bonds are high-quality and intermediate to longer-term in nature. The stocks in this fund try to replicate the Russell 1000 Index of the 1,000 largest company stocks in the United States, although the fund emphasizes stocks with lower dividends to reduce taxable distributions. Selling of stocks with capital gains is also minimized to reduce those taxable distributions as well. As with Vanguard's other index funds, this portion of the fund is managed by Gus Sauter and his army of computers.

If you live in a high-tax state, instead of buying this Vanguard fund, you may be better off buying a state and federally tax-free municipal bond fund if a good one's available for your state (see Chapter 8 to find out) and pairing it with a tax-friendly stock fund.

funds, for example, (which I describe in more detail in the upcoming section "Vanguard's Funds of Funds") invests portions of its assets in various Vanguard stock and bond funds that focus on different types of securities.

Without further ado, the following sections describe some stupendous hybrid funds. They're loosely ordered from those that generally take less risk to those that take more. Higher-risk hybrid funds tend to hold greater positions in stocks and/or make wider swings and changes in their investments and strategies over time.

Vanguard Wellesley Income

This is among the most conservative and income-oriented of the hybrids. This fund typically has about two-thirds of its assets in high-quality bonds, with the other third in high-yielding, large-company stocks. Since its inception in 1970, the majority of this fund's returns have come from dividends. Like many of the other conservative Vanguard funds, this one is managed by Wellington Management and the dynamic duo of Earl McEvoy and John Ryan, who have about 50 years of investment experience between them.

This fund is ideal for people who have either retired or are on the verge of retiring — or anyone else who wants a high rate of current income but also some potential for growth from their investments. The main drawback of this fund is that it is somewhat interest rate-sensitive because it tends to hold intermediate to longer-term bonds and higher-yielding stocks. Its stocks, however, are more value-oriented large-company stocks and are among the more stable of stocks. Its high-quality bonds also don't go through the gyrations that junk bonds do. Expense ratio is 0.3 percent. $3,000 initial minimum, $1,000 for retirement accounts. ☎ 800-662-7447.

Vanguard's Funds of Funds

A *fund of funds* is simply a mutual fund that invests in other individual mutual funds. Although the concept is not new, it has become increasingly attractive to investors who are overwhelmed by the number of fund choices out there or who want to diversify. Vanguard offers some excellent funds of funds.

Begun in 1985 — and thus the oldest of the funds of funds — the Vanguard Star fund is diversified across nine different Vanguard funds: six stock, two bond, and one money market fund. Its targeted asset allocation is 63% in stocks, 25% in bonds, and 12% in the money market fund. This fund emphasizes value more than growth. It is also very U.S.-focused, seldom holding more than a few percent in foreign stocks. The Star fund's diversification comes cheap: The average expense ratio of the underlying funds is 0.4 percent (there's no additional charge for packaging them together). The initial investment requirement is just $1,000 for both retirement and non-retirement accounts.

Realizing that in the case of asset allocation, one size does not fit all, Vanguard introduced the LifeStrategy series of funds in 1994. Although each of the four LifeStrategy funds draws from numerous Vanguard stock and bond funds, they differentiate themselves by their target asset allocations. The LifeStrategy Income portfolio, the most conservative of the bunch, has 80 percent in bonds and 20 percent in stocks whereas the LifeStrategy Growth portfolio, at the other end of the risk spectrum, invests 80 percent in stocks and 20 percent in bonds. The asset allocations of the other two portfolios — Conservative Growth and Moderate Growth — fall in between these extremes.

Unlike the Star fund, the more aggressive LifeStrategy funds allow more exposure to international markets: up to 15 percent for the Growth portfolio. In addition, by relying more heavily on index funds than the Star fund does, the LifeStrategy funds come through with an even lower average expense ratio of 0.3 percent. Minimum initial investment is $3,000 ($1,000 for retirement accounts). ☎ 800-662-7447.

Dodge & Cox Balanced

This particular fund is one of the older balanced funds, having started in 1931. It wasn't until the 1980s that Dodge & Cox started marketing and registering the fund for sale in states throughout the United States. The company has never been all that aggressive or interested in building a huge mutual fund (the fund is available in about half the states, mostly larger ones). Although never at the top of the fund heap, this fund has not had a down year since 1981.

Like Dodge & Cox itself, this fund is conservatively run, investing primarily in large-company value stocks and high-quality, intermediate-term bonds. Typically, it invests 60 percent in stocks and the rest in bonds. A small portion of the fund (less than 10 percent) may be invested overseas and less than 5 percent may be invested in junk bonds.

This fund has always been managed using a team approach, so if you like to be able to rattle off the name of a star fund manager who's investing your money, this is not the fund for you (although you can impress others by saying that the minimum account size that Dodge & Cox normally accepts is several million dollars). This fund has an almost Vanguard-like 0.6 percent expense ratio. Minimum initial investment is $2,500 ($1,000 for retirement accounts). ☎ 800-621-3979.

Vanguard Wellington

Wellington is the oldest hybrid fund: It dates back to the summer of 1929 (which means that it even survived the Great Depression!). This fund typically invests about two-thirds in large-company stocks, with the other third in high-quality, intermediate- to longer-term bonds.

This fund is co-managed by Wellington Management's Ernst H. von Metzsch and Paul Kaplan, who together have five plus decades of investment management experience. Up to 10 percent of this fund's assets can be and often are invested internationally. Its expense ratio is 0.3 percent. Minimum initial investment is $3,000 ($1,000 for retirement accounts). ☎ 800-662-7447.

Fidelity Asset Manager

Fidelity offers a number of hybrid funds that invest overseas as well as in the United States. They differ from Vanguard's offerings by making more radical shifts in strategies and investments held. Fidelity is one of the few companies that has the research capabilities to allow a fund manager to invest intelligently in many different markets.

Managed by a team, Asset Manager typically has about one-half of its assets in stocks, with a healthy portion of those overseas. Most of the rest of the fund is invested in bonds (with a healthy helping of the bonds being junk).

The expense ratio is 0.8 percent annually. Minimum initial investment is $2,500 ($500 for retirement accounts). ☎ 800-544-8888.

Fidelity Puritan

One of Fidelity's oldest funds (it began in 1947), this fund is managed by Bettina Doulton. Like Fidelity's Asset Manager fund, Puritan is a worldwide hybrid fund. Puritan typically has about 50 to 60 percent in stocks that tend to be value-oriented. The fund historically has invested a fair amount in foreign stocks.

The bonds in this fund are similar to those in Asset Manager in that 20 to 25 percent of them are junk bonds. Most of the bonds are intermediate-term. The expense ratio is 0.7 percent. Minimum initial investment is $2,500 ($500 for retirement accounts).☎ 800-544-8888.

Other noteworthy hybrids

Lindner Dividend most closely resembles Vanguard Wellesley in that it focuses on maximizing income. Lindner does this by investing in higher-yielding stocks (including international) and bonds (including convertibles). The expense ratio is 0.6 percent. Minimum initial investment is $2,000 ($250 for retirement accounts). ☎ 800-995-7777.

T. Rowe Price Balanced is a decent fund if you're investing through that company. It's sort of like a conservative version of Fidelity's hybrid funds, because it invests about 20 percent of its stocks overseas and 20 percent of its bonds in junk. The expense ratio is 0.9 percent. Minimum initial investment is $2,500 ($1,000 for retirement accounts). ☎ 800-638-5660.

Computers amok: Recommended index funds

Index funds, which I discuss in detail in Chapter 6, are passively managed — that means an index fund's money is invested, using computer modeling, to simply track the performance of a particular market index, such as the Standard & Poor's 500. When you buy into an index fund, you give up the possibility of outperforming the market, but you also guarantee that you won't underperform the market either.

"Beating the market" is extremely difficult; most actively managed funds are unable to do it. The best index funds, however, have an unfair advantage — they have the lowest operating expenses in the business. In Chapter 6, I talk more about the virtues of index funds and what kind of role they should play in your portfolio. The following sections cover the best stock index funds available.

Vanguard's index funds

John C. Bogle, Vanguard's founder and former CEO, was the first person to take the idea of indexing to the mutual fund investing public; he has been a tireless crusader for index funds ever since. Today, Vanguard continues to be the index fund leader with the lowest operating expenses (which directly translates into higher index fund returns) and the biggest index fund selection around.

Vanguard's less aggressive index fund is a hybrid fund, **Vanguard Balanced Index.** Sixty percent of this fund's assets are invested in stocks according to the Wilshire 5000 Index; the other 40 percent are invested in bonds to replicate the performance of the Lehman Brothers Aggregate Bond Index. The fund has a 0.2 percent annual operating expense ratio.

The flagship of Vanguard's index fleet, the **Vanguard Index 500** fund invests to replicate the performance of the popular stock market index — the Standard & Poor's 500 Index — which tracks the stocks of 500 large companies in the United States. These 500 stocks typically account for about three-quarters of the total value of stocks outstanding in the U.S. market. I don't enthusiastically recommend this to those wanting to index some or even all of their U.S. stock fund investments. The reason: You miss out on medium and smaller size companies, and the larger stocks in this fund tend to pay higher dividends than their smaller brethren, thus making this fund a bit tax unfriendly for non-retirement account investors. The expense ratio on this fund is a razor thin 0.19 percent (that's right — less than two-tenths of one percent!).

A more diversified and tax-friendlier fund than Vanguard's Index 500 is the **Vanguard Index Total Stock Market,** which replicates the performance of the Wilshire 5000 Index. This index comprises the entire U.S. market of large-, medium-, and small-company stocks. Smaller companies tend to pay lower dividends so this fund pays lower taxable dividends than the Standard & Poor's 500 fund. This fund also has a wafer thin expense ratio of 2 percent.

The **Vanguard Total International Fund** seeks to replicate a combination of two international indexes: the Morgan Stanley Capital International Index (which is comprised of established economies) and the Select Emerging Markets Index. At 0.4 percent, this fund's expense ratio is higher than other Vanguard index funds but still a pittance compared to actively managed international funds. Be aware that there is a one-time, 0.5 percent transaction fee charge when you buy into this fund. This fee is not a load (commission): Rather than going into the pockets of a salesperson, the fee is paid back into the fund itself to offset operating costs. For certain funds, Vanguard charges these transaction fees to discourage short-term trading.

The manager behind the computers who directs the investments in all of Vanguard's index funds is Gus Sauter, Vanguard's indexing guru, who has been with the company since 1987. For non-retirement accounts, the minimum initial purchase for Vanguard index funds is $3,000; for retirement accounts, it's $1,000. Vanguard's index funds assess nominal annual account fees ($10 per year) for account balances of less than $10,000 to discourage short-term trading. These fees do increase the costs of owning these funds, but total index fund fees still run far lower than those of actively managed funds. ☎ 800-662-7447

Schwab's index funds

Although their expenses are higher than Vanguard's, Schwab's index funds are worth mentioning for their tax-friendliness and low initial minimum requirements ($1,000 for non-retirement accounts, $500 for retirement accounts).

The **Schwab 1000** fund invests in a Schwab-created index of the 1,000 largest publicly traded U.S. companies. Its expense ratio is 0.5 percent. The **Schwab International Index** invests in another Schwab-created index of 350 large-company stocks outside the United States. The expense ratio is 0.6 percent.

Both of these funds are tax-friendly: Whenever they need to sell securities because of changes in the index or shareholder redemptions, they make sure to offset capital gains with losses. To achieve this result, these funds have been given the flexibility to deviate occasionally from index weightings by small amounts.

"Tax-friendliness" is only a concern for non-retirement account investing. For retirement accounts, Vanguard's lower expenses give it the definite edge. ☎ 800-435-4000.

Recommended U.S.-focused stock funds

This section focuses on the better actively managed funds that invest primarily in the U.S. stock market. I say *primarily* because some "U.S." funds venture into overseas investments.

Of all the different types of funds offered, U.S. stock funds are the largest category. To see the forest amidst the trees, remember the classifications I cover earlier in the chapter. Stock funds differ mainly in terms of the size of the companies they focus on and whether those companies are considered "growth" or "value" companies.

Some of these funds may invest a little overseas. The only way to know for sure where a fund is currently invested (or where the fund may invest in the future) is to ask. You can start by calling the 800 number of the mutual fund company that you're interested in. You can also read the fund's annual report (which I explain how to do in Chapter 4). A prospectus, unfortunately, won't give you anything beyond general parameters that guide the range of investments; it won't tell you what the fund is currently investing in or has invested in.

I've tried to order these funds from those that are more conservative to those that are more aggressive.

Dodge & Cox Stock

Another of the fine but few funds offered by Dodge & Cox, this fund focuses on large-company value stocks. Unlike most U.S. stock funds today, it does little trading, often less than 10 percent of its portfolio annually. Like the Dodge & Cox Balanced Fund, this fund is managed by a team and does not try to time the markets. Its annual expense ratio is a low 0.6 percent. Initial minimum investment is $2,500 ($1,000 for retirement accounts). ☎ 800-621-3979.

T. Rowe Price Spectrum Growth

T. Rowe Price offers a number of good stock funds, both U.S. and international, and this fund of funds offers a simplified way to invest in them. The U.S. stock funds in this fund cover the spectrum of company sizes. The fund also offers an international stock fund and the New Era fund, which invests in natural resource stocks and provides a good inflation hedge. Typically, international stocks comprise about 30 percent of this fund's holdings.

This fund of funds is managed by regular meetings of a committee made up of fund managers within the company. Slight changes in allocations among the different funds are made based on expectations of how a particular sector will fare in the future. The expense ratio of the funds in this fund generally averages out to 0.9 percent, and there's no additional fee charged for the fund's packaging. Minimum initial investment is $2,500 ($1,000 for retirement accounts). ☎ 800-638-5660.

What to do about your Mutual Qualified, Shares, and Beacon fund holdings

In the first edition of this book, I recommended three Mutual Series funds: Mutual Qualified, Mutual Shares, and Mutual Beacon. The excellent track record of these funds is largely attributable to the manager of all three — Michael Price. He has taken the concept of value investing to the extreme, often investing in "turnaround situations": companies that are on the ropes and even in bankruptcy. Not as dangerous as it sounds, the strategy has edged out the market averages over the past decade plus — no small feat in the mutual fund business.

However, in 1996, Price sold his funds to the Franklin/Templeton fund family. Although Price continues to manage all three funds, I no longer recommend them to new investors. Franklin is a load fund family and has attached front-end sales charges to the purchase of these funds and has also jacked up the annual operating expense ratio. High fees like this harm a fund's performance.

I still mention these funds in case you already own them. For existing shareholders, the funds remain no load and have retained the older, lower operating expenses. As long as the funds continue to perform well, holding them is fine.

Fidelity's overabundance of funds

Although Vanguard is closing the gap, Fidelity is still the largest mutual fund company in America. Fidelity's success and reputation were built on U.S. stock fund management. Peter Lynch, who managed the Fidelity Magellan fund during the 1980s, is the manager who really got Fidelity noticed. In addition to Magellan, Fidelity had numerous U.S. stock funds that were beating the market averages. As the company grew explosively, Fidelity's ability to produce market-beating returns began to wane during the 1990s for three reasons. First, a number of the star managers left. Second, some of the stellar fund managers struggled to find good places to invest all the new money. Third, the cost savings in managing an increasingly larger mountain of money (in the form of a lower operating expense ratio) was not being shared with Fidelity's customers.

I still like a number of Fidelity funds, but one does need to choose funds carefully at Fidelity. Fidelity is the Procter & Gamble of mutual funds. Just as P&G comes up with scores of different brands of laundry detergent that are pretty much the same, Fidelity offers a maddening array of more-or-less similar funds. In selecting among these better offerings within the Fidelity family, pay close attention to fees, both ongoing and up-front sales charges. On all of the following funds that have sales charges, those charges can be avoided by purchasing the fund inside a tax-sheltered retirement account.

If you're investing outside of a tax-sheltered retirement account, avoid the funds with sales charges. They ain't worth it — you have plenty of good alternatives available. Also be aware that Fidelity funds do lots of trading, so they tend to produce high rates of capital gains distributions — which increases the tax burden for non-retirement account investors.

For investors looking for stock funds that pay modest dividends, Fidelity offers several good choices. **Fidelity Equity-Income Fund** invests in larger company value stocks and tends to pay a decent dividend, currently in the range of 2 percent. One of the ways that this fund gooses its dividend is through investing part of its portfolio in bonds, including convertibles. The fund also invests overseas and lately has had about 15 percent of its stock investments there.

This fund is managed by Stephen Petersen. Petersen has managed this fund only since 1993, but before he came to this fund, he had managed a similar fund plus another for large institutions in Fidelity's institutional division since 1987. Annual expenses equal 0.7 percent.

Fidelity is Fidelity's original fund, dating back to the Depression years — 1930. This is not "the Fidelity fund without a name," although if you say "I want to invest in the Fidelity fund," most people will say something like, "That's great . . . which one?" This fund pays a modest dividend of around 1.5 percent, invests less than 10 percent in bonds, and invests a small portion overseas.

This fund is managed by one of the few but increasing number of women in the mutual fund field, Beth Terrana, who has more than a decade of experience managing similar funds (Growth & Income and Equity-Income funds) at Fidelity. Until the Reagan years, investors had to pay a whopping 8.5 percent load to get into this fund, but today it's load-free and charges a 0.6 percent per year operating fee.

Fidelity Disciplined Equity is one of the few Fidelity U.S. stock funds that actually stays focused on U.S. stocks. It invests in a mixture of mostly large- but also medium- and small-company stocks. These stocks are selected largely by a computer model developed by fund manager Brad Lewis for the specific purpose of selecting stocks that seem underpriced in relationship to a company's overall financial picture.

Lewis has managed this fund since 1988. The fund's operating expenses are a reasonable 0.7 percent. If you like this fund's and Lewis's approach and want some foreign stock exposure, you're in luck: Since 1990, Lewis has managed a near-clone of this fund called **Fidelity Stock Selector,** which has some investments overseas.

Taxes on stock funds

For mutual funds held outside of retirement accounts, you gotta pay income tax on dividends and capital gains that are distributed. This is another reason that most investors are best off sheltering more money into retirement accounts (see Chapter 6).

If your circumstances lead you to have money that you want to invest in stock funds outside of retirement accounts, then by all means do it. But pay close attention to the dividend and capital gains distributions that funds make. I've indicated which funds are "tax-friendly."

In addition to the tax-friendly index funds discussed earlier in the chapter, also check out the **Vanguard Tax-Managed Capital Appreciation Fund**, which, like the Schwab 1000 Fund, invests in the universe of the 1,000 largest company stocks in the U.S. stock market. Unlike the Schwab 1000 Fund, though, Vanguard's offering selects and samples from among the 1,000 companies. Like the Schwab fund, it seeks to minimize capital gains distributions by holding onto appreciating stock and, if it needs to sell some stocks at a profit, offsetting those sales by selling other stocks at a loss.

You shouldn't go into the Vanguard Tax-Managed Capital Appreciation Fund unless you plan to hold your investment for five years. Why? Because you'll get clipped with a transaction fee of 1 to 2 percent for such an early exit. The minimum initial investment is also a hefty $10,000. If you want the flexibility of selling within five years without cost, or if you don't have 10 grand burnin' a hole in your wallet, use the Schwab 1000 fund.

Fidelity Low Priced Stock specializes in investing in small-company, value stocks. As you may guess from its name, it buys stocks that have low share prices. At least two-thirds of the fund's investments are in these stocks. Lower-priced stocks tend to coincide with smaller companies, but not always: The price per share of a stock may bear little resemblance to the size of the issuing company because companies can "split" their stock and issue more shares, which cuts the price per share.

This fund has been managed since its inception in 1989 by Joel Tillinghast, who also worked as an analyst and assistant on several other Fidelity funds beginning in 1986. Avoid this fund's 3 percent sales charge by purchasing this fund *inside of a retirement account*. Annual operating expenses are 1.0 percent. For all the Fidelity funds mentioned in this section the minimum initial investment requirement is $2,500 for non-retirement accounts and $500 for retirement accounts. ☎ 800-544-8888.

Fidelity funds of funds — about time!

If Fidelity were a restaurant, you probably wouldn't be ready when the waiter came to take your order: Fidelity's menu of funds is truly overwhelming. Perhaps more than any other fund family, Fidelity has long been a perfect candidate for a fund of funds. In 1996 (I'd like to think in part due to prodding from folks like myself) Fidelity gave in and now offers funds of funds, called Freedom Funds.

There are five Freedom funds: Freedom Income, Freedom 2000, Freedom 2010, Freedom 2020, and Freedom 2030. The Freedom Income Fund is the most conservative, targeting 40% of its assets to fixed income funds, 40% to money market funds, and 20% to equity funds. At the other end of the scale is the Freedom 2030 Fund, the most aggressive, with 85% of its assets in equity funds and 15% in fixed income funds. The asset allocations of the other three funds fall between these extremes (the higher the number in the fund title, the greater its percentage of stock funds).

All the Freedom Funds draw from a fixed pool of Fidelity funds such as Capital & Income, Government Securities, Intermediate Bond, Blue Chip Growth, Disciplined Equity, Equity Income, Growth Company, Diversified International, and Fidelity Overseas.

On top of the operating expenses of the underlying funds, Fidelity has tacked on a 0.1% management fee for bundling the funds together. It's a reasonable expense, although more expensive than Vanguard's or T. Rowe Price's funds of funds (which don't charge bundling fees).

Other noteworthy U.S.-focused stock funds

Warburg Pincus Emerging Growth focuses on smaller company stocks and makes some investments overseas. It's managed by Elizabeth Dater, who has been managing this fund since its inception in 1988; and Stephen Lurito, who joined Dater in 1993 as co-manager. The Warburg Pincus company was in the private money management business first and then jumped into the mutual fund fray in the mid-80s. Expense ratio on this fund is a bit high — 1.2 percent. If you go through discount brokers, normally you can purchase this fund without transaction fees. Minimum initial investment is $2,500 ($500 for retirement accounts). ☎ 800-927-2874.

Neuberger & Berman: Guardian, Partners, and Focus are three stock funds run by Neuberger & Berman, a New York-based private money manager that's also been in the mutual fund business for decades. These three funds are similar in that they invest in a mixture of small- to large-cap stocks. The Focus and Partners funds tend to focus more on small- and medium-size company stocks, whereas Guardian holds more large-company stocks. Annual operating expense ratio on all three is a very competitive 0.8 percent, and they can be purchased through discount brokers, normally without a transaction fee. Note the low $1,000 initial investment minimums, ($250 for retirement accounts). ☎ 800-877-9700.

Vanguard Primecap is one of the few growth-oriented stock funds that doesn't trade its portfolio heavily, trading typically 10 percent of its fund per year. It invests in companies of all sizes and even invests a bit overseas. This fund has been managed since its inception by Howard Schow and Theo Kolokotrones (say that name five times real fast!) of Primecap Management, a Southern California investment management company. Schow and Kolokotrones have more than six decades of investment experience between them. The expense ratio for this reasonably tax-friendly fund is a competitive 0.6 percent. Minimum initial investment is $3,000 ($1,000 for retirement accounts). ☎ 800-662-7447.

Columbia Growth and **Columbia Special,** like some of the other solid mutual funds offered by companies such as Dodge & Cox and Warburg Pincus, are managed by a firm that got into the mutual fund business after managing money for the already-rich-and-famous. Both of these funds are fairly aggressive and tend to take their lumps in down markets. Columbia Growth invests in a broad array of primarily larger- and medium-size U.S. stocks. Columbia Special focuses more on smaller- to medium-size company growth stocks that have low to no dividends; it is the more volatile and aggressive of the two funds. Both may invest small amounts overseas, typically less than 10 percent. Both funds are team-managed. Growth's annual operating expenses total about 0.7 percent per year; Special's total about 0.9 percent. Growth's initial minimum investment is $1,000 for all accounts; Special's is $2,000.☎ 800-547-1707.

Brandywine invests in high-growth companies of all sizes and has done very well over the years — a moot point, however, if you can't afford its high initial minimum of $25,000. The fund is head-managed by Foster Friess, who oversees about two dozen researchers divided into 8 teams, each of which is responsible for a portion of the portfolio. Be aware that the fund can be volatile. Annual operating fees are 1.0 percent. ☎ 800-656-3017.

Recommended international funds

For diversification and growth potential, funds that invest overseas should be part of an investor's stock fund holdings. Normally, you can tell you're looking at a fund that focuses its investments overseas if its name contains words such as *international, global, worldwide,* or *world.*

As a general rule, you should avoid foreign funds that invest in just one country, such as India or Indonesia or Italy. As with investing in a sector fund that specializes in a particular industry, this lack of diversification defeats the whole purpose of investing in funds. Funds that focus on specific regions, such as Southeast Asia, are better but still problematic because of poor diversification and higher expenses than other, more-diversified international funds.

Should I invest in the Warren Buffett fund?

It's widely known now that Warren Buffett is a heck of an investor. As Chairman and CEO of the Nebraska-based firm Berkshire Hathaway, which invests in other companies' stocks and also owns several other businesses, Buffett's stock market investments have earned in excess of 20 percent per year on average over recent decades.

Because Buffett and his firm invest in many other companies' stocks, investing in his firm's stock is sort of like investing in a mutual fund. So if he's so shrewd a money manager, should you buy into his stock? Probably not. Here's why.

Because of Buffett's renowned stock-picking acumen, Berkshire Hathaway stock, unlike a true mutual fund, sells at a hefty premium to the value of the underlying stocks that Buffett and crew invest in. This stock commonly sells at more than 30-plus times its annual earnings, which is high even for a growth company. In addition, one share of Berkshire Hathaway stock costs about $35,000 because Buffett doesn't like stock splits. He thinks that splits would encourage people with a short-term focus (although this is debatable).

If you want to invest with Buffett but not pay the inflated premium to buy his "stock fund," you could find a list of stocks that Buffett is currently invested in and buy them individually. This is pretty easy to do because Buffett invests in a relatively small number of stocks (typically a dozen or less), holds them for a long time, and discloses his holdings every year in his firm's annual report.

If you're wondering if I would engage in this investment strategy with my own money, the answer is no. Keep in mind that just because you replicate Buffett's portfolio doesn't mean that you're replicating his performance. As I just mentioned, you'll be buying stocks that Buffett bought very cheaply a long time ago; the prices of those stocks have gone up quite a bit since then — that's why he's so rich! Chances are, in fact, you'll be buying those stocks at a premium, which is exactly what Buffett doesn't do.

Moreover, you'll never know what and when Buffett buys next. It would be self-defeating for him to advertise to the world that he thinks a company is undervalued before he even buys it. So he buys first and people hear about it later. And believe me, the stock price of that company will probably be higher by the time you hear about it.

And what does the Oracle of Omaha have to say on the subject of owning stocks? Buffet's advice may surprise you: "Most investors, both institutional and individual, will find that the best way to own common stocks is through an index fund that charges minimal fees."

If you want to invest in more geographically limiting international funds, take a look at T. Rowe Price's and Vanguard's offerings, which include funds that focus on broader regions such as Europe, Asia, and the volatile but higher-growth emerging markets in Southeast Asia and Latin America.

In addition to the risks normally inherent in stock-fund investing, international securities and funds are also influenced by changes in the value of foreign currencies relative to the U.S. dollar. If the dollar declines in value, that helps the value of foreign stock funds. Some foreign stock funds hedge against currency changes. Although hedging helps to reduce volatility a bit, it costs money to do, so I wouldn't worry about it if I were you. Remember, you're investing in stock funds for the long haul. And in the long haul, your international stock funds' performance will largely be driven by the returns generated on foreign stock exchanges, not currency price changes.

The following sections offer my picks for diversified international funds that may meet your needs. Compared to U.S. funds, there are fewer established international funds, and they tend to have higher annual expense ratios. So I've listed fewer options for you (don't forget the two foreign stock index funds, Vanguard Total International fund and Schwab International Index fund, which I discuss in the index section in this chapter). Beware of unproven managers and fund companies that are advertising the heck out of newly developed international funds. Newer funds in this area also tend to have high expenses, which will depress your returns.

T. Rowe Price International Stock

The international stock fund of T. Rowe Price, a pioneer in international investing, has performed well since its inception in 1980. It invests primarily in larger companies in larger, established economies, but it also invests modest amounts (10 to 20 percent) in emerging international stock markets.

This fund is team-managed by the firm of Rowe Price-Fleming (a joint venture with Fleming, a London-headquartered private money management firm). The team is led by Martin Wade, who has three decades of experience in international stock investing. The fund uses numerous managers around the globe, each of whom is responsible for researching stocks in specific countries. The annual operating fee is an internationally reasonable 0.9 percent. Initial minimum investment is $2,500 ($1,000 for retirement accounts). ☎ 800-638-5660.

Vanguard International Growth

Like T. Rowe Price International Stock, Vanguard International Growth invests primarily in large companies with growth potential, mainly in established countries. It also invests about 10 to 20 percent in emerging markets.

International Growth is managed by London-headquartered Schroder Capital Management, which has research offices around the world focused on specific countries. The team is led by Richard Foulkes, who has managed this fund since its inception in 1981. This fund has a Vanguard-thin expense ratio of 0.6 percent and has been reasonably tax-friendly. Initial minimum investment is $3,000 ($1,000 for retirement accounts). ☎ 800-662-7447.

Warburg Pincus International Equity

This fund invests in an eclectic mix of small-, medium-, and large-company value stocks in both established economies and emerging markets (which often make up a third or so of the fund).

This fund is managed by Richard King, who has three decades of international investment experience and has managed this fund since it began in 1989. At 1.3 percent, annual operating expenses are slightly higher than those for some of the fund's peers, but expenses have continued to fall as the fund's assets have grown. This tax-friendly fund is available through most discount brokers without transaction fees. Initial minimum investment is $2,500 ($500 for retirement accounts). ☎ 800-257-5614.

USAA International is well-diversified internationally and focuses on larger company stocks. This fund has been managed since its inception in 1988 by David Peebles. Expenses for this tax-friendly fund are a tad high at 1.1 percent, but they're coming down as assets grow. Initial minimum investment is $3,000 ($250 for retirement accounts). ☎ 800-382-8722.

Tweedy Browne Global Value invests mainly in smaller- and medium-size value stocks worldwide, primarily in established countries. Although it can invest in the United States, its U.S. holdings are expected to be small (less than 20 percent of the fund). The parent company has an excellent reputation, managing money privately since the 1920s; this fund itself has been in existence only since 1993 but has done well. Operating expenses, consistently lowering as the fund grows in size, are still a bit on the high side at 1.4 percent. Initial minimum investment is $2,500 ($500 for retirement accounts). ☎ 800-432-4789.

One of a kind: Recommended specialty funds

Specialty funds don't fit neatly into the other categories I discuss in this chapter. These funds are often known as *sector* funds because they tend to invest in securities in specific industries.

Specialty or sector funds should be avoided in most cases. Investing in stocks of a single industry defeats a major purpose of investing in mutual funds — you give up the benefits of diversification. Also, just because the fund may from time to time be dedicated to a "hot" sector (a sector fund or two is often at the top of short-term performance charts), you can't assume that the fund will pick the right stocks and/or bonds within that sector.

Another good reason to avoid sector funds is that they tend to carry much higher fees than other mutual funds do. Many sector funds also tend to have high rates of trading or turnover of their investment holdings. Investors holding these funds outside of retirement accounts may have to turn over a tidy portion of their returns to the IRS.

The only types of specialty funds that may make sense for a small portion (10 percent or less) of your investment portfolio are funds that invest in real estate or precious metals. These types of funds can help diversify your portfolio because they can do better during times of higher inflation — which often depresses general bond and stock prices. Don't feel obligated to invest in these sector funds, however, because diversified stock funds tend to hold some of these specialty investments.

Utility funds are popular with investors who want more conservative stock investments, and I discuss these funds in this section, too.

Real estate investment trust funds

Do you want to invest in real estate without the hassle of being a landlord? Invest in real estate investment trusts (REITs), which are stocks of companies that invest in real estate. These funds typically invest in properties such as apartment buildings, shopping centers, and other rental properties. Of course, it's a hassle to evaluate REIT stocks, but you can always (you guessed it) invest in a mutual fund of REITs!

REITs are small-company stocks and usually pay decent dividends. As such, they are not appropriate for higher-tax-bracket investors investing money outside of retirement accounts. Most of the larger, diversified U.S. stock funds that I recommend earlier in this chapter have a small portion of their fund's assets invested in REITs, so you'll have some exposure to this sector with investing in a REIT focused fund.

Fidelity Real Estate, the oldest REIT fund, has been managed by Barry Greenfield since its inception in 1986. Greenfield is an investing veteran who has been with Fidelity since 1968. This fund has expenses of 0.9 percent per year. Initial minimum investment is $2,500 ($500 for retirement accounts). ☎ 800-544-8888.

Cohen & Steers Realty Shares has been managed by Martin Cohen and Robert Steers since the fund began in 1991. This fund is best purchased through most discount brokers, where the minimum initial investment is much lower (typically $2,000) instead of the normal $10,000. Discounters also offer it without transaction charges. Annual expenses are 1.1 percent. ☎ 800-437-9912.

Utility funds

Utility funds tend to attract older folks who want to earn good dividends and not have the risk of most stock investments. And that's what utility funds are good for. But this once-staid industry is being shaken up by increased competition.

In a sense, these funds are superfluous. Most diversified stock funds contain some utilities, and those investors who want income can focus on better income-producing funds such as Wellesley Income in the hybrid group.

But if you want a pure play on this relatively stable industry, consider **Fidelity Utilities,** which has been around since 1987 and sports a good track record investing in utilities of all shapes and sizes, including some overseas stocks. Since 1992, this fund has been managed by John Muresianu, who has been with Fidelity since 1986. Its expense ratio is a 0.8 percent annually. Initial minimum investment is $2,500 initial minimum ($500 for retirement accounts).☎ 800-544-8888.

Gold & silver — precious metals funds

Over the millennia, gold and silver have served as mediums of exchange or currency because these metals have intrinsic value and cannot be debased. These precious metals are used not only in jewelry but also in less-frivolous applications such as manufacturing.

As investments, gold and silver do well during bouts of inflation. For example, during the1970's, when inflation zoomed up in the U.S. and stocks and bonds went into the tank, gold and silver company stocks skyrocketed. People were concerned that our government was going on a money-printing binge.

Over a *very* long term, precious metals are lousy investments. They don't pay any dividends, and their price increases just keep you up with, but not ahead of, increases in the cost of living. Although this is better than keeping cash in a piggy bank or stuffed in a mattress, it's historically not been as good as bonds, stocks, and real estate.

If you want to invest in precious metals, don't buy the bullion itself; storage costs and the concerns over whether you're dealing with a reputable company make buying bullion a pain. Also avoid futures and options (see Chapter 1), which are gambles on short-term price movements.

Among the better funds are the **Vanguard Gold & Precious Metals Fund,** which, like most gold funds, invests in mining companies' stocks worldwide, because many are outside the U.S. in countries such as South Africa and Australia. This fund has one of the best track records among precious metals funds and has been around since 1984. Annual operating expenses for this tax-friendly fund are 0.5 percent. Minimum initial investment is $3,000 ($1,000 for retirement accounts).☎ 800-662-7447.

ERIC'S PICKS

American Century Global Gold invests only in gold companies in North America. Around since 1988, this fund has been managed by Bill Martin since 1992. Annual expenses are a reasonable 0.6 percent. This fund can be purchased through most discount brokers without a transaction charge. Initial minimum investment is $2,500 ($1,000 for retirement accounts). ☎ 800-345-2021.

REMEMBER

If you expect high inflation, or if you just want an inflation hedge in case you expect the end of civilization as we know it, stick with a gold fund. But these funds have wild swings and are not for the faint of heart or for the majority of your portfolio. To illustrate why, consider this: In 1993, the Vanguard Gold fund rocketed up 93 percent, whereas in both 1992 and 1990, it lost almost 20 percent.

"Socially Responsible" Funds

Socially responsible mutual funds appeal to investors who want to marry their investments to their social principles and avoid supporting causes that they feel are harmful. These funds attempt to look at more than a company's bottom line before deciding to commit their investors' capital. Many of these funds consider such factors as environmental protection, equal employment opportunity, the manner in which a company's employees are treated, and the level of honesty a company displays in its advertising.

I can certainly understand the desire to put your money where your mouth is; unfortunately, however, socially responsible funds have failed to bridge the gap between theory and practice. If you blindly plunk down your money on such a fund, you may be disappointed with what you're actually getting. Bear with me as I explain.

The problems with socially responsible funds

The biggest problem is that the term *socially responsible* means different things to different people. Sure, there are some industries that most socially conscious investors can agree on as "bad." The tobacco industry, associated with hundreds of thousands of deaths and billions of dollars of health-care costs, is an obvious example, and socially responsible funds avoid them. But most industries aren't so easy to agree on.

For example, McDonald's is the world's largest fast-food (hamburger) company as well as a stock that is held by the *Domini Social Equity Index,* one of the more popular of the socially responsible funds. Domini considers

McDonald's socially responsible because of its support for children's charities, participation in recycling programs, hiring and promotion of women and minorities, and purchase of hundreds of millions of dollars in goods and services from woman- and minority-owned businesses.

But how socially responsible is a company whose business depends on beef? It's certainly not the best for people's health, and cattle raising is tremendously land- and water-intensive. Moreover, some may also question the screening and awarding of contracts based on gender and ethnicity. Others may blame McDonald's for running small local restaurants out of business and contributing to the sterile "strip-mall culture" of our communities.

Or consider Toys "R" Us, the giant toy retailer and another stock that is widely held by socially responsible funds for many of the same reasons that McDonald's is. But this company sells widely criticized video games that are quite violent and keep kids away from homework. Gun control supporters argue that selling toy guns encourages kids to use the real thing. Investors who agree should consider Toys "R" Us a socially *ir*responsible company — and that's before we consider the heaps of plastic (made from petroleum) and the drive toward overconsumption that the toy industry generates.

Pick any company, put it under a magnifying glass, and you can find practices that are objectionable to somebody's (perhaps yours) moral consciousness. Of course, that's a poor argument for throwing in the towel. I'm simply warning you that you may be hard-pressed to find a mutual fund manager whose definition of social responsibility is closely enough aligned to yours. Keep in mind that a mutual fund, by its very nature, is trying to please thousands of individual investors. That's a tall order when you throw moral consciousness into the picture.

It's a small world after all

Even if you can agree on what's socially irresponsible (such as selling tobacco products), funds aren't always as clean as you would think or hope. We live in a global economy where it's increasingly difficult to define a company's sphere of influence. Although a fund may avoid tobacco manufacturers, it may invest in retailers that sell tobacco products, or the paper supplier to the tobacco manufacturer, or the advertising agency that helps pitch tobacco to consumers. (These kinds of definitional problems have caused the major mutual fund companies to steer clear of offering socially responsible funds. Neither Vanguard nor Fidelity offers these funds.)

To top if off, lagging performance

Socially conscious funds, which have been around since the early 1970s, have developed a relatively small following despite the continued boom in mutual funds. Today there are a few dozen of these mutual funds, but their total assets under management are less than 1 percent of all fund assets.

Because of the small sizes of these funds, they're forced to charge relatively high operating expenses. Not surprisingly, socially responsible funds have generally underperformed their morally neutral peers.

Ways to express your social concerns

Some funds that are not labeled "socially responsible" still meet many investors' definitions of socially responsible. These other funds usually carry lower fees and produce better returns. For example, GNMA bond funds invest in mortgages that allow people to purchase their own homes. Municipal bond funds buy bonds issued by local governments to fund projects that most would consider good — such as building public transportation, libraries, and schools. See Chapter 8 for my specific bond fund recommendations.

Among the funds that label themselves as socially responsible, the pickings are slim. Here are two that are worth your time if you really want to try to be socially responsible in your investing:

- **PIMCO Total Return III** invests mainly in U.S. bonds using the same philosophy as PIMCO Total Return (which I describe in Chapter 8). Annual expense ratio is 0.5 percent. This fund must be purchased through discount brokers.
- **Domini Social Equity Index** is a quasi-index fund that invests in Standard & Poor's 500 stocks that meet its definition of socially responsible. Annual expense ratio is rather high for an index fund at 1.0 percent partly because of the small amount of money under management. ☎ 800-762-6814.

REMEMBER

If you consider investing in socially responsible funds, make sure that you look well beyond a fund's marketing materials. If you find a socially responsible fund that interests you, call the mutual fund company and ask it to send you a recent report that lists the specific investments that the fund owns. Otherwise, you may be blissfully ignorant, but not as socially responsible as you may like to believe.

You can always consider alternative methods of effecting social change, such as through volunteer work and donations to causes that you support. You can also exercise a means of change that people the world over are dying for, a means that is guaranteed to all American citizens by the Constitution and is exercised today by only a minority of American adults — the right to vote!

Chapter 10

Working It Out — Sample Portfolios

In This Chapter

- Establishing your financial goals
- Handling life changes
- Investing in retirement
- Managing a windfall

This is the chapter where the rubber hits the road. If you read Chapters 7, 8, and 9 where I discuss the details of money market, bond, and stock funds and everything in between, the concepts and individual funds may be swirling around your brain like random pieces of paper in a city alley during a windstorm. (Chapter 6 covers several important investment selection topics as well, including asset allocation. If you haven't read that chapter, please do so now — otherwise, you'll be less able to make use of the guidance in this chapter.)

In this chapter, I talk through some real live cases. (Of course, the names and details have been changed to protect the innocent!) This chapter should bring a lot of things together for you; at least I hope that it calms the whirlwind.

My goal in going through these cases is to illustrate useful ways to think about investing in funds and to provide you with ideas and specific solutions to investment situations. You may think that you'll benefit most from reading only those cases that seem closest to your current situation, but I encourage you to read as many cases as your time allows — perhaps even all of them. Each case raises somewhat different issues, and your life and your investing needs will change in the years ahead.

Don't worry if your situation doesn't perfectly match one of these cases; in fact, it probably won't be a perfect match. After all, you're uniquely you. However, I do think that the principles illustrated here are general enough to be tailored to just about anyone's specific situation.

Throughout these cases, I hope to show

- How your investing decisions fit within the context of your overall finances (that's one of the constant themes of this book, you know)
- How to consider the important tax impact of your investing decisions
- How to recognize situations in which you may need to make other financial moves prior to (and maybe even instead of) investing in mutual funds

Remember, you must first determine where you stand with regard to your own important financial goals, such as retirement planning (the fund-related ins and outs of which I cover in Chapter 3), as you put together your investment portfolio.

The examples that follow are arranged somewhat by level of difficulty, from the simpler cases to the more complex.

Starting Out

If you're just starting to get your financial goals together, you're hardly alone. If you're still in school or otherwise young and new to the working world, *good for you* if you want to get on the right investing road now! Regardless of your age, though, remember that it's never too late. Just get started.

Beginning at ground zero: Melinda

Melinda is in her 20s, works as an architect, earns decent money, lives in New Jersey, and has no debt and no savings yet because she just started her first job. Financially speaking, she's a blank slate, but because she made a New Year's resolution to get her finances in order, she wants to do something.

Her employer offers her health and disability insurance and a profit-sharing retirement plan, which only her firm may contribute to, but to which small contributions have been made in the past. She wants to invest in mutual funds but doesn't want hassle in either paperwork or complications on an ongoing basis.

On a monthly basis, she figures that she can save $600. She wants to invest for growth. With her money earmarked for long-term future needs such as retirement, she sees no need to invest conservatively (even though she does want some of her investments more conservatively invested). She's in the 28 percent federal tax bracket now, but as her experience in her field increases, she expects to earn more and soon will edge into the 31 percent federal tax bracket.

Recommendations: Melinda should consider investing $2,000 annually in a Roth IRA (see Chapter 3). In her case, a regular IRA contribution won't be tax-deductible because her employer offers a retirement plan under which she is considered covered and because she earns more than is allowed to make a tax-deductible contribution to a regular IRA.

She's willing to be aggressive, so she could invest her first two years' IRA contributions in a couple of good funds that invest exclusively in stocks at Fidelity — maybe, for example, Fidelity Disciplined Equity or Stock Selector and Fidelity Low Priced Stock.

Melinda could establish her IRA account through Fidelity's discount brokerage division, which allows purchasing Fidelity and non-Fidelity funds through one account. Because Fidelity assesses a $12 fee if an IRA fund balance is less than $2,500, sticking with two funds over a few years so as to build each fund's balance above $2,500 would be a wise move. Warburg Pincus International Equity or USAA International would be a good foreign fund to add.

Like everyone else, Melinda should have an emergency source of cash. Although the mutual funds that she's investing in outside her retirement account are liquid and can be sold any day, she runs a risk that an unexpected emergency could force her to sell when the markets are hungover.

With family to borrow from if needed, she could make do with, say, a cushion equal to three months' living expenses. She could even postpone building an emergency fund until after she funds her IRA. (Normally I would recommend establishing the emergency fund first but since she has family she could borrow from, I believe that it's okay to go for the long-term tax benefits of funding the IRA account.) Because she won't keep a large emergency balance, she could keep her emergency fund in her local bank account, especially if the balance helps keep her checking account fees down. Otherwise, she could invest in Vanguard's New Jersey Tax-Free Money Market Fund.

If Melinda lived in a state without a good state-specific money market fund (see Table 7-1 in Chapter 7), she could simply use the Vanguard Municipal Money Market fund, which is federally tax-free.

For longer-term growth, Melinda could invest her monthly savings as follows (the following funds are reasonably tax-friendly, which is important because she's investing outside a retirement account and is in a reasonably high tax bracket):

50%–70% in Vanguard Index Total Stock Market

30%–50% in Vanguard International Growth or Total International Index

These two funds pay very low dividends and, historically, have made modest capital gains distributions. They require a $3,000 minimum initial investment so Melinda needs to save the minimum before she can invest. After the minimum is met and invested in each fund, she can have money deducted electronically from her bank checking account and invested in these mutual funds.

Silencing student loans: Stacey the student

Stacey is a 25-year-old graduate student in psychology with three years to go before she gets her well-deserved degree. She's hoping that all this education will fetch her a decent income when she finally gets out of school.

Her current income amounts to about $16,000 per year. She's also sitting under $15,000 of student debt from her undergraduate days. Both of her loans are in deferment so she's not obligated to make payments until she finishes graduate school: One is incurring interest at 8.75 percent per year; the other is subsidized, meaning that the government is paying the interest until she gets out of school.

Fortunately, Stacey has the starving-student-thing down cold. She's so savvy at living cheap that despite her low income she has an extra $150 to play with at the end of every month. (Stacey has an emergency reserve already in place.)

Stacey would like to be debt-free sooner rather than later, so her first instinct is to use that money to start paying down those student loans. But Stacey is also excited about investing for her future. Because half of her student loan interest is subsidized, she's wondering if she'd come out ahead by using her extra money to open and invest in an IRA account.

Recommendations: Stacey should be proud of herself. Living below her means on such a small income, as well as thinking about her financial future, is commendable. She is asking good questions.

TIP

Getting started with $100 per month or less to invest

Although most mutual funds' minimum initial investment amount of a couple of thousand dollars is quite small compared to private money managers, who have six-figure to several-million-dollar entrance requirements, the amount may still loom large if you're just starting to save and invest. You want to get on with the program, and you don't want to risk giving in to the temptation to spend your savings if it's sitting around in your bank account until you can save enough for high fund minimums.

Here's a way around the problem. Some fund companies allow you to invest in their funds without meeting the minimum initial investment requirements as long as you enroll in their automatic investment program. You can do the trick with these by having a small amount per month deducted from your bank account and sent electronically to the fund company. Call the fund family's toll-free number to see if they offer an automatic investment plan for a fund you're interested in.

Also remember that fund retirement account minimums are significantly lower — often as low as $500 per month, some even less. A final strategy is to save for several months until you have enough for some of the funds recommended in Chapters 7 through 9 that have $1,000 minimums.

Before 1998, tax considerations would have tilted the balance in favor of funding the IRA because the contributions are tax deductible. But now, thanks to the tax bill passed by Congress in 1997, student loan interest payments are also tax-deductible, just like IRA contributions. So either way, whether she funds the IRA or the student loans, she gets a comparable tax break.

With taxes out of the picture, her decision comes down to a comparison of the student loan interest rate to the potential return of her IRA investments. Because she'll be investing for retirement, which is decades away for a 25-year-old, Stacey's time horizon is long enough to focus largely or almost entirely on stocks. As I discuss in Chapter 1, stocks historically have returned about 10 percent per year. Measured against the 8.75 percent interest she is accruing on her unsubsidized student loan, Stacey can perhaps come out a little ahead by holding off on student loan payments and investing in stocks through an IRA account.

I say that it's really Stacey's call as to which option — paying down the 8.75 interest student loan or investing in good stock mutual funds through an IRA — makes her feel more comfortable. Financially, the choice is a toss-up. It's worth noting, however, that the annual savings of 8.75 percent that comes from paying down the student loan is a sure thing, whereas the stock market annual average returns of 10 percent are an expectation and in no way guaranteed.

If Stacey decides to go the IRA route, because she has such a long time horizon, her fund(s) should focus almost entirely on stocks. Ideally, her fund(s) should be diversified across large-, medium-, and small-company stocks as well as international investments. Stacey's situation is ideally suited for a fund of funds. Here are two sufficiently diversified funds with low enough initial minimum requirements:

- T. Rowe Price Spectrum Growth: $50 minimum with automatic investment plan
- Fidelity Freedom 2030: $500 minimum with automatic investment plan

Living month to month with debt: Mobile Mark

Mark is a 42-year-old renter who says that he has no desire to own a home. He doesn't want the feeling of being tied down in case he ever wants to move, something he's done a lot of over the years. Currently, he lives in California. Feeling that he has "hit middle age," Mark wants to start socking away money regularly into investments. He has a large folder filled with mutual fund ads and prospectuses but found most of the material confusing and intimidating. He has about $5,000 in a bank IRA invested in a certificate of deposit.

Mark feels insecure living month-to-month and being so dependent on his paycheck. One of the reasons he's feeling some financial pressure is that, in addition to his monthly rent, he has an auto loan payment of about $300 per month and total credit card debt of $6,000. He also doesn't have any family he can depend on for money in an emergency.

Recommendations: Although Mark has the best of intentions, he's a good example of someone who has managed to get his financial priorities *out* of order. Mark's best and most appropriate investment now is to pay off his credit card and auto loan debt and forget about fund investing for a while. These debts have interest rates ranging from 10 to 15 percent, and paying them off is actually his best investment.

Like millions of others, Mark got into these debts because credit is so easily available and encouraged in our society. Such easy access to borrowing has encouraged Mark to spend more than he has been earning. Thus, one of the first things he should do is figure just where his money goes in a typical month. By using his credit card statement, checkbook register, and memory of items he has bought with cash, Mark can determine how much he is spending on food, clothing, transportation, and so on. He needs to make some tough decisions about which expenditures he'll cut so that he can "save" money to pay off his debts.

Like Melinda (the 20-something architect in the first example), Mark should also build an emergency reserve. If he ever loses his job, becomes disabled, or whatever, he'd be in real financial trouble. Mark has no family to help him in a financial pinch, and he's close to the limits of debt allowed on his credit cards. Because he often draws his checking account balance down to a few hundred dollars when he pays his monthly bills, building up his reserve in his checking or savings account to minimize monthly service charges makes the most sense for him now. Recently, Mark eliminated about $100 per year in service charges by switching to a bank that waives these fees if he direct-deposits his paycheck.

Mainly by going on a financial austerity program — which included sacrifices such as dumping his expensive new car and moving so that he could walk or bike to work — within three years, Mark became debt-free and had accumulated several thousand dollars in his local bank. Now he's ready to invest in mutual funds.

Recommendations: Because his employer offers no retirement savings programs, the first investment Mark should make is to fund a $2,000 individual retirement account (IRA). Mark does not want investments that can get clobbered: He thinks that he has been late to the saving game and doesn't want to add insult to injury by losing his shirt in his first investments. Being a conservative sort, Mark thinks that Vanguard makes sense for him. For his IRA, he can divide his money between a hybrid fund such as Vanguard Wellington (70 percent) and an international stock fund such as Vanguard International Growth (30 percent). In addition to his new $2,000 contribution, Mark also should transfer his $5,000 bank CD IRA into these funds.

Now debt-free, Mark thinks that he can invest about $400 per month in addition to his annual IRA contribution. His income is moderate, so he's in the 28 percent federal tax bracket. He wants diversification, but he doesn't have a lot of money to start his investing program. He has set up automatic investment plans whereby each month the $400 is invested as follows (note that many of these funds have a minimum initial investment requirement of $1,000 and that some of them waive that minimum if you invest via electronic funds transfer):

30% in American Century-Benham CA Tax-Free Intermediate or Long-Term Bond fund

30% in T. Rowe Price Spectrum Growth

20% in Neuberger & Berman Focus

20% in Warburg Pincus International Equity or Vanguard International Growth

Competing goals: Gina and George

George works as a software engineer and his wife Gina works as a paralegal. They live in Virginia, are in their 30s, and have about $20,000 in a savings account, to which they currently add about $1,000 per month. This money is tentatively earmarked for a home purchase that they expect to make in the next three to five years. They figure that they will need a total of $30,000 for a down payment and closing costs; they are in no hurry to buy because they plan to relocate after they have children in order to be closer to family (the allure of free baby-sitting is just too powerful a draw!).

Justifiably, they're pleased with their ability to save money — but they're also disappointed with themselves for leaving so much money earning so little interest in a bank. They figure that they need to be serious about investments because they want to retire by age 60, and they recognize that kids will cost money.

George's company, although growing rapidly, does not offer a pension plan. In fact, the only benefits his company does offer are health insurance and a 401(k) plan that George is not contributing to because plan participants cannot borrow against their balances. Gina's employer offers health insurance, $50,000 of life insurance, and disability insurance — but, like George's employer, Gina's employer does not offer a retirement savings plan.

Recommendations: Deciding between saving for a home or funding a retirement account and immediately reducing one's taxes is often a difficult choice. In George and Gina's case, however, they can and should do some of both. At a minimum, George can save 10 percent of his income in his company's 401(k) plan. Wanting to be somewhat aggressive and considering his age, George could invest about 80 percent in stock funds with the balance in bonds among his 401(k) plan's mutual fund investment options.

Here are his 401(k) plan options and how he should invest:

0% in the money market fund option

20% in Vanguard Bond Index Total Bond Market

0% in T. Rowe Price New Income (another bond fund that has much higher management fees than Vanguard's and mediocre investment returns)

15% in Fidelity Magellan (available without its normal sales charge)

15% in Janus

15% in Vanguard Equity Income

35% in Harbor International (an excellent international fund that's currently closed to new investors but still available through some 401(k) plans such as this one)

0% in a so-called guaranteed investment contract (GIC) which is not a mutual fund but a fixed-return insurance contract (See the sidebar on "Investing money in company-sponsored retirement plans" for a discussion of these investment options.)

If George contributes the maximum amount through his employer's 401(k) and he and Gina still want to invest more in retirement accounts, they can invest $2,000 each, per year, into an IRA.

Gina shouldn't worry that, if she and George divorce, George would get all the money in his 401(k) plan. As with non-retirement account assets, these assets can be split between a divorcing husband and wife. A more significant concern would occur if, say, George is an isolated dunce and refuses to talk to Gina about the investment of this money for their retirement and makes some not-so-smart moves such as frequently jumping from one fund to another. (Try talking about this issue with your spouse. If you don't get anywhere with your spouse, pay a visit to your local marital counselor.)

What about their $20,000 that's sitting in a bank savings account? They should move it, especially because George is a fan of USAA, having benefited from their terrific insurance programs as a member of a military family. Initially, he and Gina can establish a tax-free money market fund such as the USAA Tax-Exempt VA money market fund as an emergency reserve.

Because they don't plan to need the down-payment money for the home for another three to five years, they can invest some of their savings — perhaps as much as half — in the USAA Tax-Exempt Intermediate-Term Bond fund. Even though they will pick up a little more yield, they need to know that the bond fund share price declines if interest rates rise (for that weighty subject, see Chapter 8).

George should get some disability insurance to protect his income (it turns out that his employer offers a cost-effective group coverage plan). Before Gina becomes pregnant, George and Gina should also purchase some term life insurance.

If George and Gina had little or no money saved and couldn't both save for the home and get the tax benefits of their retirement account contributions, they'd have a tougher choice. They should make their decision based on how important the home purchase is to them. Doing some of both (saving for the home and in the retirement accounts) is good, but the option of not using the retirement account and putting all their savings into the home down-payment "account" is fine, too.

TIP

Investing money in company-sponsored retirement plans

In some company-sponsored plans, such as 401(k)s, you are limited to the predetermined investment options your employer offers. In most plans, the mutual funds are decent and make you happy that you didn't have to do the legwork to research them. Plans differ in the specific options they offer, but these basic choices are common:

- **Money market funds:** Offer safety of principal because they don't fluctuate in value. However, you run the risk that your investment will not keep up with or stay ahead of inflation and taxes (which are due upon withdrawal of your money from the retirement account). *In most cases, skip this option.*

  However, one situation in which you might use this option is if you already have a large lump of money accumulated and want a parking place for gradual investment into riskier investments. For regular contributions coming out of your paycheck, money funds make little sense.

  If you use the borrowing feature that some retirement plans allow, you may need to keep money in the money market investment option.

- **Bond mutual funds:** Pay higher yields than money funds, but carry greater risk because their value can fall if interest rates increase. However, bonds tend to be more stable in value than stocks. Aggressive, younger investors should keep a minimum amount of money in these funds, whereas older folks who want to invest more conservatively may want to invest more money this way.

- **Guaranteed-investment contracts (GICs):** Backed by an insurance company that typically quotes you an interest rate a little lower than on bond funds, GICs have no volatility (that you can see). The insurance company, however, normally invests your money mostly in bonds and a bit in stocks. GICs are generally better than keeping your retirement money in a money market or savings account, both of which usually pay a couple of percent less in yield. (See Chapter 8 for more on GICs.)

- **Balanced mutual funds:** Invest in a mixture primarily of stocks and bonds. This one-stop shopping concept makes investing easier and smoothes out fluctuations in the value of your investments — funds investing exclusively in stocks or bonds make for a rougher ride. *These funds are solid options and, can be used for the majority of your retirement plan contributions.*

- **Stock mutual funds:** Invest in stocks, which usually provide greater long-term growth potential but also wider fluctuations in value from year to year. Some companies offer a number of different stock funds, including those investing overseas. Unless you plan to borrow (if your plan allows) against your funds — for example for a home purchase, you probably should have a healthy helping of stock funds.

- **Employee Stock Options (ESOPs):** Offer employees the option of investing in their company's stock (not all companies make these investment plans available). Generally, I would avoid this option for the simple reason that your future income and other employee benefits are already riding on the success of the company. If the company hits the skids, you may lose your job and your benefits. You certainly don't want the value of your retirement account to depend on the same factors. If you expect your company to conquer the competition, though, investing a portion of your retirement account is fine if you're a risk-seeking sort — but no more than 25 percent. If you can buy the stock at a discount compared to its current market value, so much the better.

Wanting lots and lotsa money: Pat and Chris

Pat and Chris earn good money, are in their 40s, and live in South Dakota. Pat is self-employed and wants to sock away as much as possible in a retirement savings plan. He figures that he can invest at least 10 percent of his income. Chris works for the government, which offers a retirement plan with the following options: a money market fund, a government (big surprise!) bond fund, and a stock fund that invests in larger-company U.S. stocks only.

Pat and Chris want diversification and are willing to invest aggressively. They want convenience, and they're willing to pay for it. In addition to Pat's retirement plan, they want and are able to save additional money to invest for other purposes such as Chris's dreams of buying a small business and investing in real estate. They currently own a home that has a mortgage that could easily be supported by one of their incomes. Neither depends on the other's income.

Pat also has an $8,000 IRA account, which is currently divided between the Prudential Growth Opportunity Fund (Class B) and the Prudential GNMA (Class A). Pat has not contributed to the IRA for six years now. He also owns a universal life insurance plan, which he bought from Prudential as well. He bought the life insurance plan five years ago when he no longer could make tax-deductible contributions to his IRA; the life insurance plan is better than an IRA, according to Pat's broker, because he can borrow from it. The broker told Pat last week that his life insurance plan is "paid up" (he need not put any more money into the plan to pay for the $20,000 of life insurance coverage) and has a cash value of $3,300, although he would lose $1,200 (due to surrender charges) if he cashed it in now.

ERIC'S PICKS

Recommendations: First, Pat should get rid of Prudential and his current broker. The broker has sold Pat crummy mutual funds. The Prudential funds have high fees and dismal performance relative to their peers. He could transfer his Prudential fund monies into Vanguard Star or Wellington.

Pat doesn't need life insurance because no one depends on Pat's income. Besides, it's a lousy investment (for the compelling reasons why you're better off not using life insurance for investing, see Chapter 1). Pat should dump the life insurance and either take the proceeds or roll them over into a variable annuity (which I explain later in this chapter).

Pat can establish a Keogh retirement savings plan and stash away up to 20 percent of his net self-employment income per year. A paired plan that offers a high degree of flexibility from year to year in the required contribution is his best bet (see Chapter 3 for more on Keoghs). He could establish his Keogh plan through a discount brokerage account that offers him access to a variety of funds from many firms. Over the years, he could divide up his Keogh money as follows:

15% in PIMCO Total Return

15% in Vanguard Bond Index Total Bond Market

10% in Vanguard Index Total Stock Market

10% in Warburg Pincus Emerging Growth

20% in T. Rowe Price Spectrum Growth

15% in Vanguard International Growth

15% in Warburg Pincus International Equity or USAA International

TIP

Because Chris doesn't have international stock funds as an investment option, Pat can invest more in these than he normally should if he were investing on his own. In Chris's retirement plan, contributions could be allocated this way: approximately a third into the bond fund and the balance in the stock fund.

As for accumulating money for Chris to purchase a small business or to invest in real estate, Pat and Chris should establish a tax-free money market fund, such as the Vanguard Municipal Tax-Free Money Market fund, for this purpose. As could George and Gina earlier this chapter, Pat and Chris can invest in a short- to intermediate-term tax-free bond fund if they anticipate not using this money for at least several years and want potential higher returns.

Changing Goals and Starting Over

Life changes, so your investing needs may need to change as well. If you have existing investments, some may no longer make sense for your present situation. Perhaps your investment mix is too conservative, too aggressive, too taxing, or too cumbersome given your new responsibilities. Or maybe you've been through a major life change that's causing you to reevaluate or begin to take charge of your investments. The following sections offer some examples sure to stimulate your thinking about an investing makeover.

Funding education: The Waltons

One of the biggest life changes that makes many adults think more about investing is the arrival of a child or two. And after considering all the fear-mongering ads and articles about how they're going to need a gazillion dollars to send their little bundles of joy off to college in 18 years, many a parent goes about investing in the wrong way.

The Waltons — Bill, 36, and Carol, 40, along with their two children, Ted, 1, and Alice, 3 — live in the suburbs of Chicago in a home with a white picket fence and a dog and cat. They own a home with a mortgage of $100,000 outstanding. Their household income is modest because they both teach.

The Waltons have $40,000 in five individual securities in a Shearson brokerage account they inherited two years ago. They also have $20,000 in two Shearson limited partnerships, now worth less than half of what they paid for them five years ago. Bill and Carol prefer safer investments that don't fluctuate violently in value.

They have $25,000 invested in IRAs within a load domestic stock fund and $10,000 in a load foreign stock fund outside an IRA. Bill has not been pleased with the foreign fund, and Carol is concerned about supporting foreign countries when so many Americans are without jobs. Both like conservative, easy-to-understand investments and hate paperwork. They also have $10,000 apiece in custodial accounts for each of the kids, which Bill's dad has contributed for their educational expenses. Bill's dad would like to continue contributing money for the kids' college expenses.

Bill just took a new job with a university that offers a 403(b) retirement savings plan, which he can get with many of the major mutual fund companies. He was not saving through his old employer's 403(b) plan because, with the kids, they spend all their incomes. Carol's employer does not have a retirement savings plan.

Recommendations: First, Bill should be taking advantage of his employer's 403(b) plan. Though he may *think* that he can't afford to, he really can. If need be, he should dump the individual securities and use that money to help meet living expenses while he has money deducted from his paycheck for the tax-deductible 403(b) account. (Always consider the tax consequences if you consider selling securities held outside of a retirement account. In the Waltons' case, these securities have only been held for a couple of years and were worth approximately the amount of their tax cost basis — see Chapter 13 for more on tax basis.)

Fidelity would be a fine choice for Bill's 403(b) because he can purchase their solid stock funds without those pesky and costly sales charges he'd get if he were investing in a non-retirement account. He could allocate his money as follows:

25% in Fidelity Puritan

25% in Fidelity Asset Manager

25% in Fidelity Equity-Income

25% in Fidelity Stock Selector

Bill and Carol could hold onto their load domestic stock fund investment that they have in their IRAs: This fund has a solid track record and reasonable annual fees of 0.7 percent. Its only drawback is its sales load of 5.75 percent, which is water under the bridge for Bill and Carol because it was deducted when they first bought this fund.

Their foreign stock fund is not a good fund and has high ongoing management fees. They should dump this fund and invest the proceeds in some better and more diversified international stock funds, such as Vanguard International Growth. And regarding Carol's concerns about supporting foreign companies, any companies today have operations worldwide. If she's strongly against investing overseas, I suppose that she can choose not to invest her IRA money overseas, but her portfolio will likely be more volatile and less profitable in the long run. Foreign stocks don't always move in lockstep with domestic ones, and some foreign economies are growing at a much faster rate than our economy.

TIP

Regarding custodial accounts, Bill and Carol need to remember that the amount of money their kids will qualify for in financial aid decreases as more money is saved in their names. Bill's dad should hold onto the money himself or give it to Bill and Carol. (This latter option has the added benefit of increasing Bill's ability to fund his 403(b) account and take advantage of the tax breaks it offers.) Bill and Carol (and you as well, if you have children) should read Chapter 3, which has important information you should know before you invest in funds for college.

The limited partnerships are bad news. Bill and Carol should wait them out until they are liquidated and then transfer the money into some good no-load mutual funds.

Rolling over (but not playing dead): Cathy

It's a surprise to her as much as it is to her friends and family: Cathy has a new job. Although she was happily employed for many years with a respected software company, she got smitten with the entrepreneurial bug and signed on with a well-funded start-up software company. Her 401(k) plan investment of about $100,000 is invested in the stock of her previous employer. The company is waiting for Cathy's instructions for dealing with the money. It's been nine months since she got sucked into the vortex of the insane hours of a start-up company.

Nearing 40, tired but invigorated from those long days at her new company, Cathy has resolved to make some decisions about where to invest this money. She is comfortable investing the money fairly quickly after she thinks she has a plan. Cathy wants to invest somewhat aggressively; although she enjoys working hard, she happily imagines a time when she doesn't need to work at all. She likes the idea of diversifying her investments across a few different fund families. She also wants to minimize her paperwork by setting up as few accounts as possible while at the same time minimizing transaction fees.

Recommendations: Cathy should sell her stock through her old employer and transfer cash. This sale will save on brokerage commissions. Having her retirement money in one company's stock like this is risky.

For the best of both worlds, Cathy can establish an IRA through Vanguard's brokerage divisions, which would give her access to all the great Vanguard funds, plus access for a small fee to non-Vanguard funds. She could invest the money as follows:

25% in Vanguard Bond Index Total Bond Market

25% in Vanguard Index Total Stock Market

10% in Vanguard Total International

10% in Dodge & Cox Stock

10% in Fidelity Disciplined Equity or Stock Selector

10% in Vanguard International Growth

10% in Warburg Pincus International Equity

Wishing for higher interest rates: Nell, the near retiree

Nell is a social worker. Now 59 and single, she wants to plan for a comfortable retirement. In addition to owning her home without a mortgage, she has $150,000 currently invested as follows:

$40,000 in a bank money market account

$75,000 in Treasury bills that will mature this month

$35,000 in an insurance annuity that's invested in a "guaranteed investment contract and" yielded 6.75 percent last year through her employer's non-profit retirement savings 403(b) plan.

Nell currently earns $30,000 per year and has received pay increases over the years that keep pace with inflation. She has $250 per month deducted from her paycheck for the annuity plan. Her employer allows investments in the retirement plan through almost any insurance company or mutual fund company she chooses. She's also saving about $800 per month in her bank account. She hates to waste money on anything, and she doesn't mind some paperwork.

Nell is concerned about outliving her money; she does not plan to work past age 65. She is terrified of investments that can decrease in value, and she knows a friend who lost thousands of dollars when the stock market crashed in 1987. She says that her CDs and Treasuries were terrific in the early 1980s when she was earning 10 percent or more on her money. She's concerned now, though. She keeps reading and hearing that many large, reputable companies (such as IBM and Sears) are laying off thousands of workers, but the stock market seems to be rising to ever-higher levels. She wishes that interest rates would rise again.

Recommendations: First, Nell should stop wishing for higher interest rates. Interest rates are primarily driven by inflation, and high inflation erodes the purchasing power of one's money (see Chapter 8). The problem here is that Nell's portfolio is poorly diversified. All of her money is in fixed-income (lending) investments that offer no real potential for growth and no real protection against further increases in the cost of living.

Even though she's planning to retire in six years, she's certainly not going to use or need all of her savings in the first few years of retirement. She won't use some of her money until her 70s and 80s. Thus, she should invest some money in investments that have growth potential.

Nell also could and should invest more through her employer's retirement savings plan because she is saving so much outside that plan and already has a large emergency reserve. In fact, she should invest the maximum, 20 percent of her salary. She also can do better to invest in no-load funds for her 403(b) plan instead of through an insurance annuity, which carries higher fees. Vanguard and its hybrid funds (which are far less volatile because they invest in many different types of securities) are logical choices for her to use for her 403(b). I'd recommend the following investment mix for Nell's 403(b):

25% in Vanguard Wellesley Income

25% in Vanguard Star

25% in Vanguard Wellington

25% in Vanguard LifeStrategy Growth

In addition to putting future money into these mutual funds, Nell should also decide whether she wants to transfer her existing annuity money into these funds as well. First, she should check her annuity account statement to see whether the insurance company would assess a penalty for transferring her balance. (Many insurance companies charge these penalties to make up for the commissions they have to pay to insurance agents for selling the annuities.)

If the penalty is high, she might delay the transfer a few years; these penalties tend to dissipate over time (because the insurer has use of your money long enough to earn enough to compensate for the agent's commission). If, however, the annuity is a subpar performer (a likelihood given its high fees), she may want to go ahead with the transfer despite a current penalty. (See Chapter 11 for how to do proper transfers.)

With the $115,000 in money outside of her retirement accounts, Nell can gradually invest (perhaps once per quarter over two years) a good portion of this money into a mix of funds that, overall, is more conservative than the mix she's using for her 403(b). She can be more conservative because she would likely tap the non-retirement money first in the future. She should reserve $25,000 in Vanguard's U.S. Treasury money market fund, which pays 1.5 percent more than her bank account; Nell would like to have her emergency reserve in an investment that's government-backed.

Nell can use taxable funds for the other $90,000 because

- She's in a low-to-moderate tax bracket.
- She is nearing retirement.
- Investing solely in tax-friendly funds wouldn't meet her needs (the stock funds would have to be growth-oriented — increasing the risk beyond Nell's comfort level).

I recommend that she invest the money as follows:

15% in Vanguard Bond Index Total Bond Market

20% in Dodge & Cox Balanced

15% in Lindner Dividend

10% in American Century-Benham GNMA

20% in T. Rowe Price Balanced

20% in Fidelity Puritan

TIP

If you're older than Nell, you can use a similar but more conservative mix of funds. For example, if you're in your 70s, for the 403(b), you could substitute the Vanguard Life Strategy Income fund in place of the LifeStrategy Growth fund. For the non-retirement money, you could shift the Fidelity Puritan money to the Vanguard Bond Index fund.

Lovin' retirement: Noel and Patricia

Noel and Patricia, age 65, are retired, healthy, and enjoying their long days unfettered by the obligations of work. They take long road trips together to pursue their hobbies. Noel is an avid fisherman, and Patricia is a wildlife photographer.

Together, they want about $4,500 per month to live on. Social Security provides $1,500 per month, and Noel's pension plan kicks in another $1,500 per month. That leaves an extra $1,500 per month that must come from their $400,000 nest egg, currently comprised of

$260,000 in bank CDs

$40,000 in a money market

$100,000 in IRAs, most of it in hybrid funds and bonds

They're earning about 6 percent per year on these investments and are in a low tax bracket.

Noel and Patricia have an outstanding $50,000 mortgage at 8 percent interest.

Recommendations: A good portfolio for a retiree must not only provide an income for today's expenses but also protect income for the years down the road. Noel and Patricia are managing to get by on the current income from their investments, but with only 20 percent of their nest egg invested for growth in stocks, they have left themselves quite exposed to the ravages of inflation. Their retirement could easily last another 25 plus years. Unless they allocate their assets more aggressively, their nest egg may not last that long.

They can accomplish all their goals if they are able to boost their returns from 6 percent to 8 percent (you have to crunch some numbers to figure out where you stand in terms of retirement planning; see Chapter 3). Averaging 8 percent annual returns shouldn't prove difficult; Noel and Patricia can boost their stock allocation to about 50 percent.

First, however, when the CDs mature, Noel and Patricia should go ahead and pay off the remaining $50,000 of their mortgage. Even if they invested a bigger portion of their portfolio in potentially higher returning investments such as stocks, they can't expect to get an overall return much better than 8 percent, the interest rate they are currently paying on the mortgage. True, the tax deductibility of mortgage interest effectively reduces that interest rate a bit, but don't forget that they must pay income tax on investment dividends and profits as well as on retirement account withdrawals, which effectively reduces the rate of return on their investments.

As evidenced by their current investment choices, Noel and Patricia are conservative, safety-minded investors. And although they could be more aggressive, Noel and Patricia can't be too aggressive, given their ages. Thus, paying off their mortgage, which carries an 8 percent interest rate, makes good sense. In addition to the psychological satisfaction of owning their home free and clear, by eliminating their monthly mortgage payment, Noel and Patricia will reduce their cost of living, taking pressure off their need to generate current investment income.

They can also afford to move quite a bit of money out of their money market fund into higher yielding bonds funds; $9,000 in the money market, enough to cover six months of expenses together with their Social Security and pension checks, is plenty.

So, after paying off the mortgage and withdrawing cash from the money market, they'll have $141,000 to invest in funds in a non-retirement account. They could invest it as follows:

20% in PIMCO Total Return or Vanguard Bond Index Total Bond Market

20% in Vanguard Wellesley or Lindner Dividend

20% in Dodge & Cox Balanced

30% in Vanguard Balanced Index

10% in T. Rowe Price International Stock

With their IRAs, they could keep their financial affairs really simple and use a fund of funds such as Vanguard's LifeStrategy Moderate Growth.

The dreaded "d"s: Downsizing, divorce, disability, and death

Life isn't always what we hope that it will be. Sometimes it changes suddenly. You lose your job, your health, or a loved one. Everyone reacts differently to these events. Some maintain a balanced and positive perspective. Others get depressed, panic, and make rash decisions.

If you're making financial decisions you haven't had to make before, you owe it to yourself to be educated about your options and the pros and cons of each. Be especially careful about hiring financial help because you're in danger of being too dependent and blindly following advice.

The only step you should rush to take is to raise an emergency reserve if you need one. Be careful about selling any investment that you've made a profit on. In one case, a client I had just started working with got laid off. From his perspective, the layoff came out of nowhere; it was a complete shock. He was married and he and his wife were raising their two children. They were heavily in debt, having stretched to buy the most expensive home they could afford and having leased two expensive cars. They had decent savings, but all the money was in the stock market. Luckily for them, this scenario occurred back in 1992 when the market was doing well. This guy's first move was to sell some of their stock to raise cash to tide them over if finding a job took a while. This move made sense and was all that he needed to do immediately. The rest of their investments could be left alone.

Dealing with a Mountain

Sometimes the financial forces are with you and money *pours* your way. Hopefully, this windfall will happen for good reasons rather than due to a negative event. Regardless, a pile of money may overwhelm you. The good news is that a lump sum gives you more financial options. The following sections describe the way a couple of people handled their sudden wealth.

I got money, lots and lotsa money: Cash-rich Chuck

Chuck is a successful Pennsylvania entrepreneur in his late 30s. Starting from scratch, he opened a restaurant eight years ago. Today, he's reaping the fruits of his labor. After several relocations and remodels, Chuck has built himself quite an operation, with 40 employees on the payroll. It's difficult for him to believe, but his restaurant's profit is now running at around $500,000 per year. Not surprisingly, money has been piling up at a fast rate. He now has about $800,000 resting in his business bank checking account paying next to no interest.

He owns a home with a mortgage of about $250,000 but has no money in retirement savings plans. Chuck doesn't want to set up a retirement savings plan at his company because he would have to make contributions for all of his employees in a plan such as a SEP-IRA or a Keogh (which I cover in Chapter 3).

Chuck has been planning to open another location. He figures that a second location will cost around $400,000, but, as he says, "You just never know with construction work what the total tab may be."

Recommendations: The first thing Chuck should do is get his pile of money out of the bank and into a safer investment. Bank accounts are federally insured only up to $100,000 — so if his bank fails (and banks have and will continue to fail), he'll have a lot to cry over. Besides, money funds pay much better interest than his checking account does.

Chuck has several options for investing his excess money. The first is to pay for the cost of a second location; with his savings, he can likely buy a second location with cash. But he faces a couple of drawbacks to using too much or all of his cash on a second location:

- The issue of liquidity: You can't write checks on a piece of real estate (unless you establish a home equity line of credit).
- The issue of diversification: One advantage to not using all of his savings on a second location is that he can invest some of his savings in investments other than his business.

Another option for Chuck is to pay off his home mortgage. Yes, he gets a decent tax-deduction for his mortgage interest on Schedule A of his Form 1040 — although some of the tax write-off is lost because of his high income. However, because Chuck has all this extra cash, paying off the mortgage saves interest dollars. That would leave $550,000 in his money fund.

If he paid down his mortgage and didn't want to pay all cash for his second restaurant location, he could take out a business loan — but that loan would likely be at a higher interest rate than the rate he pays on a mortgage for his home (because banks consider small business loans riskier). However, because some of the home mortgage interest is not tax-deductible, the options are close to a financial wash in Chuck's case. So he could pay off the mortgage and perhaps use some of his remaining money to pay for part of the second location, and the rest could be financed with a business loan.

He should keep a good cushion — say, around $200,000 — for operating purposes for his business. Some entrepreneurs, including those who have gone on to achieve great success, have violated these principles and more by not only pouring all their savings into their business but also borrowing heavily. I say: to each his own. There's nothing wrong with going for it if you're willing and able to accept the financial consequences. However, if the going gets tough and you don't have a safety net (such as family members who could help with a small short-term loan), be careful.

Because Chuck uses his current bank account for keeping his excess cash as well as for check writing, he could establish a tax-free money market fund with check-writing privileges (some brokerage accounts, such as those offered by Fidelity and Schwab, offer unlimited check writing — see Chapter 7 for more on money funds). Beyond the money market fund, Chuck could begin to invest some money ($100,000 to $200,000) in reasonably tax-friendly mutual funds through Vanguard's brokerage division:

20% in Vanguard PA Tax-Free Insured Long-Term

50% in Vanguard Tax-Managed Capital Appreciation

10% in Warburg Pincus International Equity or USAA International

10% in Schwab International Index

10% in Vanguard International Growth

Inheritances: Loaded Liz

About a year ago, Liz, who is in her 40s, came into a significant inheritance when her mother passed away. She received about $600,000; $150,000 of this sum was a portfolio of individual large-company, higher-yielding stocks, and the balance came as cash. The stock portfolio is being managed by an out-of-state advisor, who charges 1.5 percent per year as an advisory fee and places trades through a brokerage firm. Despite the fact that the portfolio usually has only about eight stocks in it, trade confirmations come in about once per month.

Liz currently is a college professor and makes about $50,000 per year. She has approximately $40,000 invested in the TIAA-CREF retirement plan, with 80 percent in the plan's bond fund and 20 percent in its stock fund. She's saving and investing about $400 per month in the plan because that's the amount she can afford. Liz also has $110,000 in a bank IRA that will mature soon.

Liz currently owns a home and is happy with it. It has a mortgage of about $90,000 at a fixed rate of 9 percent. She would like to retire early, perhaps before 60, so that she can travel and see the world. She's wary of risk and gets queasy over volatile investments, but she's open to different types of funds. She likes to use many different companies but doesn't want the headache of tons of paperwork. Liz prefers doing business over the phone and through the mail because she's too busy to go to an office.

Recommendations: First, Liz should maximize her retirement contributions even though she thinks that she's saving all that she can afford. She has all this extra money now that she could draw upon and use to supplement her reduced take-home pay if maximizing her retirement contributions doesn't leave enough to live on.

This extra cash also affords Liz another good move — getting rid of the mortgage. It's costing her 9 percent interest pre-tax (around 6 percent after tax write-offs) and she'd have to take a fair amount of risk with her investments to better this rate of return.

Liz also needs to invest her money more aggressively, particularly inside her retirement accounts. All of her IRA and 80 percent of her employer's retirement plan money are in fixed-income investments. In the TIAA-CREF plan, she can invest 30 percent in the bond fund, 40 percent in its stock fund, and 30 percent in its global equities fund. She could transfer her IRA account to a discount broker and invest it as follows:

40% in Vanguard Star

20% in Fidelity Asset Manager

20% in T. Rowe Price Spectrum Growth

10% in Neuberger & Berman Guardian

10% in Warburg Pincus International Equity

After paying down the mortgage and keeping an emergency reserve of $40,000, as well as another $70,000 for remodeling, Liz would have $250,000 in cash plus the stocks. She should sell the stocks because their dividend income is taxable and she's paying 1.5 percent per year (plus commissions) to have her account managed. The account has underperformed the S&P 500 by an average of 3 percent per year over the past five years. She could transfer these shares to Vanguard's discount brokerage division and then sell them there to save on commissions as well as to have money at Vanguard to invest in their funds. Then Liz could invest the remaining $400,000 once per quarter over the next three years as follows:

20% Vanguard Muni Intermediate-Term Bond fund

20% Vanguard Tax-Managed Balanced

Liz might do well to invest the remaining 60 percent in a variable annuity. As I explain in Chapter 3, these tax-sheltered investments are beneficial to folks like Liz who have excess money to invest and have many years over which they'd like the money to compound tax-deferred. Within the annuity, she could invest the remaining 60 percent as follows:

20% Vanguard Balanced

25% Vanguard Equity Index

15% Vanguard International

Chapter 11

Application, Transfer, and Other Neat Forms

In This Chapter

- Explaining application basics
- Opening multiple accounts
- Applying for checks and debit cards
- Understanding retirement account forms
- Establishing an automatic investment program
- Asking for help

You're human — so odds are good that you absolutely, positively *don't* like paperwork. Unfortunately, when you invest money, paperwork is required. But don't despair. In this chapter, I show you how to do the fund application and transfer forms.

Although the subject of this chapter may seem dreary, I explain some extra-nifty things that perhaps you didn't know you could do with fund investing. And, unlike dealing with IRS tax forms year after year, fund paperwork is not unpleasant to deal with. You won't have much (if any) ongoing paperwork to do, except for filing the taxes owed on mutual fund distributions held outside of retirement accounts — but that's the subject of Chapter 13.

The examples I've chosen for this chapter use some of the better firms recommended in this book. Because particular types of applications are so similar from firm to firm, you should know how to fill out a Dodge & Cox IRA application, for example, if I show you how to complete the same type of application for T. Rowe Price, or any other such firm.

Non-Retirement Accounts

As I discuss in Chapter 5, you can purchase most of the excellent mutual funds I recommend in this book either directly from the mutual fund company that is selling them or through a discount brokerage firm. Though you'll see many similarities among the applications in this section, you'll also see that brokerage account applications are a different type of animal than mutual fund company applications. Don't worry, though — I show you how to handle them both.

Application basics

Suppose that you've read the chapters in Part II of this book and you've decided that you want to open a Vanguard Municipal Money Market fund to hold your emergency fund reserves. You call them up on their 800 number (☎ 800-662-7447) and ask them to "Please send me your account application materials for the Vanguard Municipal Money Market fund."

Several days later, you get a wad of materials in your mailbox; the envelope has enough density and heft to make a great fly swatter! But don't be intimidated. Most of the stuff in the package is marketing propaganda — the fund company wants to convince you to send them gobs of your money, although some of the material may be educational. Hunt around until you find the document that says something like "Account Registration Form" or "New Account Application" or "Application." It should look something like Figure 11-1.

Here's how to complete a new account application for a non-retirement account:

1. **Your Account Registration.** Choose an appropriate box, and enter the name of the individual or organization who is registering the account.

   - **Individual or Joint Account.** Most people choose this box, which is the option whether you're opening the account for yourself or for yourself and someone else jointly. "Joint tenants with rights of survivorship" is the default classification for jointly registered accounts. A *joint tenancy with rights of survivorship* establishes the following conditions:
     - The person you've jointly registered the account with can do everything that you can do on the account, such as calling and inquiring about account balances, performing transactions, and writing checks. Neither party needs the other's permission (although it's possible to establish the account so that both signatures are required for check writing).
     - Each account holder has an equal interest in the account.

Vanguard
MUNICIPAL BOND FUND

Please do not write in this space. ____/____ DLR# Branch UEXR 1 2

Alpha Code | Soc Code | St Code | Tax Rate | RR | CR | CC

ACCOUNT REGISTRATION FORM

BEFORE YOU COMPLETE THE ACCOUNT REGISTRATION FORM, PLEASE BE SURE TO READ THE INSTRUCTIONS ON THE REVERSE SIDE.

Mail to: The Vanguard Group
Vanguard Financial Center, Valley Forge, PA 19482

For help with this application, or for more information, call us toll-free: **1-800-662-7447.**

PLEASE PRINT, PREFERABLY WITH BLACK INK.

1 YOUR ACCOUNT REGISTRATION (Check one box)

☐ **Individual or Joint Account**

Owner's Name: First, Initial (if used), Last

Owner's Date of Birth — Owner's Social Security Number

Joint Owner's Name: First, Initial (if used), Last

Joint Owner's Date of Birth — Joint Owner's Social Security Number

Joint accounts will be registered joint tenants with the right of survivorship unless otherwise indicated.

☐ **Gift or Transfer to Minor**

Custodian's Name (One Name Only: First, Initial (if used), Last)

Minor's Name (One Name Only: First, Initial (if used), Last)

under the ____________ Uniform Gifts/Transfers to Minors Act
(State of Minor's Residence)

Minor's Social Security Number

☐ **Trust**

Trustee(s)' Name

Name of Trust Agreement

Beneficiary's Name

Taxpayer ID Number — Full Date of Trust Agreement

☐ **Corporation, Partnership, or Other Entity**

Type: ☐ Corp. ☐ Unincorp. Assn. ☐ Partnership ☐ Other

Name of Corp. or Other Entity

Taxpayer ID Number

2 YOUR ADDRESS

Do you have other Vanguard accounts? ☐ Yes ☐ No

Street or P.O. Box Number

City — State — ZIP

Citizenship: ☐ U.S. ☐ Resident Alien ☐ Non-resident Alien ______ Specify Country

( ) Daytime Phone — ( ) Evening Phone

Name of Employer ____________

Occupation ____________

3 YOUR INVESTMENT ($3,000 minimum per Portfolio)

Money Market (45):	$ ______	Intermed.-Term (42):	$ ______
Short-Term (41):	$ ______	Long-Term (43):	$ ______
Limited-Term (31):	$ ______	Insur. Long-Term (58):	$ ______
High Yield (44):	$ ______	Total Investment :	$ ______

4 YOUR METHOD OF PAYMENT

☐ Check payable to: **The Vanguard Group-(Portfolio No. ______)**
(See Section 3 above for appropriate Portfolio number.)

☐ Exchange $______ From ____________
Name of Vanguard Fund

Account Number ____________

Account Previously Established By:

☐ Phone Exchange ☐ Wire on (Date) ____________

Account Number ____________

5 DIVIDEND AND CAPITAL GAINS PAYMENT OPTIONS (Check one box)

Unless a box is checked, all distributions will be reinvested in shares.

☐ Reinvest both income dividends and capital gains in shares.
☐ Pay income dividends in cash and reinvest capital gains in shares.
☐ Pay both income dividends and capital gains in cash.
☐ Send income dividends and capital gains to my bank account via Dividend Express.
☐ Send income dividends to my bank account via Dividend Express and reinvest capital gains in shares.

Important: If you select Vanguard Dividend Express, please provide your bank's telephone number in Section 6 below and attach a voided, preprinted check from your checking account or a preprinted deposit slip from your checking or savings account. A canceled check or deposit receipt will not be accepted.

6 WIRING AND FUND EXPRESS OPTIONS

To arrange for the wire redemption or Fund Express service, please provide your bank's telephone number below and attach a voided, preprinted check from your checking account or a preprinted deposit slip from your checking or savings account. A canceled check or deposit receipt will not be accepted. Passbook savings accounts are not eligible for Fund Express.

( ) ____ - ______
Bank Telephone Number

Please indicate the type of service you wish to establish:

☐ **Wire Redemption**
☐ **Automatic Investment Plan (AIP):** On the ______ day each month*, transfer $ ______ from my bank account to my Vanguard account.
☐ **Automatic Withdrawal Plan (AWP):** On the ______ day each month*, transfer $ ______ from my Vanguard account to my bank account.
*If you wish to arrange a payment frequency other than monthly (e.g., every other month, quarterly, semi-annually, or annually), please circle your choice and indicate the month payments are to begin ____________
☐ **Special Purchases and Redemptions (SPR):** To purchase or redeem shares at any time, using a bank account to clear the transaction.

7 SIGNATURE (Sign below)

By signing this form, I/we certify that:

- I/We have full authority and legal capacity to purchase Fund shares.
- I/We have received a current prospectus of the Fund and agree to be bound by its terms.
- Under penalty of perjury, I/we also certify that —
  a. The number shown on this form is my correct taxpayer ID number.
  b. I am not subject to backup withholding because (i) I have not been notified by the Internal Revenue Service that I am subject to backup withholding as a result of a failure to report all interest or dividends, or (ii) the IRS has notified me that I am no longer subject to backup withholding. **(Cross out item "b", if you have been notified by the IRS that you *are* subject to backup withholding because of underreporting interest or dividends on your tax return.)**
  c. If I/we have chosen a Fund Express option, I/we authorize Vanguard, upon telephonic request, to pay amounts representing redemption(s) made by me/us or to secure payment of amounts invested by me/us by initiating credit or debit entries to my/our account at the bank named above. I/We authorize the bank to accept any such credits or debits to my/our account without responsibility for the correctness thereof. I/We further agree Vanguard will not be liable for any loss, liability, cost, or expense for acting upon my/our telephonic request.

PLEASE SIGN HERE: (If joint account, both owners must sign.)

x ____________ Signature (Owner, Trustee, Etc.) — Date

x ____________ Signature (Joint Owner, Co-trustee) — Date

Welcome to Vanguard!

8 CHECKWRITING OPTION

SUBJECT TO CONDITIONS ON REVERSE SIDE
I/We apply for the privilege of writing checks against this Vanguard Fund account. I/We guarantee the genuineness of each signature and understand this request is subject to conditions on reverse side.
ALL REGISTRANTS (MINORS NOT ACCEPTED) MUST SIGN HERE:
(exactly as you will sign checks)

Signature of Owner, Trustee, Etc. — Date

Social Security Number or Employer ID Number

Signature of Joint Owner, Co-trustee, Etc. — Date

Social Security Number or Employer ID Number

Indicate Number of Signatures Required on Checks ____________
(Unless a number is indicated, only one signature will be required on checks.)

Figure 11-1: Completing an account application.

Source: The Vanguard Group

- If you should die, the entire account balance goes to the other person registered on the account without the hassles and expense of going through probate.

A rarely used option is to register the account as "tenants in common." To arrange a *tenancy in common,* you can have a legal document drawn up specifying that each tenant owns a certain percentage of the account. Unlike shares of ownership for joint tenants with rights of survivorship, the shares for tenants in common need not be equal. If you die, the account is restricted; your share of the account is distributed to the person whom you selected to receive it, and the surviving account holder is required to set up a new account for his or her share.

If you go to the trouble of setting up the account registration as tenants in common, just write in the margin in this section of the form that you want the account set up this way, or attach a short letter that presents the same request. The fund company doesn't want or need to see the legal document which you should keep with your will or other important personal financial documents.

- **Gift or Transfer to Minor.** If you want to open an account in your child's name, check the second box. As the parent, you are the *custodian;* your child is the *minor.* Your state's name is necessary because two different sets of laws govern custodial accounts: the Uniform Gift to Minors Act (UGMA) and the Uniform Transfer to Minors Act (UTMA). Each state allows one or the other. The hitch: Your child is legally entitled to the money in the account when he or she reaches the so-called age of majority (which is, depending on the state, between the ages of 18 and 21). Please read the college investing section in Chapter 3 before putting money into your child's name.
- **Trust.** Generally, you know if you have a trust because you're either the one who sets it up or you are the recipient of assets that are part of a trust. There are many types of trusts. For example, some folks, by the time they get older, have set up a *living trust* that allows their assets to pass directly to heirs without going through probate. If you have a trust agreement, provide the pertinent details at this point in the form.
- **Corporation, Partnership, or Other Entity.** If you want to open a mutual fund account for your corporation, local rotary club, or whatever, use this registration section. You need a taxpayer ID number. If your organization doesn't have one, call the IRS at % 800-TAX-FORM and request Form SS-4.

2. **Your Address.** This part's EZ. You may be wondering why they ask for your phone numbers, the name of your employer, and your occupation. The fund company wants your phone numbers so that it can call you if needed regarding an account issue. The rest of this information is partly required by

fund regulators and partly just desired by the fund company for their own "market research"; they want to know about the people who invest in each of their specific types of funds. If you wish to maintain your privacy, you can skip this stuff and the fund company will still happily open your account. (***Note:*** The fund company does not share this information with the IRS.)

3. **Your Investment.** Here's where you tell 'em which fund you want. But be careful here. In the example at the beginning of this section, the person was interested in the money market fund, which is the first line in the left column. On the line, simply write the amount you want to deposit.

To ensure that the money is deposited into the correct fund, check the account statement that you receive when you open your account. Although it doesn't happen often, fund companies (and you!) occasionally make mistakes.

4. **Your Method of Payment.** Generally, you need to send a check to open your account. Make it payable to the fund (include the fund number if the company numbers its funds as Vanguard does). Don't worry about someone stealing the check or a mail thief cashing it (remember that you make the check payable to the fund). Alternatively, you could open this account by exchanging money from another account that you already have at the company, in this case, at Vanguard.

After you have an account open, you can do exchanges by telephone into other accounts. Exchanges save you the hassle of filling out more application forms every time you open new funds at the same company (although different account types, such as IRAs, do require separate account applications).

Make sure that you have another source of cash during the time it takes for the fund company to open your money fund and send your first check. Sometimes people send in almost all their money and then, in a few days, they wish that they had kept some back.

5. **Dividend and Capital Gains Payment Options.** Most mutual funds make dividend and capital gains payments. If you're not living off this income, it's usually best to reinvest these payments by purchasing more shares in the fund. To reinvest, just check the first box. This strategy eliminates the hassle of receiving and cashing checks often and then figuring out where to invest the money (but it does not change the taxability of a fund's distributions).

On the other hand, if you're retired, for example, you may want the distributions on your fund sent to you so that you can spend it on whoopee cushions and sports cars. On this form, you can choose to have the money sent to you as a check through the mail. Or, even better, the fund can electronically transfer the money to your bank account. This method gets you the money quicker and requires less mail to open and fewer checks to sign and schlep to the bank.

6. **Wiring and Fund Express Options.** This section allows you to establish some other options. *Wire redemption*, if established, allows you to request that money be wired to your bank account. Use this feature if you unexpectedly need money fast. Your mutual fund and your bank may charge for wiring services, though, so don't use wiring as your regular way to move money back and forth to your bank.

If you want to make regular deposits into one of your fund accounts, you can select the *automatic investment plan.* This choice authorizes the fund to instruct your bank to send a fixed amount on a particular day of the month (or some other time period). You can do the same in reverse by withdrawing money on a regular schedule, too. The minimum is $50 (the amount is stated on the other side of this application — it should be stated here to make your life easier). If you want to establish this service for multiple funds, simply attach a letter with your added instructions.

Special purchases and redemptions is an electronic funds transfer — it's like a paperless, electronic check that allows you to move money back and forth between your bank and mutual fund accounts. This process usually takes a full two days to complete because, like a check, the transaction is cleared through the Automated Clearing House (wiring can typically be done same day or next day). The mutual fund and the bank should not charge for this service because it's just like a check (which means that it costs less than wiring).

To establish these additional services, remember to attach a preprinted deposit slip or blank check (write "VOID" in large letters across the front of the check so that no one else can use it).

7. **Signature.** Don't forget to sign the form. A missing signature delays the opening of your account. (The fund company will mail the application back to you!) Attach your check to the application with a paper clip or staple, and pop everything into the postage-paid envelope that should have come with the application. If you can't find the envelope, the addresses and phone numbers for the funds in this book are in the Appendix.

8. **Check-writing option.** This is a useful feature to sign up for on a money market fund. Most money funds limit check writing to amounts of $250 or more.

I don't recommend establishing check writing for bond funds because it creates tax headaches. Every time you write a check on a bond fund, the transaction must be reported on your annual tax return (because the price of the bond fund fluctuates, you'll be selling at different prices than you bought) — yuck! Keep enough cash in your money fund and just write your checks from there.

TIP

Opening many fund accounts without getting writer's cramp

As you see in Part II of the book, some of the larger fund companies have a number of good funds, so you may want to invest in multiple funds at one company. Through a comprehensive account application form, *most* fund companies let you invest in multiple funds without having to complete a mountain of paperwork.

However, not all fund companies offer these comprehensive account application forms. You are supposed to fill out a separate application for each fund you plan to invest in, but you don't need to. Here are several ways around this paperwork nightmare:

- Establish a money market fund first. Then you may do exchanges by phone into any other funds you want. When you call to order the money fund materials, ask for the prospectuses for the other funds that you're interested in. When you do telephone exchanges, fund companies are required by the SEC to ask if you've received the prospectus before they will allow an exchange.
- Some fund companies allow you to attach a separate piece of paper to one application with instructions to the fund company to open "identically registered accounts in the following funds." Next to each fund name, list the amount you want to invest. Don't forget to sign the page and attach your check.
- Open a discount brokerage account through a firm such as Charles Schwab & Company, Jack White & Company, or Fidelity that allows telephone exchanges (a subject I cover in the "Discount brokerage accounts" section).

Discount brokerage accounts

As I discuss in Chapter 5, discount brokerage firms offer you the opportunity, through a single account, to invest in hundreds of funds from many fund companies. Brokerage firms are different from mutual fund companies. The first difference is that brokerage accounts allow you to hold and trade individual securities, such as stocks and bonds. This feature is handy if you hold individual securities and want them in the same account as your mutual fund.

WARNING!

Another difference is that, in addition to offering mutual funds, brokerage accounts allow you to invest in riskier types of securities and engage in riskier investing strategies. Many brokerage firms, for example, allow investing in options (see Chapter 1), which are volatile, short-term, gambling-type instruments. Keep your distance.

Most of the sections on a typical brokerage application are the same as those on a mutual fund application as I describe in the "Application basics" section earlier in the chapter. The following sections explain the main differences that may give you cause for pause.

Margin what?

Brokers offer (and sometimes encourage) *margin trading.* Just as you can purchase a home and borrow some money to finance the purchase when you can't afford to pay all cash, you can do the same with your investments. When you buy a home, most banks require that you make a 10 to 20 percent down payment on the purchase price. When you invest in a brokerage account, you need to make a 50 percent down payment.

Buying investments on margin, which may only be done for non-retirement accounts, is not something I recommend. First, you pay interest. Although the rate is competitive — nothing approaching the worst credit cards — it still ain't cheap. Typically, the rate is a bit less than you would pay on a fixed-rate mortgage on your home.

Also, if your investments fall significantly in value (25 to 30 percent), you get a *margin call,* which means that you'll need to add more cash to your account. If you can't or don't, you'll be forced to sell some investments to raise the cash. Of course, if your securities' prices increase in value, you'll earn money not only on the "down payment" you invested, but also on the borrowed money invested. (That's called *leverage.*) Margin borrowing can't be done in retirement accounts, which is where you should be doing most of your investing (because of the tax benefits).

Excessive margin buying and borrowing was one of the reasons that the stock market crashed so precipitously during the Great Depression. Back then, stocks could be purchased with just 10 percent down.

Borrowing on margin can be useful as a short-term source of money. Suppose that you need more short-term cash than you have in a money fund. What to do? Rather than sell your investments, just borrow against them with a margin loan. This move makes sense especially if you'd have to pay a lot of tax on profits were you to sell appreciated investments.

Getting too personal?

You'll notice in Figure 11-2 in sections 1 and 2 of the brokerage application that several questions ask for financial information that most people consider to be confidential: driver's license number, income, net worth. "Why," you may rightfully ask, "are they being so nosey? Do they really need to know this stuff?"

All brokerage firms ask for this kind of information because of the so-called "Know your customer rule" imposed by regulators. Because brokerage accounts allow you to do some risky stuff, regulators believe that brokerage

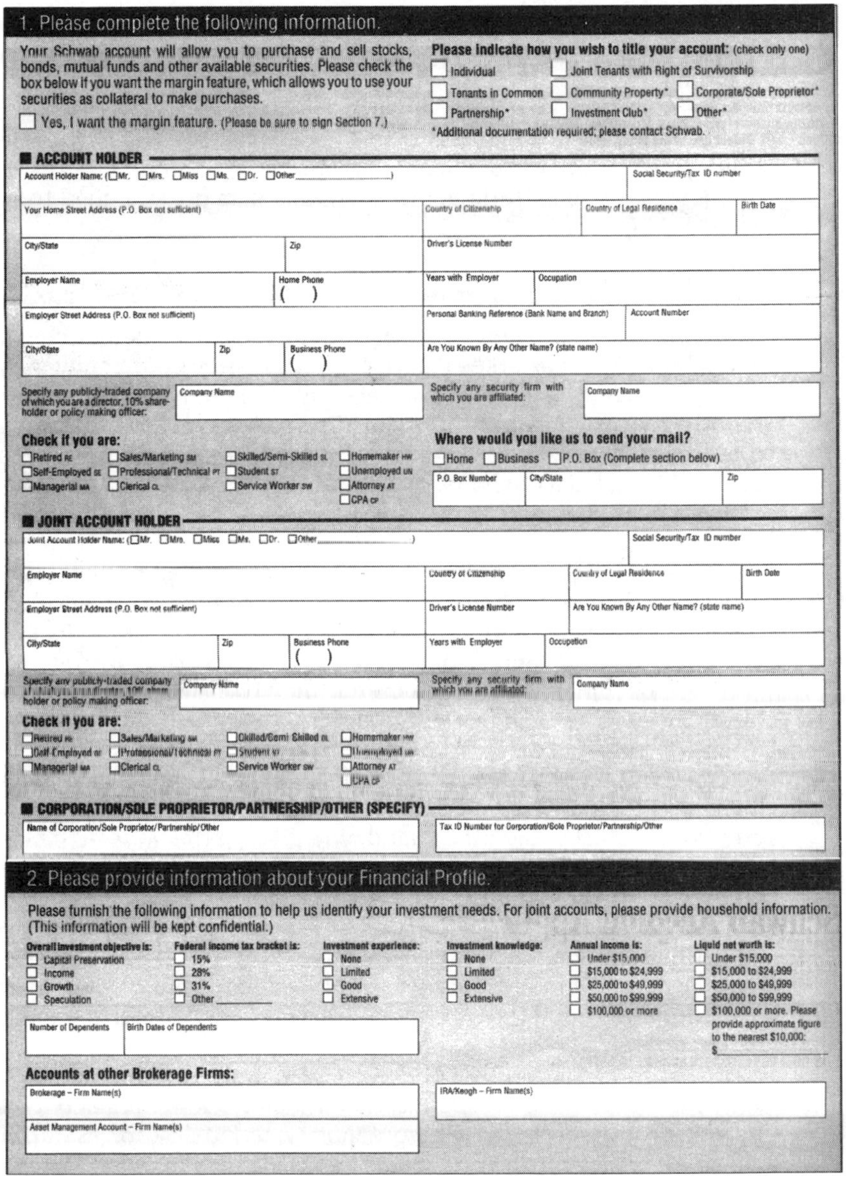

1. Please complete the following information.

Your Schwab account will allow you to purchase and sell stocks, bonds, mutual funds and other available securities. Please check the box below if you want the margin feature, which allows you to use your securities as collateral to make purchases.

☐ Yes, I want the margin feature. (Please be sure to sign Section 7.)

Please indicate how you wish to title your account: (check only one)

☐ Individual ☐ Joint Tenants with Right of Survivorship
☐ Tenants in Common ☐ Community Property* ☐ Corporate/Sole Proprietor*
☐ Partnership* ☐ Investment Club* ☐ Other*

*Additional documentation required; please contact Schwab.

ACCOUNT HOLDER

Account Holder Name: (☐Mr. ☐Mrs. ☐Miss ☐Ms. ☐Dr. ☐Other________) | Social Security/Tax ID number

Your Home Street Address (P.O. Box not sufficient) | Country of Citizenship | Country of Legal Residence | Birth Date

City/State | Zip | Driver's License Number

Employer Name | Home Phone ( ) | Years with Employer | Occupation

Employer Street Address (P.O. Box not sufficient) | Personal Banking Reference (Bank Name and Branch) | Account Number

City/State | Zip | Business Phone ( ) | Are You Known By Any Other Name? (state name)

Specify any publicly-traded company of which you are a director, 10% shareholder or policy making officer: Company Name

Specify any security firm with which you are affiliated: Company Name

Check if you are:

☐Retired RE ☐Sales/Marketing SM ☐Skilled/Semi-Skilled SL ☐Homemaker HW
☐Self-Employed SE ☐Professional/Technical PT ☐Student ST ☐Unemployed UN
☐Managerial MA ☐Clerical CL ☐Service Worker SW ☐Attorney AT
☐CPA CP

Where would you like us to send your mail?

☐Home ☐Business ☐P.O. Box (Complete section below)

P.O. Box Number | City/State | Zip

JOINT ACCOUNT HOLDER

Joint Account Holder Name: (☐Mr. ☐Mrs. ☐Miss ☐Ms. ☐Dr. ☐Other________) | Social Security/Tax ID number

Employer Name | Country of Citizenship | Country of Legal Residence | Birth Date

Employer Street Address (P.O. Box not sufficient) | Driver's License Number | Are You Known By Any Other Name? (state name)

City/State | Zip | Business Phone ( ) | Years with Employer | Occupation

Specify any publicly-traded company of which you are a director, 10% share holder or policy making officer: Company Name

Specify any security firm with which you are affiliated: Company Name

Check if you are:

☐Retired RE ☐Sales/Marketing SM ☐Skilled/Semi-Skilled SL ☐Homemaker HW
☐Self-Employed SE ☐Professional/Technical PT ☐Student ST ☐Unemployed UN
☐Managerial MA ☐Clerical CL ☐Service Worker SW ☐Attorney AT
☐CPA CP

CORPORATION/SOLE PROPRIETOR/PARTNERSHIP/OTHER (SPECIFY)

Name of Corporation/Sole Proprietor/Partnership/Other | Tax ID Number for Corporation/Sole Proprietor/Partnership/Other

2. Please provide information about your Financial Profile.

Please furnish the following information to help us identify your investment needs. For joint accounts, please provide household information. (This information will be kept confidential.)

Overall investment objective is:	Federal income tax bracket is:	Investment experience:	Investment knowledge:	Annual income is:	Liquid net worth is:
☐ Capital Preservation	☐ 15%	☐ None	☐ None	☐ Under $15,000	☐ Under $15,000
☐ Income	☐ 28%	☐ Limited	☐ Limited	☐ $15,000 to $24,999	☐ $15,000 to $24,999
☐ Growth	☐ 31%	☐ Good	☐ Good	☐ $25,000 to $49,999	☐ $25,000 to $49,999
☐ Speculation	☐ Other ________	☐ Extensive	☐ Extensive	☐ $50,000 to $99,999	☐ $50,000 to $99,999
				☐ $100,000 or more	☐ $100,000 or more. Please provide approximate figure to the nearest $10,000: $________

Number of Dependents | Birth Dates of Dependents

Accounts at other Brokerage Firms:

Brokerage – Firm Name(s) | IRA/Keogh – Firm Name(s)

Asset Management Account – Firm Name(s)

Figure 11-2: Getting to know all about you — brokerage account application.

Source: Charles Schwab & Company, Inc.

firms should make at least a modest effort to determine whether their clients know enough and have a sufficient financial cushion to make riskier financial investments.

Make your paperwork go faster and your investing less dangerous and skip this stuff! If you're not signing up for the risky account features such as margin and options trading, the brokerage firm doesn't need to know this personal information.

Neat brokerage account options — checks and debit cards

Some brokerage accounts offer additional features, such as check writing and a VISA debit card (see Figure 11-3), that allow more convenient ways for you to access the money in your account. The only challenge is that you have to request the application for the special type of brokerage account that offers these features. At Fidelity, for example, its souped-up brokerage account is called a Cash Management Ultra Service Account; Schwab's is called a SchwabOne account.

Debit cards look just like credit cards and are accepted by retailers the same way as credit cards. There's one important difference, however. When you make a purchase with your debit card, the money is generally sucked out of your brokerage account money fund within a day or two. You may also use your VISA debit card to obtain cash from ATMs (which usually costs you a buck or so).

TIP

You can use debit cards instead of credit cards. Doing so may simplify your financial life by saving you from writing a check every month to pay your credit card bill. On the other hand, you give up the *float* — the free use, until the credit card bill is due, of the money that you owe — because debit cards quickly deduct the money owed from your account.

As with a money market mutual fund account, you may obtain checks to write against the money market fund balance in your brokerage account. Don't forget to complete the signature card for check writing.

Some brokerage accounts come with even more features that make organizing your finances easier, such as unlimited check writing and a bill payment service. These services cost more money; at Fidelity, for example, you must put more money into your account ($10,000 instead of $5,000), pay a $5 monthly service fee, and also pay an annual account fee of $24 if you don't place at least one trade per year.

Discount brokerage account transfers

You may have cash, securities, and most mutual funds transferred into a new brokerage account that you establish. (If you haven't opened an account yet, you also need to complete an account application form.) All

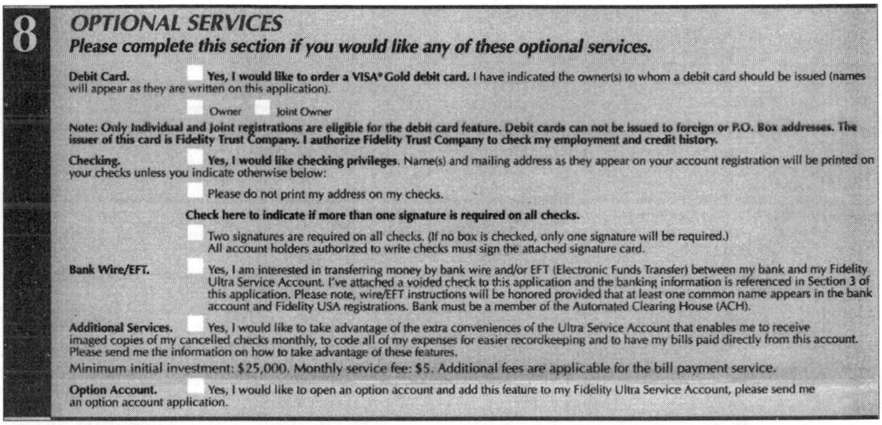

8 **OPTIONAL SERVICES**

Please complete this section if you would like any of these optional services.

Debit Card. ☐ **Yes, I would like to order a VISA® Gold debit card.** I have indicated the owner(s) to whom a debit card should be issued (names will appear as they are written on this application).

☐ Owner ☐ Joint Owner

Note: Only Individual and Joint registrations are eligible for the debit card feature. Debit cards can not be issued to foreign or P.O. Box addresses. The issuer of this card is Fidelity Trust Company. I authorize Fidelity Trust Company to check my employment and credit history.

Checking. ☐ **Yes, I would like checking privileges**. Name(s) and mailing address as they appear on your account registration will be printed on your checks unless you indicate otherwise below:

☐ Please do not print my address on my checks.

Check here to indicate if more than one signature is required on all checks.

☐ Two signatures are required on all checks. (If no box is checked, only one signature will be required.) All account holders authorized to write checks must sign the attached signature card.

Bank Wire/EFT. ☐ Yes, I am interested in transferring money by bank wire and/or EFT (Electronic Funds Transfer) between my bank and my Fidelity Ultra Service Account. I've attached a voided check to this application and the banking information is referenced in Section 3 of this application. Please note, wire/EFT instructions will be honored provided that at least one common name appears in the bank account and Fidelity USA registrations. Bank must be a member of the Automated Clearing House (ACH).

Additional Services. ☐ Yes, I would like to take advantage of the extra conveniences of the Ultra Service Account that enables me to receive imaged copies of my cancelled checks monthly, to code all of my expenses for easier recordkeeping and to have my bills paid directly from this account. Please send me the information on how to take advantage of these features.

Minimum initial investment: $25,000. Monthly service fee: $5. Additional fees are applicable for the bill payment service.

Option Account. ☐ Yes, I would like to open an option account and add this feature to my Fidelity Ultra Service Account, please send me an option account application.

Figure 11-3: Extra services give you more ways to access your funds.

Source: Fidelity Investments

you need is an account transfer form (see Figure 11-4) for the brokerage firm into which you're transferring the assets. Using one of these forms saves you the hassle of contacting brokerage firms, banks, and other mutual fund companies from which you want to move your money. Using this form also saves you the bother and risk of taking possession of these assets yourself.

Here's the information you need to know to complete a transfer form like the one in Figure 11-4.

A. **Information about your (new) brokerage account.** Fill in your name as you have on your account application or as it's currently listed on your account if it's already open. If you're sending in your account application with this transfer form, you won't have an account number yet, so just write "NEW" in the space for your account number.

B. **Information about the account you are transferring.** Write the name of the brokerage, bank, or fund company that holds the assets you want to transfer; also enter the account number of your account there. *Title of account* simply means your name as it appears on the account you are transferring.

Complete one of the following. Complete the relevant section for the brokerage account, mutual fund, or bank account you are moving.

TIP

C. **Brokerage Account Transfer.** Here, you have to decide whether you want to transfer your entire account — which makes your administrative life easier by eliminating an account — or only a part of it. (Another advantage of closing accounts at firms such as Prudential, Merrill Lynch, Dean Witter, Smith Barney Shearson, and Paine Webber is that many of them charge an annual account fee.)

Charles Schwab
Account Transfer Form Schwab Clearing Number: 0164

(Schwab completes.)
❑ Brokerage
❑ IRA
❑ Rollover
❑ Keogh/Qualified Pension Plan
❑ Broker change only
❑ ACAT
❑ Non-ACAT Full
❑ Partial
❑ Mutual Fund

A. Information about your Schwab account. If opening an account, please attach an account application to this form.

Name ____

Your Schwab Account Number ____ Your Social Security or Tax ID Number ____

B. Information about the account you are transferring. (Please refer to your statement for the following information and attach a complete copy of your statement to this form.)

❑ Check here if these assets come from a Qualified Plan.

Name of Firm or Fund Company ____

Your Account Number ____

Broker Clearing #
(Schwab completes.)

Name(s) and the title of the account as shown on your statement ____

Custodian or trustee of this account (Schwab completes.)

Please select only one of the following: section C, D or E.
(Please use a separate form for each account you transfer.)

Non-ACAT transfers only (Schwab completes.)
❑ Deliver all securities in kind and uninvested credit balance.
❑ Issue a certificate for all whole shares, liquidate all fractional shares and discontinue dividend reinvestment.

❑ **C. Brokerage or Trust Account Transfer.** (Please check appropriate box.)
❑ I wish to transfer my entire account. (Please skip to signature section.)
❑ I wish to transfer only the following assets from my account. (Please do not complete the following information if you are transferring your entire account. Section to be used for partial transfers only. Please attach additional forms if necessary.)

Description of Asset (Partial transfers only. NOT TO BE USED FOR MUTUAL FUNDS.)	Quantity (Indicate # of shares or "All.")	Description of Asset (Partial transfers only. NOT TO BE USED FOR MUTUAL FUNDS.)	Quantity (Indicate # of shares or "All.")

❑ **D. Mutual Fund Transfer.** (Please use one form for each mutual fund company.)
Indicate below how you would like your shares transferred and your dividends and capital gains credited. If you do not otherwise indicate below, Schwab will transfer all shares and reinvest your dividends and capital gains.

Name of Fund	Fund Acct. #	Quantity (Indicate # of shares or "All.")	Handling (Check one.)		Credit Capital Gains and Dividends as (Check one if transferring shares.)		Omnibus Account (Schwab completes.)
			Transfer my shares.	Sell my shares, transfer cash.*	Reinvested shares	Cash	

*Requests to sell mutual fund positions are dependent upon the delivering firm receiving and processing the request and may take several weeks to complete.

❑ **E. Bank, Savings & Loan or Credit Union Transfer.** (Check one)
❑ I am only transferring cash.
Please transfer:
❑ All cash in account.
❑ Only $____.
❑ I have a CD that I want to transfer. Please:
❑ Liquidate it IMMEDIATELY. I am aware of and acknowledge the penalty I will incur from any early withdrawal.
❑ Liquidate it AT MATURITY. Maturity Date____/____/____ (Please submit 2-3 weeks before maturity date.)
Month Date Year

F. Please sign this section.

"If this account is a qualified retirement account, I have amended the applicable plan so that it names Charles Schwab & Co., Inc. as successor custodian.

Unless otherwise indicated in the instructions above, please transfer all assets in my account to Charles Schwab & Co., Inc. I understand that to the extent any assets in my account are not readily transferable, with or without penalties, such assets may not be transferred within the time frames required by NYSE Rule 412 or similar rule of the NASD or other designated examining authority.

Unless otherwise indicated in the instructions below, I authorize you to liquidate any nontransferable proprietary money market fund assets that are part of my account and transfer the resulting credit balance to the successor custodian. I authorize you to deduct any outstanding fees due you from the credit balance in my account. If my account does not contain a credit balance, or if the credit balance in the account is insufficient to satisfy any outstanding fees due you, I authorize you to liquidate the assets in my account to the extent necessary to satisfy that obligation. If certificates or other instruments in my account are in your physical possession, I instruct you to transfer them in good deliverable form, including affixing any necessary tax waivers, to enable the successor custodian to transfer them in its name for the purpose of sale, when and as directed by me. I understand that upon receiving a copy of this transfer instruction, you will cancel all open orders for my account on your books.

I affirm that I have destroyed or returned to you credit/debit cards and/or unused checks issued to me in connection with my securities account."

Disposition of money market fund assets other than liquidation and transfer: ____

IMPORTANT: Please be sure to attach a complete copy of the latest statement of the account you are transferring.

X ____
Your Signature Date

X ____
Joint Account Holder Signature Date

Delivering Agents: Please refer to the reverse side of this form for delivery instructions.

Letter of Authorization (Schwab completes.)
To the prior trustee or custodian: Please be advised that Charles Schwab & Co., Inc. will accept the above captioned account as successor custodian.

Successor Custodian Authorized Signature	Date	Date of Trust

Figure 11-4: Brokerage account transfer form.

Source: Charles Schwab & Company, Inc.

If you're doing a partial transfer, simply list the assets you want to transfer — for example, IBM stock — and list the number of shares, such as 50 or All. With partial transfers that include the transfer of mutual funds, you have to go through the hassle of completing one of these silly forms for each company whose funds you're moving. These funds get listed in the next section, D.

You won't be able to transfer (into your new brokerage account) mutual funds that are unique (or *proprietary*) to the brokerage firm you're leaving. Funds that cannot be transferred include funds such as Prudential, Merrill Lynch, Dean Witter, Smith Barney Shearson, Paine Webber, and so on. If there are no adverse tax consequences, you're better off selling these funds and transferring the cash proceeds. Check out Chapter 12, which walks you through the issues to consider if you're debating whether to hold or sell a fund.

If you were sold some of those awful limited partnerships, check with the discount brokerage to which you're transferring your account to see if they will be able to hold them. Discounters will likely charge you a fee ($25 to $50) to hold LPs, but many of the lousy firms that sold them to you in the first place also charge you for the privilege of keeping your account open with them. If the costs are about the same, I'd move the LPs to your new account to cut down on account clutter. Another alternative is to speak with the branch manager of the firm that sold them to you and ask that they waive the annual account fee for continuing to hold your LPs there.

D. **Mutual Fund Transfer.** As I explain in the last section, only certain companies' funds may be transferred into a brokerage account. You need to complete one of these forms for each company's funds you're transferring. For each fund you're transferring, list the fund name, your account number, and the amount of shares you want transferred or sold.

If you are transferring the fund "as is" instead of selling it, you need to tell the new firm whether you want the fund's dividends and capital gains distributions reinvested. Unless you need this money to live on, I'd reinvest it.

E. **Bank, Savings & Loan, or Credit Union Transfer.** Use this section on the form to move money from banks and the like. A potential complication occurs when the money is coming from a certificate of deposit. In that case, send in this form several weeks before the CD is set to mature.

If you're like most people and do things at the last minute, you may not think about transferring a CD until the bank notifies you by mail days before it's due to mature. Here's a simple way around your inability to get the transfer paperwork in on time: Instruct your bank to place the proceeds from the CD into a money market or savings account when the CD matures. Then you can have the proceeds from the CD transferred whenever you like.

F. **Please sign this section.** Sign it and don't forget to attach a copy of a recent statement of the account you're transferring, as well as your account application if you haven't previously opened an account. At this point . . . you're done! Mail the completed application in the company's postage-paid envelope and the transfer will hopefully go smoothly. If you have problems, see Chapter 14 for solutions.

Retirement Account Paperwork

The applications for retirement accounts pose new challenges. The first part of these applications is just like a non-retirement account application, except that it's easier to fill out. Retirement accounts are only registered in one person's name: You can't have jointly registered mutual fund accounts.

Because mutual fund company retirement account forms are so similar to brokerage account retirement forms, I just use the mutual fund company forms as examples in this section.

Retirement account applications

Individual Retirement Accounts (IRAs) are among the most common accounts you might use at a mutual fund company. This section explains what you need to know to complete an IRA application (SEP-IRAs for the self-employed are quite similar). I use the T. Rowe Price mutual fund IRA application as an example (see Figure 11-5).

If you plan to transfer money from a retirement account held elsewhere into the one you're opening, you need to be careful about two details before you start:

- Make sure that the retirement account type you're opening (such as an IRA or SEP-IRA) matches the type you're transferring (unless you're moving money from a 401(k) plan, in which case you would be sending that money into an IRA account because you can't open a 401(k) as an individual).
- If you want to transfer individual securities from a brokerage account, you need a *brokerage* account application for whatever type of retirement account you're opening, not a mutual fund account application.

1. **IRA Registration.** An easy section — but make sure, especially if you're going to be transferring IRA money from another firm into your mutual fund IRA, that you list your name exactly as it appears on the account you're transferring. Otherwise, the firm that has your IRA may make the transfer problematic by causing delays and making you complete yet more forms.

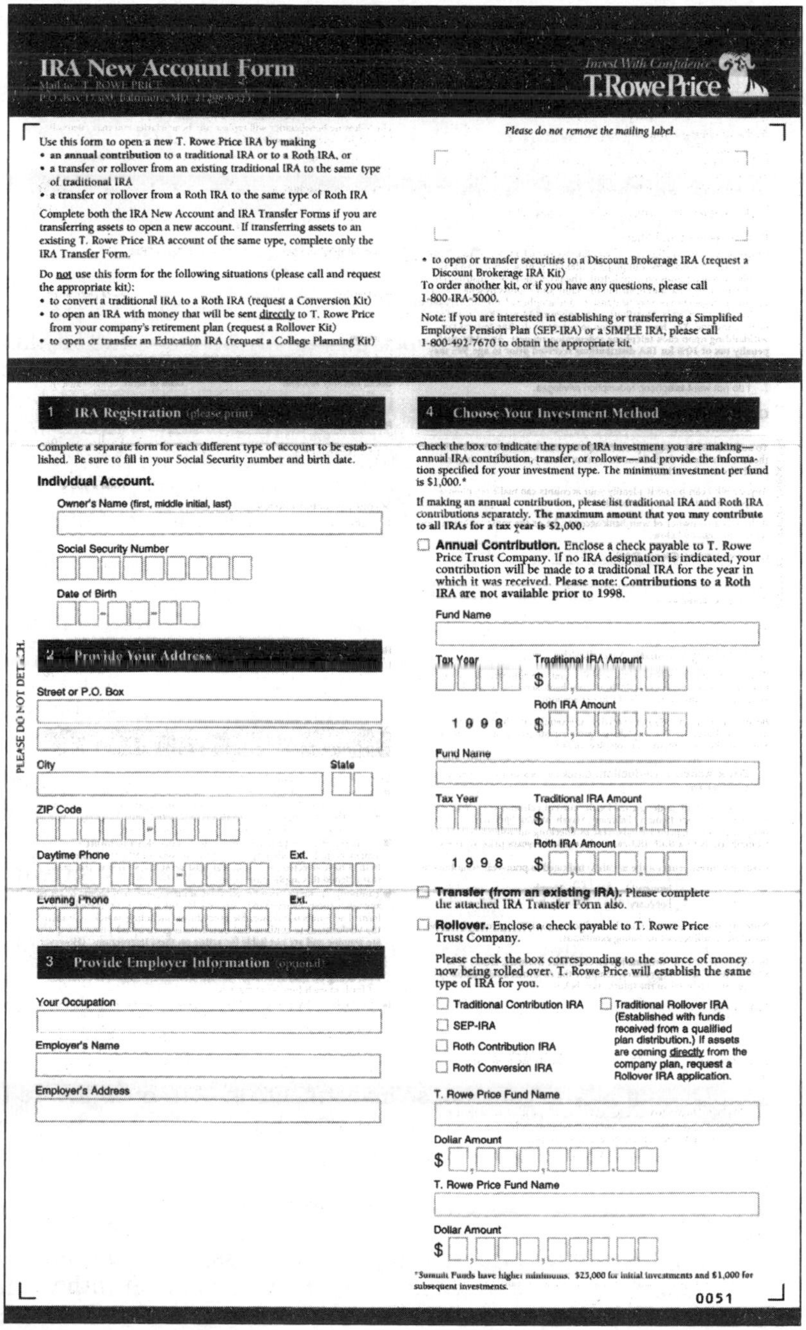

Figure 11-5: Mutual fund IRA application form.

Source: T. Rowe Price

2. **Provide Your Address.** See, this isn't so hard. Enter your mailing address and phone numbers.

3. **Provide Employer Information.** You don't have to provide this information if you don't want to.

4. **Choose Your Investment Method.** Choose one of three methods, each one corresponding to a little check box along the left side of the column. Here's what each of these little boxes allows:

- **Annual Contribution.** This is the box you check if you're opening up a new IRA account with money previously held outside any kind of retirement account. You must specify which kind of fund(s) you want to buy, how much you'll be contributing (up to $2,000), which kind of IRA you want to open (traditional or Roth), and which tax year you're making your contributions for. You have until the time you file your tax return (the deadline is April 15) to make a contribution for the previous year. (I explain the various types of retirement accounts, including IRAs, in Chapter 3.)
- **Transfer (from an existing IRA).** If you want to move an IRA from another investment firm or bank into your new mutual fund IRA, check this box. You also need to complete an IRA transfer form (which I explain in the "stuff to do before transferring retirement accounts" section). This is the best way to move an existing IRA because it presents the least hassle and the fewest possibilities of a tax screw-up.
- **Rollover.** Withdrawing the money yourself from another IRA and sending it yourself to the new account is not a good way to transfer your IRA. The big danger is that if you don't get the funds back into the new account within 60 days, you'll owe mega-taxes (current income tax plus penalties).

  If you're rolling over money from an employer-sponsored plan such as a 401(k), you can check the small box labeled "Traditional Rollover IRA." Tax advisors usually recommend that money coming from your employer's plan should go into a rollover account. This choice allows you to someday transfer the money back into another employer's plan. Of course, you can choose investments in your own IRA, so this may sound like a silly reason to use a "Rollover IRA." An advantage to establishing a contributory IRA, instead, is that you can add to it with future IRA contributions. You can also merge it with other IRA accounts.

  Don't request that your employer issue you a check because your employer must withhold 20 percent for taxes. If you want to roll the full amount over — a wise move — you must come up with the missing 20 percent when you deposit the money into your IRA. Otherwise, you owe tax and penalties on it. Establish your IRA and then instruct your employer to send your money directly to that account.

5. **Select Your Account Service Options** (see Figure 11-6). Here, you can pick and choose from the various service options that come with your IRA account. Some of them, such as telephone/computer exchange, are automatically available with your account unless you specify otherwise. In this section, you can also set up an automatic investment plan; contributions to your IRA can be regularly deducted from either your bank checking account or your paycheck itself.

6. **Designate Your Beneficiaries.** Here's where you specify who gets all of this retirement money if you work yourself into an early grave or haven't spent all of it by the time you go. In most cases, people name their spouses, kids, parents, and siblings. You may also list organizations such as charities that you want to receive some of your money; providing their tax identification number and address is a good idea (just include this information on a separate piece of paper).

If your children are under 18, they don't have access to the money. The money is controlled by a guardian that you identify through your will. If you die without a will, a guardian will be assigned by the courts.

Your *primary beneficiaries* are first in line for the money, but if they've all crossed the finish line by the time that you do, your *contingent beneficiaries* receive the money.

7. **Provide Your Signature.** Don't forget to sign and attach any checks.

Stuff to do before transferring retirement accounts

If you have money in a retirement account in a bank, brokerage firm, other mutual fund company, or in a previous employer's retirement plan, you can transfer it to the mutual fund(s) of your choice. Here's a list of steps for transferring a retirement account. ***Note:*** If you're doing a rollover from an employer plan, please heed the differences indicated:

1. **Decide where you want to move the account. Check out Chapter 5 and Part II.**
2. **Obtain an account application and asset transfer form.** Call the toll-free number of the firm you're transferring the money to and ask for an *account application and asset transfer form* for the type of account you're transferring to — for example, an IRA, SEP-IRA, Keogh, or 403 (b).

5 Select Your Account Service Options

Services selected here will apply only to the account(s) established with this form.

A. To Exchange Fund Shares

Unless you check the box below, you can use the telephone/computer to make exchanges between identically registered T. Rowe Price IRA accounts. Anyone who can properly identify your accounts can make telephone/computer exchanges on your behalf.

☐ I do **not** want telephone/computer exchange privileges.

B. To Redeem Fund Shares

Unless you check the box below, you can use the telephone to redeem IRA fund shares. Anyone who can properly identify your accounts can make telephone redemptions on your behalf. The proceeds of any distribution will be made payable and mailed to the name and address in which your account is registered or may be transferred to another identically registered T. Rowe Price account. **Distributions from your IRA may be treated as taxable income. You have the option to accept or decline federal tax withholding upon each telephone redemption request. An additional penalty tax of 10% for IRA distributions received prior to age 59½ may also apply.**

☐ I do not want telephone redemption privileges.

ATTACH YOUR VOIDED CHECK HERE

C. To Make Electronic Transfers Between Your Bank and T. Rowe Price

To authorize electronic telephone/computer transfers, write "VOID" across the face of a blank check from the bank account you will be using and attach the check to this form.

Anyone who can properly identify your accounts can make telephone/computer purchases on your behalf.

If there is a co-owner of your bank account, he or she must authorize this service by signing below.

Co-owner's Name (Please Print)

Co-owner's Signature

D. To Set Up Automatic Asset Builder

By checking either or both of these boxes, you can authorize T. Rowe Price to transfer money automatically from your bank account or paycheck into your IRA account (minimum of $50 per account).

Be sure investments do not exceed your annual contribution limit. If you overcontribute, the IRS may charge you a substantial penalty. See "IRA Summary & Agreement" for complete details.

☐ **Bank Account Deduction.** Check this box to invest from your bank account.

Contributions will be designated for the current calendar year. However, you may have your January, February, March, and/or April contributions designated for the prior calendar year by checking the following box(es). **Contributions to a Roth IRA cannot be made for years prior to 1998.**

Credit my investments for the month(s) indicated as prior-year contributions.

☐ January ☐ March
☐ February ☐ April

Note: April contributions must be credited to your IRA on or before your tax filing deadline, not including extensions.

Be sure to review the information on electronic transfers, attach your voided check, and, if necessary, complete the co-owner's information in Section 5C. Then fill in the information below.

Fund Name

Dollar Amount $ ☐,☐☐☐.☐☐

Day of month you would like to invest: ☐☐

☐ **Payroll Deduction.** Check this box to invest through payroll deduction. **Contributions will be designated for the calendar year in which they are received.**

Fill in the information below, and we will mail you instructions to forward to your payroll department.

Fund Name

Dollar Amount $ ☐,☐☐☐.☐☐

This selection may be changed at any time by written instruction from you.

6 Designate Your Beneficiaries

Complete this section to designate your beneficiaries. Secondary beneficiaries receive distributions only if no primary beneficiaries survive you.

The following beneficiaries will replace any beneficiaries you may currently have on file with T. Rowe Price for the same type of IRA.

If you are opening more than one type of IRA, this beneficiary designation will apply to both.

Primary Beneficiaries

1. Name

Social Security Number — Date of Birth

Relationship — % of Distribution %

2. Name

Social Security Number — Date of Birth

Relationship — % of Distribution %

Total = 100%

Secondary Beneficiaries

1. Name

Relationship — % of Distribution %

2. Name

Relationship — % of Distribution %

Total = 100%

7 Provide Your Signature

By signing this form, I certify that:

- I have received, read, and agree to the terms of the prospectus for each fund in which I am investing. I have the authority and legal capacity to purchase mutual fund shares and establish this custodial IRA, am of legal age in my state, and believe each investment is a suitable one for me.
- I received, read, and agree to the T. Rowe Price IRA Disclosure Statement and Custodial Agreement for the type of IRA (traditional or Roth) I have selected in Section 4 at least seven days prior to the date that I signed this application.
- I authorize T. Rowe Price Funds, their affiliates, and their agents to act on any instructions believed to be genuine for any service authorized on this form. The Funds use reasonable procedures (including shareholder identity verification) to confirm that instructions given by telephone/computer are genuine and are not liable for acting on these instructions. (However, if these procedures are not followed, it is the opinion of certain regulatory agencies that the Funds may be liable for any losses that may result from acting on instructions given.) All services are subject to conditions set forth in each fund's prospectus.
- By completing Section 5, I authorize T. Rowe Price to initiate debit entries to my account at the financial institution indicated and for the financial institution to debit the same to such account through the Automated Clearing House (ACH) System, subject to the rules of the financial institution, ACH, and the Fund. T. Rowe Price may correct any transaction error with a debit or credit to my financial institution account and/or Fund account. This authorization, including any credit or debit entries initiated thereunder, is in full force and effect until I notify T. Rowe Price of its revocation by telephone or in writing and T. Rowe Price has had sufficient time to act on it.

Please Sign Here:

Owner's Signature — Date

Spouse's Signature — Date

Any resident of a community property state (AZ, CA, ID, LA, NV, NM, TX, WA, or WI) who is married should obtain his or her spouse's consent to establish this account.

Thank you for your investment. You will receive a confirmation statement shortly

0052

Figure 11-6: Fill out this form to select account service options and to name your IRA's beneficiaries.

Source: T. Rowe Price

TIP

Establishing retirement accounts when you're pressed for time

Okay, so you procrastinate — you're human. Perhaps it's April 14th or 15th and you want to establish an IRA, but you need to do it, like, now. You don't have time to call a toll-free number, wait for days to get the application in the mail, and then wait even more days until the fund company receives your check. All is not lost; here are several proven ways out of your pickle:

- **Visit a branch office.** Companies such as Fidelity and Schwab have numerous branch offices. Call them to find the location of the one nearest you. You may also be near other companies' main offices. Check the Appendix of this book for phone numbers and addresses.

  Believe it or not, some branch offices are kept open late on tax day. Fidelity, for example, keeps some of its branches open until midnight.

- **Use an express mail service.** Although not a low-cost option, if you have a couple of days and a chunk of money at stake, Federal Express or some other overnight express mail service may be worth the cost and save you the time of going to a branch office.

- **Go to your local bank.** Establish your retirement account in a savings or money market type of account at the bank. Later, when the dust has settled and you have breathing room, call your favorite fund company for its application and transfer forms to move the money.

  Bank employees will more than likely try to talk you into a CD or one of the mutual funds that they sell. Skip the CD, because you're looking for a very short-term parking place for your retirement contribution. Bank mutual funds tend to be commission-based (load) funds and are not among the best choices.

- **File for a tax extension.** If you're opening a non-IRA retirement account, such as a SEP-IRA or a Keogh, consider buying yourself more time by filing for an extension. Although you must still pay any outstanding tax owed by the April 15th deadline, filing for an extension by using IRS Form 4000 gets you four more months to file your Form 1040 and establish and fund your retirement accounts. (***Note:*** This extension does not apply to normal IRAs; April 15th is the absolute deadline.) Come the middle of August and you're still disorganized or otherwise not ready to get the job done, you can file for one last extension (Form 2688) for yet another two months. October 15th, then, is your final deadline for making your contribution.

If you're self-employed, be aware that you need to file the paperwork for a Keogh retirement account by December 31st — there are no extensions (although, as with other retirement accounts, you do have until the time you file your tax forms to fund the Keogh). You can use the strategies I discuss in this sidebar to get the job done by year end.

You can tell which account type you currently have by looking at a recent account statement; the account type is given near the top of the form or in the section with your name and address. If you can't figure it out on a cryptic statement, call the firm that currently holds the account and ask a representative which type of account you have (just be sure to have your account number handy when you call).

3. **Figure out which securities you want to transfer and which you need to liquidate.** Transferring existing investments in your account to a new investment firm can cause glitches because not all securities may be transferable. If you're transferring cash (money market assets) or securities that trade on any of the major stock exchanges, transferring isn't a problem.

   If you own publicly traded securities, it's often better to transfer them *as is* to your new investment firm, especially if the new firm offers discount brokerage services. (The alternative is to sell them through the firm you're leaving, which may be more expensive.)

   If you own mutual funds unique to the institution you're leaving, check with your new firm to see if it can accept them. If not, you need to contact the firm that currently holds them to sell them.

4. **(Optional) Let the firm from which you're transferring the money know that you're doing so.** (You don't need to worry about this step if you're rolling money out of an employer plan.) If the place you're transferring from does not assign a specific person to your account, you definitely should skip this step. If you're moving your investments from a brokerage firm where you've dealt with a particular broker, though, the decision is more difficult. Most people feel obligated to let their representative know that they are moving their money.

   In my experience, calling to tell your representative the "bad news" is usually a mistake. Brokers or others who have a direct financial stake in your decision to move your money will try to sell you on staying. Some may try to make you feel guilty for leaving, and some may even try to bully you. What to do? I say write a letter if you want to let them know you're moving your account. It may seem the coward's way out, but writing usually makes your departure easier on both sides. With a letter, you can polish your explanation, and you don't run as much risk of putting the broker on the defensive. Just say that you've chosen to self-direct your investments.

   But then again, telling an investment firm that its charges are too high or that it sold you a bunch of lousy investments that it misrepresented to you may help the firm to improve in the future. Don't fret this decision too much. Do what's best for you and what you're comfortable with. Brokers are not your friends — even though they may know your kids' names, your favorite hobbies, and your birthday — it is a *business* relationship.

TIP

Retirement plan applications for the self-employed: SEP-IRAs and Keoghs

If you're self-employed, consider opening a Simplified Employee Pension Individual Retirement Account (SEP-IRA) or Keogh plan. Why? Because most self-employed people can generally make larger tax-deductible contributions into these accounts than they can into a regular IRA. (You can find the pros, cons, and contribution limitations of SEP-IRAs and Keoghs in Chapter 3.)

SEP-IRA applications are virtually identical to IRA applications, so just follow the instructions for the IRA applications in the section, "Retirement account applications" (in fact, some firms use the same application form). At those firms that use SEP-IRA applications that differ from IRA applications, you may see references to "Employer Contribution" as the main difference. You, as the self-employed person, are your own employer. If you have other employees, they may be eligible for SEP-IRA contributions under your plan (the maximum waiting period is three years of service — "a year of service" is a year in which an employee earns $400). When employees become eligible for contributions, you set up accounts for them (with their names on them) — they don't establish accounts on their own.

Keogh account applications are more complicated. You must complete more paperwork, particularly if you set up the combined profit-sharing and money purchase pension plans that I explain in Chapter 3.

A few items appear on a Keogh application that you won't find on an IRA application. First, you must supply an *employer tax identification number*. Say what? If your business has obtained a tax identification number from the IRS, plug that in. Otherwise, most small business owners use their Social Security number.

You also need the name(s) of the *plan administrator*, the person(s) responsible for determining which employees are eligible in the plan, making contributions into the accounts, and other tasks. If you're a sole proprietor, you're the administrator. In larger businesses, the administrator is the business owner(s).

The Keogh plan documents also ask if your company operates, for tax purposes, on a calendar year (which ends on December 31) or a fiscal year (which has some other end date for the year). Employees are eligible to participate after they have completed two years of service. Different plans define a year of service differently, but most use 500 or 1,000 hours as the threshold.

Retirement account transfer forms

Transferring retirement accounts generally isn't too much trouble. In most cases, all you need to do is complete a transfer form. You can use a mutual fund transfer form to move money that's in a bank account, in another mutual fund, or in a brokerage account. You may only use this form to move investment money that you want liquidated and converted to cash prior to transfer.

Figure 11-7 shows the form used for transferring money into a mutual fund IRA. Use one of these forms for each investment company or bank you are transferring IRA money out of. If you're transferring individual securities (for example, stocks or bonds) or want brokerage account features, you need a brokerage account transfer form (and brokerage application forms).

1. **Account Ownership.** List your name as it appears on the account you're transferring (look at a recent statement for that account). Write in your Social Security number and the date you entered this here world.

2. **Address.** List the address as it appears on the account you're transferring. Add your phone numbers in case the mutual fund firm needs to get in touch with you if questions arise.

3. **Type of IRA.** Look at a statement for the account you're transferring and see which type of IRA you have. If you can't figure it out, either call that company and ask them which of the three types you have or just leave it blank, send it to the mutual fund, and let them figure it out!

4. **Where IRA Will Be Invested.** Here's where you tell the fund company which fund you want the money invested in. If you are opening a new IRA, check the first box. If you already have an IRA at Fidelity, check the second box.

In Part B of the form, list the funds that you want the transferred money invested in and the percentage of the money that is to go into each (the percentages must total 100 percent). If you want to divvy up the money into more than two funds, list the additional funds on a separate piece of paper and attach that sheet to the form.

5. **IRA Being Transferred.** Here, you tell the fund where your IRA is currently held. If it's in another fund, list the name of the fund (if you're transferring more than one fund from the same company, just squeeze those names into the space). If it's money in a CD that you're moving, try to send this form several weeks before the CD is scheduled to mature. If you don't get around to sending the form until right before your CD matures, buy yourself more time by directing your bank to place the CD proceeds into a money market or savings type account from which you then can do the transfer.

List the firm where the IRA is currently being held. *Custodian* is simply the term for the company holding your IRA — for example, First Low Interest Bank & Trust or Prune Your Assets Brokerage. You probably won't have a clue as to which person or department handles transfers. If you don't, you can call the company and try to find out. But my advice is: Don't bother. Most funds don't burden you with having to find this information out — the funds should know from other transfers they've done with that firm. If they don't, let them do the work to find out.

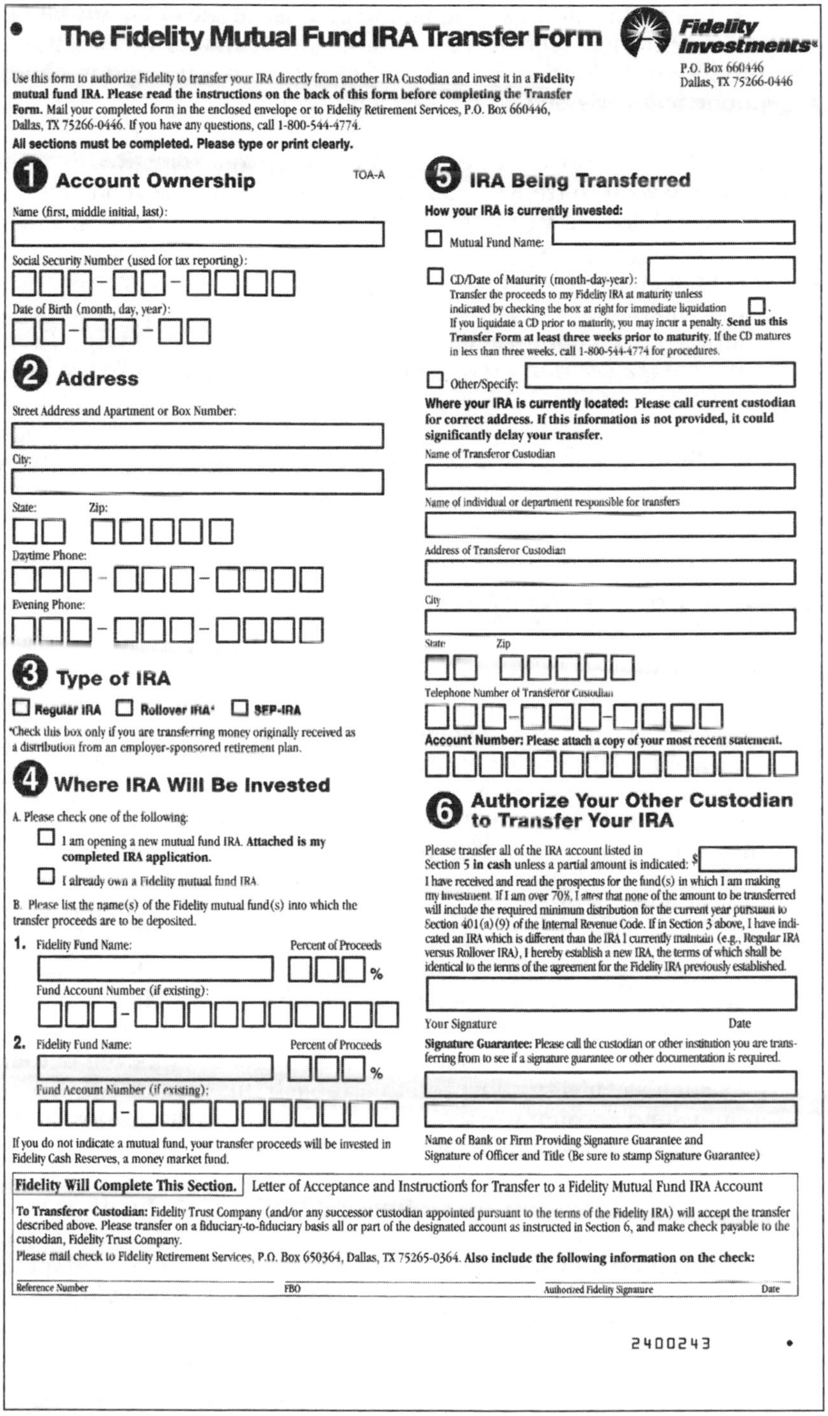

The Fidelity Mutual Fund IRA Transfer Form

Fidelity Investments®
P.O. Box 660446
Dallas, TX 75266-0446

Use this form to authorize Fidelity to transfer your IRA directly from another IRA Custodian and invest it in a **Fidelity mutual fund IRA**. Please read the instructions on the back of this form before completing the Transfer Form. Mail your completed form in the enclosed envelope or to Fidelity Retirement Services, P.O. Box 660446, Dallas, TX 75266-0446. If you have any questions, call 1-800-544-4774.

All sections must be completed. Please type or print clearly.

1 Account Ownership TOA-A

Name (first, middle initial, last):

Social Security Number (used for tax reporting):

□□□ - □□ - □□□□

Date of Birth (month, day, year):

□□ - □□ - □□

2 Address

Street Address and Apartment or Box Number:

City:

State: Zip:

□□ □□□□□

Daytime Phone:

□□□ - □□□ - □□□□

Evening Phone:

□□□ - □□□ - □□□□

3 Type of IRA

□ Regular IRA □ Rollover IRA* □ SEP-IRA

*Check this box only if you are transferring money originally received as a distribution from an employer-sponsored retirement plan.

4 Where IRA Will Be Invested

A. Please check one of the following:

□ I am opening a new mutual fund IRA. **Attached is my completed IRA application.**

□ I already own a Fidelity mutual fund IRA.

B. Please list the name(s) of the Fidelity mutual fund(s) into which the transfer proceeds are to be deposited.

1. Fidelity Fund Name: Percent of Proceeds

□□□ %

Fund Account Number (if existing):

□□□ - □□□□□□□□□□

2. Fidelity Fund Name: Percent of Proceeds

□□□ %

Fund Account Number (if existing):

□□□ - □□□□□□□□□□

If you do not indicate a mutual fund, your transfer proceeds will be invested in Fidelity Cash Reserves, a money market fund.

5 IRA Being Transferred

How your IRA is currently invested:

□ Mutual Fund Name:

□ CD/Date of Maturity (month-day-year):
Transfer the proceeds to my Fidelity IRA at maturity unless indicated by checking the box at right for immediate liquidation □.
If you liquidate a CD prior to maturity, you may incur a penalty. **Send us this Transfer Form at least three weeks prior to maturity.** If the CD matures in less than three weeks, call 1-800-544-4774 for procedures.

□ Other/Specify:

Where your IRA is currently located: Please call current custodian for correct address. If this information is not provided, it could significantly delay your transfer.

Name of Transferor Custodian

Name of individual or department responsible for transfers

Address of Transferor Custodian

City

State Zip

□□ □□□□□

Telephone Number of Transferor Custodian

□□□ - □□□ - □□□□

Account Number: Please attach a copy of your most recent statement.

□□□□□□□□□□□□□□□□□

6 Authorize Your Other Custodian to Transfer Your IRA

Please transfer all of the IRA account listed in
Section 5 **in cash** unless a partial amount is indicated: $
I have received and read the prospectus for the fund(s) in which I am making my investment. If I am over 70½, I attest that none of the amount to be transferred will include the required minimum distribution for the current year pursuant to Section 401(a)(9) of the Internal Revenue Code. If in Section 3 above, I have indicated an IRA which is different than the IRA I currently maintain (e.g., Regular IRA versus Rollover IRA), I hereby establish a new IRA, the terms of which shall be identical to the terms of the agreement for the Fidelity IRA previously established.

Your Signature Date

Signature Guarantee: Please call the custodian or other institution you are transferring from to see if a signature guarantee or other documentation is required.

Name of Bank or Firm Providing Signature Guarantee and
Signature of Officer and Title (Be sure to stamp Signature Guarantee)

Fidelity Will Complete This Section.	Letter of Acceptance and Instructions for Transfer to a Fidelity Mutual Fund IRA Account

To Transferor Custodian: Fidelity Trust Company (and/or any successor custodian appointed pursuant to the terms of the Fidelity IRA) will accept the transfer described above. Please transfer on a fiduciary-to-fiduciary basis all or part of the designated account as instructed in Section 6, and make check payable to the custodian, Fidelity Trust Company.

Please mail check to Fidelity Retirement Services, P.O. Box 650364, Dallas, TX 75265-0364. **Also include the following information on the check:**

Reference Number	FBO	Authorized Fidelity Signature	Date

2400243

Figure 11-7:
Form to transfer your IRA into mutual funds.

Source: Fidelity Investments

List the mailing address and phone number of the company where your IRA is currently held, and also list your account number there. Attach a copy of the statement for the account you want to move. If you don't know the phone number, don't worry — it ain't critical.

6. **Authorize Your Other Custodian to Transfer Your IRA.** Sign the form. If you only want to transfer some of the cash from the account, fill that amount in the little box. If you want to transfer everything, leave the box empty.

It's a pain in the posterior, but some firms that you're transferring out of may require that you burn a chunk of your day to go get your signature guaranteed at your local bank (this is not done by a notary). Fortunately, most companies don't require this effort — but the only way to know for certain is to call and ask.

Stuff this transfer form (along with an application form if you're opening a new IRA) in the envelope and send it off.

Automatic Investing Forms

You may have noticed earlier in this chapter that some mutual fund applications include sections that allow you to establish an automatic investment program. This program allows the fund to electronically transfer money from your bank account at pre-determined times. You'll probably need to complete a separate form to establish this service if your fund company doesn't have this option listed on its original application, you didn't fill out that part when you opened the account, or you're investing through a discount brokerage firm. Figure 11-8 is an example (see the explanation in "Application basics," earlier in this chapter, for how to complete this process).

If you have a pile of money sitting in a money market fund and you want to ease it (some call it dollar-cost averaging) into mutual funds, you can use the services most fund companies and discount brokers offer for this purpose. They may have separate forms to fill out or, even better, companies such as Fidelity allow you to establish this service by phone after your money fund account is open (see Chapter 6 for a discussion of the pros and cons of dollar-cost averaging).

If you're investing outside a retirement account into fund(s) at different points in time, here's a hint: For tax record-keeping purposes, save your statements that detail all the purchases in your accounts. (Most mutual fund companies also provide year-end summary statements that show all the transactions you made throughout the year.)

Vanguard
FUND EXPRESS

Please print, preferably with black ink.

1. **YOUR NAME AND ADDRESS** *(Please provide the information exactly as listed on your Vanguard Fund account.)*

Name ____________________

Street ____________________

City ____________________ State ____________ ZIP ____________

Daytime Telephone Number ____________________ Evening Telephone Number ____________________

2. **YOUR BANK INFORMATION** *(Please be sure that your bank is a member of the Automated Clearing House (ACH) network.)*

Bank or Credit Union ____________________

Branch ____________________ Branch Telephone Number ____________________

Please indicate the bank account to be used with your Fund Express transactions:

Checking account # ____________________

OR

Statement savings account # ____________________

OR

NOW account # ____________________

IMPORTANT: Please attach a voided preprinted personal check. A cancelled check is not acceptable.

3. **YOUR FUND EXPRESS SERVICE**

Vanguard Fund Express may be used for the following:

- **Automatic Investment Plan (AIP)**—transfers money from your bank account to your Vanguard account on a monthly, bimonthly, quarterly, semi-annual, or annual basis. (Maximum: $100,000; minimum: $50)
- **Automatic Withdrawal Plan (AWP)**—transfers money from your Vanguard account to your bank account on a monthly, bimonthly, quarterly, semi-annual, or annual basis. (Maximum: $100,000; minimum: $50)
- **Special Purchases and Redemptions (SPR)**—enables you to transfer money between your Vanguard account and your bank account by toll-free telephone. (Minimum: $100 purchase and $1,000 redemption)

(over, please)

Please indicate below the Vanguard accounts for which Fund Express is being established, the type of service (AIP, AWP, or SPR), the dollar amount to be transferred (for automatic plans *only*), the transfer schedule (for automatic plans *only*), and the date you wish the transfers to begin (for automatic plans *only*).

Fund Name	Account Number*	Service** (please circle)	Dollar Amount	Transfer Schedule†	Start Date†† (month/day)
		AIP AWP SPR	$		
		AIP AWP SPR	$		
		AIP AWP SPR	$		
		AIP AWP SPR	$		

* If the Vanguard account registrations do not exactly match the bank account registration (including spellings, abbreviations, and initials), all registered shareholders of the Vanguard accounts must have their signatures guaranteed in Section 5 below by an authorized officer of a bank that is a member of the Federal Deposit Insurance Corporation (FDIC), a trust company, or a member of a domestic stock exchange.

** AIP and AWP cannot be established concurrently.

† A monthly, bimonthly (every other month), quarterly, semi-annual, or annual schedule may be selected. If no schedule is indicated, assets will be transferred on a *monthly* basis.

†† The Fund Express service will not begin until *three weeks after* your application has been processed by Vanguard. If the start date you selected falls within this processing period, the transfers will not begin until the next date in your designated schedule.

4. **SHAREHOLDER SIGNATURE(S)** *(Important: **All registered shareholders must sign exactly as registered.**)*

I/We authorize Vanguard, upon telephonic request, to pay amounts representing redemption(s) made by me/us or to secure payments of amounts invested by me/us by initiating credit or debit entries to my/our account at the bank I/we have indicated. I/We authorize the bank to accept any such credits or debits to my/our account without responsibility for the correctness thereof. I/We further agree that Vanguard will not be held accountable for any loss, liability, cost, or expense for acting upon my/our telephonic instructions.

It is understood that this authorization may be terminated by me/us at any time by *written* notification to Vanguard *and* to the bank. The termination request will be effective as soon as Vanguard has had a reasonable amount of time to act upon it.

____________________ ____________________

Account Owner's Signature / Date Joint Owner's Signature / Date

5. **SIGNATURE GUARANTEE** *(If applicable)*

As stated in Section 3 above, if your bank account registration **does not exactly** match the registration of all of the Vanguard accounts you have listed above, all registered shareholders must have their signatures guaranteed below.

____

Authorized Signature of Registered Vanguard Shareholder

____

Authorized Signature of Registered Vanguard Shareholder

Authorized Officer to place stamp here

____

Guarantor's Signature

____

Title

Figure 11-8: Investing on auto-pilot.

Source: The Vanguard Group

If you don't save your statements, it won't be the end of the world — if you're investing through most of the larger and better fund companies, which now are able to tell you your average cost per share when you need to sell your shares.

Other Safety Nets

If you get stuck or just can't deal with filling out forms on your own — not even with the comfort and solace you get from this book — you have two safety nets:

- **Call the fund company's or discount broker's toll-free number and ask for help.** (The number is usually listed at the top of the first page of the application.) Providing assistance is one of the many tasks those phone representatives are paid to do. If you get someone who's impatient or incompetent, simply call back and you'll get someone else. (If this happens with the companies recommended in this book, please write and let me know!)

  If you're dealing with a problem that can't be solved during the first phone call and you're working with a representative on it, jot down the person's name and extension number. And don't forget to ask which office location they're in. Some of the larger fund companies route their toll-free calls to various offices, so you never know where your call has ended up unless you ask.

- **Visit a branch office.** After all, accessibility is one of the reasons that branch offices exist. Not all companies have them — see Chapter 5 for more details.

Part III
Maintaining a Great Fund Portfolio

The 5th Wave   By Rich Tennant

In this part . . .

This part covers stuff that other mutual fund books leave you to figure out for yourself, including how to maintain a fund portfolio after it's up and running. Here you discover how to evaluate the performance of your funds, how to decide when to sell, how to understand tax forms that your mutual fund companies send you, and how to fix the rare but downright aggravating technical glitches and problems that pop up in any investing program.

Chapter 12

Evaluating Your Funds: Sell, Hold, or Buy More?

In This Chapter

- How to read (and understand) the finer points of fund statements
- Which figures tell you whether your funds are winning or losing
- How to compare the performance of your fund to the real competition
- How to decide whether to sell, to hold, or to buy more of a fund

After you've explored different funds, filled out the application forms, and mailed in your money, the hard part is over. Congratulations! You've accomplished what millions of people are still thinking about but haven't gotten off their blessed keisters to do (probably because they haven't read this book yet!).

Now that you've started investing in funds (or even if you've been doing so for years), of course, you want to know how you're doing — specifically, you want to know how much money you're making. It's not that you're greedy; after all, a desire to make money spurred you to invest in funds in the first place. You'd just like some feedback about how your funds are doing.

You may also be interested in evaluating funds you already owned before you and I "met." You may be wondering if your prior holdings are greyhounds, basset hounds, or mongrels.

In this chapter, I explain how to evaluate the performance of your funds and decide what to do with them over time. I also explain why most of the statements you get from fund companies make your head spin and leave you clueless as to how you're doing. I start with the first thing that you receive after you invest money in a fund: an account statement.

Understanding Your Fund Statement

Every mutual fund company has its own unique statement design. But they all report the same types of information, usually in columns. The following sections present the type of entries you find on your statement, along with my short explanations of what they all mean (see Figure 12-1).

Trade date or date of transaction

The trade date (or date of transaction) is the date that the mutual fund company processed your transaction. For example, if you mailed a check as an initial deposit with your account application, you can see which date they actually received and processed your check. If the fund company receives your deposit by 4:00 p.m. EST, it will purchase shares that same day

THE Vanguard GROUP.

December 31, 1997, year-to-date   Page 17 of 21

Vanguard Selected Value Portfolio

(800) 662-2739 - Client Services
Fund number: 934
Account number: 9850839956
Statement number: 001158511

ACCOUNT VALUE	On 12/31/1996	On 12/31/1997
	$ 0.00	**$ 2,001.08**

Trade date	Transaction	Dollar amount	Share price	Shares transacted	Total shares owned
	Balance on 12/31/1996		$ 10.91		.000
3/21	Exchange from MM-PRIME	$ 1,000.00	10.68	93.633	93.633
6/17	Check purchase	765.00	12.22	62.602	156.235
12/19	Income dividend .05	7.81	11.86	.659	156.894
12/19	ST cap gain .225	35.15	11.86	2.964	159.858
12/19	LT cap gain .235	36.72	11.86	3.096	162.954
	Balance on 12/31/1997		**$ 12.28**		**162.954**

Income dividends	$ 7.81
Short-term gains	35.15
Long-term gains	36.72
Total income year-to-date	$ 79.68
Purchases year-to-date	$ 1,765.00

The current Fund distribution was payable on December 24, 1997.

IMPORTANT TAX NOTE
Because of changes in federal tax law, long-term capital gains distributed in 1997 may be taxed at different rates, depending on how long the fund held an asset and when it was sold. Vanguard will mail Form 1099-DIV by January 31, 1998, providing information for properly reporting capital gain distributions.

Figure 12-1: A typical statement.

Source: The Vanguard Group

in the bond and/or stock funds that you intended the check for. Money market funds work a little differently than bond and stock funds. Money market fund deposits don't start earning interest until the day after the company receives your money. Why the wait? Because the fund company must convert your money into federal funds.

Transaction description

In the transaction description column, you find a brief blurb about what was actually done or transacted. For example, if you mailed in a deposit, this item may simply say something like *purchase,* or *purchase by check.* If you moved money into a fund from your U.S. Treasury money market fund by phone, this item may say *phone exchange from U.S.T. money fund.*

For retirement accounts, companies use slightly different lingo in the transaction column. Often, new purchases are referred to as a *contribution* (such as *1998 IRA contribution*). A transfer of money into your retirement account from another investment company or bank is typically called an *asset transfer.* You may also see an entry for an annual maintenance fee charge (try to pay these fees outside the account so that more of your money continues compounding inside the retirement account).

During the year, you may also see entries labeled *dividend reinvestment,* which simply means that the fund paid a dividend that you reinvested by purchasing more shares of that same fund in your account (see details in the section, "Dividends," later in the chapter if you're not sure what a dividend is). Dividends also may be paid out as cash — the fund company can send a check to you or it can electronically deposit the money into your bank checking account. In either case, the transaction description says something like *income dividend cash.*

Funds pay capital gains, too, so in this column you also see phrases such as *capital gains reinvest.* In order to please the IRS, capital gains are specified, for example, as short-term capital gains or long-term capital gains, for which different tax rates apply. (See Chapter 13 for the reasons the IRS cares, and the consequences for your tax return.)

On the statement for a money market fund, you may see entries such as *check writing redemption* to show the deduction of a check that has cleared your account.

Dollar amount

The dollar amount column simply shows the actual dollar value of the transaction. If you sent in a $5,000 deposit, look to make sure that the correct amount was credited to your account. Fund companies calculate and credit the appropriate amount of dividends and capital gains to your account. There's no way — and really no need — to check these distributions. At any rate, I'm not aware of a fund company making a mistake with these, other than possibly a delay (a few days beyond the promised deadline) in crediting shareholder accounts.

Share price or price per share

The share price (or price per share) column shows the price per share that the transaction was conducted at. When you're dealing with a no-load (commission-free) fund such as those that I recommend in this book, you get the same price that everyone else who bought or sold shares that day received. Money market funds always maintain a level price of $1 per share.

TIP

If you're concerned that a load was charged, check with the company to see the buy (bid) price and sell (asked) price on the day you did a purchase transaction. If a load was not charged, these two prices should be identical. If a load was charged, the buy price is higher than the sell price, and the purchase on your statement was done at the buy price.

Share amount or shares transacted

The share amount (or shares transacted) column simply shows the number of shares purchased or sold in the particular transaction. The number of shares is arrived at by default: The fund company takes the dollar amount of the transaction and divides it by the price per share on the date of the transaction. For example, a $5,000 investment in a bond fund at $20 per share gets you 250 shares. You detail-oriented types will be happy to know that fund companies usually go out to three decimal places in figuring shares.

Shares owned or share balance

If money was added to or subtracted from your account, the share balance changes by the amount of shares purchased or redeemed and listed in the prior section, "Share amount or shares transacted."

In one unusual instance, the number of shares in an account changes even though no transactions have occurred: when a fund *splits*. If it splits 2 for 1, for example, you receive two shares for every one that you own. This split doesn't increase the worth of the investments you own; the price per share in a 2-for-1 split is cut by 50 percent.

Why do funds split? It's a gimmick. In the world of individual securities, stock splits are often associated with successful, growing companies; likewise, mutual fund splits are usually trying to cash in on positive connotations. The fund company wants potential buyers to think that the fund has done *so* well that the company has split its shares in order to reduce the price; that way, new investors won't think that they're paying a high price. But the high price doesn't matter because fund minimum investment requirements determine whether you can afford to invest in a fund, not the share price. (*Reverse splits* can be done as well to boost the price per share.)

Account value

Typically, on a different part of the account statement separate from the line-by-line listing of your transactions, fund companies show the total *account value* or market value of your fund shares as of a particular day — usually at the end of a given month. This value results from multiplying the price per share by the total number of shares that you own.

Four out of five fund investors care about total account value more than the other totals (at least according to my scientific surveys of fund investors that I work with!). So you'd think that the fund companies would list on your statement how this value has changed over time. Well, they don't, and that's one of the reasons why examining your account statement is a lousy way to track your fund's performance over time. Some companies, such as Fidelity, show how your current account value compares to the value when your last statement was issued. This comparison sheds some useful light on your account's performance, but it still doesn't tell you how you've done since you originally invested. See the later section, "Am I Winning or Losing?," for how to determine your funds' performance.

Interpreting Discount Brokerage Firm Statements

Discount brokerage statements look a bit different than those produced by mutual fund companies. In a discount brokerage statement, the portfolio overview and the transaction details are usually listed in separate sections (see Figure 12-2):

PORTFOLIO POSITION DETAIL

CATEGORY	ST	LONG/ SHORT	QUOTE SYMBOL	QUANTITY	INVESTMENT DESCRIPTION	LATEST PRICE	MARKET VALUE
MUTUAL FUNDS	C	Long	PTTRX	1210.897	PIMCO TOTAL RETURN FUND	9.7500	$11,806.25
	C	Long	SRFBX	989.962	STEINROE TOTAL RETURN FUND	24.5300	$24,283.77
	C	Long	TBGVX	973.236	TWEEDY BROWNE GLOBAL VAL GLOBAL VALUE FUND	12.0100	$11,688.56
	C	Long	CUIEX	636.451	WARBURG PINCUS INTL EQTY	19.6400	$12,499.90
MONEY FUNDS	C	Long		37.22	SCHWAB MONEY MARKET FUND	1.0000	$37.22
Net Portfolio Value					$60,315.70		

ACCOUNT TRANSACTION DETAIL

DATE	TRANSACTION	QUANTITY	DESCRIPTION	PRICE	AMOUNT
*****			Opening Cash Balance		$.00
11/01	Reinvested Shares	5.953	PIMCO TOTAL RETURN FUND	9.8000	($58.34)
11/01	Div For Reinvest		PIMCO TOTAL RETURN FUND		$58.34
11/11	Reinvested Shares	10.569	STEINROE TOTAL RETURN FUND	25.0200	($264.44)
11/11	Div For Reinvest		STEINROE TOTAL RETURN		$264.44
*****			Ending Cash Balance		$.00

Source: Charles Schwab & Co., Inc.

Figure 12-2: Discount brokerage account statement.

- **The Portfolio Position Detail section** lists funds from different companies. As on a mutual fund statement, the *number of shares (quantity), price per share (latest price),* and *market value* of the funds held as of the statement date are listed.

  Long simply means that you bought shares and you're holding those shares. (You may — although I don't recommend it — actually *short* shares held in brokerage accounts. Shorting shares simply means that you sell the shares first, hope that they decline in value, and then buy them back.) The *C* in this example means that this is a cash holding (as opposed to one purchased with borrowed money).

- **The Account Transaction Detail section** confuses most people because each transaction seems to be repeated. The apparent repetition occurs because of the silly accounting system of debits and credits that brokerage firms use. Note that this account shows that 5.953 shares of PIMCO Total Return were purchased at $9.80 per share for a total purchase of $58.34. Where did this odd amount of money come from for the purchase? The next line tells you — the fund paid a dividend of $58.34. It would be logical and more understandable if these two lines were reversed, wouldn't it? First the money comes in and then it's reinvested into purchasing more shares!

Am I Winning or Losing?

Now that you know how to read your statement, it's time for a more important and interesting issue: determining how much money you're making. Probably the single most important issue that fund investors care about — how much or little they're making on their investments — is not easy to figure from those blasted statements that fund companies send you. That is, it isn't easy to figure unless you know the tricks regarding what to look for and what to ignore.

The misleading share price

You probably know someone who's always got his head buried in the financial section of a newspaper, the part that reports on share prices of individual stocks and how much they have gone up or down since the day before. He's always checking on how his stocks are doing, and he's either cheering or groaning depending on the size of the numbers after the plus or minus sign.

Unfortunately, mutual fund share prices are also reported in many newspapers. I say "unfortunately" because all too many fund investors, perhaps taking a cue from individual stock owners, look to daily or other short-term-oriented sources of fund pricing information.

If you follow the price changes in your fund(s) every day, week, month, or other time period, you won't know how your fund is doing. And you won't know because mutual funds make distributions. When a fund makes a distribution to you, you get more shares of the fund. But distributions create an accounting problem because they reduce the share price of a fund by the exact amount of the distribution. Therefore, over time, following just the share price of your fund doesn't tell you how much money you've made or lost.

REMEMBER

The only way to figure out exactly how much you've made or lost on your investment is to compare the *total value* of your fund holdings today to the total dollar amount you originally invested. If you've invested chunks of money at various points in time, this exercise becomes much more complicated. (Some of the investment software I recommend in Chapter 16 will help if you want your computer to crunch the numbers. Frankly, though, you have easier, less time-consuming ways to get a sense of how you're doing — and I get to those ways soon.)

Total return nuts and bolts

The *total return* of a fund is the percentage change in the overall value of your investment over a specified period. For example, a fund may tell you that its total return during the year that ended December 31st was 15 percent. Therefore, if you invested $10,000 in the fund on the last day of December of the prior year, your investment is worth $11,500 after the year just ended.

The following sections explain the three components that make up the total return on a fund: dividends, capital gains, and share price changes.

Dividends

Dividends are income paid by investments. Both bonds and stocks can pay dividends. As I explain in Chapter 8, bond dividends tend to be higher. When a dividend distribution is made, you can receive it as cash (which is good if you need money to live on) or reinvest it into more shares in the fund. In either case, the share price of the fund drops by an amount that exactly offsets the payout. So if you're hoping to strike it rich by buying into a bunch of funds just before their dividends are paid, don't bother.

If you hold your mutual fund outside a retirement account, the dividend distributions are taxable income (unless they come from a tax-free municipal bond fund). If you're ready to buy into a fund outside of a retirement account that pays a decent dividend, you may want to check to see when the fund is next scheduled to pay a dividend. For funds that pay quarterly taxable dividends, you may want to avoid buying in the weeks just prior to a distribution. (See the Appendix of this book for funds' historic distribution schedules.)

Capital gains

When a stock or bond mutual fund manager sells a security in the fund, any gain realized from that sale (the difference between the sale price and the purchase price) must be distributed to fund shareholders as a *capital gain.* Typically, funds make one annual capital gains distribution in December. Some funds make two per year, typically making the other one around mid-year.

As with a dividend distribution, you can receive your capital gains distribution as cash or as more shares in the fund. In either case, the share price of the fund drops by an amount to exactly offset the distribution.

For funds held outside retirement accounts, all capital gains distributions are taxable. As with dividends, capital gains are taxable whether or not you reinvest them in additional shares in the fund.

Sometimes you invest in bond and stock funds outside retirement accounts. When you do, determine when capital gains are distributed if you want to avoid investing in a fund that is about to make a capital gains distribution. (Stock funds that appreciated greatly during the year are most likely to make larger capital gains distributions. Money funds don't ever make these distributions.) Investing in a fund that is soon to make a distribution increases your current-year tax liability for investments made outside retirement accounts. About a month before the distribution, fund companies should be able to estimate the size of the distribution. (Also, see the Appendix.)

Share price changes

You also make money with a mutual fund when the share price increases. This occurrence is just like investing in a stock or piece of real estate. If your fund is worth more today than when you bought it, you have made a profit (on paper, at least). To realize — or lock in — this profit, you need to sell your shares in the fund. A fund's share price increases if the securities that the fund has invested in have appreciated in value.

The total return

After you've seen all the different components of total return, you're ready to add them all up. For each of the major types of funds that I discuss in this book, Table 12-1 presents a simple summary of where you can expect most of your returns to come from over the long term. The funds are ordered in the table from those with the lowest expected total returns and share price volatility to those with the highest.

Table 12-1 Components of a Fund's Returns

	Dividends +	*Capital Gains* +	*Share Price Changes*	*=Total Return*
Money market funds	All returns come from dividends	None	None	Lowest expected funds return but principal risk is nil
Shorter-term bond funds	Moderate	Low	Low	Expect better than money funds but more volatility
Longer-term bond funds	High	Low to moderate	Low to moderate	Expect better than short-term bonds but with greater volatility
Stock funds	None to moderate depending on stock types	Low to high depending on trading patterns of fund manager	Low to high	Highest expected returns but most volatile

Easiest ways to figure total return

As I explain in the section, "How to Read Your Fund Statement," earlier in the chapter, fund companies make it almost impossible for you to determine your total return from the information they provide on their statements. Fund companies would make everyone's life easier if they reported not only the current value of each fund held but also the amount originally invested; the percentage difference would be the total return. Most fund companies say that their computer systems aren't set up to allow for this type of report — but tell us something we don't already know! In this age of technology, there's no reason why fund companies can't make the appropriate changes to their computer systems. Eventually, you'll probably start to see some companies do what I'm suggesting — even though I don't predict financial market movements, I do predict fund industry practices!

Regardless of the time period over which you're trying to determine your funds' total return, here are the simplest ways to figure total return without getting a headache:

TIP

- **Call the fund company's toll-free number.** The telephone representatives can provide you with the total return for your funds for various lengths of time (such as for the last three months, the last six months, the last year, the last three years, and so on).
- **Examine the fund's annual and semi-annual reports.** These provide total return numbers.
- **Keep a file folder with your investment statements.** That way, you can look up the amount you originally invested in a fund and compare it to updated market values on new statements you receive. You can make a handwritten table or enter the figures in the software I describe in Chapter 16.
- **Check fund information services and periodicals.** Fund information services and financial magazines and newspapers carry total return data at particular times during the year. Some, such as *The Wall Street Journal,* carry this information daily.

TIP

How often should I check on my funds?

I recommend that you *don't* track the share prices of your funds on a daily basis. It's time-consuming, nerve-racking, and will make you lose sight of the long term. Worse, you'll be more likely to panic when times get tough.

When you take an airplane trip across the country, do you have to hear from the pilot over the public address system every 60 seconds that the weather and other conditions are okay? I didn't think so. If you did, you wouldn't enjoy the flight, and the incessant updates would serve little purpose other than to make you nervous.

A weekly, monthly, or even quarterly check-in is more than frequent enough to follow your funds. I know many successful investors who check on their funds' performance twice or even just once a year.

Which total return figures are best for the long-term?

Fund companies typically report fund total returns in one of two ways. The *absolute return* measures the total percentage increase from the beginning to the end of the time period being looked at. The *annualized return* measures the average increase *per year* during the specified time period.

Over a five-year period, for example, the absolute return of the Blue Chip Stock fund may be 98 percent, which translates to an annualized return of about 14.6 percent.

Don't be fooled by a more impressive sounding absolute return. Remember, both numbers are measuring the same real return. Beware of fund companies that exploit the eye-catching qualities of absolute return numbers to make themselves look good in their marketing literature. 200 percent, 300 percent! Sounds spectacular, but it doesn't mean anything unless the time period and the performance of comparable funds and benchmarks are taken into account. If the time period is long enough, just about any fund's absolute return figure, especially if it's for a stock fund, is impressive-looking, even if it's below average.

Annualized return numbers are much more useful — and therefore more common — for comparative purposes. Because a time factor — per year — is built into the number, a glance at the annualized return gives you a much better idea of how a fund has performed, and a much easier time comparing that performance to similar funds for similar time periods.

If you've made numerous purchases in a fund, you may want to know your effective rate of return when you also factor in the timing and size of each purchase. The only way to make this calculation is with software. However, you don't need to know the exact rate of return for your overall purchases in order to successfully evaluate your fund investments. Comparing your funds' performance over various time periods to relevant *performance benchmarks* is sufficient. (Benchmarks? See the next section.)

If you've just started investing in funds — or even if you've held funds a long time — you need to realize that what happens to the value of your stock and bond funds in the short term is largely a matter of luck. Don't get depressed if your fund or funds drop in value the day after you buy them or even over the first three or six months. When you invest in bond and stock funds, you should focus on returns produced over longer periods — periods of at least one year, and preferably longer.

Your funds' performance

Whenever you examine your funds' returns, compare those returns to appropriate *benchmark indexes*. Although many stock market investors may have been happy to earn about 10 percent per year with their investments during the 1980s and early 1990s, they really shouldn't have been because the market averages or benchmark indexes were generating about 15 percent per year.

Each mutual fund should be compared to the benchmark that is most appropriate given the types of securities that a fund invests in; for the bond and stock funds that I recommend in Chapters 8 and 9, I provide descriptions of the types of securities that each fund invests in. The following sections offer a brief rundown of the benchmark indexes you'll find useful. (I provide benchmarks for the types of funds most people use for longer-term purposes such as retirement account investing.)

Bond benchmarks

A number of bond indexes exist (see Table 12-2) that differ from one another mainly in the maturity of the bonds that they invest in, for example, short-term, intermediate-term, and long-term indexes.

Table 12-2 Bond Indexes

Year	*Lehman Short-Term Bond Index*	*Lehman Intermediate-Term Bond Index*	*Lehman Long-Term Bond Index*	*Lehman GNMA Index*	*First Boston High Yield (Junk Bond) Index*
1988	6.3%	7.5%	9.7%	8.8%	13.6%
1989	11.7%	14.9%	17.5%	15.7%	0.4%
1990	9.7%	8.2%	6.5%	10.6%	-6.4%
1991	13.2%	17.7%	19.5%	16.0%	43.7%
1992	6.8%	7.9%	8.5%	7.4%	16.7%
1993	7.1%	12.2%	16.2%	6.6%	18.9%
1994	-0.7%	-4.5%	-7.1%	-1.5%	-1.0%
1995	12.9%	21.4%	29.9%	17.1%	17.4%
1996	4.7%	2.7%	0.1%	5.5%	12.4%
1997	7.1%	7.9%	14.5%	9.5%	12.6%
5-year average	**6.1%**	**6.7%**	**10.0%**	**7.3%**	**11.8%**
10-year average	**7.8%**	**8.3%**	**11.1%**	**9.4%**	**11.9%**

There are also many more specialized indexes than those listed here, for example, indexes for municipal bonds, Treasury bonds, and so on. So if you're looking at these different types of funds, take a look in the fund's annual report to see which index they compare the fund's performance to. Don't assume that they are using the most comparable index.

U.S. stock benchmarks

The major U.S. stock indexes (see Table 12-3) are distinguished by the size of the companies (large, small, all sizes, and so on) whose stock they are tracking. The Standard & Poor's 500 Index tracks the stock prices of 500 large-company stocks on the U.S. stock exchanges. These 500 stocks account for about 70 percent of the total market value of all stocks traded in the U.S. The Russell 2000 Index tracks 2,000 smaller-company U.S. stocks. All stocks of all sizes on the major U.S. stock exchanges are tracked by the Wilshire 5000 Index. (Trivia fact: Actually, *more* than 5,000 stocks are in the Wilshire 5000 Index, which had 5,000 stocks in it when it was created more than 20 years ago — now more than 6,000 stocks are in the index.)

Table 12-3 U.S. Stock Indexes

Year	*Standard & Poor's 500*	*Russell 2000*	*Wilshire 5000*
1988	16.5%	24.9%	17.9%
1989	31.6%	16.2%	29.2%
1990	-3.1%	-19.5%	-6.2%
1991	30.4%	46.1%	34.2%
1992	7.6%	18.4%	9.0%
1993	10.1%	18.9%	11.3%
1994	1.3%	-1.8%	-0.1%
1995	37.6%	28.4%	36.4%
1996	23%	16.5%	21.2%
1997	33.4%	22.4%	31.4%
5-year average	**20.3%**	**16.4%**	**19.3%**
10-year average	**18.0%**	**15.8%**	**17.6%**

If you're evaluating the performance of a fund that invests solely in U.S. stocks, make sure to choose the index that comes closest to representing the types of stocks that the fund invests in. Also, remember to examine a stock fund's international holdings. Suppose, for example, that a particular stock fund typically invests 80 percent in U.S. stocks of all sizes and 20 percent in the larger, established countries overseas. You can create your own benchmark index by multiplying the returns of the Wilshire 5000 index by 80 percent and the Morgan Stanley EAFE international index (which I discuss in the next section) by 20 percent, and then adding them together.

International stock benchmarks

When you invest in funds that invest overseas, you gotta use a comparative index that tracks the performance of international stock markets. The *Morgan Stanley EAFE* (which stands for Europe, Australia, and Far East) index tracks the performance of the more established countries' stock markets. Morgan Stanley also has an index that tracks the performance of the emerging markets in Southeast Asia and Latin America (see Table 12-4).

Table 12-4 International Stock Indexes

Year	*Morgan Stanley EAFE*	*Morgan Stanley Emerging Markets*
1988	28.6%	40.4%
1989	10.8%	65.0%
1990	-23.2%	-10.6%
1991	12.5%	59.9%
1992	-11.8%	11.4%
1993	33.0%	74.9%
1994	8.1%	-7.3%
1995	11.2%	0.2%
1996	6.4%	15.2%
1997	2.1%	-16.4%
5-year average	**11.7%**	**9.4%**
10-year average	**6.6%**	**19.2%**

You should know that emerging markets are volatile and risky. As I discuss in Chapter 9, diversified international funds that invest in both established and emerging markets offer a smoother ride for investors who want some exposure to emerging markets. More-diversified funds also aren't as constraining on a fund manager who believes, for example, that emerging markets are overpriced.

If you do invest in the more diversified international funds that place some of their assets in emerging markets, remember that it's not fair to compare the performance of those funds solely to the EAFE index. So how do you fairly compare the performance of this type of fund?

Well, if an international fund typically invests about 20 percent in emerging markets, then multiply the EAFE return in the table by 80 percent and add to that 20 percent of the *Emerging Markets* index return. For 1993, for example: 33.0% (*.8) + 74.9% (*.2) = 41.4%. With this computation formula, you can see how any international fund that invested in emerging markets in 1993 couldn't help but look good in comparison to the EAFE index. (The numbers in Table 12-4 also tell you not to be too impressed with an emerging markets fund that boasted of a 70 percent return in 1993 — if it did, it was below average!)

TIP

The hard part is finding out the percentage of assets a fund typically has invested in emerging markets. Most international funds don't report the total of their investments in emerging markets. For the international funds I recommend in Chapter 9, I provide some general idea of the portion they have invested in emerging markets. Also, you can peek at a fund's recent annual or semi-annual report, in which the fund managers detail investments held for each country.

Don't get too focused on performance comparisons. Indexes don't incur expenses that an actual mutual fund does although, as you may know, expenses among funds vary tremendously. Remember all the other criteria — such as the fees and expenses and the fund company's and manager's expertise — that you should evaluate when you consider a fund's chances for generating healthy returns in the years ahead (see Chapter 4).

Deciding Whether to Sell, Hold, or Buy More

I am often asked, "How do I know when I should sell a fund?"

TIP

The answer is relatively simple: *Sell only if a fund is no longer meeting the common-sense criteria (which I outline in Chapter 4) for picking a good fund in the first place.* Stick by your fund like a loyal friend as long as it is

- Generating decent returns relative to appropriate benchmarks and the competition (even one or two year's of slight underperformance are okay if the fund's five- and ten-year numbers are still comparatively good)
- Not raising the fees that it charges and not charging more than the best of the competition
- Still managed by a competent fund manager

The only other reason to sell a fund is if your circumstances change. For example, suppose that you're 50 years old and you inherit a big pot of money. You hadn't been planning to retire early, but with oodles of money suddenly at your disposal, maybe now you're thinking that early retirement ain't such a bad idea after all. This change in circumstances may cause you to tweak your portfolio so that you have more income-producing investments and fewer growth investments.

Tweaking Your Portfolio

Over longer periods of time, you may need to occasionally tweak your portfolio to keep your investment mix in line with your desires (see the asset allocation discussion in Chapter 6).

Suppose that at the age of 40 you invest about 80 percent of your retirement money in stock funds with the balance in bonds. By the age of 45, you find that the stock funds now comprise an even larger percentage (maybe 85 percent) of your investments because they have appreciated more than the bond funds have. *You* are also appreciating (in age that is) and should in fact be reducing your stock allocation as you get older.

Using the asset allocation guidelines in Chapter 6, you decide that at the age of 45, you now wish to have about 75 percent of your money in stock funds. The solution is simple: Sell enough of your stock funds to reduce your stock holdings to 75 percent of the total and invest the proceeds in the bond funds. Don't forget to factor the tax consequences into your decisions when you contemplate the sale of funds held outside retirement accounts (see Chapter 13).

REMEMBER

Trying to time and trade the markets to buy at lows and sell at highs rarely works in the short-term and never works in the long-term. If you do a decent job *up front* of picking good fund companies and funds to invest in, you should have fewer changes to make over the long haul.

If you have a good set of funds, keep feeding money into them as your savings allows. But, over time, there's no reason to use just a few funds. So, as your portfolio value grows, add a new fund or two to broaden your overall mix. Holding a couple (or several) of each different type of fund makes a lot of sense. (I cover the common sense of fund diversification in much depth in Chapter 6.)

Chapter 13

Understanding Yucky Tax Forms for Mutual Funds

In This Chapter

- Form 1099-DIV and distributions from mutual funds
- Tax forms and issues to understand when selling funds
- Form 1099-R and good stuff to know about retirement fund withdrawals

Let's face it: You invested in a mutual fund to make some money. But guess who starts licking his chops when he hears about money being made? That's right: good ol' Uncle Sam. And state governments, too.

In Chapter 12, I explain the different ways that mutual funds can make you money: either through distributions (capital gains and dividends) or through appreciation. Either way, if the fund that made the money is being held outside a tax-shielded retirement account, then federal and state governments will demand a portion of your fund's distributions and of your profits when you sell shares in a fund for more than you paid for them.

Whether you make money through distributions or appreciation, once each year you'll get one or more tax forms that tell you how much money you made on your mutual funds held outside of retirement accounts. (Remember, you don't need to file anything with funds held inside retirement accounts.) These forms are sent to you from the mutual fund companies or brokerage firms where you're holding these funds. Come April (or whenever you get around to completing your tax returns), you must transfer the information on these fund-provided tax forms to your income tax return, where you calculate how much tax you actually owe on the money you made from your mutual funds.

If you cringed when you read the words "tax forms," then you've obviously battled these ugly beasts before. I sometimes wonder if the people who write tax forms come from another planet; that would perhaps explain their use of what appears to be a non-human form of communication. But don't despair. I devote this entire chapter to helping you interpret the hieroglyphics on these sometimes intimidating documents.

There are rewards for toughing out this chapter. I show you how to use a fund's tax forms to help you discover whether your mutual fund money is being invested in the most tax-friendly way. I also give you some tips on reducing your tax bill if you have to sell some mutual funds.

If the subject of taxes hasn't put you to sleep, perhaps you've noted my repeated use of the qualifying phrase, *for funds held outside retirement accounts*. The easiest and most effective way to avoid paying tax on money you've made with a mutual fund is simply to hold that fund inside rather than outside a retirement account (see Chapter 3). Not only do you avoid the tax, you also avoid having tax forms arrive in your mailbox. (After you retire, you do have to pay tax on money you withdraw from a retirement account. That payment involves another tax form, which I discuss in this chapter.)

Mutual Fund Distributions Form: 1099-DIV

If you're an employee of a company, you're probably familiar with the IRS Form W-2, that little piece of paper that comes in late January or early February and sums up the amount of money your employer paid you over the previous year. You are required to report this income on your income tax return.

Form 1099-DIV is similar to a W-2, but instead of reporting income from an employer, it reports income from mutual funds you hold outside of retirement accounts. By income, I mean capital gains and dividend distributions, which I explain in Chapter 12.

Like the W-2, Form 1099-DIV should arrive in your mailbox in late January or early February. You should get one for every non-retirement account you held money in during the tax year. Call the responsible company if you don't get one for an account you think that you should. (And if you're tired of receiving these forms from so many fund companies, take a peek at Chapter 5, where I explain the paperwork-friendly benefits of consolidating your mutual fund holdings into a discount brokerage account.)

Also like the W-2, a copy of each of your 1099-DIVs is sent to the IRS and your state authorities, so don't get any ideas about fudging the information on your tax return.

Figure 13-1 is a sample Form 1099-DIV, which I'll use to walk you through the form. First, notice that the distributions are divided into various boxes. (Actually, most mutual fund companies display this information in columns, but they're still called boxes.) This division is done because different parts of your distributions are taxed at different rates, and the IRS wants to know what is what.

☐ CORRECTED (if checked)				
PAYER'S name, street address, city, state, ZIP code, and telephone no.		1 Ordinary dividends $ 2a Total capital gain distr. $	OMB No. 1545-0110 1998 Form 1099-DIV	Dividends and Distributions
PAYER'S Federal identification number	RECIPIENT'S identification number	2b 28% rate gain $	2c Unrecap. sec. 1250 gain $	Copy B For Recipient
RECIPIENT'S name		2d Section 1202 gain $	3 Nontaxable distributions $	This is important tax information and is being furnished to the Internal Revenue Service. If you are required to file a return, a negligence penalty or other sanction may be imposed on you if this income is taxable and the IRS determines that it has not been reported.
Street address (including apt. no.)		4 Federal income tax withheld $	5 Investment expenses $	
City, state, and ZIP code		6 Foreign tax paid $	7 Foreign country or U.S. possession	
Account number (optional)		8 Cash liquidation distr. $	9 Noncash liquidation distr. $	
Form 1099-DIV		(Keep for your records.)	Department of the Treasury - Internal Revenue Service	

Figure 13-1: Form 1099-DIV reports dividends and capital gains your funds paid.

Jump into these boxes and see what you find.

Box 1: Ordinary dividends

True to its name, ordinary dividends includes all the money you made from dividend distributions (see Chapter 12). All types of mutual funds pay dividends, which account for all of a money market's return, most of a bond fund's return, and part of a stock fund's return.

Untrue to its name, however, ordinary dividends also includes *short-term capital gains distributions* — profits from securities that the mutual fund bought and sold within a year. Why are these short-term capital gains lumped together with your dividend income? Because they're both taxed at your ordinary income tax rate.

TIP

The distributions reported as ordinary dividends are taxed at your highest possible rate, up to 39.6 percent on your federal income tax return depending on your annual income. If you're in a higher tax bracket, you don't want to see big ordinary dividends. You'd be better off with investments that do not produce so much taxable income (Chapters 7 and 8 explain how to select tax-friendly money market and bond funds). For stock mutual funds, if you're seeing big ordinary dividends, your fund may be making lots of trades. Outside of retirement accounts, regardless of your tax bracket, there's no reason to own mutual funds that generate lots of short-term capital gains. Chapter 9 gives recommendations for tax-friendly stock funds.

Box 2a: Total capital gains distributions

Long-term capital gains distributions are profits from securities sold over 12 months after their purchase. Long-term capital gains are taxed at a lower rate than regular income, dividends, and short-term capital gains. Thanks to the 1997 tax law changes, the federal tax rate on the longest of the long-term gains (that is from securities held more than 18 months) is capped at 20 percent for those in a tax bracket of 28 percent or higher, and 10 percent for those in the 15 percent tax bracket.

TIP

You can count the lower tax rate on long-term capital gains as one more benefit of the buy-and-hold investing strategy. Not only does this strategy typically generate higher returns than short-term trading, but for investments held outside of retirement accounts, it's gentler on your tax bill as well (see Chapter 6). The tax relief and the potential for higher returns are why mutual funds that tend to buy-and-hold their securities are preferable for non-retirement accounts.

Box 2b: 28% rate gain

If you've been paying close attention, you may have noticed a gap in the capital gains timeline. Short-term capital gains (which are captured in Box 1 for ordinary dividends) are profits from securities held one year or less. Long-term capital gains are profits from securities held longer than 18 months. So what about profits from securities held between 12 months and 18 months?

Good question. Too bad Congress didn't think harder about it when they drafted the new tax laws. There used to be two capital gains tax categories, but Congress has added a third. Profits on the sale of securities that are held between 12 and 18 months are taxed at your normal income tax rate up to a maximum of 28 percent. For lack of an official term, I call these *mid-term* capital gains.

These mid-term gains are reported on the 1099-DIV in Box 2. The number here represents that portion of the number in Box 2a that is a mid-term rather than a long-term gain. To figure out the amount of long-term gain, subtract the second number from the first number.

TECHNICAL STUFF

Starting in the year 2006, another capital gains tax bracket will join the party. For securities acquired after the year 2000 and held longer than five years, the long-term federal capital gains rate will drop to 18 percent for those in the 28 percent tax bracket and higher. Beginning in the year 2001, for those in the 15 percent tax bracket, the capital gains rate drops to 8 percent. Good news for long-term investors, I suppose, but bad news for tax return filers trying to make sense of their tax forms.

Box 3: Nontaxable distributions

You rarely see numbers in the "nontaxable distributions" section of Form 1099-DIV. (You may think that this is where funds report tax-free dividends, for example, that are paid on municipal bond funds — but they're not reported on Form 1099-DIV because they're not taxable!) This box is where funds report if they made distributions during the year that repaid a shareholder's original investment. Like the principal returned to you if a bond or CD you've invested in matures, this chunk of money is not taxable — hence the term here, *nontaxable distributions.*

For shares held outside of retirement accounts, these nontaxable distributions factor into your computation of the gain or loss when the shares are sold. For purposes of calculating any gain, if and when you sell these shares, you must subtract the money returned to you from the amount you originally paid for these shares.

Why the hubbub over the Fidelity Magellan accounting error?

Late in 1994, Fidelity Investments announced that its Magellan stock fund, the nation's largest mutual fund, would pay its shareholders a capital gains distribution of $4.32 per share in late December. This announcement didn't strike anyone as out of the ordinary because many stock funds make distributions late in the year.

So why did everybody eventually make such a big deal out of that distribution? Well, it turns out that Fidelity — more specifically, Fidelity's accounting department — made a mathematical error. The actual capital gains distribution that should have been reported and that was ultimately paid out at year-end was . . . nothing! The mistake crept into Fidelity's figures through a simple human error. In totaling the gains and losses on the securities sold during the year, Fidelity's bean-counters overlooked a minus sign in front of a security sold at a loss. So a *losing* transaction was initially and incorrectly counted as a profitable one!

The resulting publicity surrounding this snafu was a small nightmare for Fidelity. Some of the reporting was poorly informed — one story, in fact, questioned whether Magellan fund manager Jeff Vinik, who makes investing decisions for the fund and has nothing to do with the accounting, would be held personally responsible for this error!

Ultimately, this fiasco was a nonevent or even good news for some fund shareholders. If the fund had made a capital gains distribution of $4.32 per share, shareholders holding this fund outside a tax-sheltered retirement account would have had to pay tax on the distribution! Those shareholders holding Magellan inside retirement accounts shouldn't have cared either way.

Box 4: Federal income tax withheld

It's bad news if your funds report that federal income tax was withheld. It means that you're being subjected to the dreaded *backup withholding.* If you don't report all your mutual fund dividend income (or don't furnish the fund company with your Social Security number), your future mutual fund dividend income is subject to backup withholding of *31 percent!* To add insult to injury, in the not-too-distant future, you will receive a nasty notice from the IRS listing the dividends you didn't report. You end up owing interest and penalties.

Find out right away what's going on here. It's possible that either you or the IRS made a mistake. It's possible that you didn't provide a correct Social Security number or that you have been negligent in reporting to the IRS your previously earned taxable income. Fix this problem as soon as you can. Call the IRS at ☎ 800-829-1040.

Don't despair about the tax that was withheld by your fund. The withholding wasn't for naught — you'll receive credit for it when you complete your Form 1040 on the line "Federal income tax withheld."

Box 6: Foreign tax paid

When I first recommended to my parents that they invest in international mutual funds, they actually took my advice — which goes to show you that there really is a first time for everything! Come the following April, dear old Dad turned into a tax-preparing grump. Why? He got a Form 1099-DIV for the international stock fund they invested in, and the form had an amount in the foreign tax paid section.

If you invest in an international mutual fund, the fund may end up paying foreign taxes on some of its dividends. The foreign taxes paid by the fund are listed on Form 1099-DIV because the IRS allows you two ways to get some of this money back. You can choose one of the following:

- Deduct the foreign tax you paid on Schedule A (the "Other taxes" line).
- Claim a credit on Form 1040 ("Foreign Tax Credit" line).

The latter move may be more tax-beneficial, but it is also more of a headache because you need to complete *another* IRS Form, Form 1116, which is a bona-fide doozie.

TIP

Get out last year's tax return

With all the fuss and muss over mutual fund distributions, you should note how the rest of your non-mutual fund investments are positioned. Although taxes aren't everything, you may be paying much more than you need to.

Look at your Form 1040 to see how much taxable interest income you had to pay tax on. On Forms 1040 and 1040A, this figure goes on line 8a. If you filed 1040EZ (don't you just love that name?), the figure goes on line 2.

Now find out the rate of interest you were being paid that generated this interest income. If it came from money in a bank account, odds are quite good that you could be earning more in a money market mutual fund. (See Chapter 7.)

When You Sell Your Mutual Fund Shares

Besides distributions, the other way to make money with a mutual fund is through appreciation. If the price of your shares moves higher than the price at which you bought them, then your investment has appreciated. Your profit is the difference between the amount you paid for the investment and the amount the investment is currently worth. For investments held outside of retirement accounts, that profit is taxable.

However, you don't actually owe any tax on the appreciation until you sell the shares and lock up your profit. Then you must report that profit on that year's tax return and pay capital gains tax on it. Conversely, when you sell a fund investment at a loss, it is tax deductible. You should understand the tax consequences of selling your fund shares and always factor taxes into your selling decisions.

What's confusing to some people about this talk of capital gains and losses is that each year your fund(s) may have been paying you capital gains distributions (see the last section) which you also owed tax on. So you may rightfully be thinking, "Hey! I'm being taxed twice!"

It's true that you are being taxed twice, but not on the same profits. You see, the profits the fund distributed, which resulted from the fund manager selling securities in his fund at a profit, are different than those profits that you've realized by selling your shares.

You have no control over fund distributions. They happen at regular intervals — at least once a year — whether you like it or not, and you must pay taxes on them when they occur from non-retirement account holdings. Taxes on fund appreciation, on the other hand, can be indefinitely delayed if you choose. As long as you hold the investment and don't sell it, the federal and state governments can't get their hands on the profit — one more advantage of buy-and-hold investing. In fact, if you hold an appreciated asset outside of retirement accounts, that asset can be transferred at your death to your heirs and the capital gain is eliminated for tax purposes.

Of course, the other way to avoid taxes on appreciated mutual funds is to hold them inside retirement accounts; then you don't have to worry about capital gains taxes at all.

Your fund's "basis"

Suppose that you sell a fund. In order to compute the taxable capital gain or the deductible capital loss, you have to compute your fund's tax basis. *Basis* is the tax system's way of measuring the amount you originally paid for your investment(s) in a mutual fund. I say investments (plural) because you may not have made all your purchases in a fund at once; you may have reinvested your dividends or capital gains or bought shares at different times.

For example, if you purchase 100 shares of the Its Gotta Rise Mutual Fund at $20 per share, your cost basis is $2,000, or $20 per share. Simple enough.

But now suppose that this fund pays a dividend of $1 per share (so that you get $100 in dividends for your 100 shares), and suppose further that you choose to reinvest this dividend into purchasing more shares of the mutual fund. The price of shares has gone up to $25 per share since your original purchase, so the reinvested $100 buys you four new shares. You now own 104 shares which, at $25 per share, are worth $2,600.

But what's your basis now? Your basis is your original investment ($2,000) plus subsequent investments ($100) for a total of $2,100. Thus, if you sold all your shares at $25 per share, you'd have a taxable profit of $500 (current value of $2,600 less $2,100 — the total amount invested or *basis*).

For recordkeeping purposes, save your statements detailing the purchases in your accounts. Most mutual fund companies provide year-end summary statements that show all transactions throughout the year. For purchases made now and in the future, fund companies also should be able to tell you your average cost per share when you need to sell your shares.

Mutual fund accounting 101

If you understand the concept of *basis* for your fund investments, it's time to put that understanding to work. Here I'm going to walk you through the different ways commonly used by taxpayers and approved by the IRS to calculate your basis when you sell your non-retirement account mutual fund investments.

If you sell all your shares of a particular mutual fund that you hold outside a retirement account at once, you can ignore this issue. (After reading through the accounting options that the IRS offers, you have more incentive to sell all your shares in a fund at once!)

Be aware that after you elect one of the following *tax accounting methods* for selling shares in a particular fund, you can't change to another method for the sale of the remaining shares. If you plan to sell only some of your fund shares — and it would be advantageous for you to, for example, specify that you're selling the newer shares first — then choose that method. But, regardless of the method you choose, your mutual fund capital gains and capital losses are recorded on Schedule D of IRS Form 1040.

Specific identification method

The first fund basis option that the IRS allows you to use when you sell a portion of the shares of a fund is the so-called *specific identification* method. Here's how it works. Suppose that you own 200 shares of Global Interactive Couch Potato fund (you laugh — but there really is a fund with a name similar to this!), and you want to sell 100 shares. Suppose further that you bought 100 of these shares ten years ago at $10 per share, and then another 100 shares two years ago for $40 per share. (I'm assuming that you didn't make any other purchases from reinvestment of capital gains or dividends — more on this issue later.) Today, the fund is worth $50 per share. Being a couch potato has its rewards!

Which 100 shares should you sell? The IRS gives you a choice. You can identify the *specific* shares that you sell. With your Global Interactive Couch Potato shares, you may opt to sell the last or most recent 100 shares you bought. Selling the most recent shares will minimize your tax bill because these shares were purchased at a higher price. If you sell this way, you must identify the specific shares you want the fund company (or broker holding the shares) to sell. Use either or both of the following ways to identify the 100 shares to be sold:

- Original date of purchase
- Cost when you bought the shares

You may wonder how the IRS knows whether you specified shares before you sold them. Get this: The IRS doesn't know. But if you are audited, the IRS will ask for proof that you identified the shares to be sold before you sold them. It's best to put your sales request to the fund company in writing and keep a copy for your tax files.

The "first-in-first-out" method

Another method of accounting for which shares are sold is the method the IRS forces you to use if you don't specify before the sale which shares are to be sold: the *first-in-first-out* (FIFO) method. FIFO means that the first shares you sell are simply the first shares that you bought. Not surprisingly, because most stock funds appreciate over time, the FIFO method leads to paying more taxes sooner. In the case of the Global Interactive Couch Potato fund, FIFO considers that the 100 shares sold are the 100 that you bought ten years ago at the bargain-basement price of $10 per share.

Although you will save taxes today if you specify selling the shares that you bought later at a higher price, don't forget (the IRS won't let you) that when you finally sell the other shares, you'll owe taxes on the larger profit. The longer you expect to hold these other shares, the greater the likely value you'll derive from postponing realizing the gain. Of course, you always run the risk that the IRS will raise tax rates in the future or that your particular tax rate will rise.

The average cost method

Had enough of fund accounting? Well, you're not done yet. The IRS, believe it or not, allows you yet another fund accounting method: the *average cost method.* If you bought shares in chunks over time and/or reinvested the fund distributions (such as from dividends) into more shares of the fund, then tracking and figuring which shares you're selling could be a real headache. So the IRS allows you to take an average cost for all the shares you bought over time.

If you sell all your shares of a fund at once, you can use the average cost basis method. This method may also be preferred when you sell a portion of a fund that you hold. Because many fund companies calculate this number for you, you can save time and possible fees paid to a tax preparer to crunch the numbers.

Regardless of which tax cost accounting method you choose for your fund sales, be careful not to overpay your capital gains tax. Remember that the maximum tax rate for long-term (investments held more than 18 months) capital gains is 20 percent (10 percent if you're in the 15 percent federal tax bracket).

Fund sales reports Form 1099-B

When you sell shares in a mutual fund, you'll receive Form 1099-B early in the following year. This document is fairly worthless because it doesn't calculate the cost basis of the shares that you sold. Its primary value to you is that it nicely summarizes and reminds you of all the transactions that you need to account for on your annual tax return. This form, which is also sent to the IRS, serves to notify the tax authorities of which investments you sold so that they can check your tax return to see if you report the transaction.

If some of the sales listed on your Form 1099-B are from check-writing redemptions, stop writing checks on those funds! Keep enough stashed in a money market fund and write checks only from that type of account. Money market fund sales are not tax reportable because a money fund's share price doesn't change. Thus, you get fewer tax headaches!

Deciding when to take your tax lumps or deductions

If funds held outside of retirement accounts increase in value, you won't want to sell them because of the tax bite. If, on the other hand, they decline in value, you may not know whether to sell them and, thus, lock in your losses. So how do you decide what to do and what role taxes should play in your decisions? As I cover in Chapter 12, several issues can factor into your decision to sell a fund or hold onto it. Taxes are an important consideration. So, what do you need to know about taxes?

You do need to realize that taxes are important, but don't let them keep you from doing something you really want to do. Suppose, for example, that you need money to buy a home or take a long postponed vacation — and selling some mutual funds is your only source of money for this purpose. I say go for it. Even if you have to pay state as well as federal taxes totaling, for example, 35 percent of the profit, you'll have lots left over. Before you sell, however, do some rough figuring to make sure that you'll have enough money to accomplish your goal.

If you hold a number of funds, give preference to selling your largest holdings (that is, those with the largest total market value) with the smallest capital gains. If you have some funds that have profits and some with losses, you can sell some of each, subject to IRS rules, in order to offset the profits with the losses.

You cannot claim more than $3,000 in short-term or long-term losses in any one year. If you sell funds with losses that total more than $3,000 in a year, you must carry the losses over to future tax years. This situation not only creates more tax paperwork, but it also delays taking the tax deduction. So try not to have *net losses* (losses plus gains) that exceed $3,000 in a year.

INVESTIGATE

Selling for tax deductions and the famous *wash sale rule*

Some tax advisors advocate doing *year-end tax-loss selling*. The logic goes something like this: If you hold a mutual fund that has declined in value and you hold that fund outside a retirement account, you should sell it, take the tax write-off, and then buy the fund (or something similar) back.

I don't think that this selling just for taking a tax loss is worth the trouble, particularly if you plan on holding the repurchased shares for a long time. Remember that by selling and buying back the shares, you've lowered your basis, which will increase the taxable profit after you sell the repurchased shares (assuming, of course, that they appreciate).

If you sell a fund for a tax loss and buy back shares in that same fund within 30 days of the sale, you can't deduct the loss. Why? Because, if you do, you violate the so-called *wash sale rule*. The IRS will not allow deduction of a loss for a fund sale if you buy that same fund back within 30 days. As long as you wait 31 or more days, no problem. If you're selling a mutual fund, you can easily sidestep this rule simply by purchasing a fund similar to the one you're selling.

What to do when you can't find the amount you paid for a fund

When you sell a mutual fund that you've owned for a long time (or that someone gave you), you may have no idea of its original cost (also known as its *cost basis*).

If you can't find that original statement, start by calling the firm where the investment was bought. Whether it's a mutual fund company or brokerage firm, they should be able to send you copies of old account statements. You may have to pay a small fee for this service. Also, increasing numbers of investment firms (particularly mutual fund companies) automatically calculate and report cost-basis information on investments you sell. Generally, the cost basis they calculate is the average cost for the shares that you purchased.

Retirement Fund Withdrawals and Form 1099-R

Someday, hopefully not before you retire, you'll need or want to start enjoying all the money that you will have socked away into great mutual funds inside your tax-sheltered retirement accounts. The following sections explain what you need to know and consider before taking money out of your mutual fund retirement accounts.

Minimizing taxes and avoiding penalties

Although there are many different retirement account types (IRAs, SEP-IRAs, Keoghs, 401(k)s, 403 (b)s, and so on), as well as many tax laws governing each, the IRS declared one rule that makes understanding taxes on withdrawals a little easier. All retirement accounts allow you to begin withdrawing money, without penalty, after age $59\frac{1}{2}$. (Why they didn't use a round number like 60 is beyond me.)

WARNING!

If you withdraw money from your retirement accounts prior to age $59\frac{1}{2}$, in addition to paying current income tax on the distribution, you also must pay penalties — 10 percent of the amount of the taxable distribution at the federal level and whatever penalties your state charges. (The penalty is computed on Form 5329 — Return for Additional Taxes Attributable to Qualified Retirement Plans.)

TECHNICAL STUFF

There are exceptions to the early withdrawal penalty: For employer's retirement plans such as 401(k)s and 403(b)s, penalty-free withdrawals before the age of $59\frac{1}{2}$ are allowed if any of the following conditions apply:

- You've stopped working after you reach age 55 (whether by retirement or termination).
- The withdrawal was mandated by a qualified domestic relations court order.
- You have deductible medical expenses in excess of 7.5 percent of your adjusted gross income.

Early IRA distributions are also exempted from a penalty if they're paid because of death or disability, paid over your life expectancy, or rolled over to another IRA. Withdrawing money from an IRA for a first-time home purchase (up to $10,000) or higher education expenses is also permitted.

TIP

Issues to consider before making retirement account withdrawals

Generally speaking, most people are better off postponing withdrawals from retirement accounts until they need the money. But don't delay if waiting means that you must scrimp and cut corners — especially if you have the money to use and enjoy.

On the other hand, if you have other money you can use, tap those funds first. The longer your retirement account money is left alone, the longer it can grow without being taxed. Suppose that you retire at age 60. In addition to money inside your retirement accounts, you have a bunch available outside as well. If you can, you're generally better off using the money outside of retirement accounts *before* you start to tap the retirement account money.

If you're not wealthy, odds are good that you'll need (and want) to start drawing on your retirement account soon after you retire. By all means, do it. But have you figured out how long your nest egg will last and how much you can afford to withdraw? Most folks haven't. It's worth taking the time to figure how much of your money you can afford to draw on per year, even if you think that you have enough. Many good savers have a hard time spending and enjoying their money in retirement. Knowing how much you can safely use may help you loosen your purse strings.

One danger of leaving your money to compound inside your retirement accounts for a long time — after you're retired — is that the IRS *requires* you to start making withdrawals by April 1st of the year following the year you reach age 70½. If you don't, you pay a whopping 50 percent penalty on the amount that you should have taken out but didn't. (***Note:*** This requirement does not apply to the new Roth IRAs.)

It's possible that because of your delay in taking the money out — and the fact that it will have more time to compound and grow — you may need to withdraw a hefty chunk each year. Doing so could push you into higher tax brackets in those years that you are forced to make larger withdrawals.

If you want to plan how to withdraw money from your retirement accounts in order to meet your needs and minimize your taxes, hire a tax advisor to help. If you have a lot of money in retirement accounts, as well as the luxury of not needing the money until you're well into retirement, tax planning will likely be worth your time and money.

Of course, you'll pay current income taxes, both federal and state, when you withdraw money that hasn't previously been taxed from retirement accounts. The one exception is for withdrawing money early from the new Roth IRA accounts for a home purchase — in this case, you do not owe any income tax on the withdrawn investment earnings.

Making sense of Form 1099-R for IRAs

If you receive a distribution from your mutual fund IRA, the mutual fund company or brokerage firm where you hold your funds will report the distribution on Form 1099-R (see Figure 13-2). These distributions are taxable unless you made nondeductible contributions to the IRA (a situation I cover momentarily). Here's a rundown of these boxes on your 1099-R:

- **Box 1, Gross distribution:** The amount of money that you withdrew from your IRA. Make sure that this figure is correct: Check to see if it matches the amount withdrawn from your IRA account statement. This amount is fully taxable if you've never made a nondeductible contribution to an IRA — that's an IRA contribution in which you didn't take a tax-deduction and therefore filed Form 8606 (Nondeductible IRA Contributions, IRA Basis, and Nontaxable IRA Distributions).
- **Box 2a, Taxable amount:** The taxable amount of the IRA distribution. However, the payer of an IRA distribution doesn't have enough information to compute whether your entire IRA distribution is completely taxable or not. Therefore, if you simply enter this amount on your tax return as being fully taxable, you overpay on your taxes if you have made nondeductible contributions to your IRA. If you made nondeductible contributions, compute the nontaxable portion of your distribution on Form 8606, which you need to attach to your annual tax return.

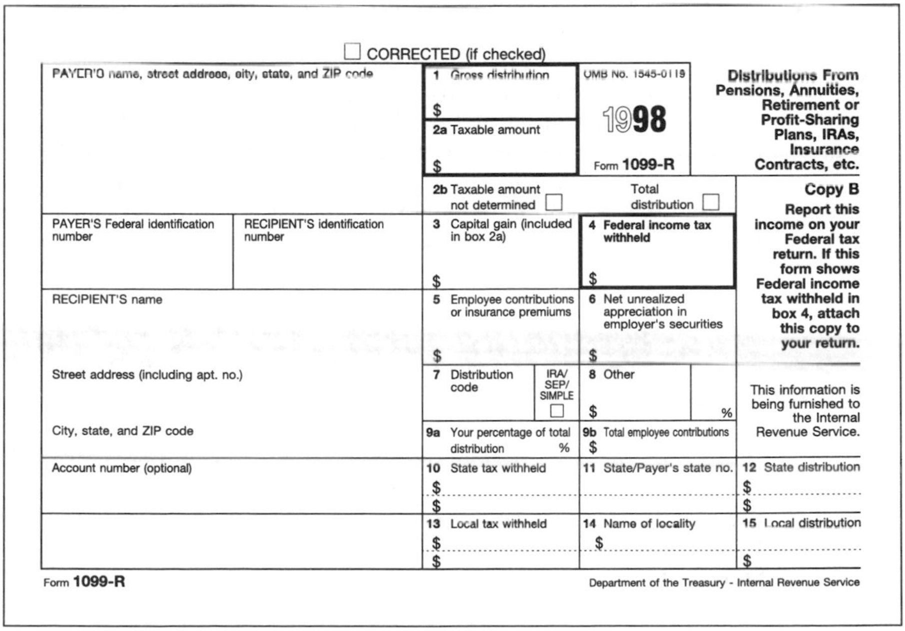
☐ CORRECTED (if checked)

PAYER'S name, street address, city, state, and ZIP code

1 Gross distribution $

2a Taxable amount $

OMB No. 1545-0119

1998

Form 1099-R

Distributions From Pensions, Annuities, Retirement or Profit-Sharing Plans, IRAs, Insurance Contracts, etc.

2b Taxable amount not determined ☐ Total distribution ☐

Copy B Report this income on your Federal tax return. If this form shows Federal income tax withheld in box 4, attach this copy to your return.

PAYER'S Federal identification number

RECIPIENT'S identification number

3 Capital gain (included in box 2a) $

4 Federal income tax withheld $

RECIPIENT'S name

5 Employee contributions or insurance premiums $

6 Net unrealized appreciation in employer's securities $

Street address (including apt. no.)

7 Distribution code IRA/SEP/SIMPLE ☐

8 Other $ %

This information is being furnished to the Internal Revenue Service.

City, state, and ZIP code

9a Your percentage of total distribution %

9b Total employee contributions $

Account number (optional)

10 State tax withheld $ $

11 State/Payer's state no.

12 State distribution $ $

13 Local tax withheld $ $

14 Name of locality $

15 Local distribution $ $

Form 1099-R

Department of the Treasury - Internal Revenue Service

Figure 13-2: Here's where funds report your retirement plan distributions.

Making non-IRA account withdrawals

Retirement account withdrawals and benefits from non-IRA accounts — such as 401(k), SEP-IRA, or Keogh plans — are taxed depending on whether you receive them in the form of an annuity (paid over your lifetime) or a lump sum. The amount you fill in on your 1040 tax return is reported on a 1099-R that you receive from your employer or another custodian of your plan, which may include an investment company such as a mutual fund company or discount broker.

If you didn't pay or contribute to your employer's retirement plan, or if your employer didn't withhold part of the cost from your pay while you worked, then the amount you receive each year is fully taxable. The amount that you contributed and for which you received a deduction — such as contributions to a 401(k), SEP-IRA, or Keogh — isn't considered part of your cost.

If you made nondeductible contributions to your retirement plan or contributions that were then added to your taxable income on your W-2, then you are not taxed when withdrawing these contributions because you've already paid tax on that money. The rest of the amount you receive is taxable.

As they often do with our needlessly complicated tax laws, the IRS gives you at least two ways to compute the amount that you owe tax on. These two ways are known as the *General Rule* and the *Simplified General Rule.* The details of these parts of the tax code are beyond the scope of this book — if you're in this boat, pick up a copy of *Taxes For Dummies* (published by IDG Books Worldwide, Inc.), which I co-authored with David Silverman.

If you receive a total distribution from a retirement plan, you receive a Form 1099-R. If the distribution qualifies as a lump-sum distribution, Box 3 shows the capital gain amount, and Box 2a minus Box 3 shows the ordinary income amount. Code A is entered in Box 7 if the lump sum qualifies for special averaging. If you don't get a Form 1099-R, or if you have questions about the form, contact your plan administrator.

Understanding form 1099-R for non-IRAs

You report non-IRA retirement account distributions on Form 1099-R, which is the same one used to report IRA distributions. Sometimes people panic when they receive a 1099-R and they intend to rollover their retirement account money into a fund from, say, their employer's retirement plan after they leave their job. Don't worry. As you'll hopefully soon see, you received this form because you *did* do a legal rollover and therefore won't be subjected to the tax normally levied on distributions.

The following highlights how some of the other boxes on distributions for non-IRA retirement accounts come into play:

- **Box 3:** If the distribution is a lump-sum and you were a participant in the plan before 1974, this amount qualifies for capital gain treatment.
- **Box 4:** This box indicates Federal Income tax withheld (you get credit for this amount when you file your tax return).
- **Box 5:** Your after-tax contribution is entered here.
- **Box 6:** Securities in your employer's company that you received are listed here. This amount is not taxable until the securities are sold.
- **Box 7:** If you are under $59^1/_2$ and your employer knows that you qualify for one of the exceptions to the 10 percent penalty, the employer enters:

  Code 2 — separation from service after 55

  Code 3 — disability

  Code 4 — death

  Code A — qualifies for lump-sum treatment

  Code G — direct rollover to an IRA

  Code H — direct rollover to another retirement plan
- **Box 8:** If you have an entry here, seek tax advice.
- **Box 9a:** This amount is your share of a distribution if there are several beneficiaries.

Chapter 14

Common Fund Problems and How to Fix 'Em

In This Chapter

- Dealing with telephone representatives
- Getting money into and out of funds
- Fixing paperwork and other problems

Sooner or later, just as minor problems crop up with bank accounts, you may have a little snafu that you need to get fixed with your mutual funds. Who you gonna call? Usually the toll-free number of the company holding the account, which you can call to talk with a telephone representative.

Established fund companies and discount brokerages have hundreds and, in some cases, thousands of telephone representatives who field phone calls and process stuff you send them in the mail. Most of the bigger and better companies recommended in this book do a good job of training their employees, so you should receive competent assistance. But keep in mind that these people are human — that is, not perfect. Some are more competent than others at getting the job done right the first time.

When you call companies to ask a question or express a concern, you may end up speaking with someone who doesn't know how to fix your problem, gives you the runaround, or worse — gives you incorrect information. Here's what you can and should do to ensure that you get accurate solutions without investing a lot of your time:

TIP

- **Know the representatives' limitations.** Fund company representatives are there to provide information and assistance. Don't depend on them for tax advice. (Most of the larger fund companies have retirement account specialists who have more detailed knowledge about tax issues relating to those accounts.)

- **Talk to someone else.** If you don't get clear answers or answers that you're satisfied with, don't hesitate to ask for a supervisor. Or you can simply call back on the toll-free line, and you're sure to get another representative. This is a proven way to get a second opinion to make sure that the first person knew what he or she was talking about.
- **Take names and notes for thorny problems.** If you're dealing with a problem that could cost you big bucks if not properly solved, make sure to take notes of your conversation. Write down the name of the representative you spoke to, the office he or she is located in, and his or her telephone extension. That way, you have some proof of your good efforts to fix things when you need to complain to or are summoned by a higher authority (for example, a supervisor, the IRS, and so on).

Although I can't guarantee that this chapter is a page-turner, it can help bail you out and soothe your nerves when you just don't know how to get a problem fixed.

Messed-Up Deposits and Purchases

With all the sound-alike fund names, you can very well have your money deposited into the wrong fund at some firms. That's why it's a good idea to look at the statement that confirms your purchase to verify that the deposit amount and the fund into which the money was deposited are both correct.

If the fund company makes a mistake, they should cheerfully fix the problem. (They may need to do a bit of research first.) They should credit the correct amount to the fund you requested as of the date the money was originally received.

TIP: If the bond or stock fund you intended to buy has declined in value since the deposit should have been made, you get to invest with the benefit of hindsight. Ask that, when the deposit is corrected, it be done as of today. On the other hand, if the fund has appreciated, then you can insist that the original date of purchase be used!

If the screw-up was your fault, sometimes fund companies will gracefully overlook this and give you what you had intended (having lots of money with the company will help your chances of this happening). Because companies are leery about people who may take advantage of this generosity by jumping out of funds that declined in value, the company judges each situation to determine whether or not it appears to be an honest mistake.

Specifying Funds to Buy at Discount Brokers

When you invest through most mutual fund companies, their account application and other forms allow you to indicate what fund(s) you wish to make your deposit into. Not so at discount brokerage firms.

If you want your deposit to a discount brokerage to be immediately invested into a particular fund or funds, write out your instructions and send them in with your deposit. For example, if you mail in $2,000 for an IRA deposit to a discount brokerage firm and you want the money divided between, say, the Neuberger & Berman Guardian fund and the Warburg Pincus International Equity fund, here's how to word the letter:

> Dear Sir or Madam:
>
> Enclosed please find a check in the amount of $2,000 that I would like invested in my IRA account as a 1998 contribution (reference your account number or specify if new application is attached) as follows:
>
> $1,000 into Neuberger & Berman Guardian (NGUAX)
>
> $1,000 into Warburg Pincus International Equity fund (CUIEX)
>
> Please reinvest dividends and capital gains.
>
> Thanks a million,

Note the reference about what to do with dividends and capital gains distributions. Try to be as precise as possible with the fund names. The ultimate in precision for a broker is the fund's *trading symbol.* (Trading symbols for funds recommended in this book are listed in the Appendix.)

Making Deposits in a Flash

Maybe you have an account open and just need to feed it in a hurry. Most often this happens when you need to fund a retirement account, but it may also happen if you've overdrawn an account by writing a check.

If you're dealing with a company that has a branch location near you, simply write a check and deposit it at their office. If the fund company isn't in your neighborhood, don't despair. The next-best and fastest way to get money into a fund account you previously established is by wiring it from your bank account.

If you have already set up the wiring feature on your fund account, first call your fund company to see what information you need to provide to your bank in order for the wire to be correctly sent. This information usually includes the name of the bank your fund uses for wires, that bank's identification number (the ABA #), the title and account number of the fund company's account at that bank, your name as it appears on your fund account, the name of that fund, and your own account number. Wiring usually costs money on both ends.

If you don't have the wiring feature established on your account, establishing this feature will take some time because you must request, fill out, and mail a special form.

Another option that most fund accounts offer is electronic funds transfer — like a paperless check. Electronic funds transfer usually takes a day longer than a wire, but it is free. Simply call your fund company and tell them how much money you want to move. As with wiring, if you don't have this feature set up, you can establish it by requesting and filling out a form from the fund company.

Verifying Receipt of Deposits

When you send money to a fund company, how do you know if the fund company received your money? Unlike when you use a bank ATM, you won't get a deposit slip with your transaction — at least, not right away. Fund companies mail you a statement, usually the day after the deposit is received and processed, showing you the transaction. You can keep a log of deposits on paper or with a computer program and check them off as received, once a month, or quarterly.

If you can't wait for the mail, you can call the fund company's toll-free number and verify receipt over the phone. Many of the larger fund companies have automated phone systems that allow you to check on stuff like this quickly, without waiting for a live person to talk to.

Getting Money Out in a Hurry

For non-retirement accounts, if you have a money market fund with check-writing privileges, writing a check to get money in a hurry is simple and costs nothing. Another option, which can be used on all types of accounts, is to call the fund company and request a *telephone redemption*. The day after the next financial market close, a check should be cut and mailed to you. If you need the check faster than the mail service can get it to you, you can provide your express mail company (for example, FedEx) account number. Some fund companies also allow you to pick up redemption checks at their headquarters. Call to see if they provide this service.

Banks and other recipients of checks from your account may hassle you by placing a hold for an unreasonable number of days on the funds from your checks. For checks that you write yourself, the hold is understandable because the check recipient has no way of knowing if the money will be in the account when the check is ready to clear. But if the check was issued by the fund company, then the money has already been taken from your account, so the check is almost as good as cash to recipients — they just need to wait a couple of days for receipt of the funds.

TIP

Banks normally place up to a five-day hold on out-of-state checks. (Odds are that your fund company clears checks through an out-of-state bank.) If a bank doesn't make the money available to you quickly, ask to speak to the branch manager or some other higher-up. Gently remind him or her that you can move your bank accounts to a less bureaucratic bank.

Wiring and electronic funds transfers are other alternatives that you may prefer because you don't need to wait for a paper check to clear. If you just realize that you need money to close on a home purchase tomorrow, these are your best bets. See the section "Making Deposits in a Flash," earlier in this chapter, for how these services work.

For retirement account withdrawals, requests need to be made in writing. Perhaps you need to withdraw money before the end of December to meet the IRS's mandatory withdrawal requirements after age 70½. The good news here is that you don't need to have received the funds before the end of the year. As long as the distribution is made by the end of December, it doesn't matter to the IRS if the check takes several days to reach you.

INVESTIGATE

Why did my fund plunge?

You shouldn't follow your funds every day, and on the days that you do check the price per share, it typically goes up or down a few cents. One day, usually soon after you talk with a friend and mention how pleased you are with your fund's returns, you receive a rude awakening.

"It dropped $1.21 per share!"

That's what one of my clients said to me after noticing the price of one of her international stock funds in December. Guess what? The fund made a distribution that reduced the price per share but increased the number of shares. So she wasn't losing money after all.

If you follow your funds through the daily newspaper and you see such a large price drop, look again to see if any special letters are printed after the fund's name, such as *x*, which indicates that a fund paid its dividend, and *e* for payment of a capital gains distribution.

Checks Lost in the Mail

TIP

Checks and other stuff can get lost in the mail. If you wrote a check and made it payable to the fund company, there's no big need to stop payment. If you're depositing checks with your fund company that someone else wrote to you, they may want to stop payment when you report to them that the check is lost, and you want it reissued if they are concerned that you might cash it.

What's a bigger pain is having to redo account applications that you may have sent with the check(s). If you do tons of applications and transfer forms, you may want to keep copies.

Registered mail and certified mail don't eliminate the problem of lost mail. They just indicate whether or not the mail was received. I wouldn't waste the money or the time needed to go to the post office to use these mail services.

Changing Options After You Open Your Account

Perhaps now you wish you had check writing on your money market fund. Or you want to establish a regular monthly investment plan so that money is sent electronically from your bank account to some funds. How do you add these features after you've opened an account?

Although you can add some features over the phone, most features, particularly those that require your signature — such as check writing — can only be set up through short forms that you request by phone. Previously established options, such as reinvestment of dividends, can be changed over the phone.

Changing the registration of your accounts is more of a pain. A letter is generally required, for example, if you marry and change your name or want to add your spouse to the account. A *signature guarantee* may be required — these are provided by banks and brokerage firms. Don't confuse this requirement with getting something notarized, which is different.

Making Sense of Your Statements and Profits

Can't understand your fund statement? Don't know how much money your fund is making for you? Welcome to a large and not very exclusive club. See Chapter 12 for the full scoop.

TIP

If you want a tax, financial, or legal advisor — or a savvy relative — to help you keep an eye on your investments, you can ask that he or she be listed on your account as an *interested party* to receive duplicate statements. Simply write to the fund company and include the accounts you'd like the interested party to receive statements for and provide that person's name and mailing address.

Changing Addresses

Normally fund companies require that you make a change of address in writing, but over time more fund companies are establishing security procedures that allow you to make a change of address by phone. The safeguards include a requirement that you prove that you are who you say you are on the phone (give your mother's maiden name and all that); the fund companies also mail confirmations of the changed address to both old and new addresses.

Finding Funds You Forgot to Move with You

Every year, people literally throw away hundreds of millions of dollars in investments, including investments in mutual funds. You may have done this if you've moved around a lot without systematically sending changes of address to fund companies and placing mail-forwarding orders with the post office. After fund companies try for a long time to send mail to your old address, they eventually throw in the towel, and your account becomes dormant. No more statements are sent for a number of years, after which time your account is considered abandoned!

By law, the mutual fund company must transfer your abandoned money to the treasurer's office (called *escheatment*, for you Scrabble and Trivial Pursuit buffs) of the state in which the fund company does business or the state in which the last registered address appeared on your account. This transfer may happen from within a few years to more than a decade after the fund company loses contact with you. If you don't claim the money within a certain number of years after that, the state gets to keep it.

TIP

If you vaguely recall that you had funds with a particular fund company way back when, call the company. You don't need to remember the specific funds you invested in. By using your name, Social Security number, old mailing addresses, and personal stuff like that, the fund company's computer system can find your accounts and determine whether they were turned over to the state. You can also try contacting the state treasurer's office in the states in which you have lived to see if they have any of your abandoned accounts. If you find your accounts, please write to me in care of the publisher and let me know — these things make me feel all warm and fuzzy inside.

Account Transfer Snags

Transferring accounts from one investment firm or bank to another can be a big pain. Even obtaining the correct transfer paperwork and completing it is a challenge — that's why I explain how to do it in Chapter 11.

BEWARE

Problems happen most often with retirement accounts and with brokerage account transfers. Some firms are reluctant to give up your money and so they drag their feet, doing everything they can to make your life and the lives of employees who transfer accounts at your new investment company a nightmare. The biggest culprits are the supposed "full service" brokerage firms (for instance, Prudential, Salomon Smith Barney, Dean Witter, and Merrill Lynch) that employ commission-based brokers. They've lost a lot of money flowing out to no-load and discount brokers' mutual funds, and they do what they can to hang on. The unfortunate reality is that they will cheerfully set up a new account to accept your money on a moment's notice, but they will drag their feet, sometimes for months, when it comes time to relinquish your money.

TIP

Don't let this foot-dragging on the part of brokerage firms deter you from moving your money into a better investment firm. Remember that the transfer should, under securities industry regulations, be done within 30 days. If it's not, hammer the villains! Should the transfer not be complete within a month, get in touch with your new investment firm to determine what the problem is. If your old company is not cooperating, a call to a manager there may help to get the ball rolling. To light a fire under their behinds, tell the manager at the old firm that you're sending letters to the National Association of Securities Dealers (NASD) and the Securities and Exchange Commission (SEC) if they don't complete your transfer within the next week. Then do it.

In addition to uncooperative brokers, certain assets present problems with transfers. If you purchase any mutual funds at, say, Dean Witter that are Dean Witter house mutual funds, in addition to buying into what I consider to be a relatively crummy family of funds, you also can't transfer their funds as they are. You must first have them liquidated through Dean Witter so that the cash proceeds can be transferred. Most annuities work the same way.

TIP

Transfer individual securities, such as stocks and bonds, to a discount broker. That way, if you later decide to sell them, you save on commission charges. Limited partnerships generally can't be liquidated, and everybody charges decent-sized fees to hold them — another reason not to buy them in the first place. If you want less account clutter, transfer these to the discount broker you're otherwise going to be using.

Eliminating Fund Marketing Solicitations

Some mutual fund companies fill your mailbox with tons of marketing materials on all sorts of new funds, old funds, and everything but the kitchen sink.

TIP

If you do business with many companies and their marketing folks are driving you batty, call your fund companies and ask them to code your account on their advanced computer systems so that you won't receive anything other than statements. Fund companies are required under Securities and Exchange Commission regulations to honor such a request. Fund companies are happy to oblige — they don't want irritated customers.

As for all the other junk mail you get thanks to firms that sell mailing lists, fight back — and spare a couple of trees — by sending a request not to receive junk mail to the Direct Marketing Association, Mail Preference Service, P.O. Box 9008, Farmingdale, NY 11735-9008.

TIP

Some fund companies and brokers may call you at home soliciting your purchase of investments. They tend to focus on people with large cash balances sitting in their accounts. As former First Lady Nancy Reagan said to kids about using drugs, "Just say no!" To stop fund sellers from calling you in the future, you have the Telephone Consumer Act on your side. This act allows you to request the fund company (or anyone else who solicits you by phone, for that matter) to cease and desist! The fund company then notes on its computers to stop calling you.

Digging Out from under All Those Statements

If you're being buried in paperwork from statements and transaction confirmations from too many fund companies, consider consolidating your fund holdings through a discount broker. There are tradeoffs involved — you pay more in fees for the convenience these accounts offer (see Chapter 5).

Getting Statements from Older Accounts

Perhaps, for reasons of nostalgia or taxes, you need copies of a statement that's more than a year old. Most companies should have no problem providing it. They may, however, charge you something like $10 per fund per year requested. So be choosy. The main reason you'd request a statement is to research how much you originally invested in a mutual fund held outside of a retirement account. If you've sold or are thinking about selling shares of the fund, you may have to figure out the fund's cost basis for tax reporting purposes (see Chapter 13). In the future, be sure to keep your statements so you don't need to ask for copies.

REMEMBER

If you're going to sell *all* the shares that you hold in a fund, check to see if your firm can report the average cost of the shares sold. If their accounting system can do this, you're golden and you don't need to bother with getting the old statements. (See Chapter 13 for more details on tax issues to consider when selling funds.)

Part IV
Evaluating Information and Advice

The 5th Wave By Rich Tennant

"Perhaps you'd like to buy these magic beans, or this charm that will give you good luck, or this stock that promises a 200% return on your investment in less than 18 months."

In this part . . .

This part covers other stuff you may *want* to know but don't really *need* to know. Perhaps you've received tons of junk (er, I mean, direct) mail from Mr. Fund Knowitall, or you've just watched Ms. MarketTiming Guru on television, and now you want to know whether you should follow their prognostications and pearls of wisdom. Or maybe you're one of those impatient types who wants to know now (instead of waiting till your fund company sends you statements) how your funds are doing. This part lets you indulge such gluttonous desires to the hilt. Here you master techniques for evaluating gurus and newsletters, and you turn your computer into an investment intelligence agency.

Chapter 15

Fund Ratings, Gurus, and *Still More* Funds

In This Chapter

- Investment Newsletter Hall of Shame
- Use and abuse of fund ratings
- The best newsletters and information sources
- The scoop on closed-end funds

My father loves data and analyzing things. He likes to figure out how things work. When he was still working (he's now retired), he was a mechanical engineer (impressively, he worked his entire career in one field). He loves to make charts and graphs. During the months that I wrote the first edition this book, he was poring over a veritable truckload of data and information on mutual funds and investing.

So I wrote this chapter for people like my dad. Even if you're not an engineer by training, there may be a bit of a data lover in you. The challenge as you navigate the landscape of mutual fund data, newsletters, references, and gurus is discerning the good from the merely mediocre — as well as the downright useless and dangerous information and advice. Unfortunately, more of the latter are out there waiting to trip you up.

Stuff to Avoid

Why start with the bad stuff? Simple. So much bad investment advice is out there, and odds are good that you may currently be using some of it, or thinking of using it, or it may be pitched to you in the future. Finding out the tricks of the trade enables you to better identify the good stuff. But if you're pressed for time and can't bear to see the ugly side of the investment newsletter business, skip ahead to the good sources that I recommend later in this chapter (I cover software and online services in Chapter 16).

Market timing doesn't work — and neither do crystal balls

Many fund investors believe that they can increase their chances of success if they follow the prognostications of certain gurus. Many gurus say (or imply) that they can tell you when you should be in or out of the markets or particular investments. Whenever a guru near you treats you to such "wisdom," just repeat after me:

> *"No one can predict the future."*
>
> *"No one can predict the future."*
>
> *"No one can predict the future."*

If you can remember this one simple fact — a fact supported by mountains of evidence and plenty of good old-fashioned common sense — you will dramatically increase your chances for successful investing in funds, and you will decrease the odds of making major mistakes. *And* you'll have a much clearer vision about which resources to use for further reading and research about funds.

As I explain in Chapter 6, the strategy of market timing is doomed to failure in the long run. Newsletter writers should be given no more credibility than you would give some palm-reader on the street. (In fact, when Morningstar once likened market timing to astrology, it was an astrology buff that turned out to be the most offended.)

Take a look at the performance track record of investment newsletters. According to the *Hulbert Financial Digest* (see the next section), which looks at risk as well as return, only two newsletters have managed to keep ahead of the market averages over the past decade (and none have done so over the past 15 years). And these two newsletters only managed to do so by a few *tenths* of one percent per year (and that doesn't take into account the cost of subscribing to a newsletter). The worst investment newsletters, on the other hand, have underperformed the market averages by dozens of percentage points; some would even have caused you to lose money during a decade when the financial markets performed extraordinarily well.

Of course, you'd never know about newsletters' dismal performances if all you ever listened to were the claims made by newsletter writers themselves. Most claim that they avoided investing when the stock market crashed in 1987, and they even claim that they told their loyal followers to sell everything just before the bottom fell out. They also usually go on to proclaim that they avoided other major declines and bought at every bottom in the market.

But we're also #1 according to . . .

Newsletters also cite rankings from other organizations (such as *Timer's Digest)* in their efforts to justify their claims of *numero uno* status. Again, the same problems that force newsletters to qualify in the Hulbert ratings come into play with other newsletter rankings. Given enough time periods and categories of newsletters, many newsletter writers can claim the coveted #1 spot at some time or another.

Newsletters also refer to awards they've won from the Newsletter Publisher's Association (NPA). My advice: Ignore NPA awards. They're meaningless. They have nothing to do with the performance of a newsletter's advice. And because the NPA is an association made up of the newsletters themselves, they're just giving themselves a pat on the back! Not a very objective way to dole out awards, eh? (The association isn't very large and it is always doling out awards, which doesn't hurt newsletter writers' chances of winning, either.)

And, of course, there are the inevitable customer testimonials. Curiously, though, testimonials almost always parrot the promotional material for the newsletter, and they never include the person's name. All they provide are the person's initials, such as B.S., and good old B.S.'s home, such as Brooklyn, N.Y. Some of these testimonials are made up — so they really are B.S.!

Newsletters writers don't know anything that isn't already reflected in the prices of securities. If newsletter writers did have a knack for unearthing information that no one else typically knew, they'd be too busy investing their own money and making millions off their predictions to waste their time publishing a newsletter.

Rated #1 by the Hulbert Financial Digest

Mark Hulbert started a useful business in the 1980s. Almost every investment newsletter was making outrageous claims about the success of its previous predictions. But how could you, the potential new subscriber, know if a newsletter was telling the truth or blowing smoke? Answer: You couldn't.

Not until Mark Hulbert came along, that is. He tracks the actual performance of the newsletters' investment picks. For each newsletter, he creates a portfolio based exactly on the newsletter's recommendations. So, over time, Hulbert knows exactly how the newsletters' picks have done.

Has the *Hulbert Financial Digest* stopped the outrageous claims of the investment newsletters? No, but they seem to be slowly getting better, thanks to Hulbert's influence. The problem is that people still believe the marketing hype of the newsletters and never bother to check with Hulbert's service.

Hulbert's service has created another problem, however. Many newsletters can claim to be #1 by selecting short time periods when they actually were #1, even though they have underperformed the rest of the time. And some falsely lay claim to #1 status by simply comparing their performance to all those that are worse while ignoring the ones that perform better!

Hire us as money managers

Many newsletter writers publish newsletters as a means of drawing people into their money management business. For some, that's the only reason they produce the newsletter. So they don't really want to teach you too much about investing; they want to convince you that your money is best off in their hands — which means that their articles are usually trying to tell you that investing is complicated and market timing is everything.

Some newsletters that are already short on content plug their money management service *right in the newsletter.* One monthly that sells for more than $100 per year publishes issues that typically are 20 pages long, 16 pages of which are filler; performance numbers for funds are an example of this filler — numbers that you can get for a few bucks a month by picking up one of the many financial magazines that contain this data. In the four pages of articles in the typical newsletter, readers often confront a plug for the editor's money management business because (according to him) a newsletter's advice can't substitute for the daily oversight of your portfolio.

Please.

Don't believe it. Of course, this claim isn't what they told you in their marketing materials to get you to subscribe to the newsletter.

Investment Newsletter Hall of Shame

The following sections reveal some of the many examples of the really heavy stuff that gets shoveled by some of these folks to sell you on their investment newsletters. All of the following examples are drawn from real-world newsletters. However, I've changed the names to keep you focused on the types of misleading practices that marketing newsletters engage in rather than having you focus on the particular scoundrels behind each of these disreputable newsletters.

Dwayne Dweeb's Personal Finance

A veteran newsletter writer, Dweeb's newsletter marketing materials issue the following proclamation about Dweeb: "A Millionaire Maker Outsmarts the Market. Again." In a glossy, multi-page brochure, Dweeb is said to have "the highest I.Q. of them all . . . somewhere between Einstein, Mother Theresa, and an IBM mainframe."

His literature goes on to say: "The reason he can expand your money by 30 percent to 50 percent a year is sheer mental horsepower." You're also told that his newsletter is rated #1 by "both of the major rating services."

Dweeb's materials assert that he has developed a brilliant and totally awesome proprietary model, which he calls the "Master Key Indicator." His claim is that this model has predicted the last 28 (count 'em, 28) upturns in the market in a row without a single miss. The odds of doing this, according to Dweeb, are more than 268 million to 1!

But wait, it gets better. The ad goes on to claim that Dweeb's "Master Key" market timing system could have turned a $10,000 investment in 1980 into $39.1 million by 1992. That would be a return of 390,000 percent!

Does this claim sound too good to be true? You got it. This outrageous claim, if not purely fabricated, was based on *backtesting,* looking back over historical returns and creating "what if" scenarios. In other words, Dweeb didn't turn anyone's $10,000 into $39 million. Much too late after that ad appeared, the SEC finally charged Dweeb with false advertising. Dweeb settled out of court and a $60,000 fine was imposed.

Here's the real scoop on Dweeb's investing ability. In 1991, Dweeb established a mutual fund, Dweeb Personal Finance. Since then, this fund has been one of the worst growth stock funds around. His fund has underperformed about 90 percent of its peers and has underperformed the market averages every year of its existence. Looks like he should have stuck to psychology, the field he got his doctorate in.

Harry Hacker's Mutual Fund Investing

"America's #1 Mutual Fund Advisor."

I remember Hacker's name as if it were my own because for a while, it seemed, once a month I would receive a glossy color brochure more than 20 pages long from him in the mail. Like Dweeb, Hacker claims to have been rated #1 by Hulbert. Hulbert responds, "It is a fabrication. *Mutual Fund Investing* is not now, nor has it ever been, rated number one by my digest." Hulbert was so incensed by Hacker's claim that he devoted an entire column, appropriately entitled "Lies and near lies," to setting the record straight in *Forbes* magazine.

Other investment gurus and the media

I could fill an entire book with all the shameful and deceptive marketing that goes on in the investment newsletter business. Investment gurus come and go. Some of them get their 15 minutes of fame on the basis of one or two successful predictions.

Joe Granville, for example, has long been known for making outrageous and extreme stock market predictions and has been quoted in many financial publications. And his newsletter was #1, according to the Hulbert Financial Digest, in 1989. That part was true, actually. The only trouble is that, in the past decade, one of the best decades ever for the stock market (the Wilshire 5000 index of all U.S. stocks produced a return of 506 percent), followers of Granville's advice *lost* about 99 percent!

Then there's Charles Givens, whose books and interviews were chock-full of bad advice in the 1980s. His books advised people to "invest in only one mutual fund at a time" because there can be only one right type, depending on the state of the economy. He claimed that if you paid him hundreds of dollars for his audio tapes and financial library, he'd show you how to make more than 20 percent per year in the stock market.

And then consider the former Shearson stock market analyst Elaine Garzarelli, one of the thousands of gurus who supposedly predicted the stock market's crash in the fall of 1987. Garzarelli's fund, Smith Barney Shearson Sector Analysis, was established just before the crash. Supposedly, Garzarelli's indicators warned her to stay out of stocks, which she did, and in so doing saved her fund from the plunge. Shearson quickly motivated its brokers to sell shares in Garzarelli's fund. Thanks to all the free publicity she got from being interviewed just about everywhere, investors soon poured nearly $700 million into this fund.

These investors ended up being sorry. In 1988, Garzarelli's fund was the worst-performing fund among growth stock funds. From 1988 to 1990, Garzarelli's fund underperformed the S&P 500 average by about 43 percent! So even the few investors who were in her fund *before* the crash in 1987 (when Garzarelli's fund outperformed the S&P 500 by about 26 percent) still lost. The money she saved her investors by avoiding the crash she lost back (and then some) in the years that followed.

The moral of these stories is simple: Stop guru-watching. And I challenge the financial media to do their homework before they rush to interview people for predictions. Doing fewer guru pieces would be a step in the right direction as well. These pieces are detrimental to many investors because they undermine people's confidence in being able to make sense of and succeed in the financial market on their own.

Soon after Hulbert's scathing column about Hacker appeared in *Forbes,* in Hacker's next mailing he changed his tune a bit. His January of 1992 marketing materials displayed a colorful chart showing that his stock and bond fund picks returned 1,517 percent from 1975 to 1990 — for a nearly 20 percent annualized rate of return, which would have outperformed the famous Fidelity Magellan fund and Peter Lynch. This return would imply that his advice had beaten the average stock fund, which returned just 14.7 percent per year, and the average bond fund, at 9.1 percent per year, by some distance significantly greater than a country mile.

Like many fund investing newsletter writers, Hacker also said to avoid index funds — he actually calls them "blind average index" funds because, he said, they are "headed for trouble in the 1990s." Why? Simple: Hacker reasoned that index funds specialize in stocks of large, well-known companies, the very firms that made big bucks in the 1980s from corporate mergers and the like. But as I discuss in Chapter 6, index funds don't just invest in large-company stocks, and as the history of the 1990s has shown, Hacker was all wrong about future performance of index funds.

You should also note that this newsletter's "all-star team" in 1992 included world income funds in place of U.S. bond funds because, as Hacker noted, yields were much higher overseas, and these funds were growing fast "for good reason." This call proved to be another bad decision.

Hulbert's tracking of Hacker's recommendations clearly shows that if a fund investor had followed his advice, the investor would be worse off than he would have been if he had just thrown all of his money in index funds and forgotten about the investment. Hacker's portfolio returns fell well *below* the market averages.

Newsletters cost you time and money — many cost up to several hundred dollars per year. Ignore the predictions and speculations of self-proclaimed gurus (the Jeane Dixons of the investment world). Never use a newsletter for predictive advice. If people were that smart about the future of financial markets, they would be successful money managers making lots more money. The only types of publications you should consider subscribing to are those that offer research and information rather than predictions. And I discuss those publications next.

The Good Stuff

If you want to read more, by all means read more. But read *useful* information. Most of the better financial magazines and newspapers, for example, cost a fraction of the newsletters' price, and provide more useful information.

Many of the major financial publications — *Barron's, Business Week, Financial World, Forbes, Fortune, Kiplinger's Personal Finance, Family Money, SmartMoney, The Wall Street Journal,* and *Worth* — do annual mutual fund roundups. Most newspapers and many large news magazines and television programs such as those on PBS and CNBC provide fund coverage as well.

Some good newsletters are available, too. I get to those in a moment, but first I must discuss what has become a national obsession: rating mutual funds.

Mutual confusion: Misuse of fund ratings

If you check out the business and financial publications, be cautious about fund ratings. The most common mistake investors make in using even the better mutual fund publications is focusing too much on the ranking of specific funds. Allow me to illustrate my point with a person who once called me — a person who made many of the mistakes that can be made when examining fund ratings. Judging from experience, unfortunately, she has lots of company.

I got a call from a woman I'll call Ellen. Ellen asked if she should switch out of her investments in the Vanguard Wellington and Vanguard Star funds and put her money into the Fidelity Balanced fund. Fresh from a trip to the local library, she sounded like the financial equivalent of a weatherman spewing forth data on these funds' performance, saying, "Fidelity Balanced returned 19.3 percent last year and has averaged 14.2 percent over the past five years, whereas Vanguard's Wellington returned only 13.5 percent last year and 12.4 percent over the past five years and Star just 11 percent last year and 11.7 percent over the past five years." All the funds Ellen was reviewing were balanced funds, which hold a diversified mixture of stocks and bonds.

If the raw performance numbers weren't enough to confirm her sub-par investment selections, Ellen also rattled off the Lipper ratings, which "ranked" the Fidelity Balanced fund as an "A" fund, whereas Vanguard Wellington and Vanguard Star both earned the less-than-stellar grade of "C." Just as in the classroom, "A" is the highest ranking a fund can get (the top 20 percent get it) from the rankings provided by Lipper. Perhaps in order not to insult any fund companies, the bottom 20 percent get an "E" (presumably for making the *E*ffort, instead of a more common "F"). These ratings are largely worthless; they don't account for risk, and funds are lumped into broad categories. The performance rankings that wind up in some newspapers can be for periods as short as *one year* (which is the figure that Ellen saw).

Ellen also said that the Fidelity Balanced fund earned the most coveted five-star rating — the investment equivalent of a Siskel and Ebert movie rating of two thumbs up — from Morningstar. "Vanguard Wellington has four stars and Vanguard Star just three," said Ellen with dejection. A true information junkie, Ellen also cited several recent magazine rankings of funds that confirmed her suspicion that something was amiss with her fund investments.

Shooting Morningstars

Thanks to Morningstar's fund ranking system, the mutual fund universe is starting to look like a night sky with a new moon: Lots of stars are out.

Morningstar, a fund research firm, doles out from one to five stars to each fund it tracks — one star for the "worst," five stars for the "best." Investors pay a lot of attention to these stars, and the Morningstar ranking system has become a high-stakes business. Funds blessed with Morningstar's four-star and five-star ratings boast about their high ratings in ads all across the land. Now everybody in the business is more "starstruck" than a teenage girl on Hollywood Boulevard.

Morningstar's star rating system is misleading for a number of reasons. First, Morningstar's system makes some fund categories falsely look better than others. Without going into all the technicalities of Morningstar's star ratings calculations, I can tell you that Morningstar looks at what's called *risk-adjusted performance.* Risk is measured by the volatility of a fund's share price over time. Because international securities don't always move in tandem with U.S. securities, a fund's holding of both types generally lessens the volatility of the fund's value. Thus, funds that diversify in this way have an unfair leg up in the Morningstar ratings game.

Second, a fund only needs to be around for three years before it's eligible to get a star rating. Three years hardly qualifies as a long-term track record, but it's enough for an upstart fund bolstered by a great market to grab a higher rating than a fund that has been around for decades and has weathered multiple market declines. There are dozens of five-star funds that have never been through even a modest 10 percent decline in the market.

Third, Morningstar has been afflicted by a problem that pervades the academic world: grade inflation. As this book goes to press, nearly half the no-load domestic equity funds that Morningstar tracks have a four- or five-star ranking. No wonder so many mutual funds are boasting about all their stars in their advertisements; it's hardly an exclusive group.

As for predicting future performance, Morningstar rankings may be stars of the falling variety. According to *Hulbert Financial Digest,* which has tracked Morningstar rankings since 1991, five-star no-load equity funds have underperformed the market by an average of 3 percent per year.

REMEMBER

Although I've always enjoyed numbers and statistics (it's probably just a genetic condition I got from my dad), I still find it difficult to believe that some mutual fund rankings can make such wrong-headed comparisons, leading smart folks like Ellen in the wrong direction. Comparing the Fidelity Balanced fund with Vanguard's Wellington or Star fund is completely unfair and invalid! Fidelity's offering invests a significant portion of its assets overseas, sometimes up to 50 percent. Vanguard's funds focus on U.S. investments.

At the time Ellen was doing all this information gathering on her funds, international investments were kicking butt, and that portion of its portfolio was boosting the Fidelity Balanced fund's performance. But that boost didn't mean that Fidelity's fund was "better" than the Vanguard funds. To be fair, the Fidelity Balanced fund should have been compared with other balanced mutual funds that invest worldwide, not those that invest just in the United States.

Ellen actually held a couple of international funds in her portfolio. When she combined their returns with those of the Vanguard funds, she realized that her returns actually bested the Fidelity Balanced fund. Suddenly, she was happy with the funds she had. And, it's a good thing Ellen held onto her domestic balanced funds because in the mid and late 1990s, these funds handily beat the pants off of worldwide balanced funds.

Morningstar No-Load Funds

Morningstar's mutual fund publication, *No-Load Funds,* is a bit like the cities of Hong Kong and Tokyo. Every square inch of its single-page fund summaries (printed on $8^1/_2$-x-11-inch pages) is put to use and *packed* with information (rather than people as in those cities).

The most valuable benefit of these one-pagers is that they can save you time. If you want a snapshot summary of lots of data, as well as some thoughtful analysis about a fund you are considering investing in or currently own, Morningstar can't be beat. Most of the information summarized on its pages comes from a fund's prospectus and semi-annual reports. Some of the data that is provided for funds would take you hours to calculate and would require a sophisticated computer software program.

TIP

Many public libraries subscribe to Morningstar. A one-year subscription costs $175 per year; a three-month trial subscription costs $45 (you can take one of these once every two years). Morningstar also sells single pages for the individual funds of your choice ($5 per fund). Fidelity and Schwab also sell Morningstar pages — typically a few bucks per report if you buy several pages.

Morningstar produces another publication called *Morningstar Mutual Funds.* This publication covers more funds than *No-Load Funds* because it includes load funds (funds that carry commissions) as well as no-load funds. As I explain in Chapter 4, loads are an additional and unnecessary cost to buy funds that are sold through brokers. If you have load funds that you want to evaluate, *Morningstar Mutual Funds* can help (check for it at your local library or get a three-month trial subscription for $55, ☎ 800-735-0700).

Using a Morningstar bond fund page

As I mention earlier, Morningstar packs a lot of data on a page (see Figure 15-1), so folks like my father love it. However, it makes some people's heads spin. The hard part is knowing what to look at and what to make of the information. I highlight some of the more useful features to examine for bond funds that you may be considering. I jump around their page a bit so that I can work from the bigger picture issues toward more of the details.

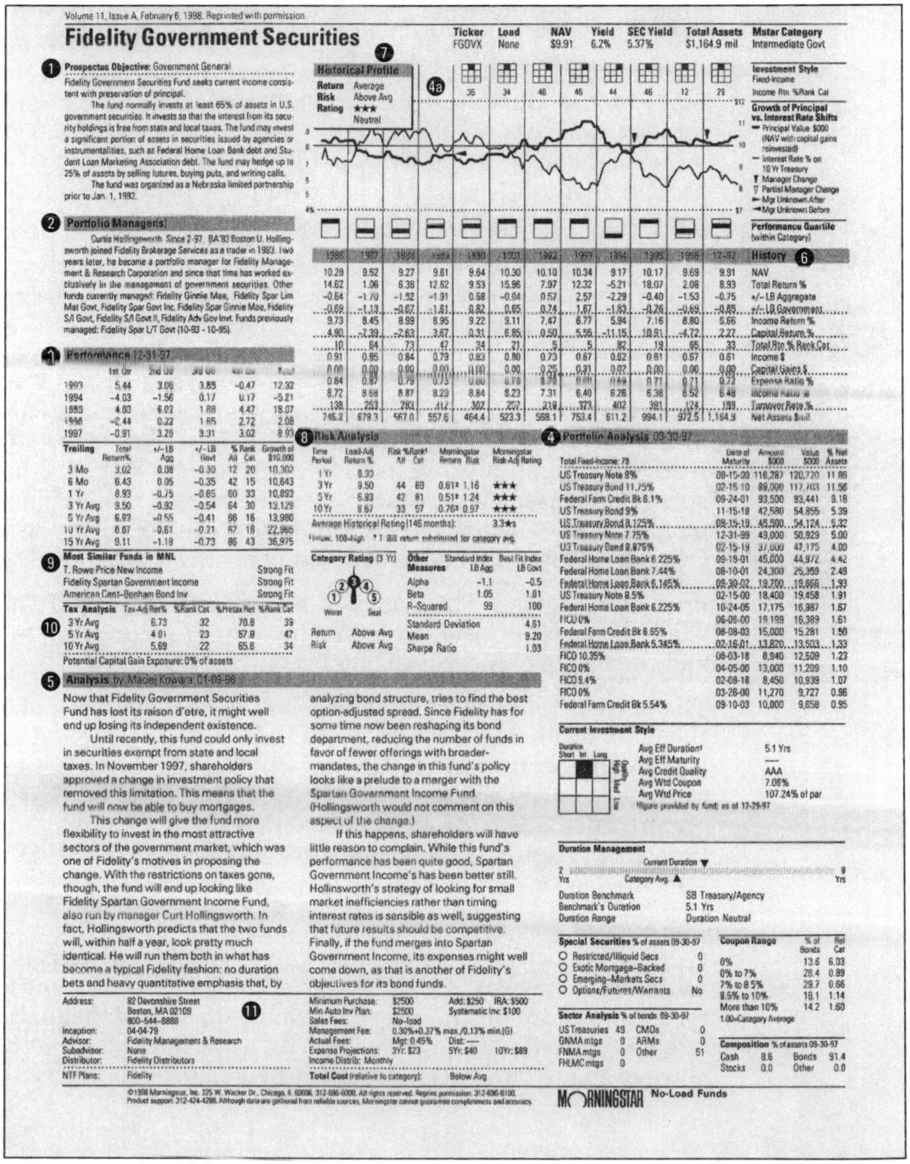
Volume 11, Issue A, February 6, 1998. Reprinted with permission.

Fidelity Government Securities

Ticker FGOVX · Load None · NAV $9.91 · Yield 6.2% · SEC Yield 5.37% · Total Assets $1,164.9 mil · Mstar Category Intermediate Govt

Analysis by Maciej Kowara 01-09-98

Now that Fidelity Government Securities Fund has lost its raison d'etre, it might well end up losing its independent existence.

Until recently, this fund could only invest in securities exempt from state and local taxes. In November 1997, shareholders approved a change in investment policy that removed this limitation. This means that the fund will now be able to buy mortgages.

This change will give the fund more flexibility to invest in the most attractive sectors of the government market, which was one of Fidelity's motives in proposing the change. With the restrictions on taxes gone, though, the fund will end up looking like Fidelity Spartan Government Income Fund, also run by manager Curt Hollingsworth. In fact, Hollingsworth predicts that the two funds will, within half a year, look pretty much identical. He will run them both in what has become a typical Fidelity fashion: no duration bets and heavy quantitative emphasis that, by analyzing bond structure, tries to find the best option-adjusted spread. Since Fidelity has for some time now been reshaping its bond department, reducing the number of funds in favor of fewer offerings with broader mandates, the change in this fund's policy looks like a prelude to a merger with the Spartan Government Income Fund. (Hollingsworth would not comment on this aspect of the change.)

If this happens, shareholders will have little reason to complain. While this fund's performance has been quite good, Spartan Government Income's has been better still. Hollinsworth's strategy of looking for small market inefficiencies rather than timing interest rates is sensible as well, suggesting that future results should be competitive. Finally, if the fund merges into Spartan Government Income, its expenses might well come down, as that is another of Fidelity's objectives for its bond funds.

Address: 82 Devonshire Street, Boston, MA 02109, 800-544-8888
Inception: 04-04-79
Advisor: Fidelity Management & Research
Subadvisor: None
Distributor: Fidelity Distributors
NTF Plans: Fidelity

Minimum Purchase: $2500 · Add: $250 · IRA: $500
Min Auto Inv Plan: $2500 · Systematic Inv: $100
Sales Fees: No-load
Expense Projections: 3Yr: $23 · 5Yr: $40 · 10Yr: $89
Income Distrib: Monthly
Total Cost (relative to category): Below Avg

MORNINGSTAR No-Load Funds

Figure 15-1: Morningstar page for a bond fund.

Source: Morningstar

Morningstar's pages are difficult to read with all of their small print. (Although my wife and I both have good eyesight, when she saw one of their pages she suggested taking it to a copy shop to enlarge it!)

1 **Prospectus Objective.** From the prospectus, this section provides a summary of the general investment objectives and limitations that a fund subjects itself to.

2 **Portfolio Manager(s).** This section highlights work and educational background of the fund's managers — good cocktail party chatter! The date the manager(s) started managing the particular fund is noted.

3 **Performance.** The first section displays the total amount that investors made or lost (from dividends, capital gains, and share price changes) for each quarter over the past five years. This section can give you a sense of the likely volatility of an investment in the fund (remember, though, that this is history, and the future will probably differ). If you get queasy looking at these numbers, then don't invest.

The second section — the trailing returns section — shows annualized total return information over longer time periods. (Total return numbers do not account for loads, but you're not going to pay any anyway, are you?) The fund's returns are also compared to benchmark indexes, which in some cases aren't so comparable. The Lehman Brothers bond index used here is an intermediate-term maturity index. This type of index isn't valid for comparing all bond funds, but it isn't bad for this fund, which typically invests in intermediate- to longer-term bonds. For some odd reason, Morningstar doesn't compare bond funds to indexes of appropriate maturities — short-, intermediate-, and long-term (see Chapter 12 for more background on benchmarks).

4 **Portfolio Analysis.** This data is summarized from a fund's most recent semi-annual report. Note the total number of securities this fund holds and the listing of the top 20 holdings.

The *Current Investment Style* box shows you which types of bonds the fund mainly holds at the moment (in this case, high-quality, intermediate-term bonds). Measures of interest rate sensitivity — average maturity and duration (both of which I explain in Chapter 8) — are provided here, as well as the average credit quality of the fund's bonds. (4a: Note the little style boxes for each year so that you can see how the fund's style has varied, if at all, over time.)

The *Special Securities* section highlights the fund's holdings in riskier types of securities, including derivatives (which I discuss in Chapter 1). All things being equal, it's best to see zeros here, but some funds use, for example, options to hedge or reduce the risk of the fund. The empty circle to the left of each risky security name indicates that the fund is allowed to hold these types of securities (a dash indicates that it can't).

Sector Analysis quantifies the fund's current holdings of the major types of bonds. See Chapter 8 for definitions. *Composition* details the fund's recent holdings of cash, bonds, and other securities. Composition is worth looking at to determine if a fund really is what it says it is.

5. **Analysis.** Each fund at Morningstar is assigned an analyst. Each analyst then uses available information, as well as interviews with fund company managers (and others) and data on the page, to summarize the fund strategies. This section is usually well worth reading, especially if you're *not* a numbers kind of person.

6. **History.** Here's a data dump of all sorts of information for the fund over more than the past decade. Here you can see how the total return, performance versus benchmarks, dividend (income), capital gains, the fund's annual operating expenses, and trading (turnover) have varied over the years.

7. **Historical Profile.** Without a doubt, this is the most overused and abused part of the Morningstar page. Funds are given ratings, based on past performance and volatility, from one (worst) to five (best) stars. I discuss some problems with Morningstar's fund ratings earlier in this chapter, in the sidebar "Shooting Morningstars." The folks at Morningstar say that ". . . funds with 3, 4, and 5 stars often make the most sense for many investors." I think that says it well — you can't really say much more about the star rating system than that. More stars are *not* necessarily better than less and vice versa.

8. **Risk Analysis.** Here you see more details for the determination of the ranking and the way the fund rates over different periods. You also see the fund's average star rating over all the months that it has received a rating. This average rating provides a sense of the consistency of the fund's rating over time.

   All sorts of other quantitative measurements of risk are presented here. One of the more useful is *beta,* which helps you calibrate the volatility of a fund compared to relevant benchmarks. The overall bond market benchmark is assigned a beta of 1.00. Thus, a fund with a beta of 1.2 implies that it is 20 percent more volatile on average (perhaps because it invests in longer-term bonds or lower-credit quality bonds).

9. **Most Similar Funds.** The section names funds that have behaved similarly to this fund. This information may help you identify comparable funds, but don't assume that these other funds are all that similar — check out the rest of the information on *their* pages.

10. **Tax Analysis.** This section provides some insightful measures of a fund's tax-efficiency or tax-friendliness. If you're investing in a fund inside a retirement account, ignore this section. If you're investing outside a retirement account, the tax-adjusted return column shows what your effective return would have been in this fund over various periods if all the dividend and capital gains distributions that a fund makes were taxed at the highest possible federal tax rate.

Potential Capital Gains Exposure measures how much, if any, unrealized profit exists. The larger the number here, the greater the potential risk of larger distributions in the future, particularly for funds that trade a lot (that is, that have a high turnover), as this one does. Make sure to examine historically how much the fund has distributed (see my discussion in "6. History," just a few paragraphs earlier).

⑪ **Address, telephone, and other stuff.** Here's where you see how to get in touch with the fund, how much is required as a minimum investment, how often it pays dividends, and so on.

Using a Morningstar stock fund page

Morningstar's stock fund pages carry much of the same types of information that their bond fund pages carry (see Figure 15-2). I won't repeat my explanations of the same sections I cover for a bond fund page (to see what I would be repeating if I *did* talk about it here, skip back to the preceding section). Sections 4 and 6 are the only sections of a stock fund page that significantly differ from a bond fund page:

④ **Portfolio Analysis.** The summary of a fund's holdings is the most important area of difference between a stock fund page and a bond fund page. That's no surprise, though, because stocks are quite different from bonds.

Similar to the bond fund page, the total number of securities held is noted, and a list of the top 25 holdings, along with the number of shares held and the way that number has changed recently, also shows up here.

Current Investment Style classifies a fund's current stock holdings based on the size of the company, as well as on whether those stocks tend to be growth, value, or both (I cover the difference among these various types of stocks in Chapter 9). A variety of statistical measures are also presented for the stocks that the fund holds. For example, you can see the average rate of growth in the earnings of the companies that this fund invests in and how that rate compares to that of the S&P 500 index.

Composition is also useful because it indicates whether a fund is holding major cash positions and whether it invests in securities other than stocks. *Market Cap* shows how the fund is allocating its holdings among stocks of various-sized companies. *Sector Weightings* breaks down a fund's stock holdings by industry and again compares the fund's holdings to those of the S&P 500 index.

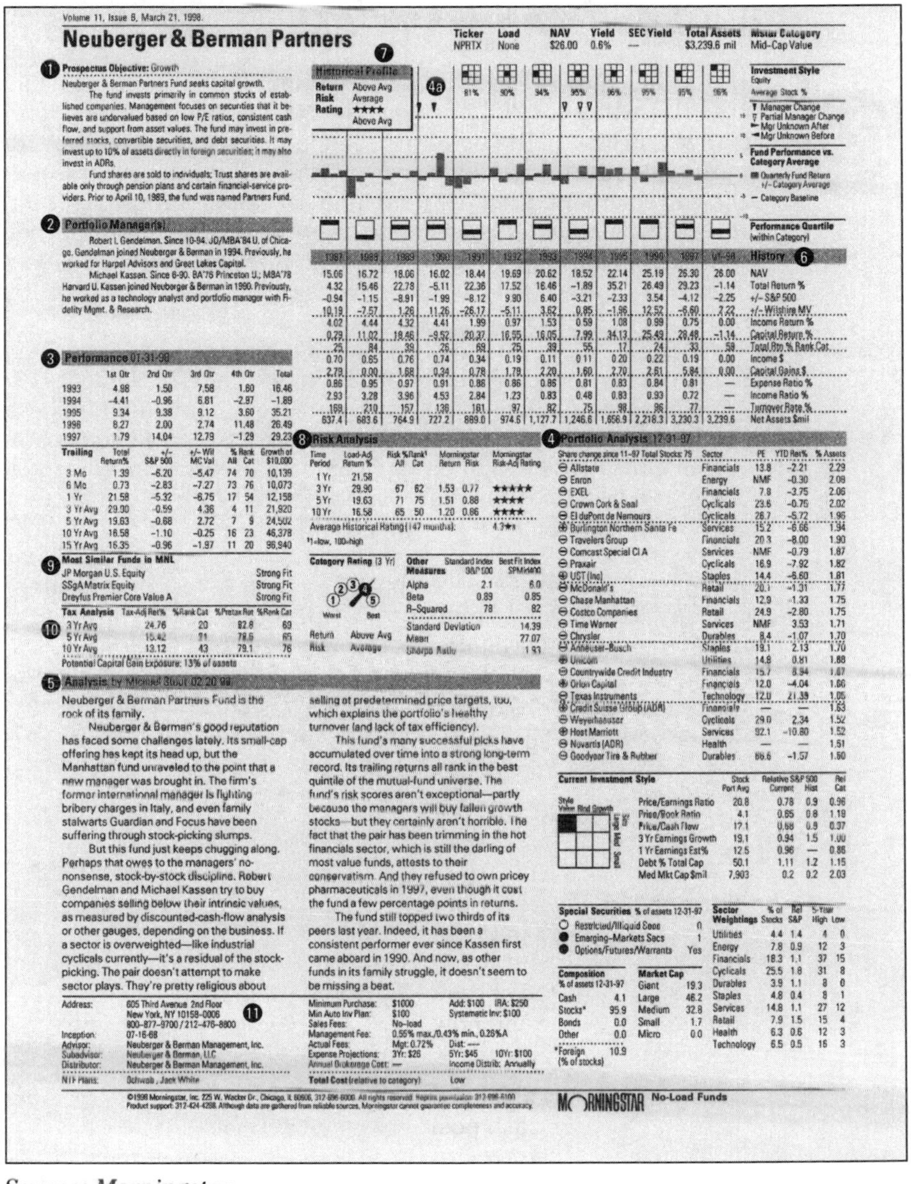

Volume 11, Issue 8, March 21, 1998.

Neuberger & Berman Partners

Ticker	Load	NAV	Yield	SEC Yield	Total Assets	Mstar Category
NPRTX	None	$26.00	0.6%	—	$3,239.6 mil	Mid-Cap Value

(1) **Prospectus Objective:** Growth

Neuberger & Berman Partners Fund seeks capital growth.

The fund invests primarily in common stocks of established companies. Management focuses on securities that it believes are undervalued based on low P/E ratios, consistent cash flow, and support from asset values. The fund may invest in preferred stocks, convertible securities, and debt securities. It may invest up to 10% of assets directly in foreign securities; it may also invest in ADRs.

Fund shares are sold to individuals; Trust shares are available only through pension plans and certain financial-service providers. Prior to April 10, 1989, the fund was named Partners Fund.

(2) **Portfolio Manager(s)**

Robert I. Gendelman. Since 10-94. JD/MBA'84 U. of Chicago. Gendelman joined Neuberger & Berman in 1994. Previously, he worked for Harpel Advisors and Great Lakes Capital.

Michael Kassen. Since 6-90. BA'76 Princeton U.; MBA'78 Harvard U. Kassen joined Neuberger & Berman in 1990. Previously, he worked as a technology analyst and portfolio manager with Fidelity Mgmt. & Research.

(7) **Historical Profile**

Return: Above Avg
Risk: Average
Rating: ★★★★ Above Avg

(4a)

81%	90%	94%	95%	96%	95%	95%	96%

Investment Style: Equity — Average Stock %

▼ Manager Change
▽ Partial Manager Change
Mgr Unknown After
Mgr Unknown Before

Fund Performance vs. Category Average
Quarterly Fund Return +/– Category Average
— Category Baseline

Performance Quartile (within Category)

1987	1988	1989	1990	1991	1992	1993	1994	1995	1996	1997	01-98	History (6)
15.06	16.72	18.06	16.02	18.44	19.69	20.62	18.52	22.14	25.19	26.30	26.00	NAV
4.32	15.46	22.78	-5.11	22.36	17.52	16.46	-1.89	35.21	26.49	29.23	-1.14	Total Return %
-0.94	-1.15	-8.91	-1.99	-8.12	9.90	6.40	-3.21	-2.33	3.54	-4.12	-2.25	+/- S&P 500
10.19	-7.57	1.26	11.26	-26.17	-5.11	3.62	0.85	-1.96	12.52	-6.60	2.22	+/- Wilshire MV
4.02	4.44	4.32	4.41	1.99	0.97	1.53	0.59	1.08	0.99	0.75	0.00	Income Return %
0.29	11.02	18.46	-9.52	20.37	16.55	16.05	7.99	34.13	25.49	28.48	-1.14	Capital Return %
25	84	39	26	69	25	39	55	17	24	33	59	Total Rtn % Rank Cat
0.70	0.65	0.76	0.74	0.34	0.19	0.11	0.11	0.20	0.22	0.19	0.00	Income $
2.79	0.00	1.68	0.34	0.78	1.79	2.20	1.60	2.70	2.61	5.84	0.00	Capital Gains $
0.86	0.95	0.97	0.91	0.86	0.86	0.86	0.81	0.83	0.84	0.81	—	Expense Ratio %
2.93	3.28	3.96	4.53	2.84	1.23	0.83	0.48	0.83	0.93	0.72	—	Income Ratio %
169	210	157	136	161	97	82	75	98	96	77	—	Turnover Rate %
637.4	683.6	764.9	727.2	889.0	974.6	1,127.7	1,246.6	1,656.9	2,218.3	3,230.3	3,239.6	Net Assets $mil

(3) **Performance 01-31-98**

	1st Qtr	2nd Qtr	3rd Qtr	4th Qtr	Total
1993	4.98	1.50	7.58	1.60	16.46
1994	-4.41	-0.96	6.81	-2.97	-1.89
1995	9.34	9.38	9.12	3.60	35.21
1996	8.27	2.00	2.74	11.48	26.49
1997	1.79	14.04	12.79	-1.29	29.23

Trailing	Total Return%	+/- S&P 500	+/- Wil MC Val	% Rank All	% Rank Cat	Growth of $10,000
3 Mo	1.39	-6.20	-5.47	74	70	10,139
6 Mo	0.73	-2.83	-7.27	73	76	10,073
1 Yr	21.58	-5.32	-6.75	17	54	12,158
3 Yr Avg	29.90	-0.59	4.36	4	11	21,920
5 Yr Avg	19.63	-0.68	2.72	7	9	24,502
10 Yr Avg	16.58	-1.10	-0.25	16	23	46,378
15 Yr Avg	16.35	-0.96	-1.97	11	20	96,940

(9) **Most Similar Funds in MNL**

JP Morgan U.S. Equity	Strong Fit
SSgA Matrix Equity	Strong Fit
Dreyfus Premier Core Value A	Strong Fit

(10)

Tax Analysis	Tax-Adj Ret%	%Rank Cat	%Pretax Ret	%Rank Cat
3 Yr Avg	24.76	20	82.8	69
5 Yr Avg	15.42	21	78.6	65
10 Yr Avg	13.12	43	79.1	76

Potential Capital Gain Exposure: 13% of assets

(8) **Risk Analysis**

Time Period	Load-Adj Return %	Risk %Rank[1] All	Risk %Rank[1] Cat	Morningstar Return	Morningstar Risk	Morningstar Risk-Adj Rating
1 Yr	21.58					
3 Yr	29.90	67	62	1.53	0.77	★★★★★
5 Yr	19.63	71	75	1.51	0.88	★★★★
10 Yr	16.58	65	50	1.20	0.86	★★★★

Average Historical Rating (147 months): 4.3★s

[1]1=low, 100=high

Category Rating (3 Yr)

1 2 3 4 5
Worst Best

Return: Above Avg
Risk: Average

Other Measures	Standard Index S&P 500	Best Fit Index SPMid400
Alpha	2.1	6.0
Beta	0.89	0.85
R-Squared	78	82
Standard Deviation		14.39
Mean		77.07
Sharpe Ratio		1.93

(4) **Portfolio Analysis 12-31-97**

Share change since 11-97 Total Stocks: 79	Sector	PE	YTD Ret%	% Assets
⊖ Allstate	Financials	13.8	-2.21	2.29
⊖ Enron	Energy	NMF	-0.30	2.08
⊖ EXEL	Financials	7.8	-3.75	2.06
⊖ Crown Cork & Seal	Cyclicals	23.6	-0.75	2.02
⊖ El duPont de Nemours	Cyclicals	26.7	-5.72	1.96
⊕ Burlington Northern Santa Fe	Services	15.2	-6.66	1.94
⊖ Travelers Group	Financials	20.3	-8.00	1.90
⊖ Comcast Special Cl A	Services	NMF	-0.79	1.87
⊖ Praxair	Cyclicals	16.9	-7.92	1.82
⊕ UST (Inc)	Staples	14.4	-6.60	1.81
⊖ McDonald's	Retail	20.1	-1.31	1.77
⊖ Chase Manhattan	Financials	12.9	-1.33	1.75
⊖ Costco Companies	Retail	24.9	-2.80	1.75
⊖ Time Warner	Services	NMF	3.53	1.71
⊖ Chrysler	Durables	8.4	-1.07	1.70
⊖ Anheuser-Busch	Staples	19.1	2.13	1.70
⊕ Unicom	Utilities	14.8	0.81	1.68
⊖ Countrywide Credit Industry	Financials	15.7	8.94	1.67
⊕ Orion Capital	Financials	12.0	-4.04	1.66
⊖ Texas Instruments	Technology	12.0	21.39	1.65
⊕ Credit Suisse Group (ADR)	Financials	—	—	1.63
⊖ Weyerhaeuser	Cyclicals	29.0	2.34	1.52
⊕ Host Marriott	Services	92.1	-10.80	1.52
⊖ Novartis (ADR)	Health	—	—	1.51
⊖ Goodyear Tire & Rubber	Durables	66.6	-1.57	1.50

Current Investment Style

Style: Value Blnd Growth; Large Med Small

	Stock Port Avg	Relative S&P 500 Current	Relative S&P 500 Hist	Rel Cat
Price/Earnings Ratio	20.8	0.78	0.9	0.96
Price/Book Ratio	4.1	0.65	0.8	1.19
Price/Cash Flow	17.1	0.88	0.9	0.97
3 Yr Earnings Growth	19.1	0.94	1.5	1.00
1 Yr Earnings Est%	12.5	0.96	—	0.86
Debt % Total Cap	50.1	1.11	1.2	1.15
Med Mkt Cap $mil	7,903	0.2	0.2	2.03

Special Securities % of assets 12-31-97	
○ Restricted/Illiquid Secs	0
● Emerging-Markets Secs	1
● Options/Futures/Warrants	Yes

Composition % of assets 12-31-97		Market Cap	
Cash	4.1	Giant	19.3
Stocks*	95.9	Large	46.2
Bonds	0.0	Medium	32.8
Other	0.0	Small	1.7
		Micro	0.0

*Foreign (% of stocks) 10.9

Sector Weightings	% of Stocks	Rel S&P	5-Year High	5-Year Low
Utilities	4.4	1.4	4	0
Energy	7.8	0.9	12	3
Financials	18.3	1.1	37	15
Cyclicals	25.5	1.8	31	8
Durables	3.9	1.1	8	0
Staples	4.8	0.4	8	1
Services	14.8	1.1	27	12
Retail	7.9	1.5	15	4
Health	6.3	0.6	12	3
Technology	6.5	0.5	16	3

(5) **Analysis** by Michael Stout 02-20-98

Neuberger & Berman Partners Fund is the rock of its family.

Neuberger & Berman's good reputation has faced some challenges lately. Its small-cap offering has kept its head up, but the Manhattan fund unraveled to the point that a new manager was brought in. The firm's former international manager is fighting bribery charges in Italy, and even family stalwarts Guardian and Focus have been suffering through stock-picking slumps.

But this fund just keeps chugging along. Perhaps that owes to the managers' no-nonsense, stock-by-stock discipline. Robert Gendelman and Michael Kassen try to buy companies selling below their intrinsic values, as measured by discounted-cash-flow analysis or other gauges, depending on the business. If a sector is overweighted—like industrial cyclicals currently—it's a residual of the stock-picking. The pair doesn't attempt to make sector plays. They're pretty religious about selling at predetermined price targets, too, which explains the portfolio's healthy turnover (and lack of tax efficiency).

This fund's many successful picks have accumulated over time into a strong long-term record. Its trailing returns all rank in the best quintile of the mutual-fund universe. The fund's risk scores aren't exceptional—partly because the managers will buy fallen growth stocks—but they certainly aren't horrible. The fact that the pair has been trimming in the hot financials sector, which is still the darling of most value funds, attests to their conservatism. And they refused to own pricey pharmaceuticals in 1997, even though it cost the fund a few percentage points in returns.

The fund still topped two thirds of its peers last year. Indeed, it has been a consistent performer ever since Kassen first came aboard in 1990. And now, as other funds in its family struggle, it doesn't seem to be missing a beat.

(11)

Address:	605 Third Avenue 2nd Floor, New York, NY 10158-0006, 800-877-9700 / 212-476-8800
Inception:	07-16-68
Advisor:	Neuberger & Berman Management, Inc.
Subadvisor:	Neuberger & Berman, LLC
Distributor:	Neuberger & Berman Management, Inc.
NTF Plans:	Schwab, Jack White

Minimum Purchase:	$1000	Add: $100 IRA: $250
Min Auto Inv Plan:	$100	Systematic Inv: $100
Sales Fees:	No-load	
Management Fee:	0.55% max./0.43% min., 0.26%A	
Actual Fees:	Mgt: 0.72%	Dist: —
Expense Projections:	3Yr: $26	5Yr: $45 10Yr: $100
Annual Brokerage Cost:	—	Income Distrib: Annually
Total Cost (relative to category)		Low

©1998 Morningstar, Inc. 225 W. Wacker Dr., Chicago, IL 60606, 312-696-6000. All rights reserved. Reprints permission: 312-696-6100. Product support: 312-424-4288. Although data are gathered from reliable sources, Morningstar cannot guarantee completeness and accuracy.

MORNINGSTAR No-Load Funds

Figure 15-2: Morningstar page for a stock fund.

Source: Morningstar

(6) **History.** Note the use of different benchmark indexes suitable for stock funds. The graph also indicates — with small arrow heads — when one of the fund's managers changed.

No-Load Fund Analyst

Those who enjoy doing more reading about funds and the financial markets should consider the *No-Load Fund Analyst* newsletter, which tracks a much smaller universe of the better no-load funds than Morningstar does. This monthly publication provides commentary and analysis of trends in the economy, happenings in the fund industry, and fund manager interviews and profiles. In an industry in which many publications claim that they can double your money in a snap if you become a subscriber, the *No-Load Fund Analyst* is a breath of fresh air: It includes no hype or inflated marketing claims.

Personal interviews and the tracking of individual fund managers are unique and valuable aspects of this publication, which tries to identify talented fund managers at some of the smaller, lesser-known funds. These funds, of course, are riskier to invest in. Also, because the *No-Load Fund Analyst* recommends funds in numerous fund families, as an investor you must be willing to deal with many fund companies or establish an account at a discount brokerage firm (see Chapter 5).

The editors' primary business has been their investment management company. They manage money for institutions and wealthy individuals in mutual funds — their minimum account size is $2 million.

The *No-Load Fund Analyst* also follows and discusses closed-end mutual funds, which I cover in Chapter 2. An annual subscription to the *No-Load Fund Analyst* costs $225. For $18.75, you can obtain a sample issue by calling 800-776-9555.

Chapter 16

Computers and Mutual Funds

In This Chapter

- Finding your way around mutual funds with software
- Recognizing the good and the bad on the Internet
- Locating the best mutual fund Web sites

Computers are infiltrating our businesses and homes at a high rate. When you invest your money, especially into mutual funds, it is *not* necessary nor advantageous for you to have a PC at your disposal to make wise investing decisions and manage your portfolio.

In fact, use of a computer when investing could prove detrimental to your investing success. Why? My experience with counseling clients and students in my courses is that heavy computer users tend to focus too much on daily price changes and the short-term news and, thus, they trade too much.

So, if you're not online yet or don't own a computer with which to play around with investing software or Internet sites, don't lament. If you decide to spend money on a PC or you already own one but don't know how it can help you invest in funds, this chapter assists you with finding out how to put it to work.

Fortunately (for both you and me), this book does not focus on computers. If you're sometimes (or all the time) perplexed by your own bundle of microprocessors, and if you've ever wanted to bludgeon those frequently aggravating boxes that we call computers, then you and I have yet another thing in common. (If you're stumped by computers, you should know, if you don't already, that helping people navigate computers is what the . . . *For Dummies* series started with. So if it weren't for computers, I probably wouldn't be writing this book.)

I've divided this chapter into two parts:

- **Software:** The information contained on the disks you load onto your computer's hard drive or CD-ROM
- **Internet sites:** Which allow you to access outside data and information via a modem

Some of the stuff I discuss does some of both. Those that do are generally placed in the category that they do more of.

Software

Most software reviewers can agree that good software must be easy to use. Software that helps you make mutual fund and other investing decisions must also provide well-founded advice and information. Not all of it does.

Which software is best for you depends on the goal you're trying to accomplish and on your level of investment expertise. The financial software in the marketplace today can help you with a variety of activities that range from simply tabulating your mutual fund's values and getting current prices to researching investment choices. You can even execute fund trades on your computer.

As I discuss later in this chapter (see the section, "Internet Sites"), thanks to advances in Internet technology, Web sites are offering more and more of the features that were once the exclusive domain of software programs. So, before you rush out to purchase a specific software program for accomplishing a certain task, check to see what the Internet has to offer in that area.

Getting-and-staying-organized software

Checkbook software programs such as Quicken, Microsoft Money, and Kiplinger's Simply Money help with checkbook accounting, expense tracking, and bill paying. But checkbook software is also useful for keeping track of your mutual fund investments. By remembering your original purchase price, as well as factoring in dividend and capital gains distributions, checkbook software automatically calculates your current rate of return, both annualized and cumulative, for each individual fund as well as your entire portfolio. Tracking your cost basis when you're dollar-cost averaging (which I discuss in Chapter 6), a daunting task without a computer, is handled by checkbook software with ease.

However — and this is a big however — in order for checkbook software to keep track of your returns, you must plug in all your transactions, distributions, and share price changes when you receive your account statements. If you have lots of funds at different accounts, this could be a tedious process, depending on how much you like detail work. Some investment companies, including Schwab and Fidelity, allow you to download your account statement details directly into your checkbook software program over your modem. But even this procedure usually requires you to work with the downloaded transactions and assign them to appropriate categories.

Checkbook software can be useful if you have accounts at numerous investment firms and want to keep tabs on your various accounts and overall performance. But remember that consolidating your investments at a larger mutual fund company or through a discount brokerage account can accomplish the same goals for you — without your having to invest hours in learning software and entering data. Also keep in mind that one of checkbook software's most attractive features — its ability to track your cost basis — is irrelevant for funds held in retirement accounts and that mutual fund companies and this day and age track your cost basis for you.

Some of the checkbook software programs have added mutual fund screeners or selectors that in my humble opinion are garbage. The reason: The screening criteria are simplistic and not enough proper guidance is offered (see Chapter 4 for the characteristics of the best mutual funds). If you want to play around with more mutual fund data and information, use the Morningstar software I discuss next or the better newsletters I discuss in Chapter 15.

Investment research software

Investment research software packages usually separate investment beginners (and others who don't want to spend a lot of time managing their money) from those who enjoy wallowing in data and conducting primary research. The best reason to use research software is to access quality information in a way that may be more cost-effective than traditional channels. Research software may allow you to peruse more information more efficiently at lower cost than accessing a paper version from the same source.

Although these packages can be cost-effective, they're still expensive. Don't jump into one of these programs until you've done a careful comparison between the information it offers and the data you need. There's no lack of information and research available through investment software packages; in fact, most offer more raw data than you'll ever use. A lot of simple investment research can be done over the Internet, so don't pay a bundle for information on a software program that you could be getting for next to nothing over your modem line.

Mutual fund data hounds will delight in the software products offered by Morningstar. However, if you're an investing and mutual fund novice, don't expect an easy time working with these sometimes jargon-laden and costly packages. Also expect to invest several hours of your time to learn how to work with a program. You can choose from the following Morningstar programs:

- **Ascent.** This is the most basic package and is aimed at the non-expert investor. Although it does provide more background for the novice than Morningstar's other programs, it's superficial. A quarterly subscription costs $95 a year, the monthly subscription is $195, and a one-time trial is $45.
- **Principia.** The next step up, here you can find most of the data provided on Morningstar's printed reports that I show you in Chapter 15. You can search and screen for funds that meet specific criteria that you enter into the program. The program also comes with a feature called the Portfolio Developer, which allows you to gather a portfolio of funds and then view a pie chart of that particular portfolio's asset allocation. A monthly subscription is $395 a year, quarterly is $195, a one-time trial is $95.
- **PrincipiaPlus.** The ultimate for the mutual fund data junkie, its interface is almost identical to Principia's, but you get more data and features. All the data available on Morningstar's printed reports comes with this program; in fact, the program lets you print out these reports on your own printer. The Portfolio Developer also allows tracking the performance of your mutual fund portfolio over time. The price for Morningstar's first class ticket is steep: Annual subscription with monthly updates is $795, quarterly updates are $495, a one time trial is $295. ☎ 800-735-0700.

Before you plunge into the data jungle and try to become the next Peter Lynch or Warren Buffet, be honest about your reasons for wanting to do research. Some investors fool themselves into believing that their research will help them beat the markets. As I say many times in this book, though, few of even the so-called "professional" investors ever beat the markets.

Retirement planning software

If you know nothing about your retirement other than that it's something you eventually want to do, it's easy to put off saving for it. Creating a retirement plan is a great way to get yourself motivated to start saving money.

Unless you were an applied math major in college, however, coming up with a useful retirement plan by using a pencil and a calculator is a complex task. There are so many factors to consider: expected rates of investment return, inflation, tax brackets, savings rates, social security benefits, retirement ages, pension benefits, life expectancies . . . and on it goes.

So if you have a computer or access to one, let your computer assist you. Computers are a great tool for retirement planning because they make testing different scenarios easy. Tinker with any variable — the inflation rate, for example, or your desired retirement income — and you can quickly see how that change affects your whole retirement plan.

Quicken Financial Planner ($40, ☎800-446-8848, also available through software retailers) allows for lots of detail in your plan. Besides looking at all the factors I mention earlier, this program lets you plan for income changes over your lifetime as well as major one-time financial events such as selling your house.

Before you shell out the $40, though, take a look at some of the better retirement calculators you can access over the Internet. Vanguard has an excellent one on its Web site (`www.vanguard.com`). Even Quicken offers a good online version (`www.quicken.com/retirement/planner`). Although these online retirement calculators don't allow for quite as much detail as Quicken's software program, they may suit you fine, especially if you're not a numbers geek or you're a long way from retiring and just looking for ballpark figures.

WARNING!

The retirement calculators built into some of the checkbook software packages, such as Quicken's, are not very good because they are too simplistic. Use the online calculators I mention in this section instead.

Trading software

The fast-growing investment behemoths Charles Schwab and Fidelity offer software packages that link you to your investment account. Both Fidelity's On-line Xpress+, also known as FOX (☎ 800-925-6809), and Schwab's StreetSmart (☎ 800-334-4455) provide up-to-date account balances, the ability to make trades and track the performance of your investments, free real-time quotes, and access to market research services such as Reuters Money Network and Dow Jones News/Retrieval.

However, before you buy one of these programs ($20 for FOX and $40 for StreetSmart), realize that both Schwab and Fidelity are offering more and more of these account access services directly through their Web sites, which, if you already have Internet access, are free. In fact, for basic services such as viewing account balances and making trades, the only significant difference between the software programs and the Web sites is speed: The software programs are a bit faster. But this distinction, too, will probably change in the not-too-distant future.

Investment news programs

If you're a real financial news and data junkie, you may enjoy tapping into services such as Reuters Money Network or Dow Jones Interactive. These packages combine a software program with online access to current news and historical data:

- **Reuters Money Network:** Offers mutual fund data from Morningstar (which is updated monthly) and research reports on stocks and bonds from Standard & Poor's. Users can also access financial information and news from Dow Jones, Reuters itself, and many other sources for a fixed monthly fee ranging from $6.95 to $19.95. For an additional $9.95 per month, you can partake of Reuters's "Personalized News Clipping Service," which culls articles from a number of publications on your specific mutual fund(s) of interest, as well as on other investments in your portfolio. ☎ 800-346-2024
- **Dow Jones Interactive:** Is the ultimate for news and information junkies. It provides access to Dow Jones Newswire and various international newswires, dozens of newspapers (with archive files going back more than five years), and hundreds of magazines. The service also offers a clipping service that can collect articles as they are written for particular topics of your choosing. *The Mutual Funds Performance Report,* which covers 1,500 mutual funds, gives you information on historical performance, assets, and basic background — not a lot of meat here.

  Everything you do through Dow Jones Interactive costs money. Most articles cost $2.95 per access. There is a special pricing plan called *The Private Investor Edition,* which provides you with 10 hours of usage per month for $29.95. This flat-rate service has two major catches, however. The first is that you can't use it weekdays between 6 a.m. and 7 p.m. Also, you don't have access to nearly as many publications. ☎ 800-522-3567 (You can also download the software from the Dow Jones Web site at `ip.dowjones.com`.)

Before you know it, you can blow a chunk of money on these programs, which tend to charge you depending on your usage level. Successful fund investing does not require a steady diet of breaking news on the financial markets. If anything, day-to-day financial news can be detrimental to a disciplined, long-term investment strategy. Buy one of these programs only because you enjoy news and data, not because you think that it will give your investing some kind of "edge."

Internet Sites

The Internet is a vast network of computers all over the world that share information. Just about anyone can plug into the Internet right from home — all you need is a personal computer and a modem.

The mutual fund industry has jumped on the Internet bandwagon. Here are some of the possible benefits available to mutual fund investors with access to the Internet:

- The Internet can give you faster access to important resources than traditional channels allow. Before the Internet, investors had only one way to get their hands on, say, a fund prospectus: Call up the fund company, give them an address, and possibly wait up to a week for the U.S. Post Office to deliver the goods. With Internet access, you can log onto the fund company's Web site and view the prospectus immediately, even print it out if you want to. The same goes for annual reports, account applications, research reports, account statements, and so on.
- The best Internet sites are similar to software programs in being "interactive." The phenomenon of retirement planning calculators is a good example. The best of these online calculators ask you questions, you plug in the answers, and on your computer screen you see your personalized plan calculated for you, complete with graphs and charts — sure beats slugging it out with a calculator and pencil over a fill-in-the-blank retirement planning workbook.
- Information on the Internet can be kept up-to-date, even up-to-the-minute. Larger companies may have an entire staff responsible for keeping their Web site current. If a prospectus is revised, or a new tax law affects a retirement planning calculation, a well-maintained Web site can reflect these changes the next time you log on. This is an advantage not only over the traditional print medium but also over software programs.

Of course, there's a flip side to every coin. The Internet has introduced plenty of hazards for mutual fund investors to be worried about, but I give you a few tips on steering clear of the pitfalls:

- After you've paid your toll to get on the Information Superhighway, everything you find there has the illusion of being "free." Don't be fooled. Somebody has to pay to put that information on the Internet, and nine times out of ten it's a company that's trying to sell you stuff that you're better off not buying. Before you ever trust an Internet Web site with information on mutual funds, find out who's paying the bucks for the site to be there. (See the sidebar, "Who's footing the bill?")
- What I identify earlier in this section as an advantage of the Internet — its capability to keep information up-to-date — is also its Achilles' heel. Too many Internet sites get so focused on the short-term that they lose sight of the big picture. For example, many Web sites are centered around daily investment price quotes and late-breaking financial news; this type of information does not serve a healthy, long-term investment strategy perspective. Don't let the Internet distract you from your focus on the investment horizon. Don't be as enamored with the Internet's up-to-the-minute updatability as most Web sites seem to be.

INVESTIGATE

Who's footing the bill?

You need to know that the Internet is primarily funded by the marketing departments of companies. Of course, there's nothing intrinsically wrong with this arrangement; magazine articles and television programs are also paid for with advertising dollars. What is problematic about the Internet, however, is that the line between advertising and content is much fuzzier and blurrier than in other mediums. In fact, some Web sites obscure the difference between content and advertising in a manner that could be called deliberate.

For example, consider a Web site that hypes itself as the "best independent mutual fund resource" and declares that "Content is what makes us different." However, this "content," such as the text that appears in the site's "Expert's Corner," turns out to be nothing more than thinly veiled marketing fodder from financial newsletter writers intent on selling you a subscription to their wares.

So how can you tell if the "objective content" you're reading on the Web is really just a paid advertisement? Begin by thoroughly checking out the fine print. In the preceding example, I found this little disclaimer in the corner: "These articles are sponsored by the featured experts. . . ." Sponsored means that the "experts" (newsletter writers) were paying to put their articles on the Web site.

If the Web page has a button that says something like "About Us," click it; sometimes you can get information on who's sponsoring the site. Also click any buttons that say something like "For Clients Only" or "How to Join Us." You may discover that the site only mentions fund companies that pay a fee to be represented.

When you read articles on "independent" sites, keep an eye out for advertisements that "spill over" into the content. For example, if an article recommends a fund company whose advertisement appears at the top of the page, go get your salt shaker.

If you can't find out who's behind a particular site, don't trust it. A Web site that has nothing to hide has no reason to be evasive. To be safe, stick with sites that are totally upfront about who's paying for them. A site whose Web address is `www.fundcompanyxyz.com` is obviously not trying to fool anybody.

- Message boards and chat rooms are a unique aspect of the Internet. The way that these mediums can facilitate communication between people in various towns, cities, and states is potentially exciting. But message boards and chat rooms are dangerous places to tread for the naive and too-trusting. Remember, there are no entrance exams or license requirements for joining a chat room or posting a message on an electronic bulletin board. The anonymity of "screen names" makes it easy to pretend to be someone you're not. Therefore, *participate cautiously*. Never trust any advice you get from a chat room or message board without verifying it through a reliable independent source.

- The possibilities on the Internet are so endless they are overwhelming, and the easiest way to find bad advice is to be unsure about what you're looking for in the first place. It pays to know what information you want before you start searching. If you enter a vague term into an Internet search engine — say, "mutual funds" — you'll probably end up more lost than you were to begin with. If, on the other hand, you enter a specific term — such as "T. Rowe Price mutual funds" — you'll probably find the information you're looking for.

That said, let me speed up your search for good resources on the Internet by recommending what I think are the best mutual fund Web sites out there. You'll recognize the names behind all these sites; they are companies I recommend throughout the book. Not surprisingly, organizations that demonstrate excellence offline seem to be the ones that do best online as well.

Vanguard.com

For educational content and high-quality advice, Vanguard's Web site (`www.vanguard.com`) is unsurpassed. Its online "University" offers an excellent crash course on fund investing. The retirement calculators — one for pre-retirement planning and one for managing investments after you've retired or are close to retiring — are among the best available, online or off. And for any development that has an effect on fund investing — for example, a tax law that changes the capital gains rate — be assured that Vanguard's site will offer a thoughtful explanation.

SchwabNow

Schwab has consistently been the industry's trail-breaker, and the Internet is one more territory where the discount broker has lead the way. Just about every advance in online account access — whether it's viewing current balances, placing trades, or obtaining research — has been pioneered by Schwab. If you're a Schwab account holder, you can be assured that Schwab's Web site (`www.schwab.com`) will offer you the very latest technology.

Morningstar.net

Morningstar's site (`www.morningstar.net`) is one of the better mutual fund Web resources. Here you can find Morningstar's well-known research reports on individual mutual funds, which feature long-term fund performance data and graphs, risk ratings, manager profiles, information on fees, and a listing of discount brokers who sell the fund. Compared to Morningstar's traditional printed report, the online version is slightly watered down — no analyst commentary and fewer statistics (for example, no Price/Earnings ratios or turnover rates). But it's hard to complain when you factor in the price tag: The online reports, unlike their printed brethren, are free. (Surprisingly, considering that Morningstar was built on the basis of research and no advertising, it is the mutual fund companies with their banner advertisements at the top of every page that "pay" for this Web site.) The site also features articles on advanced concepts of fund investing and developments in the fund industry.

Honorable mentions

Fidelity and T. Rowe Price have both put up sites worthy of their good fund offerings. On Fidelity's Web site (`www.fidelity.com`), you can find information and performance data not only on Fidelity's large family of funds, but also on hundreds of non-Fidelity funds available through its discount brokerage services. T. Rowe Price offers solid advice in its retirement planning section (`www.troweprice.com`).

Part V
The Part of Tens

"My portfolio's gonna take a hit for this."

In this part . . .

Why include lists of ten-somethings? Why not? Life is all about priorities, and more than ten of anything is too many to remember. Fewer than ten leaves you with that empty feeling you have after eating a hearty plate of bean sprouts for lunch. So — ten it is. Like Goldilocks, here you get just the right amount of information about some important fund concepts and concerns.

Chapter 17

Ten Developments in the Mutual Fund Business

To help you make better investment decisions, you should be aware of the broader trends and developments in and around the fund industry, and I discuss these trends in this chapter.

The industry is booming

Some people are troubled by the fast growth of the mutual fund industry. They believe it has been fueled by legions of baby boomers suddenly realizing that retirement is right around the corner and trying to make up for lost time. According to the doomsayers, when the current bull market ends, all these inexperienced investors are going to panic and dump their funds, leading to a market meltdown. Another doomsayers' scenario predicts that when the baby boomers hit retirement and start drawing on their nest eggs, the stock market will crash.

Such doomsaying is unfounded, and the growth in the mutual fund business has been misinterpreted. Let me set some facts straight:

- Only about half the growth of fund assets in recent years is due to new money flowing in. The other half has come from investment returns.
- The growth of the industry has been fueled not so much by "new money" as it has from a change in the way people save for retirement. More and more employers are discontinuing their company-directed pension plans and moving employees into self-directed 401(k)-type plans. Stock money that was once part of a pension plan is now directed toward mutual funds. It's not "new money" because pension funds, like mutual funds, invest in stocks and bonds, and this money is still being managed by a professional (now a fund manager rather than a pension fund manager).
- A lot of "new" mutual fund investors are "ex" individual stock holders. They aren't necessarily saving more money, just moving around money that had already been invested. Indeed, surveys show that baby boomers aren't saving enough for retirement.

- Despite their growth, mutual funds still hold only 15 percent of the total corporate equity (stock) outstanding. Mutual fund investors would be relatively small players in a massive sell-off if one ever did occur.

The fear that boomers will suddenly sell everything when they hit retirement is also bogus. Nobody sells his entire nest egg the day after he stops working; retirement can last up to 30 years, and assets are depleted quite gradually.

Criticizing funds has become a big business of its own

Take a look at a business-book best-seller list. It's obvious that spurning mutual funds in favor of picking individual stocks can help sell a lot of books. "Mutual funds are boring," these best-selling authors are saying, "Invest like me and you're guaranteed fabulous, double-digit, market-beating returns." The book-writing gurus would have you believe that it's their stock-picking prowess that has generated their double-digit returns. Baloney! Even index funds have been able to get 20 and 30+ percent returns in the U.S. stock market in recent years, a time when making an investment mistake has been difficult.

These returns are *not* sustainable. The market will cool off sooner or later, and when it does, everyone's returns — both the index funds' and the chest-thumping gurus' — will fall to more sober levels. I'm not a market timer, so I can't predict when this will happen. But I do predict that when it does, stock-picking books that claim to crush the market won't be so popular.

Fund expenses aren't getting lower

Despite the rapid growth of fund assets, overall fund average expenses aren't getting lower. However, this fact doesn't lend itself to any simplistic conclusions. Sure, some funds have gotten really big but are sticking it to their shareholders by refusing to reduce their expenses. But many funds have reduced their expense ratios over time. What has probably been keeping overall expense ratios high is the continued influx of new fund companies and new funds onto the scene. With few assets, these fund companies are forced to charge high expenses to cover their costs. (That's two counts against upstart fund companies: high costs and lack of track records.)

Index funds are starting to get the popularity they deserve

Index funds, which invest to track specific market averages, were once scorned as "guaranteed mediocrity." But investors are finally noticing that these funds are beating the majority of their actively managed peers. As a result, billions of dollars have been flowing into index funds, fund companies are offering them. In fact, the Vanguard Index 500 Fund is on pace to take over Fidelity's Magellan fund as the biggest fund in existence.

The long-term benefits of index funds — low costs and low turnover — are applicable to all markets, not just large-company stocks. Indexing makes sense for bond markets, smaller-company stocks, and international investments.

Fidelity is fumbling . . .

The undisputed king of U.S. stock-picking in the '80s, Fidelity has been sucking some wind in recent years in part because the company has become a victim of its own success. Thanks to their excellent past performance, many Fidelity funds got too popular and too big. Fidelity learned the hard way that enormous asset size makes beating the market difficult. Although Fidelity has closes some of its oversized funds to new investors, the move was long overdue.

Fidelity has been equally a victim of its own arrogance. Back in the '80s, Fidelity encouraged its stock managers to take big risks, and the strategy paid off handsomely. Unfortunately, the '90s have not been so kind to Fidelity's brand of risk taking.

Under increasing pressure from peeved investors, management took some aggressive steps. Fidelity shuffled and dismissed managers for many of its funds and instituted changes to keep funds in line with their stated purposes. The mutual fund giant is not down for the count; it still offers some excellent U.S. stock funds. But, by working for more conservative, consistent performance, Fidelity seems to be acknowledging that the glory days of the '80s are over.

. . . and Vanguard is vindicated

I received some letters criticizing the first edition of this book for recommending too many Vanguard funds. One reader asked if I was on the Vanguard payroll!

I wish that more fund companies put the interests of their shareholders first, but the fact is, Vanguard is the best on this dimension. Thanks to Vanguard's unique corporate structure, it's the only fund company that is owned by its shareholders. Profits are returned to the shareholders in the form of the lowest fund operating expenses in the business. For mutual funds whose performance depends heavily on the expense ratio — that is, money market and bond funds — Vanguard is the number-one choice.

What has changed since the first edition of this book is that Vanguard is starting to get credit for its stock funds as well. Vanguard's disciplined approach to investing — with low turnover, avoidance of market timing, and lots of indexing — has paid off with handsome stock fund returns.

Personal computers continue to change the way we invest

Companies such as Schwab and Vanguard have made the personal computer a viable way to communicate with their investors. Schwab has been a pioneer in offering its customers online access to account information, as well as the ability to place trades with the click of a mouse. Vanguard has shown how to turn a Web site into a valuable educational resource for investors. You can count on personal computers playing a bigger role in fund investing. However, the personal computer has introduced some new dangers to the fund investing scene. A low barrier of entry has allowed a lot of bad investing advice and seedy marketing pitches to proliferate on the World Wide Web. Moreover, the personal computer has duped some individual investors into believing that they can duplicate the research resources of a professional stock picker, and therefore duplicate the professional stock picker's returns. But there's a lot more to stock picking than getting stock quotes (see Chapter 2).

More funds of funds are available

I've always liked the concept of a fund of funds (a fund that invests in other mutual funds), but when the first edition of this book came out, the pickings of good funds of funds were slim: Only Vanguard Star and T. Rowe Price Spectrum Growth were available. Since then, Vanguard has added four funds of funds (the LifeStrategy series), and Fidelity has introduced a family of five funds of funds (the Fidelity Freedom funds). Look to funds of funds to become increasingly popular as folks get fed up with too many fund choices out there. See Chapter 9 for more on funds of funds.

Fund companies are merging

A lot of companies have come to feed at the trough of the booming fund industry. However, the smaller companies have been finding it tougher and tougher to compete with the bigger players. Rather than getting shoved out of the way, they have teamed up with other companies in the hopes of lowering their costs and boosting their profits. Usually, these mergers bring together companies with complementary specialties: a domestic fund company and an international fund company, for example. Fund company merging may be an encouraging trend. Too many fund companies and funds are available right now, the industry could stand some consolidation. On the other hand, I do fear (and have seen some examples of) some smaller fund company's funds that expense ratios will be jacked up once they are acquired by a bigger and perhaps greedier fund company.

Fund supermarkets are proliferating

As I discuss in Chapter 5, increasing numbers of discount brokers are offering investors the ability to invest in funds from a variety of fund companies through a single account. This one-stop shopping does come at a price, however, because many of the best funds that I recommend in this book will cost a transaction fee to buy or sell through a discount broker.

Chapter 18

Ten Negative Fund-Investing Thoughts to Overcome

Sometimes, when you invest in mutual funds, thinking too much and acting in what seems to be a sensible way are your own worst enemies. Experiencing the thoughts that I identify in this chapter is a sign that you're a normal person. But these thoughts are also something I want you to overcome. Once you do, you're well on your way to avoiding common painful and costly fund investing mistakes.

Why should I bother with so little to invest?

You gotta start somewhere. Those who have less to invest actually benefit more from mutual funds than do those investors with heftier balances (although they benefit a lot as well). With several hundred or a few thousand dollars to invest, you can't diversify well or avoid big commissions when you buy individual securities. By investing in mutual funds, you can. And you pay no more than those with big bucks to invest.

If you invest money for the longer term, especially inside retirement accounts, start with a hybrid fund or a fund of funds such as T. Rowe Price Spectrum Growth, Vanguard Star, or one of the Fidelity Freedom funds (see Chapter 9). These funds have low minimum initial investment requirements of $500 to $1,000. They'll go even lower — $50 for T. Rowe Price Spectrum Growth — if you sign up for an automatic investment plan that makes electronic withdrawals from your bank account on a regular basis. (See the example of Stacey the student in Chapter 10.)

Consider this approach: Invest just $1,000 today in good mutual funds and add just $50 per month. With funds that average a 10 percent annual return, in 20 years you'll have about $44,000! Invest over 40 years, and you'll have about $336,000. If you can manage $100 per month instead of $50, you'll have about $82,000 in 20 years, and $628,000 in 40 years!

My funds went down so I must have made a bad decision

Don't be so hard on yourself. Invest in the funds I recommend in this book and use good selection criteria in picking funds on your own. Then, if one of your funds goes down, the decline is — 99 times out of 100 — because the types of securities it focuses on (for example, bonds, U.S. stocks, international stocks) are down.

REMEMBER

If, for example, your fund is down about 5 percent over the past year, find out how similar funds have done over the same time period. If the average comparable fund is down more than 5 percent, you have cause to be happy; if comparable funds are up an average of 20 percent, you have reason to worry. See Chapter 12 for some ground rules for deciding whether to dump or hold your laggard fund.

I don't want the risk of being in investments that aren't insured

Lack of insurance, such as that from the FDIC on bank accounts, is not what makes funds risky. Mutual fund risks are driven by the price changes of the securities, such as bonds and stocks, that they invest in. Unlike banks and insurance companies, mutual fund companies can't go bankrupt (see Chapter 2).

Mutual funds that invest in municipal bonds may have insurance against the default of the bonds. Otherwise, insurance isn't necessary or available for funds.

Don't overlook other, not so obvious, types of risk. Bank accounts don't carry the price, risk, or volatility that bond and stock mutual funds do. However, bank accounts are exposed to the risk that the value of your money may not grow fast enough to keep ahead of inflation and taxes.

TIP

If you don't like volatility, even with money you have earmarked for long-term purposes, invest more of your money in balanced or hybrid funds. These funds tend to mask the volatility of their individual stock and bond components because they're all mixed together (see Chapter 9).

I'll buy the funds that are doing best now

Most people want to jump on board the winning bandwagon. But the best performers all too often turn into tomorrow's mediocre or loser funds (see Chapter 4).

TIP

The types of securities that do best inevitably change. You may actually increase your chances of fund-investing success by minimizing exposure to recent hot performers and investing more into fund types that are currently depressed.

I can do better investing in individual securities

Perhaps you've read about how investment legends like Peter Lynch and Warren Buffett make wise investments, so you figure that if you do what they do, you can, too. (After all, a ton of books out there say that you can.)

Nothing personal, but it ain't going to happen. You're probably a part-time amateur, at best. If you enjoy playing pick-up basketball games, it would be fun, if somewhat humbling, playing against the great Michael Jordan. But I assume that you'd play Jordan for the fun of it rather than an expectation or vain hope of beating him. Buying individual stocks is the same — don't do it thinking that you'll beat the better mutual fund managers.

Don't fool yourself into thinking that you're an expert just because you know more than most people about a particular industry or company. Many others have this knowledge, and if you have truly inside information that a company is about to be acquired, for example, and you invest your money based on this insider knowledge, you'll end up with a large fine or jail sentence or both.

I shouldn't invest without knowing what's happening with the economy, trade agreements, tax and budget reform . . .

Although I don't advocate sticking your head in the sand, all these big picture economic issues are well beyond your (or, really, anyone else's) ability to accurately forecast. Besides, investors' expectations are already reflected in the prices of securities in the financial markets.

By all means, read, listen to, and absorb what's going on in the world around you. But don't use this information in an attempt to time the markets.

I'm going to sell because interest rates are rising and the economy is tanking

The financial markets tend to lead these sorts of economic changes. The stock market, for example, often peaks six months to a year before the economy does. Conversely, stock prices usually head back up in advance and in anticipation of an actual economic recovery. Interest rates and bond prices typically have the same kind of interaction. By the time everyone's talking about the damage to the bond market from rising interest rates, the bond market has usually hit bottom.

Although I'm not foolish enough to think that I can predict future financial market movements, I do know that selling when bonds are "on sale" is the opposite of a wise investment strategy (see Chapter 8 to find out about bonds).

I'm going to wait for a correction for a buying opportunity

Some stock market investors like to wait for a big drop before they start investing. This strategy seems logical, especially coming on the heels of years of advancing prices. It also fits the philosophy of buying when prices are discounted.

The problem is, how do you know when the decline has run its course? A 10 percent drop? 20, 30, or 40 percent? If you're waiting for a 20 percent drop and the market only drops 15 percent before it then rises 100 percent over the coming years, you'll miss out.

TIP

Especially if you're just starting to save and invest money, forget about trying to wait and buy at lower prices. Invest regularly so that, if prices drop, you'll buy some at lower prices. That way, if prices don't decline, you won't miss out on the advance. If you have a large amount of money awaiting investment, move the money gradually — a portion every month or every quarter over a year or two into different types of funds (see Chapter 6).

I need to stay on top of my funds to make sure that nothing bad happens

There's a big difference between monitoring and obsessing. You don't need to follow the daily price changes of your mutual funds. Following the daily prices of mutual funds is a lousy way to discern the amount of return from your fund. In addition to share price changes, you must take into account dividend and capital gains distributions when you calculate a fund's performance (see Chapter 12).

WARNING!

Tracking and hovering over your funds increases your chances of panicking and making emotionally based decisions. The investors I know who bail out when prices are down almost always are those who follow prices too closely. Keep your sights on the big picture: why you bought the fund in the first place and what financial goal you are trying to fulfill.

My fund isn't in the Top Ten for its category so it's not the best

Stop looking at fund performance Top-Ten lists. Most of these lists completely ignore risk. Many of these lists rank funds based on short time periods. The funds on top are constantly changing.

REMEMBER

If a fund is taking so much risk that it's in the Top Ten, that status also means that it's risky enough to end up in the Bottom Ten some day (see the many examples in Chapter 4).

The categories that are used in these types of lists are also flawed, because many of the funds aren't really comparable. Read Chapter 12 to find out appropriate ways to evaluate and track the performance of your funds.

Chapter 19

Ten Questions More Fund Investors Should Ask

Investors and market followers ask a lot of questions. Asking questions is a good thing, because the answers, if honestly provided by knowledgeable people, will help you expand your knowledge. As I note in Chapter 18, questions based on fear are particularly important to clear up. Otherwise, you could make a bad move.

Although plenty of questions are asked, not enough of the *right* kind of questions are asked. So, here are some queries and issues to ponder so that you can become a better investor and help the fund industry and even our government become better oriented to serving your needs.

Why so many funds?

So many funds exist because so many companies and people want a slice of the profitable mutual fund pie. Investors certainly don't need this many funds and, thus far, these extra funds and the companies selling them haven't led to as much beneficial price competition as you see in other industries with as many players. The reason: Comparison shopping is difficult for the uninformed.

Over time, you are likely to see more competition, particularly on the fees that funds charge. This competition will inevitably lead to the merging of smaller companies into larger ones to help contain costs. In the meantime, take the proliferation of funds as a sign that it pays to shop around (which I've done for you to provide the recommendations in this book) because some companies are charging much more than others for the same types of funds and performance.

What is this fund going to cost me?

You don't buy groceries, dinner out, or tickets to a play or baseball game without knowing the cost. Why should mutual funds be any different?

Because funds charge you every day, week, month, and year you're in them (and load funds hit you with sales commissions on top of that), check out the amount a fund is going to cost you over, say, ten years of ownership. This information is now required in a fund's prospectus. On a $5,000 investment, you may see a range from about $10 to $1,500 (see Chapter 4 for how to read a prospectus)!

Why do some large stock mutual funds, like Fidelity's Magellan fund, still charge an annual fee of about 1 percent?

Under the management of Peter Lynch, now almost a household name, the Fidelity Magellan fund amassed the best ten-year track record among stock funds. *After* that happened (and after Lynch left), money poured into Magellan as Fidelity advertised the heck out of its performance.

Today, the Magellan fund charges an annual operating fee of about 0.7 percent. For a stock fund, that expense ratio may seem reasonable — until you consider how huge the Magellan fund is with approximately $73 billion under management. Fidelity is raking in about $510 million in annual fees from this fund. Compare this amount to 1984, when Magellan had about $2 billion in assets, was charging 1 percent annually, and was collecting about $20 million in yearly fees.

Does managing this fund cost Fidelity more than 25 times as much as it did in 1984? Of course not. Much of this extra money is going into the pockets of the owners of Fidelity. If Fidelity were sharing the extra profits that come with managing this amount of money in Magellan, the annual expense fee on this fund should be much less. As the mutual fund industry continues to grow, increasing numbers of companies and funds do not share the extra profits that come from running larger funds.

Why doesn't the Social Security system allow taxpayers to invest their money in mutual funds?

The tiny country of Chile, for example, allows taxpayers to invest their government-collected retirement money in mutual funds. This policy not only ensures the segregation of retirement funds from the rest of government spending, it also ensures healthy growth and returns on citizens' investments.

The U.S. Social Security trust fund is somewhat bogus in that the assets are part of the overall federal pool of money. The government claims that the Social Security money is invested in Treasuries, but this is not really true. The money flowing in from Social Security simply reduces the number of Treasury bonds the government needs to issue to finance the national debt.

As more people like me direct the investment of their own retirement funds, instead of having a company pension fund manager do the job, isn't there a danger we'll screw up?

Yes, individuals who direct their own retirement investments can make major mistakes. The average person has but a fraction of the training and experience in investing money that a company pension fund manager has. So people are more likely to not save enough, to underinvest in growth-oriented investments such as stocks, and to try to time the financial markets. These pitfalls are among the downsides of self-directed retirement plans such as 401(k)s.

Of course, not all pension managers do superb jobs; but as a group, they've done well. Companies like to do away with traditional pension plans because many employees don't seem to value them as they should and because the plans are expensive to maintain. With 401(k)-type plans, the responsibility and most of the "cost" of saving gets dumped onto the employee's shoulders.

REMEMBER

You must educate yourself and find out how to properly and intelligently invest your money!

Why doesn't our company retirement savings plan allow investing through the best mutual funds?

Sometimes, the well-intentioned people at a company who establish a retirement savings plan, such as a 401(k) or 403(b) plan (see Chapter 3), may not know any more than you do about investments. They may even know less or have gotten bad advice when the plan was established.

TIP

Company retirement plan investment options are often improved because of suggestions from employees like you! So, speak up with constructive suggestions and ideas.

Why isn't more money invested in index funds?

Although growing in popularity, index funds, which track the performance of the markets, still account for a minuscule portion of the total assets now invested in funds. The main reason so little money is invested in index funds is because of all the ratings and rankings of funds. So much attention is paid to which funds are at the head of the pack today that most people lose sight of the fact that, over longer time periods, index funds beat the vast majority of their actively managed peers.

Index funds also seem sort of boring and ego-deflating because you're admitting that you can't beat the market, so you're resigning yourself to the market rate of return. Swallow your ego and discover the benefits of using these funds (see Chapter 6).

Did this mutual fund or advisor invest in securities comparable to the index they are comparing themselves to?

If a fund — or an advisor's fund recommendation — looks like it has beaten the pants off a comparative index, odds are that it's using an unfair index for comparison. A fair comparative benchmark is one that invests in the same types of securities as the fund. Check out the way the fund allocates its assets. Suppose, for example, that a fund manager or an advisor who invests in funds says that he or she generated annual returns averaging 15 percent over the past five years and compares the performance to the Standard & Poor's Index of 500 large-company U.S. stocks. If the fund or advisor invested in international stocks or smaller company stocks or bonds or all the above, then the S&P 500 isn't a fair yardstick (see Chapter 12).

Can you prove that your privately managed fund or newsletter recommendations produced the returns that you claim?

Most of the time, fund managers and advisors can't prove their claims. And if they can, they'll choose short, selective time periods during which they look the best. Privately managed funds can produce proof of performance only through an independent accountant's audit. Newsletters are tracked by the *Hulbert Financial Digest*. Over long time periods, the "best" newsletters just barely keep up with the market rates of return that you can obtain with near 100 percent certainty using index funds (see Chapter 15 for more on investment newsletters).

Why don't more fund companies adopt an operating structure like Vanguard's?

Most businesses and business founders want to reap the full financial rewards if their business succeeds. That's what capitalism is all about. Fewer are as concerned about the impact that their business structure has on the customer's best interests (witness tobacco manufacturers). John Bogle, founder of Vanguard, was far more concerned about his customer's needs than maximizing profits.

What's most appealing about Vanguard's structure is that its funds have an incentive to control costs, because its funds are solely owned by its shareholders and don't kick profits back to the management company. Vanguard's incentive system has also managed to reward fund managers for producing good performance.

At other mutual fund companies, the supposedly independent boards of directors should be asking tougher questions, such as why management fees aren't being reduced as some funds mushroom in size. The problem may be that most directors are afraid that, if they raise these issues, they'll be shown the door from these cushy jobs that often pay tens of thousands of dollars per year for very little work.

Chapter 20

Ten Issues to Consider Before Hiring a Financial Advisor

Millions of people have successfully invested in mutual funds on their own. The vast majority of these folks were like you. Maybe they had an idea what a mutual fund was, but at first they weren't sure or were uncomfortable about investing in funds. Some people didn't even know what a mutual fund was — perhaps you didn't when you started reading this book. But investing in mutual funds is not difficult; common sense and a modicum of financial sense is all you need.

There's no compelling reason to hire someone like me or another financial advisor in order to invest in mutual funds. So, if you jumped to this chapter first, STOP right here! I recommend that you march back to the earlier chapters in this book and start finding out more about funds and investing. You'll be better able to understand this chapter after you've read those that come before it, not to mention the fact that you'll be improving your ability to save yourself possibly thousands of dollars in financial advisory fees.

But if you've arrived here because you just don't want to deal with handling fund investing or financial planning decisions on your own, keep on keepin' on.

Financial planner or money manager?

As you search the landscape for help, you will confront a variety of people who call themselves "advisors" and who are eager to assist you with investing your money. As I discuss in Chapter 5, those who claim to be advisors but who derive commissions from the products that they sell are salespeople, not advisors.

True financial planners generally provide objective help with a variety of issues such as retirement planning, decisions relating to the use and payoff of debt, investing, insurance, and perhaps even real estate. The charge for these services should be a fee based on the time that's involved. I talk about fees later in the chapter (see the section, "Fees — What's your advice going to cost?").

Money managers or financial advisors who perform *money management* will invest your money and charge you a fee — usually expressed as a percentage of assets under management. Some advisors only do money management, but increasing numbers of financial planners offer money management services as well.

The benefit of a good planner is that he or she should help restructure your financial situation before your money gets invested in mutual funds. If a planner provides specific mutual fund recommendations, you can implement them on your own and save yourself a bundle in ongoing advisory fees.

Using money managers can make sense for people who have finished their planning and need someone to help manage their money. Money managers will argue that, because they devote themselves full-time to investing, they are more adept at it.

But here's an increasingly common problem that has been surprisingly little discussed in the financial press: When financial planners add the second hat of money manager, a number of conflicts of interest can arise with the planning services that they offer.

First, planner/money managers may be reluctant to recommend — and, in fact, have an incentive to ignore — strategies that deplete the money you have to invest. Why? Because the more you have to invest, the greater the total money management fees they earn. All the following financial moves result in less money that you can invest with the planner/money managers, so they may not recommend these:

- Maximizing saving through your employer's retirement savings plan(s)
- Spending more on real estate — either by purchasing a larger primary home or investing in rental property
- Buying and investing in your own business or someone else's privately held business
- Paying down debt of all types, such as credit cards, auto loans, mortgages, business loans, and the like

Another problem with planners who also manage money is that they may be short on specific advice in the planning process. Sadly, I've seen more than a few cases in which people have paid planners upward of several thousand dollars for a largely boilerplate computer-generated financial plan and have received little if any specific financial planning and investment advice. If you want to invest in no-load funds, the planner should willingly and happily provide specific fund recommendations and help you build a portfolio for the fee that you pay him or her.

Active or passive management?

Much of what you're paying a planner for is the time spent reviewing your financial situation and matching your needs and goals to a suitable portfolio of funds. If your needs and situation are relatively stable and you do your homework right the first time and select good mutual funds, you shouldn't need to bounce from fund to fund.

BEWARE

If anything, constant tinkering with a mutual fund portfolio tends to lower returns. This is the same issue I cover in Chapter 15 on the perils of blindly following some newsletters' and gurus' timing advice to switch into this fund and out of that one. Trading in non-retirement accounts also increases your tax burden.

Who's in control?

If you hire a money manager, another issue you should consider is that the manager will require that you turn control of the account over to him or her. Specifically, you will sign or initial a form granting the advisor authority to execute trades in your account — otherwise known as granting a *limited power of attorney* (that's what the first line in Figure 20-1, a section of a discount brokerage application, is authorizing).

Almost all money managers manage money on what's called a *discretionary basis* — they make decisions to buy this fund and sell that fund without your prior approval. In other words, you're turning control over to them. You find out about transactions *after* they've occurred, usually when you receive the trade confirmations in the mail and through your monthly or quarterly statement.

TIP

At a minimum, before you turn control over to the money manager, make sure that you discuss your investment objectives with her. These overall goals should drive the way the manager manages your money.

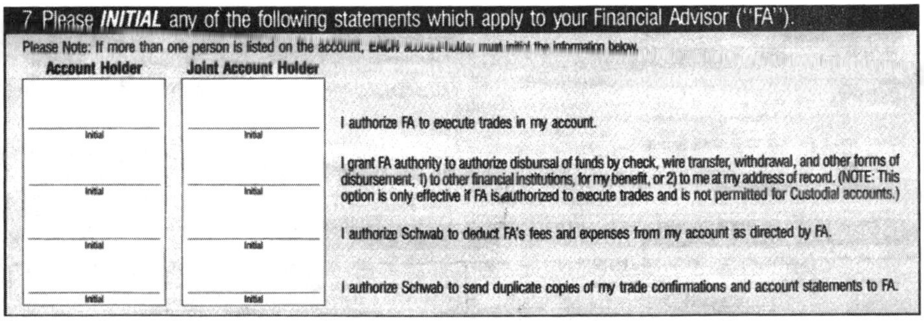
7 Please ***INITIAL*** any of the following statements which apply to your Financial Advisor ("FA").

Please Note: If more than one person is listed on the account, EACH account holder must initial the information below.

Account Holder	Joint Account Holder	
Initial	Initial	I authorize FA to execute trades in my account.
Initial	Initial	I grant FA authority to authorize disbursal of funds by check, wire transfer, withdrawal, and other forms of disbursement, 1) to other financial institutions, for my benefit, or 2) to me at my address of record. (NOTE: This option is only effective if FA is authorized to execute trades and is not permitted for Custodial accounts.)
Initial	Initial	I authorize Schwab to deduct FA's fees and expenses from my account as directed by FA.
Initial	Initial	I authorize Schwab to send duplicate copies of my trade confirmations and account statements to FA.

Figure 20-1. When you initial this section, you give your financial advisor control over investing your funds.

Source: Charles Schwab & Company, Inc.

The second line on the sample form in Figure 20-1 gives your advisor power to move money out of your account. I recommend against giving your advisor this power unless you need to withdraw money from your account frequently and find it more convenient to have your advisor do it for you.

The third line allows your advisor to have his or her ongoing fees deducted from the account. I would definitely not allow this deduction to retirement accounts because it diminishes the amount of money that you have compounding tax-deferred. For non-retirement accounts, it's up to you, although many advisors insist on this feature to make collecting their fees easier.

The fourth line requests the brokerage firm to send duplicate copies of your account statements and trade confirmations to your advisor. That's acceptable and to be expected.

Fees — What's your advice going to cost?

If you hire a planner on an hourly basis, expect to pay anywhere from $50 or so all the way up to several hundred dollars per hour. Expect to pay at least $100 per hour — you can easily pay more; planners with the $300 per hour billing rates tend to work exclusively with the affluent. Here's an example of a fee schedule for a money management firm that manages, on an ongoing basis, a portfolio of mutual funds. This firm charges a percentage of assets under management.

Amount You Invest	Fee Percentage	Annual Fee in Dollars
$100,000	1.00%	$1,000
$250,000	1.00%	$2,500
$500,000	0.95%	$4,750
$1,000,000	0.85%	$8,500
$2,000,000	0.70%	$14,000
$5,000,000	0.50%	$25,000

What's amazing to me about this type of fee schedule is that, although the percentage charge declines slightly as the amount you invest increases, look at how the total charges increase. This firm sends the same quarterly reports out to the client with $1,000,000 invested, who pays $8,500 per year, as it does to the client with $100,000 invested, who pays $1,000 per year for the same service.

This advisory firm, in fact, claims that "every client regardless of whether they have $100,000 invested or $1,000,000, receives the same personal attention." If that's true, then their fee schedule shouldn't look like it does! Either this firm ain't making any money on their small accounts, or (more likely) they're making a truckload on the larger ones. Keep this example in mind because advisors' fees are negotiable. The more you have to invest, the greater your ability should be to negotiate lower fees.

Also, ask what sort of transaction and other fees you can expect to pay in addition to the advisory fee paid to the money manager. Most money managers will ask that you establish an account at one of the discount brokerage firms, such as Schwab or Jack White, or with a mutual fund company. Ask who they use and why.

If you're going to consider hiring a mutual fund money manager, take the time to add up all the costs. Here's a quick table (see Table 20-1) to help you do the job.

Table 20-1 Adding Up All the Costs

Cost	*Annual Percentage of Your Assets*
Money manager's fee	for example, 1.0% ________
Operating fees on mutual funds invested in (don't let the advisor say that they can't figure this amount because the funds they use vary over time — they can base the calculation on their current portfolio or the amount they used over the past year)	for example, 1.0% ________
Transaction and other fees	for example, 0.2% ________
Total	for example, 2.2% ________

Remember that, over the long haul, a diversified portfolio primarily invested in stocks has usually returned around 10 percent. If you're paying a total of 2.5 percent to have your money managed, you're giving away 25 percent of your expected return. And don't forget, because the IRS sure won't, that you'll owe taxes on your non-retirement account profits, so you're giving away an even greater percentage of your after-tax returns.

How do you make investing decisions?

Throughout this book, I discuss the good and bad ways people can and have invested in mutual funds over the years. Chapter 4, in particular, walks you through the methodology and logic behind fund selection. The process isn't rocket science — it can be as simple as picking any other product or service. You want value — where can you invest in funds that meet your needs managed by a fund company and fund managers that have good track records and that charge competitive fees?

Most advisors try to factor their economic expectations and prognostications into their investment strategies. But this forecasting is much easier said than done.

The fundamental problem with some money managers is that they try to convince you that they have a crystal ball. Specifically, some will claim that they can time the markets; they say that they'll get you out of the market before it falls and put your money back in time to catch the next rise.

In Chapter 15, you can see for yourself that over long time periods, it is virtually impossible for even the acknowledged experts to beat the markets. Great investors, such as Warren Buffett and Peter Lynch, say that you can't time the markets. Believe 'em!

What's your track record?

In the world of mutual funds, fund companies must have their performance records audited and reviewed by the Securities and Exchange Commission. Most also provide an independent auditor's report.

Private money managers face no such SEC requirement. A few — very few — provide independent audits. Of course, you really want to know the performance facts about the money manager you are considering for ongoing management of your funds. What rate of return has he earned year by year? How has he done in up and down markets? How much risk has she taken, and how have her funds performed versus comparable benchmarks (see Chapter 12)? These are important questions. But it is difficult, if not impossible, to get objective and meaningful answers from the majority of investment advisors who manage money on an ongoing basis.

Money managers play a number of marketing games to pump themselves up. If all the money managers out there are telling the truth, then 99 percent of them have beaten the market averages, avoided the stock market crash of 1987, and just happened to be in the best-performing funds last year. Here are the common marketing ploys money managers use to pump up their supposed past performance, and to seduce you into turning your money over to them:

- **Select accounts.** If you can get the money manager to give you performance numbers and charts, all too often a little asterisk refers you to some microscopic footnote somewhere near the bottom of the page. If you have your magnifying glass handy, you will see that the asterisk says something like "select" or "sample accounts." What this term means, and what they should have said instead is: "We picked the accounts where we did best, used the performance numbers from those, and ignored the rest." (Interestingly, using smaller type in this way is a violation of SEC regulations.)

  Advisory firms also may select the time periods when they look best. Many of the track records being touted in sales brochures don't cover periods when the stock market took a major hit, such as Black Monday in October of 1987. Finally, and most flagrantly, some firms simply make up the numbers.

- **Free services.** Some money managers will produce performance numbers that imply that they're giving their services away for nothing. Remember, money managers charge a fee (a percentage of assets) for their services — these fees (according to SEC regulations) should be deducted from the returns that were earned to clearly show the amount you as an investor using their services would have made. Because most money managers place their mutual fund trades through discount brokers who charge transaction fees, these fees should be deducted from returns as well.

- **Bogus benchmarks.** It's bad enough that some money managers make their performance numbers higher than they really are; some also try to make themselves look good in relation to the overall market by comparing their performance numbers to inappropriate benchmarks. For example, money managers who invest worldwide (including international stocks) may compare their investment performance only to U.S.-based indexes.
- **Switching into (yesterday's) stars.** Money managers don't want to send out performance updates that show that they're sitting on yesterday's losers and they missed out on yesterday's winners. So guess what? They may sell the losers and buy into some of yesterday's winners, thus creating the illusion that they're more on top of the market than they really are (some mutual fund newsletters engage in this practice as well). This strategy, also known as *window dressing,* is potentially dangerous because they may be making a bad situation worse by selling funds that have already declined and buying into others after they've soared (not to mention possibly increasing transaction and tax costs).

What are your qualifications and training?

The answers you receive to the question of qualifications and training will vary. An advisor should have experience in the investing or financial services field — generally, the more the better. But also look for someone with intelligence and ethics who can converse with you in plain English.

In terms of credentials, check 'em out but don't be overly impressed by some, such as the C.F.P. (Certified Financial Planning) degree. Most planners with this "credential," which can be earned by taking a self-study course at home, sell financial products. Other common credentials include:

- **C.F.A. (Chartered Financial Analyst).** This is a plus because it means that the advisor should know how to analyze securities and investments and the fundamentals of portfolio management.
- **M.B.A. (Master of Business Administration).** This is a plus because it means that the advisor should have had coursework dealing with investments and finance. Find out where the M.B.A. was earned.
- **P.F.S. (Personal Financial Specialist)** is a credential conferred on accountants who pass an exam similar to the C.F.P. Those with the P.F.S. are less likely to work on commission the way many C.F.P.s do.
- **C.L.U. (Chartered Life Underwriter) and Ch.F.C. (Chartered Financial Consultant)** are insurance credentials and carry little if any value in advising on mutual funds. This credential may be a red flag that you're dealing with a salesperson or with someone who knows more about insurance than investments.

The term *Registered Investment Advisor* denotes that the advisor is registered with the U.S. Securities and Exchange Commission. The SEC does not require a test; however, it does require that the advisor file *Form ADV,* also known as the Uniform Application for Investment Advisor Registration. This lengthy document asks for specific information from investment advisors, such as a breakdown of the sources of their income, relationships and affiliations with other companies, each advisor's educational and employment history, the types of securities the firm recommends, and the firm's fee schedule. (Many states require passing a securities exam, such as a Series 2, 63, or 65.)

In a pitch over the phone or in marketing materials sent by mail, an advisor may gloss over or avoid certain issues. Although it's possible for an advisor to lie on Form ADV, it's likely that an advisor will be more truthful on this form than in marketing materials. Ask the advisor to send you a copy of Form ADV, or write the SEC for a copy: Securities and Exchange Commission, Attention: Public Reference, 450 5th St. NW, Washington, D.C. 20549. (You can also fax your request to 202-628-9001.)

What are your references?

Take the time to ask other people about how the advisor benefited them. This is a terrific way to verify the rates of return the advisor may claim (although you're smart enough to recognize that the advisor will refer you to the clients who have done the best with him). Also inquire about the advisor's strengths and weaknesses.

Virtually all money managers offer a "free" introductory consultation if you meet their minimum investment requirements. Planners who work on commission also tend to offer free sessions. So the "free" consultation ends up being a sales pitch to convince you to buy certain products or services.

Busy advisors who charge by the hour usually can't afford to burn their time for a "free" in-person session. Don't let this deter you; it's probably a good sign. These advisors should be willing, however, to spend time on the phone free of charge answering background questions. They should also send background materials and provide references if you ask.

Do you carry liability insurance?

Some advisors may be surprised by this question or may think that you're a problem customer looking for a lawsuit. On the other hand, if your advisor gets you into some disasters, you'll be glad for the insurance coverage.

Financial planners and money managers should carry *liability* (sometimes it's called *errors and omission*) *insurance.* This coverage provides you (and the advisor) with protection in case a major mistake is made for which the advisor is liable.

Appendix

How to Find Fund Companies and Discount Brokers

American Century Funds
4500 Main Street
P.O. Box 419200
Kansas City, MO 64141
☎ 800-345-2021

Brandywine Fund
3908 Kennctt Pike
P.O. Box 4166
Greenville, DE 19807
☎ 800-656-3017

Charles Schwab and Co.
101 Montgomery Street
San Francisco, CA 94104
☎ 800-435-4000

Cohen & Steers Realty Shares, Inc.
757 Third Avenue
New York, NY 10017
☎ 800-437-9912

Columbia Funds
1301 SW 5th Avenue
P.O. Box 1350
Portland, OR 97201-5601
☎ 800-547-1707

Dodge & Cox Funds
One Sansome Street, 35th Floor
San Francisco, CA 94104
☎ 800-621-3979

Domini Social Equity Fund
6 St. James Avenue, 9th Floor
Boston, MA 02116
☎ 800-762-6814

Fidelity Funds
82 Devonshire Street
Boston, MA 02109
☎ 800-544-8888
Fidelity Discount Brokerage
☎ 800-544-8666

Lindner Funds
7711 Carodelet, Suite 700
P.O. Box 11208
St. Louis, MO 63105
☎ 800-995-7777

Neuberger & Berman Funds
605 Third Avenue
New York, NY 10158
☎ 800-877-9700

PIMCO Funds
840 Newport Center Drive, Suite 360
Newport Beach, CA 92660
☎ 800-927-4648

SteinRoe Funds
P.O. Box 804058
Chicago, IL 60680
☎ 800-338-2550

T. Rowe Price Funds
100 E. Pratt Street
Baltimore, MD 21202
☎ 800-638-5660

Tweedy Browne Funds
52 Vanderbilt Avenue
New York, NY 10017
☎ 800-432-4789

USAA Funds
USAA Building
9800 Fredericksburg Road
San Antonio, TX 78288
☎ 800-382-8722

The Vanguard Group
P.O. Box 2600
Valley Forge, PA 19482
☎ 800-662-7447

Warburg Pincus Funds
466 Lexington Avenue
New York, NY 10017
☎ 800-927-2874

Jack White & Company
9191 Town Center, 2nd Floor
San Diego, CA 92122
☎ 800-323-3263

Table A-1 Bond Funds

Fund Name	Trading Symbol	(Total Return — Percent) 1988	1989	1990	1991	1992	1993	1994	1995	1996	1997	Capital Gains*	Dividends*
Taxable													
Vanguard Short-Term Corporate	VFSTX	7.0	11.5	9.2	13.1	7.2	7.1	–0.1	12.7	4.8	7.0	D	Monthly
PIMCO Low Duration	PTLDX	8.2	11.5	9.1	13.5	7.7	7.8	0.6	11.9	6.1	8.2	D	Monthly
Vanguard Index Total Bond Market	VBMFX	7.3	13.6	8.6	15.2	7.1	9.7	–2.7	18.1	3.6	9.4	D	Monthly
PIMCO Total Return	PTTRX	9.5	14.2	8.1	19.5	9.7	12.5	–3.6	19.8	4.7	10.2	D	Monthly
Vanguard GNMA	VFIIX	8.8	14.8	10.3	16.8	6.8	5.9	–1.0	17.0	5.2	9.5	D	Monthly
American Century-Benham GNMA	BGNMX	8.5	13.9	10.2	15.6	7.7	6.6	–1.7	15.7	5.2	8.7	D	Monthly
USAA GNMA	USGNX	-	-	-	-	6.1	7.1	0.0	16.7	2.9	9.5	D	Monthly
Dodge & Cox Income	DODIX	-	14.1	7.4	18.0	7.8	11.3	–2.9	20.2	3.6	10.0	D	Quarterly
Vanguard Long-Term Corporate	VWESX	9.7	15.2	6.2	20.9	9.8	14.6	–5.3	26.3	1.2	13.8	D	Monthly
Vanguard High Yield Corporate	VWEHX	13.6	1.9	-6.0	29.2	14.2	18.2	–1.7	19.1	9.6	11.9	D	Monthly
U.S. Treasury													
Vanguard Short-Term Treasury	VFISX	-	-	-	-	6.7	6.3	–0.6	12.1	4.4	6.5	D	Monthly
Vanguard Admiral Short-Term Treasury	VASTX	-	-	-	-	-	6.5	–0.3	12.2	4.5	12.2	D	Monthly
Vanguard Intermediate-Term Treasury	VFITX	-	-	-	-	7.8	11.4	–4.3	20.4	1.9	9.0	D	Monthly
Vanguard Admiral Intermediate-Term Treasury	VAITX	-	-	-	-	-	11.3	–4.2	20.5	2.1	20.5	D	Monthly
Vanguard Long-Term Treasury	VUSTX	9.2	17.9	5.8	17.4	7.4	16.8	–7.0	30.0	–1.3	13.9	D	Monthly
Vanguard Admiral Long-Term Treasury	VALGX	-	-	-	-	-	16.7	–6.9	30.0	–1.1	14.0	D	Monthly
Federally Tax-Free													
Vanguard Municipal Short-Term	VWSTX	5.6	7.0	6.6	7.2	4.7	3.8	1.6	6.0	3.7	4.1	D	Monthly
Vanguard Municipal Limited-Term	VMLTX	6.4	8.1	7.0	9.5	6.4	6.3	0.1	8.6	4.1	5.1	D	Monthly

* Capital gains and dividend schedules may change over time, but these are the typical months that the fund has, in the past, declared such distributions payable to shareholders of the fund.

Fund Name	Trading Symbol	1988	1989	1990	1991	1992	1993	1994	1995	1996	1997	Capital Gains*	Dividends*
		(Total Return — Percent)											
Vanguard Municipal Inter.-Term	VWITX	10.0	10.0	7.2	12.2	8.9	11.6	–2.1	13.6	4.2	7.1	N	Monthly
Vanguard Municipal Long-Term	VWLTX	12.2	11.5	6.8	13.5	9.3	13.5	–5.8	18.7	4.4	9.3	N	Monthly
Vanguard Municipal Insured Long-Term	VILPX	12.8	10.6	7.0	12.5	9.2	13.1	–5.6	18.5	4.0	8.7	N	Monthly
State and Federally Tax-Free													
American Century-Benham CA Tax-Free Intermediate	BCITX	5.9	7.9	7.0	10.4	7.1	10.7	–3.7	13.5	4.2	7.4	D	Monthly
American Century-Benham CA Tax-Free Long-Term	BCLTX	10.4	9.8	6.6	11.8	8.1	13.7	–6.5	19.8	3.6	9.7	D	Monthly
Schwab CA Short-Int Tax Free	SWCSX	-	-	-	-	-	-	–2.1	10.4	3.9	5.1	D	Monthly
Vanguard CA Tax-Free Insured Intermediate	VCAIX	-	-	-	-	-	-	-	13.1	5.4	7.7	D	Monthly
Vanguard CA Tax-Free Insured Long-Term	VCITX	12.1	10.5	7.0	11.0	9.3	12.8	–5.7	18.5	5.0	8.9	D	Monthly
Fidelity Spartan CT Muni Income	FICNX	10.1	10.4	6.6	10.6	8.2	12.9	–7.0	17.1	4.2	9.1	Jn,D	Monthly
Fidelity Spartan FL Muni Income	FFLIX	-	-	-	-	-	14.9	–6.7	18.6	4.0	8.8	D	Monthly
USAA FL Tax-Free Income	UFLTX	-	-	-	-	-	-	–10.0	18.9	4.4	11.2	My, N	Monthly
Fidelity Spartan MA Muni Income	FDMMX	10.7	9.3	7.4	11.3	9.3	12.9	–6.1	18.1	3.6	9.3	S,D	Monthly
Fidelity Spartan MI Muni Income	FMHTX	13.0	10.2	5.1	12.0	9.5	13.8	–7.5	15.4	3.4	9.0	F,D	Monthly
Fidelity Spartan MN Muni Income	FIMIX	12.6	9.2	7.2	8.5	7.6	12.4	–6.0	16.0	3.8	8.9	F,D	Monthly
Fidelity Spartan NJ Muni Income	FNJHX	10./9	10.4	7.1	12.3	8.7	13.1	–5.8	15.4	4.1	8.4	D	Monthly
Vanguard NJ Tax-Free Insured Long-Term	VNJTX	-	10.4	7.7	11.2	9.4	13.4	–5.2	17.3	3.2	8.6	D	Monthly
USAA NY Bond	USNYX	-	-	-	13.3	9.0	13.5	–9.1	18.1	3.8	10.6	My,N	Monthly

* Capital gains and dividend schedules may change over time, but these are the typical months that the fund has, in the past, declared such distributions payable to shareholders of the fund.

(continued)

Table A-1 *(continued)*

Fund Name	*Trading Symbol*	*1988*	*1989*	*1990*	*1991*	*1992*	*1993*	*1994*	*1995*	*1996*	*1997*	*Capital Gains**	*Dividends**
		(Total Return — Percent)											
Vanguard NY Insured Tax-Free	VNYTX	12.0	10.3	6.3	12.8	9.7	13.1	–5.7	17.7	4.1	8.7	D	Monthly
Vanguard OH Tax-Free Insured Long-Term	VOHIX	-	-	-	12.0	9.5	12.8	–5.2	16.8	4.2	8.5	D	Monthly
Vanguard PA Tax-Free Insured Long-Term	VPAIX	12.3	10.6	6.9	12.2	10.2	12.7	–4.6	16.4	4.3	8.3	D	Monthly
USAA TX Tax-Free Income	-	-	-	-	-	-	-	-	22.2	5.2	11.2	My, N	Monthly
USAA VA Bond	USVAX	-	-	-	11.7	8.5	12.6	–6.3	17.1	5.1	9.5	My,N	Monthly

Table A-2 **Stock Funds**

Fund Name	*Trading Symbol*	*1988*	*1989*	*1990*	*1991*	*1992*	*1993*	*1994*	*1995*	*1996*	*1997*	*Capital Gains**	*Dividends**
		(Total Return — Percent)											
Hybrid													
Vanguard Tax-Managed Balanced	VTMFX	-	-	-	-	-	-	-	24.5	12.2	16.6	D	Jn,D
Vanguard Wellesley Income	VWINX	13.6	20.8	3.8	21.4	8.6	14.6	–4.4	28.9	9.4	20.2	D	Mr,Jn,S,D
Vanguard Star	VGSTX	19.0	18.6	-3.6	24.1	10.5	10.9	–0.3	28.2	16.2	21.2	D	Ja,Jl
Dodge & Cox Balanced	DODBX	11.6	23.0	0.9	20.6	10.6	15.9	2.1	28.0	14.8	21.2	D	Mr,Jn,S,D
Vanguard Wellington	VWELX	16.1	21.5	-2.8	23.5	7.9	13.5	–0.5	32.9	16.2	23.2	D	Mr,Jn,S,D
Fidelity Asset Manager	FASMX	-	15.3	5.3	23.5	12.7	23.2	–6.6	18.1	12.7	22.3	D	Mr,Jn,S,D
Fidelity Puritan	FPURX	18.8	19.6	-6.2	24.4	15.4	21.4	1.8	21.4	15.2	22.4	S,D	Mr,Jn,S,D
Lindner Dividend	LDDVX	24.1	11.8	-6.5	27.3	21.1	14.9	–3.3	21.5	11.5	14.0	Mr,D	Mr,Jn,S,D
Vanguard Balanced Index	VBINX	-	-	-	-	-	10.0	–1.6	28.7	14.0	22.2	D	Jn, D
T. Rowe Price Balanced	RPBAX	9.0	20.7	7.1	22.0	7.3	13.3	–2.1	24.9	14.6	19.0	D	Mr,Jn,S,D

* Capital gains and dividend schedules may change over time, but these are the typical months that the fund has, in the past, declared such distributions payable to shareholders of the fund.

Fund Name	Trading Symbol	1988	1989	1990	1991	1992	1993	1994	1995	1996	1997	Capital Gains*	Dividends*
					(Total Return — Percent)								
U.S. Stock													
Vanguard Index 500	VFINX	16.2	31.4	–3.3	30.1	7.5	9.8	1.2	37.4	22.9	33.2	D	Mr,Jn,S,D
Schwab 1000	SNXFX	-	-	-	-	8.5	9.6	–0.1	36.6	21.6	31.9	D	Ju,D
Vanguard Index Total Market	VTSMX	-	-	-	-	-	10.6	–0.2	35.8	21.0	31.0	D	Mr,Jn,S,D
Dodge & Cox Stock	DODGX	13.8	26.9	–5.0	21.4	10.8	18.3	5.2	33.4	22.3	28.4	D	Mr,Jn,S,D
T. Rowe Price Spectrum Growth	PRSGX	-	-	-	29.8	7.2	21.0	1.4	29.9	20.5	17.4	D	D
Fidelity Equity Income	FEQIX	22.5	13.7	–14.0	29.3	14.6	21.2	0.2	31.8	21.0	30.0	Mr,D	Mr,Jn,S,D
Fidelity Fund	FFIDX	17.9	28.7	–5.0	24.1	8.4	18.3	2.6	32.8	19.8	32.1	Fe,Ag,D	Mr,Jn,S,D
Vanguard Tax-Managed Capital Apprec.	VMCAX	-	-	-	-	-	-	-	34.4	20.9	27.3	D	Jn,D
Fidelity Disciplined Equity	FDEQX	-	36.3	–0.6	35.9	13.2	13.9	3.0	29.0	15.1	33.3	D	D
Fidelity Low Priced Stock	FLPSX	-	-	–0.1	46.2	28.9	20.2	4.8	24.9	26.9	26.7	S,D	S,D
Warburg Pincus Emerging Growth	CUEGX	-	21.8	–9.9	56.1	12.1	18.0	–1.4	46.3	9.9	21.3	D	Jn,D
Neuberger & Berman Guardian	NGUAX	28.0	21.5	–4.7	34.3	19.0	14.4	0.6	32.1	17.9	17.9	D	Mr,Jn,S,D
Neuberger & Berman Partners	NPRTX	15.4	22.7	–5.1	22.4	17.5	16.5	–1.9	35.2	26.5	29.2	D	D
Neuberger & Berman Focus	NBSSX	16.5	29.8	–5.9	24.7	21.1	16.3	0.9	36.2	16.2	24.2	D	D
Vanguard Primecap	VPMCX	14.7	21.6	–2.8	33.0	9.0	18.0	11.4	35.5	18.3	36.8	D	D
Columbia Growth	CLMBX	10.8	28.9	–3.3	34.2	11.8	13.0	–0.6	32.9	20.9	26.3	D	D
Columbia Special	CLSPX	42.5	31.8	–12.4	50.3	13.7	21.7	2.3	29.3	13.0	12.7	D	D
Brandywine	BRWIX	17.7	32.8	0.6	49.2	15.7	22.6	0	35.7	24.9	12.0	O,D	O,D

* Capital gains and dividend schedules may change over time, but these are the typical months that the fund has, in the past, declared such distributions payable to shareholders of the fund.

(continued)

Table A-2 *(continued)*

Fund Name	*Trading Symbol*	*1988*	*1989*	*1990*	*1991*	*1992*	*1993*	*1994*	*1995*	*1996*	*1997*	*Capital Gains**	*Dividends**
		(Total Return — Percent)											
International Stock													
Schwab International Index	SWINX	-	-	-	-	-	-	3.8	14.2	9.1	7.3	D	D
Vanguard STAR Total International Index	VGTSX	-	-	-	-	-	-	-	-	2.4	0.9	D	D
T. Rowe Price International Stock	PRITX	17.9	23.7	–8.9	15.8	–3.5	40.1	–0.8	11.4	16.0	2.7	D	D
Vanguard International Growth	VWIGX	11.6	24.8	–12.0	4.7	–5.8	44.7	0.8	14.9	14.7	4.1	D	D
Warburg Pincus International Equity	CUIEX	-	-	-4.6	20.6	–4.3	51.3	0.1	10.3	10.6	–4.4	D	Jn,D
USAA Investment International	USIFX	-	–17.4	–9.3	13.4	–0.1	40.0	2.7	8.3	19.2	9.0	N	N
Tweedy Browne Global Value	TBGVX	-	-	-	-	-	-	4.4	10.7	20.2	23.0	D	D
Specialty (Sector)													
Fidelity Real Estate	FRESX	10.3	13.8	–8.6	39.1	19.4	12.5	2.0	10.9	36.2	21.4	Mr,D	Mr,Jn,S,D
Cohen & Steers Realty Shares	CSRSX	-	-	-	-	20.1	18.7	8.3	11.1	38.5	21.2	D	Mr,Jn,S,D
Vanguard Gold + Precious Metals	VGPMX	–14.2	30.3	–19.9	4.3	–19.4	93.3	–5.4	–4.5	–0.8	–38.9	D	D
American Century Global Gold	BGEIX	-	29.9	–19.5	–11.2	–8.7	81.2	–16.7	9.2	–2.8	–41.5	D	Jn,D
Fidelity Utilities	FIUIX	14.8	25.8	1.8	21.1	10.9	15.5	–5.3	30.6	11.4	31.6	Mr,D	Mr,Jn,S,D

* Capital gains and dividend schedules may change over time, but these are the typical months that the fund has, in the past, declared such distributions payable to shareholders of the fund.

Index

• C •

• D •

• E •

• F •

• J •

• K •

• L •

• M •

• N •

• O •

• P •

Discover Dummies Online!

The Dummies Web Site is your fun and friendly online resource for the latest information about *...For Dummies®* books and your favorite topics. The Web site is the place to communicate with us, exchange ideas with other *...For Dummies* readers, chat with authors, and have fun!

Ten Fun and Useful Things You Can Do at www.dummies.com

1. Win free *...For Dummies* books and more!
2. Register your book and be entered in a prize drawing.
3. Meet your favorite authors through the IDG Books Author Chat Series.
4. Exchange helpful information with other *...For Dummies* readers.
5. Discover other great *...For Dummies* books you must have!
6. Purchase Dummieswear™ exclusively from our Web site.
7. Buy *...For Dummies* books online.
8. Talk to us. Make comments, ask questions, get answers!
9. Download free software.
10. Find additional useful resources from authors.

Link directly to these ten fun and useful things at **http://www.dummies.com/10useful**

For other technology titles from IDG Books Worldwide, go to **www.idgbooks.com**

Not on the Web yet? It's easy to get started with *Dummies 101®: The Internet For Windows®98* or *The Internet For Dummies®*, 5th Edition, at local retailers everywhere.

Find other *...For Dummies* books on these topics:
Business • Career • Databases • Food & Beverage • Games • Gardening • Graphics • Hardware
Health & Fitness • Internet and the World Wide Web • Networking • Office Suites
Operating Systems • Personal Finance • Pets • Programming • Recreation • Sports
Spreadsheets • Teacher Resources • Test Prep • Word Processing

IDG BOOKS WORLDWIDE BOOK REGISTRATION

Register This Book and Win!

We want to hear from you!

Visit **http://my2cents.dummies.com** to register this book and tell us how you liked it!

- Get entered in our monthly prize giveaway.
- Give us feedback about this book — tell us what you like best, what you like least, or maybe what you'd like to ask the author and us to change!
- Let us know any other *...For Dummies®* topics that interest you.

Your feedback helps us determine what books to publish, tells us what coverage to add as we revise our books, and lets us know whether we're meeting your needs as a *...For Dummies* reader. You're our most valuable resource, and what you have to say is important to us!

Not on the Web yet? It's easy to get started with *Dummies 101®: The Internet For Windows® 98* or *The Internet For Dummies®*, 5th Edition, at local retailers everywhere.

Or let us know what you think by sending us a letter at the following address:

...For Dummies Book Registration
Dummies Press
7260 Shadeland Station, Suite 100
Indianapolis, IN 46256-3945
Fax 317-596-5498

...FOR DUMMIES™

BESTSELLING BOOK SERIES FROM IDG